OVID
AS AN EPIC POET

OVID

AS AN EPIC POET

BY

BROOKS OTIS

Olive H. Palmer Professor of Humanities
Stanford University

SECOND EDITION

CAMBRIDGE
AT THE UNIVERSITY PRESS
1970

Published by The Syndics of the Cambridge University Press
Bentley House, 200 Euston Road, London, N.W.1
American Branch: 32 East 57th Street, New York, N.Y. 10022

Library of Congress Catalogue Card Number: 75-96098
Standard Book Number: 521 07615 3

First published 1966
Second Edition 1970

First printed in Great Britain at the University Printing House, Cambridge
Reprinted in Great Britain by Alden & Mowbray Ltd at the Alden Press, Oxford

CONTENTS

PREFACE TO THE SECOND EDITION

Most second editions are not very different from the first and
require only a very few words of preface. But *this* second edition
is indeed different from the first and the difference must be
briefly explained. As a result partly of printed and oral criticism,
but mainly of my own dissatisfaction and reflection, I have come
to see some—and quite important—aspects of the *Metamorphoses*
in a new way or in a quite different light. I have thus substituted
a new final chapter or 'conclusion' for that (ch. ix) of the first
edition. The rest of the book or its first eight chapters are reprinted
without alteration, first because, though I would now write them
differently, they are still, in my present view, generally valid, and
second because it seems to me more honest—and perhaps more
helpful to the reader, especially to the reader of the original first
edition—to indicate exactly how and where I have changed my
mind. This I think will be apparent to anyone who carefully
reads the first eight chapters by and in the light of the new ninth
chapter.

The major change in my thinking concerns the so-called
'Augustanism' of Ovid. As I stated in the original preface I had
long abandoned the conception (set forth in an article published
in 1938) that the whole *Metamorphoses* is an 'Augustan epic', i.e.
an epic designed to celebrate or glorify Augustus in a manner
somewhat analogous to that of the *Aeneid*. I could not, from such
a perspective, account for a good half of the poem and the very
half that seemed most characteristically Ovidian and of most
literary value and importance. So I posited two 'Ovids'—an
Augustan and a comic-amatory Ovid so to speak—who continually got into each other's way. In fact I even stated (preface

to the first edition, see p. xiii) that the Augustan Ovid prevented the comic-erotic Ovid from realizing his full purpose and in fact condemned him to a good deal of inferior poetry, to 'fustian and bathos'. This is a view that I now completely repudiate. Indeed the careful reader will see that I had in fact repudiated it in chapter VIII and by implication elsewhere. In other words, the first edition reveals a major inconsistency or ambiguity though it has seemingly eluded most if not all of my critics. At any rate the inconsistency and the truth to which it pointed became very clear to me when I reread the book in the cold objectivity of print, as if, so to speak, it were just one among the many books on Ovid. In fact I must admit that my error or inconsistency seems so obvious to me now that I am somewhat amazed at my former stupidity or failure to see it. The only excuse I can offer is that one can be (I certainly was) entrapped as it were by the presuppositions of previous scholarship. What I now see is obvious enough to me now but it was far from obvious to Ovidian scholars before the present decade.

I now hold at any rate that the heroic and Augustan portions of the *Metamorphoses* are fully Ovidian and in this sense intentionally anti-Augustan. Where I once saw 'bathos', I now see rather delightful or at any rate intentional parody or comedy. There is of course a thin line between bathos and parody (which can perhaps be defined as intentional bathos) and I was in the first edition inconsistently aware of this; I nevertheless still thought of Ovid as explicitly Augustan in some parts at least of his poem even though he was as I also thought implicitly anti-Augustan. I am now convinced that the anti-Augustanism was fully intended and indeed but slightly mitigated by its obvious danger or audacity. All this is fully set forth in the new conclusion.

But there is still, as I see it, another Ovid, an amatory and purely mythological Ovid who is not simply writing parody or 'anti-epic'. In the few years since my book appeared a number of writers (and at least one of my critics) have inclined to the view that the whole *Metamorphoses* is parody or anti-epic. I have discussed the most convincing exposition of this thesis—the recent monograph of Bernbeck—at some length in a review that will shortly appear in *Gnomon*. It is surely a great achievement to have overcome the deadly seriousness with which so many scholars have taken the *Metamorphoses*; nevertheless there is a serious side to the poem and to disregard it is, I think, to err as disastrously as did those who disregarded the humour and parody. I have emphatically *not* repudiated the interpretation of Ovid's treatment of human love that is particularly set forth in chapter VII.

The fear I expressed in my first preface (see p. xii) that some readers might overestimate the importance of my plan or schema for the poem (especially as described in the seemingly elaborate charts or diagrams) has certainly been justified. I hope that the new chapter will serve to correct this sort of misunderstanding. Classical scholarship at present seems to be divided between those who will allow no design or symmetry in poetry and those who attribute a wholly excessive importance to such things. To the former I would say that, despite all legitimate disagreement as to details, there is in fact a symmetrical plan to much, if not most, of Augustan poetry; to the latter I would say that it is after all the poetry not the symmetry that really matters. But we have made some progress if we can now see the *Metamorphoses* as a good deal more than a huge uncoordinated mass of myths set forth with no more plan than that of a didactic 'handbook'.

What I am most anxious to correct is the impression that I ever set out to write the 'definitive' book on the *Metamorphoses*. The very attempt to be definitive must, in my view, undermine the vitality of any classical or great author. The concept of 'definitiveness' may have a certain justification when one is setting up a list of books for student reading; it is nevertheless essentially and radically false. We are all blinded as well as enlightened by the current doctrines of the age we live in but the importance of any great author consists precisely in the fact that he is not and cannot be confined within the scholarly or critical preconceptions of one particular age. Need I point to the history of Shakespeare, Homer, Goethe, or Virgil criticism? *Habent sua fata libelli.*

Finally let me express my gratitude to the Cambridge University Press for encouraging me to undertake this kind of second edition. I cannot but feel that it is at least a gesture in the direction of greater honesty in scholarship.

BROOKS OTIS

Stanford University
June 1969

PREFACE TO THE FIRST EDITION

This book has a rather complicated history. I became interested in Ovid when I was working with E. K. Rand at Harvard some thirty years ago. My primary concern at the time was with the MSS of the *Metamorphoses* but I subsequently published my ideas on Ovid's poetry in an article ('Ovid and the Augustans') which appeared in the 1938 *Transactions of the American Philological Association*. Then many other duties and interests intervened and it was under very different circumstances that I finally returned to Ovid. Yet without the article just mentioned, this book would probably never have been written. It is some sense a palinode, a solemn act of penance for that article.

The other and more direct origin of this book has been already explained in the preface to *Virgil* (Clarendon Press, 1964) and need not be repeated here. But wholly apart from any personal reasons, there is a much more important excuse for these pages that requires at least a brief explanation.

Despite the long-standing popularity of Ovid and his obvious influence, he has not received much attention from the literary critics and has been (as I think) often misunderstood by classical scholars. Patrick Wilkinson's excellent *Ovid Recalled* (Cambridge, 1955) has, however, done much to compensate for previous neglect. Though designed as a work of popularization, it is in fact as scholarly as it is delightful. No one in my opinion has written a more perceptive or more balanced account of Ovid's total work. But the book was not intended to be a critical discussion of the text and sources of the poems. In particular, the problem of the *Metamorphoses*—its plan, origins, style and 'epic' character—was only cursorily treated. Nor can it be said that any of Wilkinson's predecessors—such as Georges Lafaye, Richard Heinze, Edgar Martini, E. K. Rand, or Hermann Fränkel—have fully discussed, let alone 'solved', the problem. In fact the 'problem' has usually been ignored: the *Metamorphoses* has all too often been thought to be a wholly un-enigmatic work that he who runs may read.

In any event, no one, to my best knowledge, has tried to describe the 'plan' or 'structure' of the *Metamorphoses* as I have done in this book. I cannot, of course, presume to judge what other scholars will say of it. It is nothing I set out to find (its discovery was largely an accident) and I myself have regarded it with considerable suspicion. On the whole it seems to me to be a reality (it corresponds in some sense to Ovid's intentions) though of course there is much room for dispute as to details. But I am not so much concerned that it should be ignored as that it should be overrated or, more exactly, that Ovid's 'plan' should be confused with his *poetical* achievement. The true value of knowing his plan, as I see it, is that it enables us to discriminate between what he felt he had to do and what he truly wanted to do. For the 'problem' of Ovid is really why a good poet could write such an unconscionable amount of bad poetry. It has been heretofore thought, so far as I can make out, that this was simply a consequence of his own careless and prodigal genius. The careful scheme or plan of his *Metamorphoses* demonstrates, I think, that this is quite a false assumption. There was, in short, a reason for Ovid's lapses (at least those of this poem) that we can to some extent understand. Such understanding, moreover (and this is the main point I want to make), enables us to grasp his virtues, his poetical achievement, more precisely and completely than has been the case.

What I have tried to demonstrate, to put the matter briefly, is that the superficial 'continuity' of the *Metamorphoses* (its chronology, its obtrusively evident linkage of the diverse episodes, books and sections) is really only technical or artificial: it is not the *linkage* but the *order* or *succession* of episodes, motifs and ideas that constitutes the real unity of the poem. But unfortunately this unity was marred by the inherent disharmony of its two major elements—the essentially amatory element on the one hand and the Roman–Augustan element on the other. In the article men-

tioned above I committed the great error (as I now see it) of over-
stressing the second element and calling the *Metamorphoses* an
'Augustan epic', even though I was therefore quite unable to
account for its non-Augustan features. But I did not at the time
see the plan or scheme of the poem as I now do. Ovid (as I now
think) most definitely had an Augustan plan, a plan that included
both the Roman–Augustan finale in Books XII–XV and the great
epic 'panels' of the two preceding 'sections' of the poem. But
this is quite different from the 'plan' of the rest of the poem that
deals with the comedy of divine love and, above all, the pathos of
human love. In the first (the Augustan *Metamorphoses*), Ovid was
engaged on a subject most uncongenial to him and in consequence
wrote what often amounts to fustian or bathos. In the second (the
amatory *Metamorphoses*), he revealed fully his two great qualities:
his *humour* or capacity for rich comedy and his *pathos* or sympathetic comprehension of human passion. In both he was not only
Roman but unique: there is nothing in Greek or Hellenistic poetry
that duplicates them. Unfortunately, both also revealed a latent
anti-Augustanism or, more exactly, an utter lack of sympathy
with the 'serious' or 'earnest' Augustanism that was so classically
expressed in the *Aeneid* and in the great odes of Horace.

There is really nothing here that has not been known or sus-
pected before. Yet I think that a clearer sense of Ovid's plan and
a somewhat clearer understanding of his relation to his sources
(e.g. his simultaneous use of Virgil and of Hellenistic-neoteric
poetry) can bring out (as has not been brought out) both the
reason for his lapses and the nature of his successes as a poet.
Realizing that he could not write true narrative poetry in the
elegiac metre and style, he turned to epic. It was both his fortune
and his misfortune then to confront the example of Virgil and the
reality of Augustus. This was what made possible his peculiar brand
of 'epic' but at the same time kept him from writing the 'epic'
of which he was capable. It in fact condemned him to the composition of much factitious and indeed very bad poetry. But
a clearer perception of his dilemma enables us to separate the good

from the bad more sharply and explicitly and thus to 'understand'
a poet who was so Augustan, yet so disastrously opposed to his age.

The above paragraphs were written when my manuscript was
first submitted to the Cambridge University Press on 1 February,
1964. Since then, I have not been able to make more than very
slight verbal revisions of the text. Such as it was and is, it must
now stand. I cannot, therefore, take account of Walter Ludwig's
very recent monograph, *Struktur und Einheit der Metamorphosen
Ovids* (Berlin, de Gruyter, 1965), a copy of which he most kindly
sent me. It is obviously an important contribution to the subject
and, in particular, to that phase of the subject with which this
book is especially concerned. It agrees with my own view that
the *Metamorphoses* is a carefully constructed work of art with a
definite structure and plan. Yet Ludwig's 'plan' is very different
from my own. He sees no less than twelve separate sections (e.g.
he splits my third section, the *Pathos of Love*, into four separate
sections). Nevertheless when some of his sections are taken together (e.g. the first two or the last three) their plans reveal a close
resemblance to my own 'plan' for those particular portions of the
poem. In general it seems to me that he over-emphasizes the
genealogical and chronological connections and that his sections
accordingly do not take acount of the dominant motifs and ideas
of the poem. I thus see no reason to change any of my major conclusions, though I should probably want to reconsider several
details were I now to rewrite my whole book. As it is, I can only
recommend that my fellow Ovidians read and compare the two
of us.

This book is intended for the general reader as well as for the
scholar. This is why I am so glad to have secured permission to
use the admirable verse translation of the *Metamorphoses* by
Mr A. E. Watts (University of California Press, 1954). I have
not changed it (except for two trivial errors of orthography) even
when I did not wholly agree with some particular rendering.
Such piety it certainly deserves. The Latin text of the *Metamor-*

phoses used is (with slight exceptions) that of Magnus. All other
translations are my own: in a few instances I have substituted for
Watts a prose version of my own (mainly where Watts' version
was not close enough to the Latin to bring out the particular point
I wanted to make) but all the poetical renderings of the *Metamorphoses* are by Watts.

I am grateful to many people who have helped me to bring
this book to its present form. Since it was originally planned as
part of a much larger work on the 'Augustan Epic' (of which my
Virgil also formed a part), it is indebted to many of the same
colleagues and sources of financial assistance that aided the *Virgil*.
I would here, therefore, reiterate the words of thanks I said in the
preface there. But I have been especially helped in the writing of
this book by further grants from the Stanford research fund (for
typing and indexing). I am indebted most of all to the Cambridge
University Press and my friends there. Virgil is not Ovid and
Oxford is not Cambridge. But it would perhaps be wrong to
suggest that the one university is more Virgilian or Ovidian than
the other. And yet it seems to me peculiarly fitting that *Virgil*
should have an Oxonian, *Ovid* a Cantabrigian imprint. Who, at
any rate, would want to deny that Cambridge is an eminently
Ovidian place? So I am very grateful to Professor Charles Brink
(who actually suggested the Cambridge Press to me though he
knew nothing of the book's content at the time) and to all the
Ovidians of Cambridge among whom I resided for one brief
term. (For this term, the last Michaelmas term in fact, I would
thank particularly the Fulbright authorities who supported me,
the University that invited me and Caius College that offered me
its generous hospitality.) I am grateful also to the students of my
Stanford class in Ovid (some of them are now at work on Ovidian
doctoral dissertations). I am grateful to Patrick Wilkinson who
many years ago suggested that I write down some of my ideas on
Ovid, and to my colleague Hermann Fränkel who for so long
maintained the Ovid tradition at Stanford. And, going farther
back, I am grateful to E. K. Rand and the Harvard Ovidians of

his era. Stanford, Harvard and Cambridge have in fact fostered a rather lively Ovidian tradition as the names of Fränkel, Rand and Wilkinson will attest. May the tradition and the three universities that have upheld it still continue to flourish!

BROOKS OTIS

Stanford University
May 1965

LIST OF ABBREVIATIONS

AJP	*American Journal of Philology.*
CJ	*Classical Journal.*
CP	*Classical Philology.*
CQ	*Classical Quarterly.*
PW	Pauly–Wissowa–Kroll, *Realencyklopädie der class. Altertumswissenschaft.*
Rh. Mus.	*Rheinisches Museum.*
TAPA	*Transactions of the American Philological Association.*
Atti	*Atti del Convegno Internazionale Ovidiano*, vols. I and II (1959).
Castiglioni	Luigi Castiglioni, *Studi intorno alle Fonti e alla Composizione delle Metamorfosi di Ovidio* (1906).
de Cola	Maria de Cola, *Callimaco e Ovidio* (Studi Palermitani di Filologia Classica 2, 1937).
Dietze	Johannes Dietze, *Komposition und Quellenbenutzung in Ovids Metamorphosen* (Festschrift, Hamburg, 1905).
Diller	Hans Diller, 'Die dichterische Eigenart von Ovids *Metamorphosen*', *Das humanistische Gymnasium*, 45 (1934), pp. 25–37.
Fränkel	Hermann Fränkel, *Ovid, a Poet between two Worlds* (1945).
Haupt–Ehwald	Moriz Haupt, O. Korn, H. J. Müller, R. Ehwald, *Die Metamorphosen des P. Ovidius Naso*, vols. I and II (1903).
Heinze	Richard Heinze, *Ovids elegische Erzählung* (*Berichte...der Sächsischen Akad. der Wiss.*, Phil. Hist. Klasse, vol. 71 (1919), no. 7), now

reprinted in R. Heinze, *Vom Geist des Römertums* (1960), pp. 338–403.

Lafaye   Georges Lafaye, *Les Métamorphoses d'Ovide et leurs modèles Grecs* (Université de Paris, Bibliothèque de la Faculté des Lettres XIX, 1904).

Magnus   Hugo Magnus, *P. Ovidi Nasonis Metamorphoseon Libri XV* (1914).

Martini I   Edgar Martini, 'Ovid und seine Bedeutung für die Römische Poesie' (ΕΠΙΤΥΜΒΙΟΝ Heinrich Swoboda dargebracht (1927), pp. 165–94).

Martini II   Edgar Martini, *Einleitung zu Ovid* (Schriften der Philosophischen Fakultät der Deutscher Universität in Prag, vol. 12, 1933).

Morel   Willy Morel (ed.), *Fragmenta Poetarum Latinorum* (1927).

Ovidiana   *Ovidiana, Recherches sur Ovide, publiées à l'occasion du bimillénaire de la naissance du poète par N. I. Herescu* (1958).

Quirin   Wilhelm Quirin, *Die Kunst Ovids in der Darstellung des Verwandlungsaktes* (diss. Giessen, 1930).

Rohde   Alfred Rohde, *De Ovidi arte epica* (diss. Berlin, 1929).

Schanz–Hosius Martin Schanz, Carl Hosius, *Geschichte der römischen Literatur*, Part II (1935).

Wilkinson   L. P. Wilkinson, *Ovid Recalled* (1955).

CHAPTER I

THE PROBLEM

TWO great poems of epic length have come down to us from Augustan Rome: one is the *Aeneid* of Virgil; the other is the *Metamorphoses* of Ovid. Different as they are, they each represent a conquest of very similar difficulties. Both Ovid and Virgil originally belonged to literary circles that had broken with the cruder Roman past and had adopted in protest the ideas and aims of post-classical Alexandria. Both poets had eschewed the larger or epic ambitions of the earlier generation and had turned instead to the smaller or lowlier genres made popular by the Alexandrians. They had grasped, as Ennius and his age had not grasped, the difficulty of giving contemporary and fresh meaning to obsolete forms and materials. Their Augustan Rome was not Mycenaean Greece; they knew that both men and gods were not what they had been in the time of Homer. Yet in spite of their new knowledge, their vastly greater sophistication, their mastery of small-scale techniques that their predecessors would hardly have recognized, Virgil and Ovid finally transcended their Alexandrian limitations and produced as their masterpieces works of truly epic scale and design.

I have tried in an earlier book[1] to show how Virgil was able to do this, how he could convert his Homeric material into an elaborate Augustan symbolism; and how he, therefore, could breathe new life and purpose into an obsolete form and content. His Alexandrianism taught him how not to imitate Homer; his Augustanism taught him how a contemporary and poetically valid imitation was yet possible. The case of Ovid is very different. To begin with, he was a different kind of man altogether, and though also an Augustan, he belonged to a wholly different

[1] *Virgil: A Study in Civilized Poetry* (1963).

Augustan generation: Virgil was already twenty-seven when Ovid was born.[1] Both Ovid's date and temperament made it all but impossible for him to accept the Augustan ideology and identify Rome and Augustus as Virgil had done. The kind of Augustan symbolism by which Virgil had given meaning to Homer's gods and heroes was neither poetically nor historically available to him. Though it is highly probable, indeed all but certain, that he would never have conceived the idea of his epic had not Virgil set the example or, more precisely, whetted his ambition to crown his own work with a similar *chef-d'œuvre*, he was nevertheless shrewdly aware of his own difference from Virgil and of the sheer impossibility, not to say folly, of any direct rivalry with him. The *Metamorphoses* is like the *Aeneid* only in its size, its epic style and its ambitious purpose: in most other respects it is its deliberate antithesis.

And yet Ovid can also be said to have solved the same problem that confronted Virgil. What is unique about the *Aeneid* is not that it is an imitation of Homer—the Hellenistic and Roman eras were rife with such imitations—but that it is a successful epic in its own right, as intrinsically Augustan as it is ostensibly Homeric. In other words, Virgil made the old bones live: unlike his predecessors he made contemporary poetry out of quite incredible and anachronistic material. But the same thing is true of the *Metamorphoses*, however different its nature and aim may have been. Ovid put into it a very large part of the ancient mythology—all the unbelievable gods, demigods, miracles and variegated wonders —and somehow brought them alive. His escape from Alexandrian or elegiac limitations into the scope and continuity of epic brought out a wholly new verve and power, a quite new conception of narrative and, above all, an ability to unite the most disparate material in one colossal unity. In short, Ovid made the whole mythological past live in its own Augustan—or Ovidian—life. It

[1] Ovid was born 20 March 43 B.C. Biographical material with sources for it is given in Schanz–Hosius, pp. 206–10. Cf. also the excellent biographical chapters in Wilkinson, especially ch. 1. (For references by name of author only see pp. xvii–xviii above.)

is mainly, in fact, through his *Metamorphoses* that the ancient mythology has passed to us.

Our problem today is to understand Ovid's intention and performance in this great work. It cannot, I think, be said that the poem has as yet yielded up all or most of its secrets. Its special peculiarity is its apparently baffling mixture of Alexandrian and Virgilian traits. In one sense, as Edgar Martini insisted, it is the consummation of all Alexandrian and neoteric (i.e. Roman-Alexandrian) ambition. But in another, as Richard Heinze shrewdly perceived, it is quite deliberately epic and Virgilian—non-elegiac, non-neoteric and thus non-Alexandrian in its narrative style.[1] But why should it be both at once? Furthermore, the idea of a collection of metamorphoses comes obviously from didactic sources. But why put a didactic subject into the form of a continuous narrative poem (*carmen perpetuum*)? Why the metamorphosis theme at all? Or, conversely, why the concern with narrative continuity? And what, finally, is the point of its arrangement—its strange concatenation of episodes linked by the most superficial, not to say absurd, devices? Such questions are natural but they have not, on the whole, been very satisfactorily answered.[2] The purpose of this book, however, is not just to answer them but to look for the shape and meaning of the whole poem—its principle of unity.

[1] Full references to Martini and Heinze are given on pp. xvii–xviii. See the discussion in chs. II (pp. 23 f.) and III (pp. 49 f.)

[2] See the discussion in chs. II, III below.

CHAPTER II

THE LIMITATIONS OF
THE ELEGIST

THE *Metamorphoses* represented a radical break in Ovid's poetical career. He had been an elegist: he then turned to epic. To appreciate the significance of this development we must first see what his elegiac verse really was, what it meant in terms of both background and professional identity.

There can be no doubt that Edgar Martini was in part correct when he described Ovid as the fulfiller of neoteric ambitions.[1] Ovid's elegy was, so to speak, the Augustan conclusion of the poetical revolution that we associate with the 'New Poets' or 'neoterics' of the late Republic—with the names of Cinna, Calvus and Catullus. This revolution in its turn was the Roman continuation of a prior poetical revolution that had taken place in third-century Alexandria. In each place, in both Rome and Alexandria, a small group of poets had broken with an entrenched classicism and had advocated and practised new forms and styles.

I cannot here describe in any detail the Alexandrian and neoteric developments.[2] It was not merely a case of Romans imitating Alexandrians but also of Romans repeating, under very different conditions, a similar poetical experience. In each place and era (the Alexandria of about 280–260 B.C.; the Rome of about 60–50 B.C.) a group of highly critical and self-conscious poets (Philetas, Callimachus, Theocritus, etc. in Alexandria; Cinna, Calvus, Catullus and their coadjutors in Rome) rejected the pretentious attempt of their predecessors and contemporaries to 'revive' the classical Greeks (Homer in particular) and, instead, tried to achieve poeti-

[1] Martini's phrase (Martini I, p. 190) is 'der Vollender der neoterischen Bestrebungen'.
[2] Cf. my discussion in *Virgil*, pp. 10–15, 26–32.

cal excellence on a small scale and in accordance with the spirit
and character of their own non-classical eras. The result was both
to free and to inhibit the poet's *élan*. On the one hand, the Greek
classical genres and lengthy continuous narrative (epic in short)
were depreciated and, in part, rejected. On the other, a quite new
experimentalism, a refreshing reformulation of poetical genres and
metres, marked a decided revival of poetry itself.

Callimachus[1] advocated the 'short epic' and the 'Hesiodic epic'
as well as more variety of form and novelty of theme. By the
'short epic' (ἔπος τυτθόν) he meant a self-contained single poem of
about 200–500 hexameters. By the 'Hesiodic epic' he meant
either didactic (in effect a scientific or technical treatise done into
verse) or a very loosely knit collection of short, self-contained
episodes and stories (such as his own *Aitia* or *Causes*). Both forms
went with a new conception of poetry and of its traditional mythical content. The old gods and heroes were modernized and, in the
process, reduced to fugitive characters in quite un-classical
ensembles. We see Artemis only as an unpleasantly precocious
child, Theseus as the grateful guest of an old crone in a small town,
the Cyclopes as hobgoblins used by goddesses to scare their
recalcitrant offspring. Theocritus did much the same thing: whether he wrote of heroes and gods (like Hercules or the Dioscuri)
or simple Sicilian shepherds, he gave a piquantly colloquial and
peasant-bourgeois atmosphere to his idylls. Philetas wrote short
epigrams and elegies on amatory subjects in a 'modern' or senti-
mental-pathetic manner.

It was all very novel and charming, but it was also very much of
a refusal to continue the seriousness and magnitude of the classical
epic, drama or lyric. Above all, the important point for us to
grasp is that narrative verse was itself depreciated: in condemning
the *single continuous poem* (ἓν ἄεισμα διηνεκές) Callimachus in fact
condemned all truly narrative or dramatic poetry. It was not
heroic action, a serious narrative, he was interested in but an
arresting, amusing or piquant moment: how Erysichthon's

---

[1] Cf. my discussion in *Virgil*, pp. 10–15.

parents felt about his terrible hunger, how Theseus reacted to Hecale's death, how Athene comforted Chariclo for the blinding of Tiresias. Modernization, familiarity, brevity, lightness, variety, rapid transition, episodic curtailment, the startling treatment of detail—all these were part of the new Callimachean manner. There was no place left for serious narration.

The opponents of Callimachus had, certainly, much on their side since they were at least trying to maintain the classic ideal of serious, heroic poetry and genuine full-length narrative. But the brutal fact is that Antimachus and his Alexandrian follower, Apollonius of Rhodes, could not 'revive' Homer even by introducing new stylistic tricks and new subjects (such as the love theme). Theocritus rewrote episodes of Apollonius' epic (the *Argonautica*) in the new Callimachean manner and thereby showed not that he could write a better epic but that he was in touch with his age as his rival was not. Homer's heroes and gods had really died with the heroic and classical eras: they could not be revived even by a very sophisticated Alexandrian.

But the Romans began their literature in blissful indifference to the disputes and theories of third-century Alexandria. Naevius, Ennius, Accius, and Pacuvius wrote a number of grandiose epics and tragedies: it looked for a moment as if Rome, too, would have a brand-new classicism of its own. But all this of course was, despite its undoubted achievement, a crude and premature effort. Cicero tried to defend Ennius and the Roman ancients, but he was defeated by the poetical genius of his own contemporaries. Actually some of these contemporaries—the so-called 'New Poets' or 'neoterics'—owe their modern names to his depreciatory remarks about them: we do not in fact know whether there ever was a self-conscious, self-styled party of 'New' or 'neoteric' writers.[1] But it is at least true that such poets as Catullus, Calvus

---

[1] Cicero used the terms οἱ νεώτεροι (*Att.* VII, 2. 1), *cantores Euphorionis* (*Tusc.* III, 19) and *poetae novi* (*Or.* 48. 161). He refers, by the first, to users of spondaic hexameters; by the second to depreciators of Ennius; by the third to avoiders of final *us* words like *optimus* (except before a vowel). This does not prove that there was an organized or definite party of 'new poets'. Yet it is clear that Catullus

and Cinna knew each other, shared some of the same ideals, and wrote very much the same sort of verse. They took up once more the catch-phrases of Callimachus and applied them to Roman writers. It was not voluminous epics of Roman history or even warmed-up imitations of Homer and Apollonius but the Callimachean brevity and novelty that they wanted, not the slipshod and grandiose 'classic' but the perfected miniature or 'trifle'.[1]

Catullus, Cinna, Calvus and their associates and immediate followers did not, however, complete a programme, above all did not succeed in successfully latinizing Callimachus, Theocritus or Euphorion. They wrote a few arresting 'short epics' in the Euphorionic vein that the latter-day Callimachean, Parthenius, had introduced into Rome. They also wrote a mass of short lyrics and elegies on amatory and other subjects. To us, their great originality consists in their capacity to express personal feeling in lyric form. Here, of course, we have only Catullus to go on, but there is some evidence that Calvus and possibly Cinna—perhaps even Varro and Valerius Cato—wrote quite original lyrics as well.[2] Yet, from the standpoint of the next poetical generation, there were obvious defects in neoteric verse. Remarkable as is such a 'short epic' as Catullus' *Peleus and Thetis* (64), it is far from finished or perfect: its occasionally awkward prosody, its grecisms and compound adjectives, above all its medley of styles—epic, lyric, the grandiose, the familiar—give more an impression of vivid experimentation than

(38, 50, 95) was highly sympathetic with the poetical views and practice of Cornificius and Cinna; that he was *qua* poet coupled with Calvus and Varro (Horace, *Ser.* I, 10. 19; Propertius II, 25. 41 and 34. 85 f.) and to some degree with Furius Bibaculus and Valerius Cato (Morel, p. 17; Horace, *Ser.* I, 10). It is surely poets such as Catullus, Calvus, Cinna, Cornificius, P. Terentius Varro, Valerius Cato to whom Cicero refers.

[1] Cf. Catullus I. 3 (addressed to Cornelius): *tu solebas | meas esse aliquid putare nugas.* Catullus and Cinna seem to have opposed their shorter poems or 'trifles' (*nugae*, παίγνια: what is really a *jeu d'esprit* or *lusus*) to their learned (*docta*) *carmina* or 'epics' (like Catullus 64 or Cinna's *Zmyrna*). Both, however (cf. Catullus 95), were contrasted with the lengthy, voluminous epics of the Greek Antimachus or Roman contemporaries such as Volusius and Hortensius.

[2] See Gellius, *Noctes Atticae* IX, 12. 10; Propertius II, 34. 85–92; Ovid, *Tristia* II, 427 f.

7

of harmonious unity. Furthermore, the neoteric short epic was often very obscure: Cinna's *Zmyrna*, for example, was much like T. S. Eliot's *Waste Land* in needing and getting a learned commentary very shortly after its publication. It also seems to be the case that the varied metres, the occasionally daring colloquialisms, the vivid abuse, even the obvious passion of Catullus' lyrics and elegies were, in their own time, considered of no great account beside the consistent elegiac verse of Callimachus or the smooth conversational hexameters of Theocritus. No 'new poet' had even attempted anything like Callimachus' *Aitia*—four books of brilliantly facile talk and narrative, all in one elegiac style and metre.

C. Cornelius Gallus (69–26 B.C.) was the man who reduced the neoteric 'chaos' to some sort of order.[1] Before Virgil had commenced to latinize Theocritus, or Horace to transform the crude measures of Lucilius into easy, prosaic verse, Gallus had begun his four books of amatory elegies addressed to the famous courtesan Cytheris. There has been much dispute as to the nature of these books, but there can really be little doubt that they marked the beginning of the genre (amatory elegy proper) which Tibullus, Propertius and Ovid inherited. While the idea of books (collections) of elegies and a good deal of the style came from Callimachus and Euphorion, the content was at least partially derived from Catullus, Varro and Calvus. No Greek, so far as we can tell, wrote a collection of poems on his personal relations with one mistress, and no Greek, at any rate, was autobiographical in the Catullan manner. But Gallus himself was not really able to maintain the personal passion of Catullus. Undoubtedly he wrote of his own *passages d'amour* with Cytheris but undoubtedly also he padded them with many of the amatory conventions and stock motifs that we find in Greek epigram, the Greek New Comedy, and various Roman sources. Nor did he, so far as we can conjecture, use mythology for the description of his deepest feelings (as Catullus did in poem 68); he used it only as a kind of extrinsic and consciously 'poetical' decoration. In short, what had begun as

[1] The *facts* about Gallus are recorded in Schanz–Hosius, pp. 169–72.

true love poetry became with Gallus a rather self-conscious literary exercise. This is also borne out by his whole literary career: he imitated Euphorion's elegies in Latin and composed more than one Euphorionic 'little epic' in Latin hexameters. His aim was clearly to carry on—if not to complete—the Callimachean programme at Rome. The fact that his later renown was primarily based on his amatory elegies must not deceive us about his literary and Alexandrian purpose.

The example of Gallus clearly dominated the work of Propertius and Tibullus. They differed from him, however, in confining their poetical effort to the elegiac metre. For them rivalry with Callimachus came to mean only rivalry of his achievement in elegy—above all his *Aitia*. Though Tibullus, so far as we know, remained wholly within the sphere of amatory elegy, Propertius finally broke out of it and actually attempted to latinize or romanize the *Aitia*. He also experimented with the elegiac love-letter. Ovid, as fourth in the line, was thus presented with very much of a ready-made programme: first of all, the amatory elegy that Gallus had created; second, the elegiac love-letter; and third the *Fasti* or elegiac Roman Calendar into which Propertius had proposed to convert the analogously structured *Aitia* of Callimachus.

It is unnecessary here to describe in any detail the nature of Tibullus' and Propertius' amatory elegies. The extraordinary thing about these poems is their amazing conventionalization of the ideas and emotions of neoteric verse. We all know the motifs of elegiac love poetry: the lover's all-night vigil before the lady's closed door; his jealousy of the lady's husband or present patron and his suffering from the close supervision of her *custos* or guardian-slave; his occasional happy fulfilment and his more frequent deprivation; the cynical crone who wants the lady (her protégée) to jilt the poor poet and take up with a self-made soldier or politician; the lady's absence on a trip overseas or across the mountains or to the beach; the lorn lover inscribing her name on the trees or repeating it to the birds; her singed coiffure, her dangerous attempts at abortion; her occasional suffering (hair-tearing and face-scratching) at her jealous lover's hands, etc., etc. In short, the lover is really a type following a set role or script. Yet he is also most incongruously represented as a Catullan ego whose *servitium* or servile devotion to his girl is both a career and a passion. Though the girl is a courtesan, a freed-woman (*libertina*) 'on the market', so to speak, and at the disposal of the highest bidder, and though the poet-lover is openly abusing his *otium* or leisure (what he does is *desidia*, *nequitia*, not crime but dissipation)—yet, for all that, he prides himself on his devotion and regards his love as a kind of necessary ordeal or a *fatum* that he cannot escape and in fact does not want to escape. Copley and Burck have suggested that this very peculiar conception of the lover's role is Roman rather than Greek in origin.[1] In point of fact it seems (so far at least as the Augustan elegists are concerned) to come directly from Catullus.

But what was so moving and even tragic in Catullus, his degrading attachment to a worthless mistress whom he saw through but from whom he could not break—really much the same situation that Maugham has unforgettably depicted in *Of Human Bondage*—was, in amatory elegy, made into a kind of game or pose, a sort of very curious literary convention. When Catullus cried (76. 19–26):

> Me miserum adspicite et, si vitam puriter egi,
> eripite hanc pestem perniciemque mihi,
> quae mihi subrepens imos ut torpor in artus
> expulit ex omni pectore laetitias.
> Non iam illud quaero, contra me ut diligat illa,
> aut, quod non potis est, esse pudica velit:
> ipse valere opto et taetrum hunc deponere morbum.
> O di, reddite mi hoc pro pietate mea

> *Look at me, so wretched; you know the stainless life I have led; take from me then this bane, this ruinous torment that like a numbness creeps through my innermost vitals and drives*

[1] F. O. Copley, 'Servitium Amoris in the Roman Elegies', *TAPA* 78 (1947), pp. 285–300; E. Burck, 'Römische Wesenzüge der augusteischen Liebeselegie', *Hermes* 80 (1952), pp. 165–200.

all joys from my heart. I ask no more that she requite my love or, what is impossible, that she want to be chaste. I myself wish for health and to get rid of my bitter disease. Oh gods, grant me this reward for all my piety!

he meant something rather different from the lines in which Propertius re-echoes him (I, I. 25–38):

> Aut vos, qui sero lapsum revocatis, amici,
> quaerite non sani pectoris auxilia.
> Fortiter et ferrum saevos patiemur et ignis,
> sit modo libertas quae velit ira loqui.
> Ferte per extremas gentis et ferte per undas,
> qua non ulla meum femina norit iter:
> vos remanete, quibus facili deus annuit aure,
> sitis et in tuto semper amore pares.
> In me nostra Venus noctes exercet amaras,
> et nullo vacuus tempore defit Amor.
> Hoc, moneo, vitate malum: sua quemque moretur
> cura, neque assueto mutet amore locum.
> Quod si quis monitis tardas adverterit auris,
> heu referet quanto verba dolore mea!

Or you my friends who would save me from my tardy downfall—you must find the remedy for a spirit gone mad. I'll bravely endure steel and cruel fire, if only I have freedom to speak out my rage. Take me to the most distant of peoples and oceans, any place where no woman shall learn where I've gone. You stay behind, you to whom the god compliantly listens, whose love is ever secure and requited. But for me, Venus makes the nights bitter: Love never leaves me alone. This is the evil to shun. Let each man keep to his own true love and never change what he's used to. Yet if, too late, he give ear to my warning, ah with what sorrow then will he remember my words!

Here both poets represent their devotion as a cruel burden from which they long to be free, but Catullus is terribly in earnest whereas Propertius is merely stating the attitude or pose that he wants to maintain through the rest of the book (this is the first or

11

introductory piece of the whole collection). The generalization of the Catullan situation—*ulla femina*, any woman, for the unique Lesbia, the hypostasized *Venus* and *Amor*, the rhetorical and publicly admonitory character of the final distich (37–8)—and indeed the whole cast of the diction and metre (e.g. the absence of Catullus' harsh elisions) point to the real difference. Propertius is giving 'sound advice' to his friends and to the public: he is not interested in losing, at the very outset, the subject of his poems; Cynthia is at once his girl and the focus of his literary ambition. But Catullus' passionate plea for liberty—freedom from his *taeter morbus*—is a voice from quite another world.

All this means not that Propertius is inferior to Catullus but that he is a quite different kind of poet. It was much easier for critics brought up in the shadow of romanticism to see the originality of Catullus' direct passion than it was for them to see the originality of Propertius' unique use of conventional motifs. The result was that Propertius was either depreciated or misrepresented as a Catullus *malgré lui*. In fact, it has been only quite recently that his amazing ability to dominate his conventional material, to make it express not a romantic or personal passion but a peculiar irony and realism, a peculiar blend of pathos and brutality, has been at all understood. The first book of his elegies or *Monobiblos*, for example, sets the Cynthia theme in the context of his relations with his friends Tullus, Ponticus, Bassus and Gallus. The friends try to reduce Propertius' *amor* to the terms of their own comprehension but Propertius always evades them and, in the process, criticizes and corrects their self-assumed superiority. Poems 10–13, for example, juxtapose two themes: Cynthia's absence at Baiae, the great beach resort (a rather conventional motif) and Gallus' new love affair at Rome which, in a sense, serves to justify Propertius' own devotion to Cynthia. Because Gallus now has his own 'true love' (as Propertius delightedly sees) he can learn the error of his vaunted promiscuity and the value of Propertius' faithfulness to the absent Cynthia. But we cannot exhaust the meaning of these poems by any such summary descriptions: the point that Propertius is really making is that any pose or attitude (whether it be Gallus' affected promiscuity, Ponticus' literary preference of epic to amatory elegy, or his own *servitium* to love) must be related to an authentic experience and that it is a fatal error to try to divorce the experience from the pose. Now that Gallus has seen (and Propertius has seen that he has seen, I, 10) the true or *experienced* value of love, he is open to advice: *nec levis in verbis est medicina meis*—says Propertius to him—*Cynthia me docuit semper*. But Propertius does not take his own or Cynthia's 'teaching' as the last word: we must not interpret the topical *Cynthia me docuit* as an unambiguous statement of fact. Propertius meets every convention (particularly amatory conventions like this one of the girl as love's teacher) with an irony which only at certain moments gives way to pathos or regret and which always includes himself—the amatory and literary ego—and his own actions and impulses.

We do not find anything like this awareness of false and true values, this subtle critique of convention, in Tibullus. Here the pastoral idyll (Delia and Tibullus with the lambs) and the game of love as the shrewd Delia plays it, are merely juxtaposed without irony. It is a smooth, though extremely pleasing, verse in which no attempt is made to overcome the dichotomy between reality and convention or between fantasy and life.

What did Ovid do to Tibullus and Propertius?[1] The answer to this question can be discerned in the opening lines of the very first of his *Amores* (I, 1. 1–4):

> Arma gravi numero violentaque bella parabam
>   edere materia conveniente modis;
> par erat inferior versus; risisse Cupido
>   dicitur atque unum surripuisse pedem.

I was preparing to sing of arms and violent wars in epical rhythm. The matter suited the metre; the second verse equalled the first. But Cupid (they say) just laughed and snatched away one of its feet.

[1] Cf. my 'Ovid and the Augustans', *TAPA* 69 (1938), pp. 194–205 and bibliography therein.

The echo in line 1 of the first line of the *Aeneid*, *arma virumque cano*, is unmistakable. Ovid was about to write a hexameter epic, an *Aeneid*, when Cupid snatched a foot from the second hexameter line and thus made it the short or pentameter line of an elegiac couplet—the metre of love. Ovid then expostulates: love is not his subject and anyway he has no boy or girl to love. Cupid's only reply is to let go with his arrow. The humour, the literary intention, even the note of burlesque, are all quite unmistakable. Ovid's *amor* and 'wound' are conventional, poetical and quite unreal. ('Scis, dea...de volnere!' he humorously remarked of his *Amores* to Venus at the opening of *Fasti* IV.) Obviously he had no intention of writing an epic, but he knew that it was the convention for elegiac love poets to excuse themselves for not doing so. The important point, however, is that he had no girl at all when he started to write. It is amatory elegy—a literary genre, not actual love, with which he is concerned. And it is also obvious that he has no notion of taking his new genre seriously.

The whole three books of his *Amores* constitute in fact an extremely clever burlesque not only of elegiac convention but also of Augustan society and literature. The pretences that love is *servitium* or blind devotion to a harsh mistress and that the lover is helplessly unable to break with his folly (*nequitia, desidia*) are quickly reduced to absurdity. Ovid gives up to *Amor*, without a struggle; he wants a *servitium* as light as possible (I, 2. 17–20):

> Acrius invitos multoque ferocius urget
> quam qui *servitium* ferre fatentur, Amor.
> En ego confiteor: tua sum nova praeda, Cupido.
> Porrigimus victas ad tua iura manus.

> *More sharply and much more fiercely does Cupid oppress the reluctant than he does those who admit their slavery to him. So then, look, I confess! I'm your new conquest, Cupid! I hold my vanquished hands out to your shackles.*

He joins the mock triumphal procession in which *Mens Bona* and *Pudor* are the victims and *Error, Furor*, etc. are the preferred *comites* or escort of Love. He glories in his *nequitia*: 'ille ego nequitiae Naso poeta meae' (II, 1. 2). Actually, he says, it is foolish to call the lover *idle*. He is enlisted in love's army; in fact, his amatory activities keep him busier than a real soldier and constitute the antidote to idleness: 'qui nolet fieri *desidiosus* amet'.

And of course all the stock motifs are appropriately exaggerated and mocked: the closed door, the lover's repentance, the hair-dyeing, etc. There is much complaint of the lady's mercenary proclivities, her insistence on gifts and money, but Ovid does not, like Tibullus, want her to give up her sophistication and retire to the country. *Rusticitas*, country-style naïveté, is what he especially abominates. Though he repeats the lover's conventional denunciation of the greedy old crone (a sort of ex-madam) who advises his girl on how to make the most of her chances, he is actually very much of a *lena* or shrewd madam in his own right. Venus without Elegy, he declares, would be a country wench: Elegy is, in short, Venus's procuress (*lena*). It is not the crude and dirty Sabine girls (*tetricae Sabinae*) of King Tatius' time that Rome was founded for. Their day is past and Roman women have now learned to practise a sophisticated promiscuity (*habiles pluribus esse viris*). The chaste are simply the unpopular. Ladies who are not naive will even take the initiative themselves (*si rusticitas non vetat, ipsa rogat*).[1]

Thus the tone of the *Amores* is really one of relaxed and provocative malice. Ovid follows a solemn protestation of his innocence of the charge of tampering with Corinna's maid by a brazen letter of assignation to the maid in question (he will tell all if she refuses him!).[2] He parrots the conventional lover's abuse of the jealous husband, but he also insists that a lax husband spoils all his fun (*quid mihi cum facili, quid cum lenone marito?*).[3] The conventions have only become the rules or stages of an amusing game; the theory that passion is an excuse or at least a reason for dissipation and folly has been discarded because it is unnecessary.

[1] *Amores* III, 1 and 1, 8. Cf. my article, pp. 202–3.
[2] *Amores* II, 8.　　　　　　　　　　[3] *Amores* II, 19. 57.

Amatory folly or dissipation is now discovered to be not passion but a splendid sport—given, of course, the proper handicaps and a spirit of fair play.

I cannot here attempt anything like a rounded estimate of Ovid's *Amores*. Some have tried to see a serious meaning in the collection, but to me the comic spirit seems to have decidedly the upper hand. It is the extremely amusing work of a precociously clever poet who wants to shock, to make a smashing first impression. It lacks the charm of Tibullus and, above all, the ironical-pathetic use of convention we find in Propertius. It is witty rather than profound; it is full of paradox, conceit, exaggeration and a sort of insinuating *savoir-faire*. There is no passion whatsoever; the girl Corinna is obviously a fiction and the love episodes are part of a game that demands above everything sophistication and a light heart. One proof of this judgement is the very fact that Ovid could codify the 'rules' of the game in a mock-treatise (the *Ars Amatoria*) and could also apply them, in a dramatic form, to the famous heroines of Antiquity (*Heroides*).

Once he had written the *Amores*, he had to proceed to something else. So far as he was concerned, he had carried his amatory burlesque as far as it could go in that form. There was absolutely no personal or passional motivation to sustain his poetical momentum. But he showed considerable cleverness in extending the boundaries of his genre from the personal love-elegy to the dramatic and didactic subjects of his next two works. The *Heroides* consist of fictitious letters written by famous heroines at the fatal or crucial moments of their amatory careers. Propertius had composed one very similar letter (II, 3), though its writer (Arethusa) was not a legendary heroine and its subject was contemporary. The *Heroides* were therefore, as Ovid himself pointed out, a partial novelty. They are, in certain aspects, the *Amores* in another form (this is especially true of the letters of Phaedra and Helen) but they are also a good deal more and mark, on the whole, a distinct advance into new territory.

We need not here reopen the prolonged discussion of the

'rhetorical' inspiration of the *Heroides*. Obviously they are, in one sense, very like the *suasoriae* of Roman schoolboys—fictitious speeches often attributed to famous people deliberating at the crises of their careers. But Ovid was not conventional even in his schoolboy exercises. And the rhetorical bias of the *Heroides* is inherent in their very nature: that the abandoned Ariadne, for example, could write a long letter to Theseus at the moment of her awakening on the desolate beach, is patently absurd. The artificial situation almost demanded an artificial language. The chief fault of the *Heroides* is rather their empty emotionalism: most of the heroines have really nothing to write about but their loves, and their loves are after all remarkably similar. The chief inspiration of the *Heroides* is the neoteric 'short epic', and the device of the letter served to enhance and focus the fundamental weakness of this model—that is, its lack of real dramatic quality, its reduction of a story to one or two disconnected moments of static pathos. After all, Ovid's Ariadne is only a repetition of Catullus' Ariadne: in the one case the tapestry setting, in the other the artificial letter-form, fixes her in one emotional spot and compels her to heap up and reiterate her feelings in a long tirade that advances neither the emotion, the thought nor the action.

A few of the letters, however, rise far above the typical (the wearisome complaint of the reft maiden, the monotonous iteration of her woes) and show much more than a static emotionality, a merely repetitive declamation of the same thing. Thus Canace's letter to Macareus (xi) displays not only unusual emotional restraint (the moment of the incest is not dwelt upon) but dramatic movement as well: the terrible pregnancy, the fruitless attempt at abortion, the child's birth, the effort to conceal it, the discovery of the infant, the father's response, all lead inevitably to the moment of suicide that is to follow the conclusion of the letter. And the letter-form is for once credible: it is Canace's 'suicide-note' to Macareus and obviously must be put in writing. We see something (though not so much) of the same dramatic movement in the letters of Medea (xii) and Hypermnestra (xiv). Of the double letters, *Helen's reply to Paris* (xvii) shows a masterful progression from apparent refusal (at least the pretence of obduracy) to overt compliance—she yields with all the gradualness that her highly-developed sense of propriety could muster. In short, despite the monotony of his genre, Ovid had clearly shown some narrative ability in this work. But the genre had no future in itself. It was a *tour de force* which he wisely left for other things.

It is regrettable that Ovid's one drama, the *Medea*, has not been preserved. It presumably gave much greater scope to the dramatic ability he had revealed in a few of the letters though it belonged to the same period of his career. But it did not mark any real interruption of his main line of development. Elegy was still his first and primary love. At about the age of forty he wrote in this metre the didactic love poems (*Ars Amatoria, Remedia, De Medicamine Faciei*) that brought his amatory verse to a logical conclusion.[1] By and large they have been much over-praised. As Wilkinson has justly remarked,[2] the *Ars Amatoria* is, in many respects, a warmed-up and inferior version of the *Amores*. So many of the same themes are repeated and so often repeated in a much less striking way! Furthermore, the *enfant terrible* of twenty-five had now put at least fifteen years on his age. The humour and parody—the *Ars Amatoria* is, of course, mock didactic—cannot quite recapture the verve of the *Amores*, and the humour itself has become definitely more acid.

It was not so much the conventions of amatory elegy as the Augustan ideology itself that Ovid now attacked. Love was still, for him, a wonderful sport, but he was increasingly aware that there were spoil-sports. His irreverence is marked. When he speaks of the difficulty of getting a first 'date' without paying for it (*hoc opus, hic labor est, primo sine munere iungi*),[3] we cannot but

---

[1] On the chronology of Ovid's love poetry, cf. the data given in Schanz–Hosius, pp. 210–11. The first edition of the *Amores* certainly belongs to Ovid's youth (he refers, *Tristia* iv, 10. 57, to the time he first began to shave) and the *Ars* (i, 182) refers to the return of C. Julius Agrippa (the son of Julia and Agrippa) from the Orient in 1 B.C. There is a reference also to the *Naumachia* of 2 B.C. as a recent (*modo*, i, 171) event.   [2] P. 143.   [3] *Ars* i, 453.

recognize the parody of Virgil (*Aeneid* VI, 129). That Ovid should reduce such a solemn phrase (Virgil is referring to the ordeal of Aeneas' re-ascent from the underworld: it is the tremendous theme of the Augustan hero's resurrection) to such absurdity, is very suggestive. For Virgil stood for a whole way of life that Ovid could not accept. Ovid wanted no revival of Roman heroism and morality, no return to the good old days of rustic virtue and morality. The Augustan primitivism of the eighth book of the Aeneid (reflected also in Horace, Propertius and Tibullus) is replaced by a defiant modernity (*Ars* III, 113–28):

> Simplicitas rudis ante fuit; nunc aurea Roma est
>   et domiti magnas possidet orbis opes.
> Aspice, quae nunc sunt, Capitolia, quaeque fuerunt:
>   alterius dices illa fuisse Iovis.
> Curia consilio nunc est dignissima tanto,
>   de stipula Tatio regna tenente fuit;
> quae nunc sub Phoebo ducibusque Palatia fulgent,
>   quid nisi araturis pascua bubus erant?
> Prisca iuvent alios, ego me nunc denique natum
>   gratulor: haec aetas moribus apta meis,
> non quia nunc terrae lentum subducitur aurum
>   lectaque diverso litore concha venit,
> nec quia decrescunt effosso marmore montes,
>   nec quia caeruleae mole fugantur aquae,
> sed *quia cultus adest* nec nostros mansit in annos
>   *rusticitas* priscis illa superstes avis.

Formerly a crude simplicity prevailed. Now Rome is all golden and holds the vast wealth of the conquered world. See what the Capitol is now and was then: you'd call it the shrine of a different Jove! The Senate House now is worthy of its august Council. In King Tatius' time it was constructed of straw. The Palatine that now gleams under the mansions of Phoebus and of our rulers—what was it then but a pasture for oxen? Let others delight in the things of old! I glory in my modernity. This is the age that suits my character. Not because the ductile

19

*gold comes from the ground or rare shells from the distant
shores, nor because the hills shrink away as their marble is dug
out of them—nor because the blue sea waters are routed by
piles of masonry—but because* Culture *is here and the* Rusticity
of our antique sires has not lingered into our own times.

This is a far cry from the Virgilian progress of Aeneas and
Evander (*Aen.* VIII, 359–61):

> Ad tecta subibant
> pauperis Euandri, passimque armenta videbant
> Romanoque foro et lautis mugire Carinis.

> *to the dwelling they then came—*
> *humble it was, this house of Evander. On all sides they noticed*
> *cattle that lowed in the forum and in the now princely Carinae.*

Against primitive Italian rustics and their chaste wives, Ovid sets
not just wealth and luxury (the monstrous villas built over the
ocean) but *cultus*, the *cultus* that made sophisticates out of the gauche
and naive women of the past. His *Ars Amatoria*, in this sense, is an
aspect of Roman civilization, of the new culture that had finally
overcome the rude simplicity (*simplicitas rudis*), the rigid morality
and the rustic naïveté (*rusticitas*) of his ancestors.

This was a very strong dose for Augustus to swallow. Ovid
had of course declared quite explicitly that his 'lessons' were
intended only for ladies with no reputation to lose—freedwomen,
libertinae, not matrons with the head-bands (*vittae*) and long
flounces (*institae*) that proclaimed their rank and chastity.[1] But he
surely deceives no one except, perhaps, a credulous scholar or two.
Obviously the *libertinae* did constitute the main hunting-ground
of the wealthy Roman male on the prowl, but Ovid was certainly
not naive enough to suppose that legitimate Roman wives would
not read and practise his advice. The husbands whose deception he
encourages are not just male partners in various, temporary
liaisons. But, in any event, the formal restriction of his clientele is

---

[1] *Ars* I, 31–4; II, 599–600; III, 611–18.

not the main point. No one in Augustan Rome, we need suppose, was very shocked or shocked at all at the illicit love affairs and gay life of the *demi-monde*. It was, however, quite another matter to glorify it as the climax of Roman culture or to exalt the sophisticated adulteress as the very pattern of civilized behaviour. Promiscuity in practice was one thing: promiscuity in theory— promiscuity as the avowed 'teaching' of a popular poet at the very height of his career—was something else. It offended not only the official sentiments of Augustus but probably also his personal feelings and it perhaps exasperated his bitter sense of betrayal by the publicized immorality of his own daughter and granddaughter. Yet it seems quite certain that the *Ars Amatoria* alone would never have led to Ovid's exile: it needed an overt act—probably an act of voluntary or involuntary participation in some sexual scandal—to provoke the actual relegation to Tomis.[1]

Evidently Ovid reached the turning-point of his poetical career at about the time he completed the *Ars Amatoria*, i.e. about 1 B.C. He could not have lingered long over the *Remedia*, which is a kind of brief epilogue to the *Ars*. But thereafter, probably by the first year of the Christian era, he quickly shifted from amatory elegy to the production of bigger work on more serious topics. We know that he wrote a brief book of hexameters on the constellations (the *Phaenomena*) but this short essay in didactic could not have detained him long.[2] In the remaining seven or eight years before his banishment (in A.D. 8) he wrote his two major works—six books of *Fasti* and the fifteen books of the

[1] There is by now a considerable literature on the causes of his relegation to Tomis. The two main alternative theories (that his *error* was either political or sexual) have no direct evidence to support them. Ovid, however, does tell us that both his *Ars* and his *error* (*carmen et error*, *Tristia* II, 207) were responsible for the banishment and that his *error* was *seeing* something he ought not to have seen (*cur aliquid vidi? cur noxia lumina feci? Tristia* II, 103), though, like Actaeon, he was only *imprudens*, not deliberately criminal. It thus seems to me a reasonable conclusion that Ovid witnessed some sexual scandal and that his 'guilt by association' was therefore reinforced by his reputation as author of the *Ars*.

[2] Cf. Schanz–Hosius, p. 253. Lactantius (II, 5. 24) refers to it as one book, ending with three hexameters which he quotes.

Metamorphoses. Doubtless he kept the two works going simultaneously, but it seems natural to suppose that the *Fasti* came first
to his mind and was begun even if not finished (the last six books
were never written) before the *Metamorphoses*.[1] In any event the
Fasti, unlike the *Metamorphoses*, grew quite naturally out of the
elegiac tradition in which he had worked so long. Callimachus
had written four books of elegiac *Aitia* or *Causes* (basically the
causes or origins of various customs and ceremonies) and Propertius, in his fourth book, had applied the Callimachean model
to a number of Roman festivals. Ovid in effect completed the
Propertian scheme of a poetical calendar—the religious days of
each month, their rites and the stories behind the rites—and thus at
last realized, as Propertius did not, the dream of becoming a truly
Roman Callimachus. Probably also there was some political
motivation. Ovid must have had at this time his reasons for
placating Augustus—for, as it were, sweetening the flavour of the
Ars by a pious calendar.

The *Fasti* was thus a departure from amatory elegy but at the
same time a fulfilment of Propertius' and the neoterics' desire to
reduce the Callimachean *œuvre* to a Roman form. Yet the transition between the amatory and the new Callimachean Ovid is not
very abrupt. The metre and the narrative style are still elegiac.
There are still many traces of his amatory interests (e.g. the stories
of Priapus and Lotis, I, 415 f.; Ariadne, III, 463; Faunus, II, 305 f.)
and of his old frivolity (e.g. Ariadne's amusing recognition that
she was *rustica* to weep for Theseus when his infidelity had paved
the way for so much more desirable a match: *utiliter nobis perfidus
ille* (i.e. Theseus) *fuit*, III, 464). But there is also much that is new.
Virgilio Titone[2] has rightly insisted on the subtle art by which
Ovid brought out his ingenuous, rustic characters in the *Ceres–*

[1] Ovid certainly revised a few passages of the *Fasti* during his banishment (e.g.
the dedication to Germanicus I, 3, written after Augustus' decease) but elsewhere
he refers to Germanicus only at IV, 81. Yet he speaks in *Tristia* II, 551 of dedicating
the work to Augustus. Only Book I and IV, 81 f. seem to have been revised at
Tomis. The work, as a whole, is clearly pre-exilic; the revisions at Tomis are few
and slight.
[2] 'I fasti di Ovidio', *Atene e Roma* (1929), pp. 77–86.

Celeus (IV, 506 f.) and similar stories, on the idyllic and quiet charm of his description of landscape, on his delicate evocation of primitive Roman society. It is all done in a very low key, with no attempt at great drama or big scenes, but it is done very effectively. It quite lacks the subtlety and irony, the urbane familiarity of Callimachus or the brilliant burlesque and humour of Ovid's own *Amores* and *Ars* but it is, in its own style, a minor masterpiece. Nevertheless, Felix Peeters[1] is decidedly in error when he acclaims it as Ovid's greatest work: it lacks the verve and originality of the *Amores* and is utterly dwarfed by the protean *Metamorphoses*.

The fact is that Ovid's elegiac metre and the very nature of elegiac narrative constituted an almost insuperable barrier to the production of a major or serious work. Only Ovid's extraordinary ingenuity had enabled him to write so much in so intrinsically limited a style. He had in fact to contend not only with a metrical handicap but with the whole tradition that had come down to him from Callimachus and the neoterics.

Here Richard Heinze has made a major contribution to the understanding of Ovid and indeed of the whole elegiac-neoteric milieu to which Ovid belonged. Heinze was the first to describe clearly the generic or stylistic difference between elegiac and epic or hexameter narrative. Despite his evident failure to see many nuances—above all his tendency to equate 'epic' with 'seriousness' and thus to minimize the difference between the 'epic' Ovid and Virgil—his fundamental distinction remains as clear and self-evident as when he first propounded it in 1919.[2] By comparing the *Fasti* and *Metamorphoses* versions of the same legends (especially the Ceres-Proserpina story which is told at length in both works), he demonstrated the existence of a radical difference of styles. In the elegiac narrative the dominant emphasis is on a sentimental or tender emotion (e.g. pity, the ἐλεεινόν); in the hexameter or epic narrative, the prevailing tone is one of

---

[1] *Les 'Fastes' d'Ovide* (1939), p. 19. Peeters rather incorrectly cites Heinze as being of the same opinion. Cf. my review of Peeters, *AJP* 63 (1942), p. 471.

[2] Cf. the further discussion of Heinze's work on pp. 49–59. The most important critic of Heinze is undoubtedly Alfred Rohde (especially p. 15, n. 17).

solemnity, awe (δεινόν). With this primary difference of *ethos* go many other differences of content and style: the gods are 'serious' in epic as they are not in elegy; war and tragic action are accented in epic, not in elegy; the speeches in epic are long and infrequent compared to the short, truncated and frequent speeches of elegy; the epic writer conceals himself while the elegiac fills his narrative with familiar remarks to the reader or his characters; above all perhaps, epic narrative is continuous and symmetrical (each part of the action is proportionately emphasized) whereas elegiac narrative displays a marked asymmetry, a rapid passing over of a great deal of the action and a corresponding concentration on one or two aspects of it. The diction and sentence structure also differ considerably: the exalted vocabulary and the long *cola* and sentences of epic are, in elegy, reduced to a much more lowly language and to sentences that seldom exceed the length of the elegiac couplet itself (we shall revert to this point below).

Heinze not only saw the difference of styles in Ovid (*Fasti* v. *Metamorphoses*): he also traced it back to Propertius and Roman elegy and to the Hellenistic and Alexandrian elegy behind that. But here he had difficulty in keeping the distinctions clear since he could not fail to see that some neoteric and Hellenistic 'little epics' also contained features of 'elegiac narrative' as he had defined it from his Ovidian comparisons. He thus postulated an influencing of epic by elegiac style and so a 'contamination' of styles in the late Hellenistic and neoteric periods.[1] In this he decidedly over-complicated a relatively simple phenomenon. The fact is that Callimachus' elegiac and hexameter narratives are much the same, though undoubtedly his *Aitia* accentuated the familiar and light manner while his *Hecale* aspired to more objectivity and epic elevation. But there is little or no difference of narrative style between his hexameter hymns and his elegiac *Baths of Pallas*. His essential narrative was the same whatever the metre (hexameter or elegy) in which it was written. It was only in Rome after Gallus and his successors had reduced the varied metres and subjects of

---

[1] Heinze, pp. 99–101.

neoteric poetry to an elegiac uniformity that a sharp difference between hexameter and elegiac narratives began to emerge.[1]

We can best see the nature of the problem by considering various versions of two famous myths: the Cacus story and the Hylas story.[2] The former is a well-known episode of Hercules' giant-killing career: he once came to the site of Rome—then a primitive town under an Arcadian (Greek) king, Evander—with a herd of wonderful prize cattle that Cacus, the monster of the place, tried to steal. Hercules, of course, killed the thief and thus earned his place as a Roman god with an appropriate altar and ceremony. This legend is told by Virgil as an explanation of the Herculean rites that Aeneas found in progress on his arrival at the site of Rome (*Aeneid* VIII). Hercules is the θεῖος ἀνήρ, the deified hero of the Roman past and thus a prototype of the other deified heroes of the book—Augustus and Aeneas himself. All in their way saved Rome by defeating the powers of violence and barbaric fury. Hercules' adventure had, therefore, to be told with almost prophetic solemnity: Evander, who recounts it to Aeneas, not only evokes the august past but suggests the august future. He tells the story in seventy-eight lines: though they lack the fullness and detail of the main narrative, they give the action from beginning to end with symmetrical completeness.

The opening lines of Evander's speech strike the appropriate key—the ceremonies that Aeneas has witnessed are no vain superstition but a people's act of gratitude for its salvation from terrible danger (*Aen.* VIII, 185–9):

[1] The careful discrimination of poetry by metre is a characteristic of Augustan as compared with neoteric poetry. Compare Catullus' 'book' of *polymetra*, i.e. a mixed bag of lyric, elegiac and hexameter verse (almost certainly paralleled in the lost 'books' of Calvus, P. Terentius Varro, Valerius Cato and Ticidas) with Horace's 'books' of iambs, lyric metres, hexameter *sermones* and *epistulae*, Virgil's 'book' of bucolic eclogues, all in hexameters; Gallus', Propertius' and Tibullus' 'books' of amatory elegies. Each metre goes with a separate style and content: the doctrine is set forth in Horace's *Ars Poetica*, 73–98: *descriptas servare vices operumque colores* (86).

[2] On this cf. Friedrich Münzer, *Cacus der Rinderdieb* (Programm Univ. Basel, 1911); Heinze, pp. 19, 42–3. But a properly stylistic comparison of the versions of Virgil, Propertius and Ovid has not, to my knowledge, been undertaken so far.

non haec sollemnia nobis,
has ex more dapes, hanc tanti numinis aram
vana superstitio veterumque ignara deorum
imposuit: saevis, hospes Troiane, periclis
servati facimus meritosque novamus honores.

*These solemn ceremonies, feasts set by custom, and altar of
deity so grand, are not vain superstition imposed by ignorant
men not knowing the old gods—not this but our salvation
from great perils, Trojan, keeps and renews these rites and
honours.*

The repetitions (*haec, has, hanc*), the antithesis between the false
and true reasons, the emphasis on *saevis* (between two strong
caesurae), the emphasis on *servati*, the cumulation of phrases or
cola that lead to the grave conclusion (*facimus*, etc.), all produce an
effect of solemn expectation: the mood in which we must listen to
the legend has been set in advance.

We now (189 f.) get a description of the site (the terrible ruins
of Cacus' cave—*scopuli ingentem traxere ruinam*) and, in logical
sequence, of Cacus himself, the fire-breathing *monstrum* in his
dark and gory lair. The point of view is that of the terrorized
countryside to which Evander himself belonged. And it is from
this point of view that the transition to Hercules is made (*Aen.* VIII,
200–1):

Attulit et *nobis* aliquando *optantibus* aetas
auxilium adventumque dei.

Time at last brought us the awaited *deliverance, the divine
presence and help.*

We now insensibly enter a narrative tempo: Hercules was come
(*aderat*); he *was bringing with him* (*agebat*) his new cattle; *they were
already filling* (*tenebant*) the Tiber valley, when Cacus, in his inex-
haustible wickedness, turned them aside (*avertit*—present or
instantaneous perfect) and *started to hide some of them* (*occultabat*)
in his cave. When, later, Hercules was about to leave (*abitum
pararet*) and the whole landscape was filled with the lowing of the

departing cattle (*mugire*, etc.), one of the stolen cows suddenly lowed in response. The anger of the now enlightened Hercules was almost instantaneous: all we know next is that his wrath *had* flared up (*exarserat*), that he snatched up his club and was on his way. All now (*tum*) see Cacus in his first flight: he rushes to his cave and blocks the entrance behind him. Then (*Aen.* VIII, 228–30):

> Ecce furens animis aderat Tirynthius omnemque
> accessum lustrans huc ora ferebat et illuc,
> dentibus infrendens.

Lo the Tirynthian hero furious, raging, arrived; turning his countenance now here, now there, scanning the entrance, gnashing his teeth.

Thrice is Hercules foiled in his attempt to dislodge the stone that closes the door. Then he looks around (*lustrat*) and sees the huge rock that juts from the hill above the cave. He seizes it, uproots the whole hilltop and pushes away the débris, letting it fall in thunder and ravage the terrified stream-bed. But the cave is now open (241-2, *at specus et Caci detecta apparuit ingens regia*). The very covering of hell has been, as it were, broached, and the monster is at bay. He now belches forth a thick, black smoke that defies Hercules' weapons, but Hercules leaps through the thickest of the fumes and throttles Cacus till his eyes pop out and his throat goes bloodless. Then suddenly all is over and can be revealed to everybody (*panditur extemplo domus atra*): the stolen cattle and the shapeless corpse (*informe cadaver*) with its horrible face and bristling chest. No wonder that (268)

> Ex illo celebratus honos laetique minores
> servavere diem.

From that time on, we have paid him honour and each new generation has gladly kept his Day.

Propertius (IV, 9) treats the same legend as one of his Roman *aitia*. The whole story is told in the following twenty lines (1–20):

27

Amphitryoniades qua tempestate iuvencos
  egerat a stabulis, o Erythea, tuis,
venit ad invictos pecorosa Palatia montis,
  et statuit fessos fessus et ipse boves,
5 qua Velabra suo stagnabant flumine quoque
  nauta per urbanas velificabat aquas.
Sed non infido manserunt hospite Caco
  incolumes: furto polluit ille Iovem.
Incola Cacus erat, metuendo raptor ab antro,
10 per tria partitos qui dabat ora sonos.
Hic, ne certa forent manifestae signa rapinae,
  aversos cauda traxit in antra boves,
nec sine teste deo: furem sonuere iuvenci,
  furis et implacidas diruit ira fores.
15 Maenalio iacuit pulsus tria tempora ramo
  Cacus, et Alcides sic ait: 'Ite boves,
Herculis ite boves, nostrae labor ultime clavae,
  bis mihi quaesitae, bis mea praeda, boves,
arvaque mugitu sancite Bovaria longo:
20 nobile erit Romae pascua vestra Forum.'

*Once Amphitryon's son—after he had driven his bullocks out
of your stables, Erythea—came to the cattle-ridden Palatine,
the hill yet unvanquished. Tired himself he turned loose his
tired bullocks just where the Velabrum was flooded and sailors
plied their boats through urban water. But his cattle did not
stay safe from his faithless host, Cacus. By his theft Cacus
dishonoured Jove himself. Cacus was a native of the place
who went plundering from his terrible cavern: three separate
mouths had he, each emitting a different sound. He—that
there should be no evident mark of his theft—dragged the cattle
by their tails stern-foremost into his cave—but the god bore
witness. The bullocks bellowed forth the theft and Hercules'
wrath broke down the thief's turbulent doors. Thrice smitten
on all his three temples, smitten by the Maenalian club, lay
Cacus and Alcides speaks as follows: 'On now, go on, ye
cattle of Hercules, my club's last labour, booty of mine twice*

sought, twice captured. Loudly mooing make holy the Fields
of the Cattle. Noble will be your pasturage, the future Forum
of Rome.'

Of these twenty, the last five (16–20) retell Hercules' speech *after*
the event and give the *aitia* or *raisons d'être* of the Boarium and
Forum. Of the remaining fifteen, lines 3–6 give details absent
from Virgil's version and not really germane to the story proper
(the cattle on the Palatine, the boats on the Velabrum). In the rest
(twelve lines), Propertius reduces the story to its barest bones.
He devotes six lines (1–4, 7, 8) to a description of Cacus and
Hercules' arrival, only seven to the theft, the flight and the killing
of Cacus (as against sixty-three of Virgil's seventy-eight lines).
Finally we must note that the continuous action (theft, fight and
death of Cacus) occupies only five lines (11–15), since the first
mention of Cacus' treachery (7–8) is interrupted by the two
descriptive lines, 9–10.

More important still, the violence of the combat and, above all,
the violence of the combatants have been much toned down. We
are told of Hercules' weariness (*et statuit fessos fessus et ipse boves*)
but his anger and terrible vengeance are recounted in a deliberately
impersonal manner (13–15):

> Nec sine teste *deo*: furem sonuere iuvenci,
>   furis et implacidas diruit *ira* fores.
> *Maenalio* iacuit pulsus tria tempora *ramo*.

But the god bore witness. The bullocks bellowed forth the theft
and Hercules' wrath broke down the thief's turbulent doors.
Thrice smitten on all three temples, smitten by the Maenalian
club, lay Cacus.

It is not Hercules the man but a god who discovers the theft. It is
ira, anger, that opens the doors. It is through the Maenalian club
that Cacus lies prostrate with his three foreheads smashed. The
actual fight (lines 249–61 or thirteen lines in Virgil) is completely
omitted in the ellipsis between lines 14 and 15.

But the initial twenty lines are but the introduction of the seventy-four-line poem (that is, approximately equal to Virgil's *Cacus*). What Propertius describes after line 20 is the thirst of Hercules, the women's grove and spring (lines 23–30), the entrance and request of the god for water (31–50), the forbidding reply of the priestess (51–60), and the prompt vengeance of Hercules (61–70). The ritual exclusion of women from the altar of Hercules is thus explained and the *aition* appropriately ends with a brief prayer to the god. It is thus perfectly clear that Propertius' emphasis is on Hercules' rejection by the women. The Cacus story explains his thirst and briefly indicates his heroic character and achievement. But any special emphasis of the heroic exploit would detract from the homely episode to follow. Just as Callimachus was not primarily concerned, in his *Hecale*, with Theseus' heroic victory over the bull, but only with his entertainment by the humble crone, so Propertius is not here concerned with the giant-killer, the divine opponent of violence, but only with the dirty, dusty god-man and his rejection by the prim priestess. The contrast of the pleasant cabin and its watered coolness (the birds singing in the shade) with the dust-caked Hercules (*in siccam congesta pulvere barbam*) and also the contrast of the courteous god (so apologetic for his uncouth appearance) with the supercilious, rigidly legalistic priestess, constitute the effect, the 'psychological moment' of the poem. The gods are, after all, the defenders of humanity: to reject (for so-called religious reasons) the man who has achieved divinity through his service to all, is to reject the very *raison d'être* of true religion. Thus the curious ritual inhibition (no women allowed at Hercules' altar) reflects a quite profound piety after all.

But is not the difference between Virgil and Propertius simply one of theme and intention? Is there really a stylistic difference at all? The obvious answer is that the difference of theme and intention is itself a large part of the stylistic difference. The heroic and majestic *ethos* of epic, its strict continuity of narrative, its emphasis on violent action and emotion, is replaced in elegy by emotions and actions in a much lower key and of a much more delicate and gentle tonality. It is the 'off-beat' or peculiar episode (the odd detail, the seemingly unintelligible ritual) that is accented and it is, in this sense, an oblique or indirect effect that is aimed at. We can see this clearly in the other *aitia* of Propertius and in Callimachus. In the *Baths of Pallas* (*Hymn* v), for example, Callimachus describes the myth of Tiresias (he was blinded because he saw, though unwillingly, the naked Athena at her bath). But Callimachus' emphasis is not on the blinding (this is passed over in only eight lines, 75–82) but on Athene's sympathetic explanation of her act to Tiresias' grieving mother, Chariclo. Callimachus' main concern is the peculiar mixture of awful distance and human nearness that characterize a goddess, or, in concrete terms, Athene's dual status as a dread divinity and a warm-hearted friend. A ritual prohibition—no man must look at the goddess' naked statue as it is carried to the river to be washed—is thus, as in Propertius, given human as well as religious significance.

But let us now pass to Ovid. He also told the Cacus story in his *Fasti*, obviously with both Propertius and Virgil in mind. His version (thirty-six lines, *Fasti* I, 543–78) is as follows:

> Ecce boves illuc Erytheidas applicat heros
> emensus longi claviger orbis iter.
545 Dumque huic hospitium domus est Tegeaea, vagantur
> incustoditae lata per arva boves.
> Mane erat: excussus somno Tirynthius actor
> de numero tauros sentit abesse duos.
> Nulla videt quaerens taciti vestigia furti:
550 traxerat aversos Cacus in antra feros,
> Cacus, Aventinae timor atque infamia silvae,
> non leve finitimis hospitibusque malum.
> Dira viro facies, vires pro corpore, corpus
> grande (pater monstri Mulciber huius erat),
555 proque domo longis spelunca recessibus ingens,
> abdita, vix ipsis invenienda feris.
> Ora super postes adfixaque bracchia pendent,
> squalidaque humanis ossibus albet humus.

31

Servata male parte boum Iove natus abibat:
560   mugitum rauco furta dedere sono.
'Accipio revocamen' ait, vocemque secutus
     impia per silvas victor ad antra venit.
Ille aditum fracti praestruxerat obice montis:
     vix iuga movissent quinque bis illud opus.
565   Nititur hic umeris (caelum quoque sederat illis)
     et vastum motu conlabefactat onus.
Quod simul eversum est, fragor aethera terruit ipsum,
     ictaque subsedit pondere molis humus.
Prima movet Cacus collata proelia dextra
570   remque ferox saxis stipitibusque gerit.
Quis ubi nil agitur, patrias male fortis ad artes
     confugit et flammas ore sonante vomit.
Quas quotiens proflat, spirare Typhoea credas,
     et rapidum Aetnaeo fulgur ab igne iaci.
575   Occupat Alcides, adductaque clava trinodis
     ter quater adverso sedit in ore viri.
Ille cadit mixtosque vomit cum sanguine fumos
     et lato moriens pectore plangit humum.

*Lo, the hero with the club brings his Erythean cattle there;
long the journey he'd made to the spot. And while he shares
the hospitality of Evander the cattle go wandering untended
through the broad fields. Then morning came: aroused from
sleep their Tirynthian driver sees two bulls are missing from
the tally. But seek as he will he can find no sign, no clue to the
theft: Cacus had dragged the beasts stern-foremost into his
cave. Cacus was the terror and byword of the Aventine
woodland, no light evil he to his neighbours and guests.
Fierce was he in countenance, with strength to match his huge
body (Vulcan was the monster's father). For home he had a
huge cave with deep spreading recesses—a secret cave that even
wild beasts could scarce find. Over its door hung human
heads and arms affixed: the squalid foreground was white with
human bones. Having thus lost part of his cattle, the offspring of Jove was departing when the stolen ones raucously*

*bellowed to him. 'Recalled!' says he and victoriously following
the sound comes through the woods to the cursed cave. Cacus had
blocked the entrance with part of a broken mountain: scarce
twice-five yoke of oxen could have moved the obstacle.
Hercules heaves it with his shoulders (the sky itself had rested
upon them!) and with a movement dislodges the mighty bulk.
Once uprooted it terrified the sky itself in its crash; the soft
ground sank when hit by the weighty mass of it. Cacus at
first starts to fight hand to hand and fiercely wields stones and
branches. When these avail not, he betakes himself cowardly to
the arts of his father and vomits flames from his roaring mouth.
Each of these, as they come, you'd think to be blasts from
Typhoeus or the rapid flashes thrown up by the fires in Aetna.
Then Alcides goes for him: the triple-knotted club comes down
thrice, four times on Cacus' head. Cacus falls and vomits forth
smoke mixed with blood: dying, he beats the ground with his
mighty chest.*

Unlike Propertius, Ovid is not specially concerned with ritual
detail but with the fulfilment of Carmentis' prophecy: both
Hercules and Augustus are to achieve divinity; the new country of
Evander is to give new gods to heaven (*terra datura deos*). Hence
he follows Virgil in his emphasis on the hero and his exploit—the
actual conflict of Cacus and Hercules. But even so, the general
ethos of elegiac narrative is clearly evident. The first eight lines
(543–50) describe Hercules' arrival, reception, turning loose of the
cattle (*incustoditae*), recognition of the theft, and finally (in one
line) Cacus, the thief: (550) *traxerat aversos Cacus in antra feros*. All
this—save for the last line—is passed over by Virgil in the one
phrase *Alcides aderat* and a line and a half on the cattle. Virgil's
Hercules does not recognize the theft *until* he hears the missing
cow. But Virgil's Cacus had been described at some length
(seven lines) before any mention of the theft. Ovid thus emphasized the bucolic detail in isolation from the horror to come;
Virgil stressed the horror and omitted detail that would in any
way mitigate its effect. Furthermore, Ovid's belated introduction

of Cacus (his name first occurs in line 550) forces him to interrupt his narrative by an eight-line explanation of Cacus and his cave (551–8).

We then revert to the story (559): Hercules is about to leave without recouping his loss (*servata male parte boum*), when he hears the distant lowing of the stolen cattle. We now learn nothing directly of his wrath (as in Virgil) but only the somewhat jaunty remark 'accipio revocamen', almost like the English 'Message received'. There is nothing of Virgil's lines about Cacus' flight (Ovid has him stay in the cave where presumably he belongs). Ovid is here more logical or circumstantial but he quite destroys the emotional intensity of Virgil's narrative; furthermore, for this very reason, Cacus' letting down of the portal-stone cannot, as in Virgil, be made a part of the ongoing narrative but, instead, has to be introduced as a kind of 'flashback' (563–4: *ille praestruxerat*, i.e. Cacus had, before this, arranged it) that again interrupts the narrative. From here on Ovid follows Virgil, so far as the crash of the loosened rock (*fragor aethera terruit*, 567) and the smoke-screen to which Cacus resorts (571–4), but deprives both of their Virgilian point: it was not, in Virgil, the stone at the entrance but the whole hilltop that made the noise; while the smoke, instead of (as with Ovid) only delaying the impact of Hercules' club, changed the whole character of the dénouement and forced Hercules to throttle, not simply hit the monster. The result is an almost complete inversion of the epic *ethos*: the solemnity, violence, wrath, the hellish fury of the *monstrum*, the supernatural magnitude of the exploit, the contest of *inferi* and *superi* (hell and heaven), are all reduced to quite ordinary proportions.

With the reduction of the epic scale and tone goes a corresponding reduction of narrative continuity. We have already pointed out how Ovid's method of telling the story forced him to interrupt it at lines 551–8 and again at lines 563–4. But perhaps even more notable are the extra details which mitigate the intensity and sequence of the action. The pun on Cacus (Greek *kakos*, bad) in the line (552) *non leve finitimis hospitibusque malum* hardly maintains

the dignity of the style or the sense of a true monster. The conceit
of line 556—that the cave was scarce accessible even to wild beasts;
the Homeric tag in line 564 (that not even ten yoke of oxen could
have budged the stone); the familiar aside to the reader that
introduces the simile of line 573 (*spirare Typhoea credas*); not least
the explanation of Hercules' strength in line 565 (after all he'd held
up the whole sky!)—all these serve to weaken the action-sequence
and to reduce Virgil's eerie supernaturalism to a plausible, even if
rather 'tall', kind of yarn. In Virgil, for example, the effort and
struggle of Hercules are magnified (*ter...temptat...nequiquam...
in adversum nitens...concussit...avulsam solvit*, etc.); in Ovid it is
passed off in one jaunty remark (566). Finally the ellipses in
Ovid's narrative have a jerky and bathetic effect that markedly
lowers the tone. Consider the sequence (545–9):

> Dumque huic hospitium domus est Tegeaea, vagantur
>   incustoditae lata per arva boves.
> Mane erat: excussus somno Tirynthius actor
>   de numero tauros sentit abesse duos.
> Nulla videt quaerens taciti vestigia furti....

> *And while he shares the hospitality of Evander the cattle go
> wandering untended through the broad fields. Then morning
> came: aroused from sleep their Tirynthian driver sees two
> bulls are missing from the tally. But seek as he will he can
> find no sign, no clue to the theft.*

We can easily gather that Hercules had had a good night's sleep
after turning his cattle out to pasture, but the strongly marked
transition bothers us: the sleep and waking of Hercules, his early
morning counting of the cattle, etc. are quite incongruous with
anything grandiose, supernatural, tragic or heroic. Ovid therefore
emphasized, Virgil avoided such detail.

Now the point of such a comparison is not to show that elegiac
narrative is inferior to hexameter or epic narrative: the point is
rather to show that elegiac narrative was limited by its history and
literary status. It lacked the continuity, scope, seriousness and force

of epic. It revealed in short its Callimachean and neoteric provenience. It is tedious to multiply examples, but we must at least glance at the Hylas[1] story because it is one of the very best instances of what happened to a given myth when it passed from Homeric epic, through Hellenistic 'little epic', to Roman elegy.

Hylas was the beautiful boy whose abduction by the spring-nymphs reduced his lover Hercules to such anguish that he abandoned or almost abandoned the Argonautic expedition of which he had hitherto been a principal figure. Apollonius of Rhodes in his *Argonautica* (I, 1153–362) tells the story as part of a continuous epic narrative in which the principal Argonauts (e.g. Polyphemus, Telamon, Jason) and a god (Glaucus) are even more conspicuous than Hercules himself. The actual loss of Hylas is important to the story only because it also involves the loss (from the expedition) of his lover Hercules. The erotic encounter of Hylas and the nymphs is but a very small episode (actually 19 out of 210 lines) of the whole story. Theocritus then made an idyll (XIII) of the Hylas theme: he reduced its Argonautic setting to a few sketchy allusions; utterly omitted (save for a bare mention of Telamon) all characters beside Hercules, Hylas and the nymphs; and put his emphasis wholly on the love-anguish of Hercules. But of this he made a fairly well-planned narrative: we have a twenty-four-line introduction, showing Hercules' attachment to the boy; a central piece of thirty lines on the boy's abduction by the nymphs; a final piece of twenty-one lines on Hercules' anguish, search and abandonment of the ship.

Propertius (I, 20) then used the story as an example or warning to his friend, Gallus. Gallus had a favourite boy for whom Propertius warned Gallus to watch out because *saepe imprudenti fortuna occurrit amanti* (the unwary lover often has bad luck). Look what happened to Hylas! Of course, the real danger to Gallus' boy was not exactly from *nymphs*, but this fact only made the

[1] Cf. my discussion of the Hylas episode in Apollonius and Theocritus, in *Virgil*, pp. 13–15.

illustration more amusing. Such a setting explains the peculiar emphasis of Propertius. He disposes of Hercules, the lover (with whose anguish, as we have seen, Theocritus was mainly concerned), by a bare mention at the beginning (15–16) and two lines at the end (49–50). What he actually recounts is the story of Hylas and the spring. But even here his concern is not that of Theocritus. On the way to the spring, Hylas is annoyed by and has to beat off the importunate caresses of the winged Argonauts, Zetes and Calais. (This little episode again reminds us that naive and beautiful boys are endangered by more than nymphs.) At the spring he naively forgets his errand (to get water), picks the pretty flowers, amuses himself with his image in the water and finally lies down to drink. The rest is easy for the amorous nymphs (47–8):

> Prolapsum leviter facili traxere liquore:
> tum sonitum rapto corpore fecit Hylas.

As he leaned forward, lightly they drew him in through the yielding water. Then did Hylas cry out, as his body was snatched away.

The point that Propertius obviously wanted to make was that Hylas was so beautiful and naive as to be vulnerable in the extreme. Gallus should take warning and beware!

Here we have, then, an illuminating instance of the transition from Greek epic to Augustan elegy—of how an original epic narrative was progressively reduced to smaller and smaller proportions and, in the process, given an utterly different tone and meaning from that which it originally possessed. We cannot of course generalize from one or two instances, especially when, as in the Hylas story, the settings are so important. But by and large, the character of Roman narrative elegy remains remarkably constant. The main difference between Ovid and Propertius and, to a certain extent, between Callimachus and Propertius, was that the latter never attempted or achieved the scope of large work such as the *Aitia*, *Fasti* or *Heroides*. But though the limits of elegy might be stretched, they remained a barrier to both effective continuity of narrative and serious treatment of major themes. It is true that some short elegies do express grief or passion, but these are not usually narrative in any strict sense. Ovid perhaps came nearest to such narrative in a letter like that of Canace to Macareus or in such episodes of the *Fasti* as the Ceres–Demeter or Lucretia legends. But even here the limits are still evident. We shall revert later to Heinze's lengthy and admirable analysis of the *Ceres–Demeter*. Now we must insist more particularly than he on the metrical limits of Roman elegy.

The Lucretia story (II, 721–852) is perhaps the best—at least the most serious—thing that Ovid did in elegiac narrative. It has pace, vigour, passion and is quite devoid of the over-cleverness that Ovid found it so hard to do without. But its jerkiness, the check at the end of each pentameter, gives it an elliptical quality and an unintentional lightness that does not fit its content at all. In the lines (755–60):

> Desinit in lacrimas intentaque fila remittit,
> in gremio vultum deposuitque suum.
> Hoc ipsum decuit. Lacrimae decuere pudicae,
> et facies animo dignaque parque fuit.
> 'Pone metum, venio!' coniunx ait. Illa revixit,
> deque viri collo dulce pependit onus.

She burst into tears, let the taut threads go and buried her face in her bosom. This very thing gave her charm. Charming too were her chaste tears. Her face was true mate of her heart! 'Don't fear, I've come', cries her spouse. Then she revived and—sweet burden that she was—hung on her husband's neck

we have three elegiac couplets, each concluding a sentence. Furthermore, each of the pentameters contains an independent clause connected with the rest of its sentence by *et* or *que*. It is true that *hoc ipsum* (757) carries on the idea of Lucretia's tearful collapse and that the *pone metum* (759) is meant to come as a surprise, but we are none the less conscious of the checks—the pentameters really halt the action. They repeat a previous idea, or expatiate on it, or somewhat expand it; they in fact so clog the narrative that Ovid has to employ the greatest ingenuity in order to advance it at all. Actually the words *desinit in lacrimas* (755), *hoc ipsum decuit* (757), '*Pone metum, venio!*' *coniunx ait. illa revixit* (759) carry almost all the *events* of these lines: the rest is simply padding. In other words, the direct action-sequence skips every other line. Ovid's problem was to make the resultant jerkiness (the jumps from couplet to couplet) emotionally acceptable. A jerky or spasmodic content had somehow to support the jerky, spasmodic style. Thus the surprise visit of the husband, the collapse and sudden revival of the wife, are here quite effectively brought out. But elsewhere the 'jerks' often deflate the whole mood. Let us take the lines (805–16):

805 Instat amans hostis precibus pretioque minisque:
  nec prece nec pretio nec movet ille minis.
 'Nil agis; eripiam' dixit 'per crimina vitam:
  falsus adulterii testis adulter ero.
 Interimam famulum, cum quo deprensa fereris.'
810 succubuit famae victa puella metu.
 Quid, victor, gaudes? Haec te victoria perdet.
  Heu quanto regnis nox stetit una tuis!
 Iamque erat orta dies. Passis sedet illa capillis,
  ut solet ad nati mater itura rogum,
815 grandaevumque patrem fido cum coniuge castris
  evocat, et posita venit uterque mora.

Her amorous enemy besieges her with prayer, with bribe, with threat. Neither by prayer, bribe nor threat can he move her. 'There's nothing to do', he said. 'I'll take your life to slander your character. Adulterer though I be, I'll bear false witness to your adultery. I'll kill a slave and you'll be accused of being taken with him.' Smitten by fear for her honour, the girl succumbed. (Why, victor, rejoice? This victory will be your ruin. Oh, at what cost to your realm have you gained this one night!) Now day had begun: she sits with her hair dishevelled

like a mother preparing to go to the pyre of her son. She
summons from the camp her aged father and faithful husband.
Each comes without any delay.

Here the transitions between lines 810 and 811 or 812 and 813 are
too brief and rushed to allow a properly tragic note to emerge, for
again the pentameters (812, 814 are respectively an exclamation
and a simile) stand in the way of the developing action or prevent
the build-up of a properly emotional climax over several con-
secutive lines. Each couplet is a more or less independent unit: the
action has somehow to be broken down to its dimensions and
accommodated to it.

Here we come to the inherent limitation of the metre itself.[1]
Let us take Tennyson's version of Schiller's definition of the elegiac
couplet or distich:

In the hex|*ameter* | *ri*ses the | *foun*tain's | *sil*very | *col*umn,
In the pen|*tameter* | *aye* || *fall*ing in | *mel*ody | *back.*

The movement is that of rising and descending feet, the falling
pentameter, so to speak, stopping or checking the rising hexameter line. The general difficulty of over-running the couplets is
thus apparent. If one does it too often, the contradiction of sense
and metre (or movement) is apt to become oppressive and difficult. The metre is always trying to stop the ongoing narrative.
The Greeks, however, managed to effect enough liaison between
their elegiac couplets to preserve a reasonable continuity. Their
couplets, in fact, only loosely corresponded to the grammatical
and sense units.[2] But there was a special reason for Latin elegists to
stop their sentences or clauses with the couplets. This was their
insistence on coincidence of accent (the ordinary prose accent)

[1] My discussion of Ovid's use of the elegiac couplet is indebted chiefly to
Wilkinson, ch. III and *CQ*, 1940, pp. 30–43. But I have also read with profit the
articles of W. F. Jackson Knight, Ettore Paratore and, particularly, Bertil Axelson
('Der Mechanismus des ovidischen Pentameterschlusses') in *Ovidiana*.

[2] This point has, in my view, not been sufficiently emphasized by scholars. The
liaison between couplets and between the long and short lines of each couplet is
very much tighter in Greek elegiac verse. This is one of the chief reasons why the
distinction between hexameter and elegiac narrative is so much less important for
Greek poets than for Latin.

and metrical stress (ictus) in the last half of each pentameter line,[1] as in:

fálsus adṵltérii tḙstis adṵlter erọ,

where I have put the accent just above, the ictus below the line. A final neutral disyllable like *suum*, *erat* or *ero* did not matter, but the preceding or penultimate word had to show coincidence. Otherwise the line (ordinarily read with the accent, not the ictus) would not hold its metre for the Roman ear. In practice, this finally meant that pentameters almost invariably ended with a disyllable (very often in Ovid's case with a quite commonplace disyllable like *suum* or *erat*) that ensured prior coincidence. The resultant regularity of pattern tended, almost inevitably, to react on the grammar and the sense so that all coincided in one metrical-syntactical unit. Thus not only the couplets but even each line of each couplet ordinarily became quite separate entities, that is separate sentences or clauses or, at least, very clearly marked phrases.

It was still possible to over-run the couplets to some degree by constructing a long sentence out of several long clauses, as in these lines of the *Amores* (1, 12. 7–10):

> Ite hinc, difficiles, funebria ligna, tabellae,
> tuque, negaturis cera referta notis,
> quam, puto, de longae collectam flore cicutae
> melle sub infami Corsica misit apis.

> *Hence you bothersome tablets, wood fit for the pyre, and you,
> wax all filled with words of denial, wax that I think the
> Corsican bee must have gathered from tall hemlock flowers and
> sent here under cover of his infamous honey!*

[1] The fact of the coincidence is not in doubt for the great bulk of post-Catullan elegy. It is, however, notorious that some scholars (chiefly French) deny that the coincidence is due to a desire to preserve the prose stress or accent or that Latin, properly speaking, had a stress accent. Cf., on the general question, the crucial article of E. H. Sturtevant, 'Harmony and Clash of Accent and Ictus in the Latin Hexameter', *TAPA* 54 (1923), pp. 51–73. There is an excellent discussion of the whole question in Wilkinson's recent *Golden Latin Artistry* (1963), pp. 89–96, 118–34 and Appendix 1. Though I think the so-called 'pulse-accent theory' is the best explanation of what actually happened when Romans wrote and declaimed verse, I am far from happy with the term. The main point is that *ictus* and *accent* were not in actual Roman practice incompatible things.

but Ovid's tendency as he grew older was to restrict even this practice. Thus, in the Lucretia story of the *Fasti* (II, 721–852), out of some 130 lines there are but three instances of a couplet that is not an independent sentence or clause. Two of these occur in speeches; one in a formal simile (775 f. *ut...sic*). In the relatively long Ceres–Demeter story (IV, 417–620 or 204 lines) there are also three examples, but one of these is part of a catalogue of places, one part of a parenthesis, and one part of a speech. The over-running of couplets in the narrative proper (i.e. not in speech, simile, or catalogue) is extremely rare, almost non-existent, in the *Fasti*.

This explains the jerkiness on which we have already remarked. The result of Ovid's mastery of the elegiac couplet was in fact a metrical formalism that limited his narrative not only by inter-rupting its continuity but also by preventing the cumulative build-up of emotional and even intellectual effects—in short, by decidedly lowering or reducing its tone. It would have been impossible for Ovid to reproduce the mood or the emotional movement of Virgil's *Cacus* in the elegiac metre.

But the metrical limitation was after all only an expression of the more general and fundamental limitation of elegiac narrative which we have already described. Roman elegy, as we have seen, was but the exaggeration of a neoteric and Alexandrian develop-ment. There was, in fact, no essential or fundamental difference between the hexameter and the elegiac verse of Callimachus or Euphorion. In each case (despite some diversity of colour and some specific genre characteristics) the narrative was asymmetrical and limited because it was devoted to relatively light, static and small-scale effects. The *Hylas* of Theocritus was not the *Hylas* of Apollonius. More exactly, the *Hylas* of Apollonius was usable by Theocritus only as the subject of a short, asymmetrical poem from which both the narrative continuity and the elevation of epic had been eliminated. The neoterics did not, so far as we can tell, materially change this situation: their 'short epics', too, were brief, asymmetrical and essentially static compositions, not true, certainly not dramatically structured, narratives. Augustan elegy was thus a logical extension or refinement of neoteric, Callimachean and Euphorionic practice. Propertius boasted that he was Rome's Callimachus. Ovid followed, and, presumably, gladly followed in his footsteps.

The real problem lay in Ovid's genius and temperament. In one sense, elegy exactly suited him. It was the ideal metre for his *Amores* and *Ars Amatoria*—for the light, witty and somewhat frivolous things he had to say, for the pointed epigram, the clever conceit, the sentimental or cynical aside. It was perhaps less adapted to the *Heroides*, but the *Heroides* was, after all, a *tour de force* and, in large part, lay well within the elegiac and amatory domain. But in the *Fasti*, elegy began to seem not so much false as inadequate. One feels that Ovid could have done much better by the Lucretia story in another metre. In any event, Ovid had here stretched the elegiac form to its fullest capacity and had still fallen short of truly continuous narrative. Thus there was indubitably a side of Ovid that could not find its true expression in elegy. There was a real conflict between his genre (its content and metre) and his narrative genius. In other words, Ovid's specialization in elegy was belied by his interest in and command of narrative, his dramatic sense (after all, the *Medea* had been a considerable success), and his evident capacity for works of considerable scale and magnitude.

Furthermore, Ovid had ample precedent for writing a more serious kind of narrative. Virgil had, before him, graduated from bucolic and didactic to epic; Horace from satires and iambics to the classical lyric. But did Ovid have the ideas and temperament for a big classical genre? We can hardly think of Virgil as the author of an *Ars Amatoria*. It was one thing to sense, even if only inarticulately, the limits of elegy; quite another to enter a whole new world, a world of which, so far, only men of high seriousness had taken possession. Nor, last but not least, had Ovid shown any interest in the official Augustan ideology that had so obviously motivated and paralleled the Augustan revival of Greek classical forms. Here also the example of Virgil was ambiguous. What chance, what reason was there for another Augustan epic? Ovid, at any rate, seemed the very last person to attempt it. We can say in summary that, while much pointed toward Ovid's attempting a poem that would finally exceed the limits of elegy, much also pointed toward his doing it in a thoroughly unprecedented way.

CHAPTER III

THE PLAN OF OVID'S EPIC

O VID described his poem and his purpose in its first four lines (I, 1–4):

> In nova fert animus *mutatas* dicere *formas*
> corpora: di, *coeptis* (nam vos mutastis *et illas*)
> aspirate meis, primaque ab origine mundi
> ad mea *perpetuum* deducite tempora *carmen*!

> *Change is my theme. You gods, whose power has wrought*
> *All transformations, aid the poet's thought,*
> *And make my* song's unbroken sequence *flow*
> *From earth's beginnings to the days we know.*

He is to write of metamorphoses (bodies in new shapes) in one continuous song (*carmen perpetuum*) going down from the world's beginnings to his own times. Thus he announced the three elements of his epic: its narrative *continuity*, its *variety* (forms—many forms and the many stories that go with them) and its principle of *unity*, the concept of metamorphosis. But how could elements so diverse make a unity of any sort? Each metamorphosis, in fact, was bound to be a separate, discrete episode: after a woman has turned into a tree or a man into a stone, what more is there to do than to go on to another man or woman? Why try to write their stories in any sort of continuous whole? And how could there be any unity in unity's opposite, change?

There can be no doubt that Ovid knew what he was doing in using the term *carmen perpetuum*. As a more or less faithful follower of Callimachus (who had written of love *Callimachi numeris*[1] and had partially accomplished the Roman *Aitia* that Propertius had suggested) he was without question well aware that

[1] *Remedia Amoris* 381.

Callimachus had begun his *magnum opus*, the *Aitia*, with a declaration against the partisans of the single continuous poem (ἓν ἄεισμα διηνεκές). *Carmen perpetuum* is obviously Ovid's rendering of Callimachus' term into Latin. And its presence here, at the very beginning of Ovid's poem, is an assertion that Ovid is about to do precisely what Callimachus with great deliberation avoided. Callimachus advocated either the short epos (ἔπος τυτθόν) or a Hesiodic epos like the *Aitia* itself—that is to say, either single brief poems or a collection of single brief poems, but in no event one long continuous poem. It is clear also that Callimachus meant by the latter mainly a Homeric or Cyclic epic (though he disliked any lengthy narrative) since he refers to its content as 'big-sounding' and taken up with gods and heroes and the thunder of Zeus. But this was just the kind of epic that Ovid now proposed to write.[1]

On the other hand, it is quite as evident that the content of Ovid's *Metamorphoses* could not be a unity or single narrative in the usual Homeric sense. It is also in its way a collection of stories or episodes and their linkage, at first sight, seems extremely superficial. What then is really the difference between it and such poems as the *Aitia*? It has often been pointed out that Callimachus (at least in the *Aitia*'s first two books) linked his episodes in a manner rather like Ovid's (e.g. the 'swapping of yarns' between table guests at some banquet or entertainment).[2] Furthermore, the *didactic* verse of the Alexandrians and neoterics involved a kind of continuity, the orderly succession of topic after topic according to some sort of plan. But the difference, for all that, is quite clear, even though some scholars have not paid much attention to it. Ovid, in spite of his discontinuous subject-matter, did in fact regard his poem as one continuous narrative. It was not to be

[1] See Pfeiffer, *Callimachus*, I (1949), frag. 1 (pp. 1–6). On the equivalency of ἓν ἄεισμα διηνεκές and *carmen perpetuum* see especially Hans Herter, 'Ovids Kunstprinzip in den Metamorphosen', *AJP* 69 (1948), pp. 129–48. Cf. also my discussion in *Virgil*, pp. 8–15.

[2] Cf. Wilkinson, pp. 152–5. I cannot, however, agree with Wilkinson that Callimachus' *Aitia* is a *carmen perpetuum* like Ovid's *Metamorphoses*. Cf. my review (*AJP* 78 (1957), pp. 90–4) of his book and the general argument of this chapter.

didactic (that is a scientific or technical and essentially non-narrative treatise in verse) and it was not to be simply a discontinuous *pot-pourri* of narratives, but, instead, a single narrative whole.

There are two aspects of this continuity or unity that must be carefully noted. The first is perhaps the most obvious and is indeed stated in the first four lines: the poem is to go from the world's origin to his own times without a break. This meant, clearly, much more than some sort of linkage between metamorphoses: it meant a definitely historical structure, a temporal movement from the Creation to the present reign of Augustus. And indeed this is quite plain from its very start. The Creation leads to a progressive moral deterioration that is checked by the Flood; Apollo's hasty courtship of Daphne immediately follows the Flood; Jupiter's interest in Io is roughly contemporary with Apollo's in Daphne (both the girls' fathers are simultaneously shocked by their loss) but Phaethon (the hero of the following episode) is of the next generation (the contemporary of Io's young son) and Jupiter's next affair (Callisto) is a pleasant by-product of his investigation of the damage caused by Phaethon's unfortunate ride. The next three episodes (Coronis, Herse, Europa) are temporally united by brief indications of simultaneous or elapsed time (II, 534, 633, 708, 833–5). After that, Europa (Cadmus' sister) introduces the generations of Cadmean Thebes and we are, from then on, involved in successive stages of the heroic age of Greece. Last of all, Troy (Book XII) is succeeded (*via* Aeneas) by Rome and its history. There are, of course, many hitches in the succession and many, many irrelevancies, but the important thing to note is that the linkage of episodes is much more than the superficial thing it often seems: behind it always lies the historical scheme, the steady movement from Creation to Augustus.

Now it is clear that Ovid had many books at his disposal that traced the chronological course of events from the 'beginning' to the 'present' of their writing. Hesiod's *Theogony* was, for example, followed a century or so later by Pherecydes' prose treatise in which a theogony was chronologically joined to a history of the heroic age and its deeds. In the late Hellenistic period, Apollodoros of Athens wrote, in iambic trimeter, four books of *Chronika*, proceeding from the Siege of Troy to his own lifetime.[1] But it is certain that such authors were not epic poets, using their chronology as the basis of a higher narrative continuity. On the other hand, there is a great deal to indicate that Callimachus and the didactic writers of 'Hesiodic' epic were not remotely concerned with either a chronological scheme or any sort of narrative unity. It is, in fact, precisely the occasional links between the stories in Callimachus' *Aitia* that reveal most acutely their discontinuity. The poet either questions the Muses on most disparate points (why is this, that or the other ritual or custom so odd?); or tells of geographically related topics treated in part of a mythological handbook; or asks a strange Thessalian about his native customs. The tone of informal, discursive curiosity is quite unmistakable. It is also difficult to imagine that such works as Nicander's *Heteroioumena* (Transformations) or Parthenius' *Metamorphoses* were essentially different from extant didactic or 'collective' poems: the former seems to have been rather bald didactic (with the metamorphoses geographically arranged) and the latter a kind of *Aitia* specializing in *metamorphosis*. As for Boius' *Ornithogonia* (Origin of Birds) which Ovid's friend Macer put into Latin, it was quite clearly didactic of the narrowest sort (with the birds arranged by genera and species).[2]

The nearest thing to the *Metamorphoses* is, in fact, the scheme of the Silenus song in Virgil's sixth Eclogue. Silenus started by singing (VI, 31–6):

> uti magnum per inane coacta
> semina terrarumque animaeque marisque fuissent
> et liquidi simul ignis; ut his exordia primis
> omnia et ipse tener mundi concreverit orbis;
> tum durare solum et discludere Nerea ponto
> coeperit et rerum paulatim sumere formas

---

[1] Cf. 'Apollodorus' in PW.
[2] Cf. Martini I, p. 168; Lafaye, pp. 51–3.

> *how through the great void the seeds of earth, air, sea and*
> *liquid fire too were hurled together; how all beginnings came*
> *from these first substances and the soft orb of the world itself*
> *condensed; then how the land began to harden and to shut off*
> *Nereus [the sea] in its ocean bed and little by little assume the*
> *shapes of different things,*

and went on to tell of the stones cast by Pyrrha, the reign of
Saturn, the theft and punishment of Prometheus, and in addition
(*his adiungit*) of Hylas, Pasiphae, the Hesperides and a series of
metamorphoses: Phaethon's sisters, Nisus, Scylla, Tereus and
Philomela. In the middle we find, rather incongruously, the
meeting of Virgil's friend, the poet Gallus, with Linus and the
Muses, but this interrupts rather than breaks the chronological
succession. It seems clear that the chronological order here (Creation–Fall–Age of Heroes and the succeeding Metamorphoses) is
no accident, but it seems also most unlikely that the song is even
an embryo *carmen perpetuum* or reflects at all any actual poem
uniting in itself such disparate material. What it does show is the
conception of a real song or poem (not a didactic or Hesiodic epic)
embracing the span of history since the Creation and, perhaps
above all, merging in one whole philosophical, epical and neoteric
or Alexandrian elements.[1]

But there is much more to Ovid's *carmen perpetuum* than chronological continuity. There is also its style—its *epic* metre, diction and
narrative. Here Richard Heinze made the fundamental distinctions
which must, today, be somewhat restated but remain, in essentials,
perfectly valid. Heinze saw, as some of his disciples (for example,
Martini)[2] failed to see, that, whatever the nuances and variations
of Ovid's style in the *Metamorphoses*, it is still essentially one style.
The *Metamorphoses*, in other words, is not a composite of little
epics or *epyllia* but a stylistically unified whole.

[1] Cf. my discussion of the sixth Eclogue (particularly the Silenus song) in *Virgil*,
pp. 137-8. The important point is that the Silenus song is not just a catalogue (of
Gallus' *epyllia*, neoteric *epyllia* in general or various types of poetry in vogue) but
a chronologically arranged series of episodes.
[2] Cf. the works cited on p. xvii.

The chief points at issue can best be discussed, perhaps, by beginning with a brief reconsideration of Heinze's comparison of the two versions of the Proserpina story contained in the *Fasti* and *Metamorphoses* (*Fasti* IV, 417–620; *Met.* V, 341–661). Heinze summarized his results as follows:

Ovid—in the two versions of his story—has juxtaposed two types of poetic narrative, obviously with the explicit design of contrasting one with the other. In his *Metamorphoses* narrative, the strong, active emotions are emphasized—sudden love and sudden anger; in the *Fasti* the softer feelings—sorrowful lamentation and pity. In the *Metamorphoses*, the divine majesty of the characters is carefully enhanced; in the *Fasti*, divinity is humanized. The descriptions of the *Metamorphoses* accent the grandiose; those of the *Fasti*, the homely and the idyllic. In the *Metamorphoses* the style of the narrative maintains a kind of solemn dignity; in the *Fasti* it is more lively and active. The first clings closely to the objectivity of Epic; the *Fasti* give more scope to the personality of the narrator and his own contemporary point of view.[1]

All this is quite true, but it hardly gets at the real meaning of either version.

The un-epic characteristics of the *Fasti* version are evident enough; the story starts abruptly for no good reason except that the calendar demands it (IV, 417):

Exigit ipse locus raptus ut virginis edam.

The day itself demands that I recount the rape of the virgin.

[1] Heinze, p. 10 (my translation). Heinze (following Malten, *Hermes* 45 (1910), pp. 506 f.) believed that Ovid had only one (Hellenistic) source for both the *Fasti* and *Metamorphoses* versions of the story. Hans Herter ('Ovids Persephone-Erzählungen und ihre Hellenistischen Quellen', *Rh. Mus.* 90 (1941), pp. 236–68) has, however, returned to the older view of Richard Förster (*Der Raub und Rückkehr der Persephone*, 1874) that there were two sources: Nicander for the *Metamorphoses*; Callimachus for the *Fasti* (cf. on this Pfeiffer, I, p. 417). Herter is perhaps right. In any event (as he himself states) the two-source hypothesis in no way affects the validity of the stylistic distinction between *Metamorphoses* and *Fasti*. The *Proserpina* of the *Fasti* is elegiac (i.e. conforms to the over-all system of characterization in Ovidian and Augustan elegy) and the *Proserpina* of the *Metamorphoses* is epic. Whether Ovid altered one source or deliberately used two sources, his stylistic purpose (his use of two different styles in the two poems) remained the same. The differences here are substantially the same as those between Virgil's *Cacus* and Ovid's (cf. pp. 25–35 above), allowing, of course, for the fact that Ovid (even in the *Metamorphoses*) is not simply Virgilian (cf. my comparison of the epic Virgil and Ovid on pp. 73–6).

The occasion is a sacred banquet to which Arethusa has invited the mothers of the gods (*caelestum matres*). The place is Henna, Ceres' city in Sicily. While the mother (Ceres) attends Arethusa's celebration, the daughter goes on a flower-picking expedition with her companions. The flowers are enumerated at some length (eight lines). The actual rape of Proserpina by Pluto is, however, passed off in one brief couplet (IV, 445–6):

> Hanc videt et visam patruus velociter aufert
> regnaque caeruleis in sua portat equis.

> *Her uncle sees her and having seen her carries her swiftly away; bears her on his dusky horses to his kingdom,*

where, as usual, the short line merely expands the long one. The only point about the rape that Ovid really insists upon is that Proserpina's attendants are separated from her and do not notice the event. We then turn back to Ceres: her emotions are simply those of maternal grief; she is even compared to a bereaved cow (459–60). Her pursuit of Proserpina takes her through a series of Sicilian places, all of which are carefully enumerated (475 ff.). Finally she reaches Athens: here the idyllic tales of Caeleus, Metanira, and Triptolemus (taking up 58 lines out of the total 204) show how the goddess graciously adapted herself to a homely, peasant milieu. Its plot relation to the main narrative is slight, but its tone is in full accord with it. At last Ceres finds out the truth from the sun-god and the episode ends with a compromise arranged by Jupiter and provoked by Ceres' threat to leave the earth and rejoin Proserpina in the underworld. All is at length satisfactorily arranged: the next harvest is accordingly plenteous (617–18):

> Largaque provenit cessatis messis in arvis,
> et vix congestas area cepit opes.

> *And great was the harvest that came to the fields so long barren: scarce did the threshing-floor contain the garnered wealth.*

Such a narrative, it is needless to say, is told in the jerky, elliptical and familiar manner of elegy. The author reduces the main plot to the barest outline but finds time for catalogues of flowers and places and for curious descriptive touches (e.g. the acorns and blackberries that Caeleus is carrying, the vistas that Ceres sees on the aerial part of her journey (565 ff.)). The piquant detail is always more emphasized than the main event (e.g. the flower-picking, Ceres' questioning of the peasants (*hac gressus ecqua puella tulit?*), the swine who trample out Proserpina's footsteps). And the author introduces himself into the narrative with a familiarity quite out of place in a more serious genre, as in the following remarks to the *places* Ceres passes in her search (499–502):

> Effugit et Syrtes et *te*, Zanclaea Charybdis,
>   et *vos*, Nisaei, naufraga monstra, canes,
> Hadriacumque patens late bimaremque Corinthum.
>   Sic venit ad portus, Attica terra, *tuos*.

> *She fled by the Syrtes and by* you, *Zanclaean Charybdis, and* you, ye *dogs of Nisa, shipwrecked monsters, and by the broad Adriatic and by Corinth between the two seas and so came to* your *harbours, land of Attica.*

It is plain that the story is here quite subordinate to the curious embellishments and learned asides that Ovid so painstakingly inserts.

There is no point in underlining the utter difference of the *Metamorphoses* version. We are there in a divine, not a human-peasant milieu: the initial conversation of Venus and Cupid presents us at once with a supernatural and epic motivation; the flower-picking is only brought in as contrast to Pluto's stern appearance and violent passion; the witnesses—Cyane, Arethusa—are nymphs who, too, have their troubles with gods; the emotion that dominates Ceres is not only grief but divine rage and desire for vengeance (she talks to Jupiter almost like Juno herself). But most important of all, the narrative is truly continuous and concerns the major, not the minor, aspects of the story: the motivation of the *amor*, the actual rape, Ceres' search, are not interrupted and all but neglected for petty if pretty details. The inserted stories (Cyane, Ascalaphus, Arethusa) are directly related to the main narrative (Cyane expostulates with Dis; Ascalaphus spreads the news of Proserpina's pomegranate; Arethusa finally reveals the girls' whereabouts) and each in its way preserves its high tone and decorum. The diction and metre are the apt vehicle of the sentiments: the lengthy speeches with their solemn invocations (v, 489–90):

> o toto quaesitae virginis orbe
> et frugum genetrix, immensos siste labores, etc.

> *O mother of the far-sought maid, let stand*
> *Your world-wide toil; nor turn your wrathful hand,*
> *Mother of crops, against a guiltless land,*

the elaborate descriptions, with their epic repetitions, epithets, long clauses and cumulative *cola* (402–8):

> Raptor agit currus, et nomine quemque vocando
> exhortatur equos, quorum per colla iubasque
> excutit obscura tinctas ferrugine habenas
> perque lacus altos et olentia sulphure fertur
> stagna Palicorum, rupta ferventia terra,
> et qua Bacchiadae, bimari gens orta Corintho,
> inter inaequales posuerunt moenia portus

> *The car drives on: the abductor, as it flies,*
> *Calls on each horse by name, with coaxing cries*
> *To urge them on, while over necks and manes*
> *He shakes the spectral blackness of the reins;*
> *And past Palica's sulphurous pools he flies,*
> *Where boiling springs from deep-cleft chasms rise,*
> *And where the Bacchiad princes, forced to flee*
> *Their native Corinth (set 'twixt sea and sea),*
> *Between two harbours built a city wall:*
> *The Great on that side, and on this the Small,*

the careful transitions (*haud procul, paene simul, at, interea, quas dea per terras...erraverit...dicere longa mora est, tum*, etc.) all mark the

epic as opposed to the elegiac manner. Here we have no familiarity, no casual asides of a chatty author, no violent ellipsis and
asymmetry: the narrative, on the contrary, is solemn, sedate,
objective and balanced. The similarity to Virgil seems, in fact,
rather close.

All this is quite true but it is a relatively superficial truth.
A latent scepticism leads us to ask: is this episode really as epic as it
certainly seems at first sight to be? Its very introduction gives us
the answer. The legend is told to Minerva by the Muses (or by
their representative, Calliope): they had been telling her about
their singing contest with the impious daughters of Pieros; perhaps, they add, Minerva might like to hear what *they* sang in
response to the Pierides. Or perhaps she is too busy to hear it: *sed
forsitan otia non sint?* (333). But Minerva, of course, is decidedly
not too busy: she wants to hear everything in full detail. This is
surely a hint to the reader; he cannot (as we shall see) grasp the
true point of the story until he can set it in the context of the whole
Metamorphoses, but at least this rather coy introduction ('But
aren't you too busy?') may serve to warn him against too literal an
interpretation of the 'little epic' to come.

The story opens with an account of the eruption of Aetna: there
is real danger that Hades itself will be exposed by the commotion;
so Dis or Pluto appropriately makes a tour of inspection, thus
emerging for once into the sharp daylight of Sicily (356–61):

> Inde tremit tellus, et rex *pavet* ipse silentum,
> *ne pateat* latoque solum retegatur hiatu,
> immissusque dies trepidantes terreat umbras.
> *Hanc metuens cladem* tenebrosa sede tyrannus
> *exierat,* curruque atrorum vectus equorum
> ambibat Siculae cautus fundamina terrae.

> *Earth rocks; and he who rules the muted dead,*
> *Faced with the threat of ruin, shakes with dread,*
> *Lest gaping rents and cracks the daylight show*
> *To strike with fear the shivering ghosts below.*
> *Once, in such fear, he left his dark abode,*

And, drawn by coal-black horses, took the road,
And made a tour of Sicily, and scanned
Closely the deep foundations of the land.

The words *pavet...ne pateat...metuens* clearly indicate some empathetic penetration of Pluto's mind by the author. Furthermore, we, the readers, are placed at once on the scene: we catch Pluto after he had gone out (*exierat*, pluperfect) and was walking (*ambibat*) about the mountain. We stand, so to speak, in his solicitous shoes. We see that he is acting just as a respectable and conscientious ruler should. But the circumstance—the sight of Pluto in the open light of day—presents Venus with a splendid idea. It is, she tells Cupid, the right time for them to extend their power to a whole new territory and also to ward off the ominous possibility of still another virgin goddess! The advice is at once made good: Cupid shoots at Pluto and hits him with unerring aim. So we arrive at the simultaneous presence near Aetna of the love-wounded Pluto and the flower-picking Proserpina.

We see, first, the beautiful spot (385–91):

Haud procul Hennaeis lacus est a moenibus altae,
nomine Pergus, aquae: non illo plura Caystros
carmina cygnorum labentibus edit in undis.
Silva coronat aquas cingens latus omne, suisque
frondibus ut velo Phoebeos submovet ictus.
Frigora dant rami, varios humus umida flores:
perpetuum ver est.

Not far from where the walls of Enna rise
A still deep lake (they call it Pergus) lies;
Where swans as numerous pause and tune their song,
As on Cayster's current glide along.
The woods that fringe the water keep at bay
With screen of leaves the sun's relentless ray;
Boughs give their shade; the soil, well watered, blends
Its varied blooms; and springtime never ends.

Then we see Proserpina at play, wandering after the flowers.

Girlishly, she wants to excel her companions by picking the most (we now empathetically penetrate *her* mind). Into this idyllic ensemble the violent lover comes abruptly and without warning. The contrast between the grim god's hasty passion and the girl's simplicity is strongly accented (393–401):

> Dumque puellari studio calathosque sinumque
> implet et aequales *certat superare legendo,*
> 395 *paene simul visa est dilectaque raptaque Diti:*
> *usque adeo est properatus amor.* Dea territa maesto
> et matrem et comites, *sed matrem saepius,* ore
> clamat, et ut summa vestem laniarat ab ora
> collecti flores tunicis cecidere remissis;
> 400 *tantaque simplicitas* puerilibus adfuit annis:
> *haec quoque virgineum movit iactura dolorem.*
>
> *And while she heaped her baskets and her breast,*
> Competing with her playmates in the quest,
> *The girl, at one fell swoop, by Dis that day,*
> Was seen and loved and seized and borne away
> (For love's no laggard). *Ah, how terrified*
> *Was she, so young a goddess! How she tried*
> *To reach her playmates with her piteous call—*
> *Her mother too, her mother most of all!*
> *And as in grief she tore her dress, she spilled*
> *The gathered flowers with which the fold was filled;*
> And still a child in feeling as in years,
> She felt the loss an added cause for tears.

Line 396 and, above all, 400–1 are a sort of editorial comment on the contrast of *simplicitas* and *properatus amor.* The confrontation of god and maiden is obviously meant to be a thing of startling and near-comic incongruity.

But to Venus' social ambition, Pluto's incongruous passion and Proserpina's childish naïveté, a third element is added: the *shocked respectability* of the matron Cyane, who had just witnessed the whole operation. She actually instructs Pluto in the etiquette of courtship (415–19):

56

Non potes invitae Cereris gener esse: *roganda,*
non rapienda fuit. Quodsi componere magnis
parva mihi fas est, et me dilexit Anapis:
exorata tamen, nec, ut haec, exterrita nupsi.

> '*Think not*', she said,
> '*Against the mother's will the maid to wed—*
> To seize, not sue. *Anapis, if I dare*
> *Our modest selves with mighty gods compare,*
> *Loved me; but I unlike your captive here,*
> *Bestowed my hand by favour, not by fear.*'

Of course Pluto would not put up with such an intrusion, but that
Cyane should *therefore* weep herself into a fountain seems hardly
called for by his rebuff. In any event, her disappearance removes
one more witness of the rape. Her over-active tongue is quenched
and unavailable to Ceres (465–6):

> ea ni mutata fuisset
> omnia narrasset.

> *who had the will*
> *To tell her all, but not, so changed, the skill.*

The bereaved Ceres is overcome by her outraged maternity.
When she finally receives the facts from Arethusa (note the difference here from the *Fasti*) she at once tries to get redress from
Jupiter, the child's father. Pique and feminine resentment are
strong in Ceres' words (520–2):

> quod rapta, feremus,
> dummodo reddat eam. Neque enim praedone marito
> filia digna tua est—*si iam mea filia non est.*

> Let pass the theft, *so he restore her straight;*
> For—if she's mine no longer—'*tis no fate*
> *For child of yours to be a bandit's mate.*

But Jupiter in his turn dwells on the romantic and social aspects of
the match (524–9):

> si modo nomina rebus
> addere vera placet, *non hoc iniuria factum,*
> *verum amor est*; neque erit nobis gener ille pudori,

tu modo, diva, velis. *Ut desint cetera: quantum est
esse Iovis fratrem!* Quid quod non cetera desunt,
nec cedit nisi sorte mihi?

Yet here's no crime, *but would you name things right,*
A lover's ardour, *not an act of spite;*
Nor, with your favour, goddess, shall we draw
So deep disgrace from such a son-in-law.
To be Jove's brother merely, were it all
He had to boast, is that a thing so small?
But that's not all, nor does he yield to me
In aught except the lottery's chance decree.

We need not go further. Beneath the solemn epic façade there
are—it is quite obvious—very human feelings at work. This is, at
one level, a narrative of solemn gods and goddesses, of Hell and
Heaven, of violent love and fierce resentment—of all that is serious
and intense and can find its fittest expression in epic oratory and
narrative. But at another level it is a story of social ambition
(Venus), undignified love (Pluto), childish innocence (Proserpina),
matronly respectability (Cyane), womanly gossip (Arethusa),
maternal outrage (Ceres), and tactful persuasiveness (Jupiter) all
reacting upon each other in a quite delightful human comedy. In
the end, lover and mother both reach an agreeable compromise.
The rape, as Jupiter points out, is, after all, *amor* not *iniuria*. We can
quite well imagine that Minerva enjoyed the story and her
moment of leisure.

We must not, of course, take this one episode as typical of the
whole *Metamorphoses*. It does, however, illustrate three fundamental characteristics of the poem. First, the narrative and verbal
style is epic, not elegiac; there is, at least on the surface, an observance of epic decorum and narrative continuity, an avoidance of
elegiac levity and ellipsis. Secondly, the epic manner does not at
all mean the total disappearance of the author from the scene; here
Ovid resembles Virgil,[1] not Homer and later Greek epic, in his

[1] See my description of Virgilian empathy and the 'subjective' style of Virgil in
Virgil, pp. 41–61.

empathetic penetration of his characters and his personal comments on the action. But thirdly, Ovid makes a quite original use
of the Virgilian style: the poet's attitude toward characters and
events is no longer serious and intense but relaxed and comic, or at
any rate human in the broadest sense. The epic style does not so
much disguise as provocatively distort the author's essential levity.

But the difference from Hellenistic long or 'short' epic is just as
perceptible in Ovid's case as in Virgil's. An example will make this
clear. In both *Aeneid* IV (1–55) and *Met.* VII (1–148) there are
obvious references to the description of Medea's awakening
passion in the *Argonautica* of Apollonius (III, 44–470, 616–73,
740–801, 948–74). In particular, the Ovidian Medea's long speech
(11–71) recalls the speeches of her Apollonian predecessor (especially
Arg. III, 615–55). But what is in Apollonius a real battle between
Medea's desire (ἵμερος) and shame (αἰδώς)—she actually rushes to
the chamber of her sister, Chalciope, in order to offer aid to Jason,
then recoils from the door and, after three such advances and
retreats, collapses on her bed—has become in Virgil a rhetorical
debate. Dido admits her love but swears not to violate her *pudor*
or chastity, the Latin equivalent of αἰδώς (*Aen.* IV, 23–7):

> agnosco veteris vestigia flammae.
> Sed mihi vel tellus optem prius ima dehiscat
> vel pater omnipotens abigat me fulmine ad umbras,
> pallentis umbras Erebo noctemque profundam,
> ante, *Pudor, quam te violo* aut tua iura resolvo.

> *I recognize the traces of the fire of former years. But may the
> bottommost earth gape open for me or the omnipotent father
> hurl me with thunderbolt to the shades, the pale shades of
> Erebus and its night profound, ere yet I violate thee, O
> Chastity, or break thy laws!*

But after Anna's impassioned rebuttal, Dido's determination
weakens (54–5):

> His dictis impenso animum flammavit amore
> spemque dedit dubiae menti solvitque *pudorem*.

*By these words she [Anna] inflamed her [Dido's] heart with
measureless love, gave hope to her doubting mind and dissolved
her sense of shame.*

I have elsewhere[1] tried to show how completely Dido is here
seen through Virgil's eyes. The elaborate, rhetorical speeches
present, so to speak, the good and bad sides of the case. And Virgil
leaves us in no doubt as to where he stands: Dido's initial determination to maintain her *pudor* is to Virgil as admirable as Anna's
counter-plea is disastrous. We already know that Dido is *infelix*,
eaten by hidden fire, fatally wounded in her heart. We know that
Aeneas' destiny is exactly contrary to hers. In *inflaming* her love
and dispelling her shame, Anna is obviously urging on her
tragedy. We see all this from the very beginning. The author's
bias has at no time been disguised. In short, the rhetorical
speeches only reinforce or expand the highly subjective and
moralized narrative and do not attempt to give us an objective
account of what was really said or done. The contrast with
Apollonius' Medea is obvious: the latter is seen quite objectively;
her desire and shame are not so much the counters of a moral
debate as the actual emotions that at one particular moment drive
her in different directions.

Now Ovid's Medea episode is obviously indebted to both
Apollonius and Virgil. But its combination of rhetorical speech
with moralizing narrative is Virgilian, not Apollonian. In many
ways, Medea's speech is, as Hans Diller[2] has pointed out, a *plaidoyer*
built on the rhetorical antithesis of *furor* and *ratio*, with the text
(lines 10–11) carefully supplied: *ratione furorem vincere non poterat.*
It is, as such, an exceedingly clever piece of pleading, though the
contradiction between the inexperienced girl presupposed by the
beginning and the shrewdly calculating woman of the close (she
estimates just what her exact chances of marriage are) is rather
hard to accept. But, again, it is all part of a narrative that its author

[1] *Virgil,* pp. 76–8.
[2] Diller, pp. 29–32. But my analysis differs from Diller's at several crucial
points.

has edited for our benefit. The long speech turns on the word marriage, *coniugium*. Medea is recalled by the word to the fact that she is not really thinking of marriage at all. Ovid's reference to Virgil and Dido is here deliberate and provocative (*Met.* VII, 69–70):

> Coniugiumne putas speciosaque nomina culpae
> imponis, Medea, tuae?

> *So with the specious name*
> *Of marriage will Medea cloak her shame?*

Compare Virgil (*Aen.* IV, 172):

> Coniugium vocat, hoc praetexit nomine culpam.

> *She calls it marriage; by this word she hides her shame.*

And so Medea ends her speech with the pious resolve to give up such evil thoughts: *dum licet effuge crimen.* Then Ovid adds (72–3):

> Dixit. Et ante oculos Rectum Pietasque Pudorque
> *constiterant*, et victa *dabat iam* terga Cupido.

> *Here Duty, Right, and Honour stood revealed*
> *Before her eyes, and Love began to yield.*

These last two lines clearly do two things: (1) they bring the sentiments of the speech back into the narrative, and make us empathetically share Medea's thoughts and feelings. The verbs and tenses (*constiterant, dabat*) place the reader right in the action: they *had stood*...Cupid was *already giving way*. But they also (2) give the author's point of view—his conception of the action. They repeat, of course, the traditional struggle of *pudor* and *amor* and thus once more recall Apollonius and Virgil, but this struggle is now reduced to something approaching parody. The picture of Cupid withdrawing before Right, Duty and Modesty is just too pretty and too plastically allegorical to be serious. It is all part of the game: the maiden's first faint attempt to conquer her own scruples is not quite successful, but it obviously also forecasts her full surrender when she finally meets the man (76–7):

Et iam fortis erat, pulsusque *resederat* ardor:
cum *videt* Aesoniden, extinctaque flamma reluxit.

Heart-whole and brave was she: her passion's flame
Had cooled, when in her sight her loved one came.

Right, Duty and Modesty, after all, put up only a token or sham resistance! What is to Virgil the prelude to tragedy is to Ovid an opening gambit in the great game of love. But compared to Apollonius, Ovid's technique is here very Virgilian. Both Roman poets empathetically penetrate the minds of their characters, and comment on the action in a manner quite unlike the objective style of Apollonius. But Ovid's meaning—his poetical purpose— is very un-Virgilian indeed.

But though his style is not Virgilian or Apollonian, neither is it neoteric or Callimachean. Ovid, like Virgil, maintains full epic continuity—no one passage stands out asymmetrically; the on-going action is at no point stopped in the interest of a detail or a piece of static pathos. Ovid's *Medea* is, of course, rather untypical, for it is not a full-scale amatory narrative: Ovid has no desire to recall the pathology of her passion—the child murder, etc.—both because he had treated the subject elsewhere (in his drama, *Medea*) and because the preceding book had just ended with a similar child murder (Procne's of the little Itys). For this very reason, however, it illustrates rather well his special concern with epic continuity. He does not let Medea's declamatory speech in any way stop or even slow the action. It is only one move in the love-affair and that, in its turn, is the prelude to her co-operation with Jason in the winning of the golden fleece. But we can best see the difference between Ovid and the neoteric or Hellenistic 'short epic' by comparing Ovid's Scylla (*Met.* VIII, 1–151) with the Scylla of the pseudo-Virgilian but neoterically conceived *Ciris*.[1]

---

[1] The *Ciris* is almost certainly not Virgilian (cf. Rudolph Helm, 'Ein Epilog zur Cirisfrage', *Hermes* 72 (1937), pp. 78–103) but is nevertheless based on good, neoteric models. Line 165 (*Bistonis oris*) recalls a phrase from Calvus' *Io* (Morel, frag. 12: *vistinis ora*, an undoubted corruption of *Bistinis ora*). Though Ovid also had used the phrase (at *Heroides* 16. 344) it seems much more likely that the *Ciris*

The story is a very simple one. Scylla was the daughter of Nisus, king of Megara. When his city was besieged by the Cretan Minos, Scylla was overcome by a fatal passion for the besieger. She committed, in effect, parricide by cutting off the lock of purple hair from which Nisus, much like Samson, drew all his strength and power. She thus tried to buy Minos' love by the sacrifice of her father; his lock, as she thought, would be her dowry. But Minos, though profiting from the deed, would have nothing to do with the beautiful parricide. In the *Ciris* he actually punished her by hanging her in chains from his ship; in Ovid's version, he simply left her behind on the shore. Finally she was turned into a seabird.[1] In the *Ciris*, the story has the following salient features: (1) Scylla's love for Minos is given a quite external motivation (an unwitting offence of Juno), and there is no attempt to show its development when and as she encounters Minos himself (lines 158–65). (2) Her love is depicted in a quite pictorial way resembling that of Ariadne in Catullus 64 (cf. *Ciris* 165–86). (3) The major episode is a dramatic dialogue between Scylla and her nurse Carme. This is clearly Euripidean in inspiration and obviously recalls the Phaedra–Nurse scene of the *Hippolytus*. The only actual effect of this long episode, however, is to retard Scylla's original decision to sever the lock. The speeches of Scylla and Carme are for the most part set pieces of static pathos. (4) All the action intervening between her renewed decision to sever the lock and her dreadful punishment by Minos is passed over asymmetrically in only five lines (386–90). (5) Her punishment (*tum suspensa novo ritu de navibus altis*, line 389), her long final monologue (404–58) and her metamorphosis have little organic connection. We are not told *why* Minos punished her; her lament has no actual effect on

got it from the hexameter *Io*, especially since there seem to be other allusions to the *Io* in the poem (see Appendix, p. 383). There are also definite allusions to both Cinna's *Zmyrna* and Catullus' *Peleus and Thetis* in the *Ciris*. Cf. W. Ehlers, 'Die Ciris und ihr Original', *Museum Helveticum* 11 (1954), pp. 65–88 and my *Virgil*, p. 395 and Appendix, pp. 379 f.

[1] There is another version (given in *Met.* XIV) of the story in which Scylla becomes a sea-monster.

anything; her metamorphosis is attributed only to divine concern for the cruel injury to her body caused by the long sea-journey that is rather unnecessarily described at some length.

Ovid's account is by contrast a really continuous narrative unified by the poet's emotional identification of himself with Scylla (though his empathy here implies only a very moderate degree of sympathy). He does not mention the Juno incident: the episode starts with the war waged by Minos against Scylla's father Nisus and in particular with her first glimpse of Minos from the city's tower. It is the sight of the handsome king which inflames Scylla, and we follow both her vision and her emotions (19–37). The soliloquy of lines 44–80 shows the process of reasoning by which she reaches her fatal decision and, as is usual in the 'empathetic-sympathetic'[1] style of narrative, it is not sharply differentiated in point of view from the narrative proper: both the author's *description* of Scylla's emotions and her own account of them represent Scylla's psyche at work as Scylla herself sees it. Nor does the soliloquy stop the narrative action: rather it carries on the psychological process at work in Scylla to a decisive point. Though the ensuing account (81–103) of Scylla's cutting of the lock and presentation of it to Minos, of his horrified rejection of her love and departure without her, is altogether very brief, it fully preserves the narrative continuity. Minos does not devise a new mode of punishment, as in the *Ciris*, but merely leaves her behind. Scylla's brief speech when she presents the lock (90–4) and Minos' response (97–100), amply suffice to explain Minos' horrified departure without his would-be mistress. Her ensuing speech of mixed entreaty and invective is delivered before she leaps after his ship and in part motivates the leap. The actual metamorphosis results not, as in the *Ciris*, from divine pity for her injured body (without any dramatic relation to the action) but rather from the attack of Nisus (now a sea-gull) upon her as she

[1] This term is fully defined in my *Virgil* (pp. 48–61). By empathetic-sympathetic style I mean a style where the author both feels *with* (puts himself in the place of) and feels *for* (overtly sympathizes with) his characters.

clings to the ship: she is forced to release her hold and becomes a bird before she can touch the water in her fall.

This episode is in no sense the best example of Ovid's narrative art, but it certainly illustrates the difference between his style and the neoteric style of the *Ciris*. In Ovid the speeches and the narrative are woven into one whole: all—with the exception of the few lines devoted to Minos' rejection of her love—is written from Scylla's viewpoint and forms a continuous story of her changing psychological situation; even the metamorphosis is a quite logical outcome of it. In the *Ciris* the speeches have but little relation to the narrative and do not at all further the action: they merely accentuate the pathos of two *moments*—when the nurse catches Scylla outside her father's door, and when Scylla hangs in chains from the ship. Neither the awakening of her love nor her metamorphosis has any really organic connection with the narrative.

Thus the difference between Ovid's epic narrative and the Hellenistic, elegiac or neoteric narratives seems reasonably clear. There are not many places where we can compare Ovid with a Hellenistic or neoteric source, but there is no reason to suppose that even a major discovery of Hellenistic or neoteric verse would reverse our conclusions. Ovid's narrative in the *Metamorphoses* has (unlike all elegiac and neoteric narrative) the symmetry, elevation and other characteristics of epic and it has also a *subjective* slant to its apparently epic continuity which wholly differentiates it from both Homeric and Hellenistic epic.

We can, in fact, document this same point wherever we can find the Hellenistic or neoteric sources of Ovid. Even the only place where we really have Ovid's Callimachean model in full (Erysichthon: *Met.* VIII, 738–875; sixth *Hymn* of Callimachus, lines 25–117) makes the point clear.[1]

Erysichthon was the unfortunate youth who was condemned to unappeasable hunger because he cut down the tree or grove of the

[1] Cf. the accounts of Erysichthon below (pp. 203 f.) and Appendix (pp. 413 f.) Callimachus is certainly not Ovid's only model here but the main point to be made is that Ovid deliberately diverges from Callimachus.

goddess Demeter. The story is thus a very appropriate one for
Callimachus' Demeter hymn. Erysichthon is the type of the
profane who cannot understand religious respect or awe: thus they
overstep the line of right conduct and by their overstepping
(ὑπερβασία) bring calamity not only on themselves but on their
friends and household. Callimachus' emphasis is, therefore, as
Hans Diller has pointed out,[1] on the 'little world' of Erysichthon's
rather bourgeois family (he is a king's son, but the kingdom
is very small: the palace nothing more than a moderate farm-
house) and on the social milieu he brings down with his own ruin.
Callimachus has, in fact, two concerns: he first shows us what
'overstepping' really is and then shows its effect on the innocent
friends and family. Demeter is a kindly goddess who does not at
once try to overawe the *lad* (he is actually called τέκνον, 'lad') by
her divine presence: she first approaches him in the guise of an old
priestess, obviously a revered and familiar figure in the locality, and
warns him not to persist in his sacrilege. It is only when he scowls
at her and threatens to attack her too (nothing is going to stop
him from building his new banquet hall) that she doffs her disguise
and becomes the terrible divinity (57):

> Angered then beyond words, Demeter appeared as true
> goddess:
> Her footsteps trod on the earth: her head reached up to
> Olympus.

'You will now have banquets enough!' she tells him. The anger,
it is clear, is the result of his reckless impiety: the goddess does
not simply avenge the *act*; it is the bad spirit of Erysichthon that
excites her. He is obviously a person on whom divine kindness
is wasted.

We then turn to his family and household. For the hunger
(*limos*) is passed over in one line (66) and we see only its effects:
Erysichthon sits apart eating, eating—while his poor parents try
to hide their disgrace:

---

[1] Diller, p. 28.

Twenty prepared his dinner and twelve men brought him the
    wine.
Along with Demeter, Dionysus also was angry
For Dionysus is vexed at whatever vexes Demeter.
Nor did his parents send him to party or banquet,
Shamed as they were: all sorts of excuses they made for him.
Came to invite him, to the games of Athena Itonias,
Ormenid friends, but his mother refused them.
'He's not in. For yesterday he went to Crannon
After a debt of a hundred bullocks.' Came also Polyxo,
Aktorion's mother—she was getting her child's wedding ready—
To invite both Triopas and his son to it.
But the deeply grieved mother, weeping, responded:
'Triopas will come, but a boar has hurt Erysichthon,
Upon sweet-gladed Pindos; he's been nine days in his bed.'
Ah, unfortunate mother, child-loving, what lies did you not
    tell?
Someone was giving a feast: 'Erysichthon's away.'
Someone was taking a bride: 'A discus has hurt Erysichthon.'
Or, 'He fell off his chariot' or 'He's counting his sheep in
    Othrys.'

Finally we see the terrible dénouement: the father's despairing
and helpless prayer, the disappearance of all the livestock (even the
horses, even the cat that scares the mice!) and last of all the overt
disgrace—the young prince begging at the crossroads for crusts
and refuse.

Ovid's Erysichthon belongs to an utterly different world and
style. The young lad of Callimachus, his parents, sisters, and sor-
rowing household are quite absent. Ovid's hero is no boy but a
middle-aged man with a grown-up daughter: his social milieu is
virtually non-existent. He is, in fact, simply *Evil* itself, neither
individualized nor motivated and, therefore, quite unreal. A great
deal of the episode (lines 757–829, 73 out of 141 lines) describes the
process by which the *famine* was conveyed to Erysichthon (a point
passed over by Callimachus in one line). There is no attempt to

bring Demeter or Ceres on to the human scene (no dissuading priestess) but, rather, an almost immediate setting in motion of the divine chain of command: the tree bleeds and dies, the other tree nymphs (they are regular portraits of suffering innocence) appeal to Ceres; she dispatches a curiously anonymous mountain nymph (*montani numinis unam...oreada*) to *Fames*—Hunger personified. A startling description or *ekphrasis* makes much of Hunger's residence and all the paradoxical wonder of the scene: *Ceres* begging the aid of *Hunger*! Then, just like Virgil's Allecto, *Fames* comes to Erysichthon in the night. He dreams of hunger before he wakes to be hungry in sober reality. From then on the story of his famine is told in rather trite similes: the ocean absorbing streams and rivers, fire growing by what it feeds on. The use of his metamorphosis-prone daughter to swell his diminishing income (*census*) comes at the end with deliberate anticlimax. In any event, his destruction is a foregone conclusion: he literally eats himself up. The idea of social disgrace—the Callimachean beggar at the crossroads—is, of course, quite absent. The whole thing is generalized, allegorical, grandiose; there is no effort to make Erysichthon or his surroundings human.

At first sight a modern reader is tempted to wonder why Ovid wished to expose himself to such a devastating comparison. Why reduce the charming simplicity—the delicate humanity as well as religious sensitivity of Callimachus—to this absurd pastiche of Virgil? What is gained by the rhetorical exaggeration of Virtue and Vice, the grotesque personification of Famine, the elaborate divine machinery, the deliberate abstention from any sort of realistic or human detail? But a second reading shows us that Ovid is after all effective in his own quite un-Callimachean way. What he is really interested in are startling 'effects' or clever 'points': the *frisson* of the nymph as she approaches *Fames*, the paradox of *Ceres* (Food) using *Fames* (Hunger), the curious fact that blood comes from a tree, the highly-coloured contrast of *Vice* and *Innocence*, the grisly appearance and *comitatus* of *Fames*, the increase of Erysichthon's hunger by the food he consumes (841–2):

cibus omnis in illo
causa cibi est, semperque locus fit inanis edendo.

Food made him feed, and feeding made him void.

Ovid is, as it were, 'piling it on', deliberately exaggerating the epic décor and allegory to an absurdly pictorial precision and all the while turning the epic diction into clever conceits and paradoxes.

Obviously this is not typical of Ovid's general epic style. For example, he does not here, as elsewhere, show any particular empathy for his characters, though even here he cannot refrain from some empathy and especially from commenting on, from 'editorializing', the story. In the lines about Erysichthon (782–3):

> Moliturque genus poenae *miserabile, si non*
> *ille suis esset nulli miserabilis actis*
>
> *She planned a punishment, which, did his sin*
> *Not forfeit pity, pity well might win;*

or about the mountain nymph (811–12):

> Quamquam aberat longe, quamquam modo venerat illuc
> *visa tamen sensisse famem*
>
> *And though so distant, and so short the deal,*
> *She felt starvation's power, or seemed to feel,*

we see Ovid both communicating his characters' feelings and interpreting them. But actually the main purpose of the episode is not to engage the reader's empathy and sympathy. It is meant to be taken as an exaggeration, almost a parody, of epic, a bravura piece (we shall see why when we come to its context and position in the plan of the poem).[1] The important point to note now, however, is the epic continuity of the narrative: the pace never slackens long enough to dwell on the homely but peripheral details so dear to Callimachus. It is the wickedness of the act, the vengeance of the

----

[1] Pp. 203 f. below.

goddess, the terror of the punishment that in Ovid takes the place of the parents' social embarrassment and degradation. Or rather these are the things to which Ovid at least gives lip-service; whatever he may do with the epic style, he at least maintains it as a formal front and above all maintains the epic scale and pace.

Enough, perhaps, has now been said to illustrate the epic quality of the *Metamorphoses*, especially the epic continuity of narrative. It is clear, as we shall see, that the style is not uniform; that while it can approximate the high epic or Virgilian manner, it can also approach the neoteric, idyllic and even elegiac manners. Between the almost clamorously epic exploits of Perseus and Meleager or of the Lapiths and Centaurs on the one hand, and the much more homely tales of Pyramus and Thisbe, Philemon and Baucis, Salmacis or Pygmalion on the other, there is obviously a wide gulf. The important point is that Ovid never quite abandons either the continuity or the dignity of his epic narrative. Thus Polyphemus' plaintive song to Galatea turns abruptly toward Acis and almost imperceptibly merges into the story of Acis' death and metamorphosis (XIII, 854 ff.). Again, though the stories of the Minyades, especially *Pyramus and Thisbe* and *Salmacis*, are definitely below the epic level of the ensuing Ino and Perseus episodes, they are deliberately set in a frame (the impiety and metamorphosis of the Minyades themselves) that keeps them well within the continuity and perspective of the whole poem. We are never allowed to lose sight of either the restlessly continuous sweep of the poem or the pervading unity of its style.

The style, as we have just seen, is most Virgilian in its use of empathy and subjective commentary. Just as Virgil reads Aeneas' mind in such lines as (*Aen.* IV, 279–86):

> At vero Aeneas aspectu obmutuit *amens*,
> arrectaeque horrore comae et vox faucibus haesit.
> *Ardet abire fuga dulcisque relinquere* terras,
> *attonitus* tanto monitu imperioque deorum.
> *Heu quid agat? Quo nunc reginam ambire furentem*
> *audeat adfatu? Quae prima exordia sumat?*

Atque animum nunc huc celerem nunc dividit illuc
in partisque rapit varias perque omnia versat

*But Aeneas stood dumb and senseless at the sight; his hair rose
in horror; his voice stuck in his throat. He longs to take flight,
to leave the sweet land, astounded as he is by such a warning
and by the order of the gods. O what should he do? With
what word now can he dare address the furious queen? How
begin his speech to her? And his swift thoughts go here, go
there; his mind rushes in varied directions and turns everything over,*

and comments on the action in such lines as (*Aen.* IV, 169–72):

*Ille dies primus leti primusque malorum
causa fuit; neque* enim *specie famave movetur*
nec iam *furtivum Dido meditatur amorem*:
coniugium vocat, hoc praetexit nomine culpam

*That day was the beginning of death, the primal cause of many
woes. Nor is Dido moved by appearances or reputation nor
does she plan any more a hidden love. She calls it marriage;
by this word she hides her sin,*

so Ovid reads Medea's mind in the lines (*Met.* VII, 85–8):

posses ignoscere amanti.
Spectat, et in vultu *veluti tum denique viso*
lumina fixa tenet, nec se mortalia *demens*
ora videre putat, nec se declinat ab illo

*Well might a lover, without blame, adore.
As though till then unseen, his beauty caught
And held her gaze, and in her frenzied thought
He seemed not mortal: all in vain she tried
To turn her glances, and herself, aside,*

or the mind of the impassioned Tereus (*Met.* VI. 490–3):

At rex Odrysius, quamvis secessit, in illa
aestuat; et repetens faciem motusque manusque

qualia vult fingit quae nondum vidit; et ignes
ipse suos nutrit, *cura removente soporem*

But, though the Thracian prince retired, his breast,
On fire with Philomela, found no rest.
He saw again her face, her hands, her mien,
And pictured, as he wished them, charms not seen.
Feeding his own tormenting flames, he lay,
And turned and tossed the sleepless night away,

and combines both empathy and comment in the following lines about Tereus' guilty love for Philomela (*Met.* vi, 465–74):

Et nihil est, quod non effreno captus amore
ausit; nec capiunt inclusas pectora flammas.
Iamque *moras male fert* cupidoque revertitur ore
ad mandata Prognes et agit sua vota sub illa.
Facundum faciebat amor; quotiensque rogabat
ulterius iusto, *Prognen ita velle ferebat.*
Addidit et lacrimas, *tamquam mandasset et illas.*
Pro superi, *quantum mortalia pectora caecae*
noctis habent! Ipso sceleris molimine Tereus
creditur esse pius laudemque a crimine sumit

He sticks at nothing, by that rage possessed,
And scarce can lock his passion in his breast,
Or brook delay, but with fond speech recurs
To Procne's plans, and masks his hopes with hers.
Love makes him fluent: if entreaties go
Too far, he hints that Procne wished it so;
Tears too he sheds, as if she bade them flow.
O gods above, how dim is mortal sight;
How thick in human hearts the veil of night!
Tereus draws credit from his guilt, and seems
True husband, while he lays his treacherous schemes.

This is a style that is, on the whole, very un-Greek. In Virgil as in large parts of Ovid, it enabled the poet to establish an emotional continuum—to follow empathetically the thoughts and emotions of a given character and to relate events through his consciousness, while at the same time maintaining a quite personal relationship with the reader.[1] In this narrative style the objectivity of both speech (even when put in quotes) and action was greatly diminished, but the lyric intensity of the poetry was often much exalted. Here, however, the personality of the narrating poet could make all the difference. An intense and serious poet like Virgil could greatly heighten the *ethos* of his epic: a less serious poet like Ovid could considerably relax the tension. Where Ovid 'imitates' or refers to Virgil in the *Metamorphoses*, he is clearly not striving to rival Virgil on Virgil's own serious terms, but rather seeking to show how differently he could make the same thing look. We cannot, therefore, take the 'imitations' as typical of Ovid: when he approaches seriousness he is never engaged on a Virgilian subject. But they do reveal some of the salient distinctions between Virgil and Ovid.

A good instance is Ovid's retelling of the Achaemenides episode (*Aeneid* III, 588–683; *Met.* XIV, 154–222). In Virgil this was a most solemn and awe-inspiring affair.[2] Achaemenides was overlooked and abandoned by Ulysses and his crew when they fled from the Cyclopes. His squalid appearance is part of his terrible ordeal, his struggle for existence among the monsters. He asks the Trojans not for life so much as for the restitution of his humanity—even death if it be from human hands: *si pereo, hominum manibus periisse iuvabit.* Everything is here designed by Virgil to accent the uncanny and awful character of Polyphemus—*monstrum horrendum informe ingens*—and the terrible *homelessness* of Achaemenides, the human abandoned to the inhuman. Ovid's Achaemenides, however, is spruce and well-dressed (he is now at Caieta, far from Cyclops-land) and tells his story to his former shipmate with no inconsiderable relish. He cleverly comments on the incongruity of his apprehension for Ulysses' ship when he himself was not in it. He heaps up and clearly enjoys the horrors of the cannibalism.

---

[1] See my account of the subjective style in *Virgil*, ch. III *passim*.
[2] Cf. *Virgil*, pp. 262–4.

What he really congratulates himself about is his escape from a living tomb. (He can now get a better burial-place than the Cyclops' stomach!) And Ovid's Polyphemus is not, like Virgil's, an uncanny monster but a most articulate cannibal who expresses his feelings in an amusing speech.

We need not, perhaps, make too much of this obvious parody. The important point is to see it as such and not simply as an instance of Ovid's woeful inferiority to a great poet. Here, as in Ovid's retelling of the Orpheus story (*Met.* x, 1–77; xi, 1–84 and *Georgics* iv, 453–527), the conversion of Virgil's tragedy into comedy has its own weight and meaning in the *Metamorphoses* as a whole. But this does not mean that the *Metamorphoses* as a whole is only parody or bathos. It means, rather, that Ovid is not Virgil, that his values are quite different and that his 'epic style' is the medium of an altogether different poetical purpose.

We can see this in the quite distinct attitudes of the two poets toward continuity of narrative. Virgil's narrative was continuous for the very good reason that his epic was an easily comprehensible unity, a unity of mood and *ethos* as well as of plot. But Ovid's continuity was, as it were, a necessity imposed by the very diversity of his material, by his obvious lack of a comprehensive plot. He had at all hazards to preserve the appearance of steady progression and movement, even when leaping as it were from one plot to another. Hence the un-Virgilian character of Ovid's metric: he sacrificed most of the weight, gravity and *ethos* of Virgil's hexameter to rapid and unbroken movement. By increasing the number of dactyls, regularizing the pauses and, above all, reducing the elisions, he made his lines move at a very accelerated pace.

Consider, for example, Ovid's account of Achaemenides and Polyphemus (*Met.* xiv, 210–13):

> Me tremor invasit: stabam sine sanguine maestus,
> mandentemque videns eiectantemque cruentas
> ore dapes et frusta mero glomerata vomentem.
> talia fingebam misero mihi fata parari.

An ague seized me: faint with fear I stood,
And watched him, chewing now his bloody food,
And now disgorging gobbets mixed with wine;
And such a fate I fancied would be mine.

These lines obviously recall Virgil's (*Aen.* III, 630–5):

Nam simul expletus dapibus vinoque sepultus
cervicem inflexam posuit, iacuitque per antrum
immensus saniem eructans et frusta cruento
per somnum commixta mero, nos magna precati
numina sortitique vices una undique circum
fundimur...

For as soon as he, filled with his meal and buried deep in
drink, let down his drooping neck and lay athwart the cavern,
huge, drooling slaver and scraps mixed with bloody wine as he
slept, we then after praying to the gods and choosing lots for
what each should do, surround him on all sides together.

The real difference here is not to be discovered simply by counting dactyls and spondees or locating caesurae and diaereses. It is of course notable that Virgil has here three and Ovid no elisions (the proportion of elisions to the total of lines in the whole *Aeneid* and *Metamorphoses* is 15·6 per cent for Ovid and 50·3 per cent for Virgil).[1] But the point of most importance is that in Ovid the principal *cola* (i.e. the phrases or clauses that form some sort of meaningful unit) end or begin with the major (third foot) caesura or, in the case of three-part lines like 212, with the major caesurae (or diaereses) of the second and fourth feet. In Virgil this is not so: the major *cola* (or units of grammar or meaning) more often overrun the major caesurae or pauses as in the lines quoted just above. This Ovidian combination of sense-units with metrical units makes inevitably for a much smoother and quicker verse-flow—an effect which is of course accentuated by the relative preponderance of dactyls (note

---

[1] See A. Siedow, *De Elisionis usu in hexametris Latinis* (1911), p. 55.

that three of Virgil's lines, 631–3, begin with spondees; only one, 211, of Ovid's) and absence of elisions.[1] At the same time Ovid achieves a much higher coincidence of accent and ictus than Virgil: thus three of the Ovidian lines above (but only one of the Virgilian lines) unite both accents in the initial word. But even this is not all: the elaborate combination of dependent clauses and participles (*simul...expletus...sepultus...posuit iacuitque inmensus ...eructans,—nos*, etc.), such as we see here in Virgil, is generally avoided by Ovid. Thus in the lines given above, he starts a new sentence (or independent clause) in the second half of line 210 (after the main caesura) and another at the beginning of line 213 and carefully connects (in lines 211, 212) the present-participial objects of *videns* (*mandentem, eiectantem, vomentem*). The greater clarity of the grammar and hence the greater rapidity of the comprehension are apparent. Even the rhymes of line 211 (*mandentemque, eiectantemque* each beginning the two metrical halves of the line) speed up the movement.

Of course no comparison of a few lines has any probative value *per se* but in fact the example above does bring out very well the main metrical differences between the two poets, as any reader can easily see for himself. In a word, Ovid puts in everything (dactyls, regular pauses, coincidence of ictus and accent, rhyme, alliteration, grammatical simplicity and concision) that will speed up and lighten; leaves out everything (elision, spondees, grammatical complexity, clash of accent and ictus, overrunning of metrical by sense units) that will slow down and encumber his verse. There are of course numerous exceptions: at times Ovid wants to go slowly, to produce a specially Virgilian effect, to make his lines harsh or lumbering. But in general Ovid limits such special effects: he

[1] For Ovid's arrangement of *cola* cf. especially W. F. Jackson Knight in *Ovidiana* (pp. 106–20). A. G. Lee's edition of *Met.* I (1953) contains an excellent summary and bibliography of Ovid's use of the hexameter in the *Metamorphoses* (pp. 31–6). Traian Costa ('Formele Hexametrului la Ovidiu', *Publius Ovidius Naso, Biblioteca Antica Studii* II (1957): this is the Roumanian bimillennial *Festschrift* for Ovid) gives elaborate comparative statistics showing the arrangement of dactyls and spondees in the *Metamorphoses* as compared with other works of Ovid and other Roman poets. Cf. also the brief summary account in Wilkinson, p. 150.

makes, for example, much less of onomatopoeia (sound–sense correspondence) than Virgil does.[1]

But what is the meaning, the point of Ovid's *epic* style, his rapid metre, his evident concern to make his poem progress or 'go'? Is it adequately explained just by the sheer necessity of liaison between the separate episodes? Some critics have thought so and seen the whole poem as a kind of clever pastiche. 'The essential thing', says Wilkinson of his verse, 'was that the reader should glide easily on without pausing to reflect.'[2] 'The effect', says W. F. J. Knight, speaking of his smooth hexameters, 'is to make horrors humorous or at least to satirize myth and take the weight out of tragedy.'[3] To Hans Diller it is all a 'Spiel des Verstandes'.[4] Ovid hurries from story to story, from detail to detail, from effect to effect, glossing over the absence of any intrinsic or organic unity—any serious purpose—by his metrical and narrative art. What really interest him are isolated pictures or scenes (like the 'numbers' in a vaudeville): his art consists in letting each detail catch his readers' attention without ever arresting it; no one scene was of itself able to endure a long or serious examination. His narrative continuity is, in a word, delightful and superficial. From this point of view (it is not altogether false to one side of Ovid), the epic style is only a façade and the chronological pro- gression only a trick. There is no real substance to either.

We must now try to see how much truth there is to such plausible criticism. And here we come back to the great stumbling block for anyone who would find meaning in the poem's 'con- tinuity'. This is nothing less than its manifest and rampant variety. For why, after all, the variety, why the insistence on such hetero- geneous and discordant subject-matter? If from one point of view Ovid strives for unity of style and continuity of narrative, from another he strives quite as much for the most ample diversity. Indeed his attention to variety and diversity is far more explicit

[1] Cf. Wilkinson, p. 236. But there is more onomatopoeia in the *Metamorphoses* than Wilkinson seems to perceive. Cf. pp. 248–50 below.

[2] Pp. 150–1.

[3] *Ovidiana*, p. 111.   [4] Pp. 35–7.

77

and intense than even his very mixed material demanded. His is fundamentally not an inherited but a willed and aesthetically informed variety, as definite and explicit a part of his art as any other.

To a certain extent, of course, this can be explained simply by his concern not to bore his reader by repetition. After all, many of his myths were very much alike and abounded in stock motifs and characters. There is the amorous god and the fugitive virgin; the avenging god and the wicked mortal; the monotonous wail of the abandoned heroine or the thwarted *libido* of the abnormal heroine; the recurrent metamorphoses into the same stones, trees, birds or springs; the unchanging jealousy of Juno, gallantry of Jupiter or chastity of Diana; in short, the singular uniformity of both human and divine behaviour, particularly at times of emotional crisis. Only a constant variation of plot and treatment could overcome the intrinsic monotony of such themes. Furthermore, Ovid was well aware that his highest epic flights could not be indefinitely prolonged and had to be quickly relieved by lighter contrasts. He reserved his great epic pieces, like the boar-slaying of Meleager and the battle of Lapiths and Centaurs, for special parts of his poem and preceded and followed them by passages in a very different vein. His book could not be all war or love or vengeance or comedy. No one knew better than Ovid that variety was the spice of life.

Yet closer inspection quickly reveals that his variety was not an unsophisticated or simple thing. In the first book, for example, he introduces for the first time the motif of the determined virgin courted by the passionate god (Daphne and Apollo). There are several repetitions of this motif in the whole poem: indeed there is one repetition in the first book itself, two more in the second book, one in the fifth (Arethusa pursued by the stream-god Alpheus) and at least brief allusions to the theme thereafter (e.g. at the end of Book XI). It is, however, noteworthy that Ovid not only varies his use of this motif but varies it in a sequentially significant way. Thus the Jupiter–Io story has a quite different emphasis from the

Daphne–Apollo story that precedes it: in the latter the chase is the significant thing and the metamorphosis is the result of Daphne's desire to escape the pursuing Apollo; in the *Jupiter–Io* (that immediately follows it) the chase or courtship is reduced to very small compass and the emphasis is put on Juno's jealousy (of which Io's metamorphosis is a consequence). This new theme (Juno's jealousy) also dominates the following Callisto story, but here the simply comic side of Juno is much toned down. We are thus prepared for the truly savage violence of Juno in the Semele and Ino episodes (where the virgin-courtship motif has quite disappeared). It is not until Ovid deliberately returns to the mood and theme of Book I in the long Ceres episode of Book VI that we find a story (the pursuit and metamorphosis of Arethusa) that directly and fully recalls the *Daphne–Apollo* (i.e. the extensive chase and the metamorphosis that saves the girl from the god). Ovid in other words does not simply vary motifs without reference to sequence: he gradually subtracts and adds motif-elements so that in the end he has, in fact, substituted one complete motif for another and shifted the tone and mood altogether. If and when he recurs to a former motif (as in the Arethusa story) it is because he deliberately wants to recall it for a particular purpose (as we shall see).

Another very good instance of this procedure is his use of what I may call the Pentheus–Agave motif: a mother, under Bacchic possession, kills her own child. This first occurs in Book III in its traditional Bacchic form, the Pentheus story itself. In Book IV, however, Juno counterfeits Bacchic possession and uses it against the innocent Ino and Athamas (he, possessed by Juno's diabolic minion, Tisiphone, tears his own child from his wife's bosom and dashes it to pieces; she tries to leap off the cliff with her other child). Then in Book VI Procne uses a mock-Bacchic revel to liberate her raped sister Philomela and the two together kill Procne's child, the little Itys, thus avenging themselves on the villainous Tereus. Finally in Book VIII we have another mother, Althaea, who deliberately destroys her own child (she actually debates the matter in a soliloquy). We have thus progressed from the themes of religious possession and unconscious child-murder to human passion and conscious crime. The sequence of similar but constantly changing motifs has not only brought us from gods to men but from man's religious to man's erotic behaviour. We see both the likeness and the difference between divine and human vengeance.

In other words, Ovid's variety had method in it. His problem was to arrange his episodes so that they together represented some sort of sequence and plan. But it is quite clear that this plan could only with the greatest difficulty be incorporated in the ongoing or continuous narrative. Ovid had to keep up appearances, to be very careful to link each episode with the next. But the linkage in itself is often extremely superficial, often simply an ingenious *tour de force* that is not meant to demonstrate anything but the author's cleverness. Here, indeed, Ovid does approximate the easy discursiveness of Callimachus. Yet it is evident that Ovid himself puts no particular store on such transitions: they are in many cases—though not always—so absurd or far-fetched that we can hardly restrain our amusement (and so without question Ovid intended). But Ovid's main concern was obviously not with the links themselves: the links, in fact, are but a device for giving his essential plan an appearance or veneer of continuity.[1] Or more precisely, he is concerned with two very different kinds of continuity. One is the superficial narrative connection of the episodes; the other is the much more significant movement or sequence of motifs and ideas. At certain key places the two coincide (otherwise the effect would be simply schizophrenic) but there is no general coincidence. We can never discover the plan or meaning of the poem by a study of the links in themselves. Indeed, the links are in many cases awkward or improbable precisely because the arrangement of the episodes is not based on any

---

[1] The literature on the transitions of the *Metamorphoses* is not very helpful. R. Schmidt, *Die Übergangstechnik in den Met. des O.* (Diss. Breslau, 1938) and W. Klimmer, *Die Anordnung des Stoffes in den ersten vier Büchern von O.'s Met.* (Diss. Erlangen, 1932) do not penetrate beyond the links themselves or pay any attention to the order behind or concealed by the links.

obvious narrative connection between them. The real narrative, so to speak, is not to be found in the apparent or ostensible one.

We must try then to find out what Ovid's underlying plan or principle of arrangement was. It is quite clear that what was supposed to harmonize the apparently contradictory elements of variety and continuity was the concept of change or metamorphosis. In one sense Ovid interpreted this quite narrowly along the lines, doubtless, of such didactic works as Nicander's *Heteroioumena*. Thus, though he often introduced tales that were not true metamorphoses (e.g. Phaethon, Pentheus, Perseus, Proserpina, Medea, Cephalus and Procris, Meleager, the Lapiths and Centaurs) he usually followed them by, or incorporated in them, incidental metamorphoses of one sort or another. The sisters of Phaethon become poplars; Pentheus is warned by the tale of the Tyrrhene sailors; Perseus finally turns his enemy into stone; Ceres, in searching for Proserpina, encounters Ascalaphus and Arethusa; the grieving companions of the dead Meleager become birds, etc. But this practice need not be taken as more than a gesture toward the reader, as if the poet were saying: 'You insist on a metamorphosis for each story: well, here it is!' It is easy to see that Ovid is not primarily concerned with the formal requirement that each and every episode be a true metamorphosis in the conventional, literal sense of the word. He also conceived of metamorphosis in a much more philosophical way and explicitly stated his view in the long Pythagoras soliloquy whose significance for the whole poem we shall consider more particularly in Chapter VIII (*Met.* xv, 177–85):   nihil est toto, quod perstet, in orbe.
Cuncta fluunt, omnisque vagans formatur imago;
ipsa quoque adsiduo labuntur tempora motu
non secus ac flumen, neque enim consistere flumen,
nec levis hora potest: sed ut unda impellitur unda,
urgeturque eadem veniens urgetque priorem,
tempora sic fugiunt pariter pariterque sequuntur
et nova sunt semper; nam quod fuit ante, relictum est,
fitque, quod haud fuerat, momentaque cuncta novantur.

Nothing in all the world is free from change:
All is a flux of forms that come and go;
While time itself glides on with ceaseless flow;
And like a stream that cannot stop or stay,
The restless hour goes fleeting on its way.
Like wave impelled by wave, which onward speeds,
Both driven itself, and driving what precedes,
So flee the times, and follow as they flee,
For ever new: what was, has ceased to be;
What has not been, is born, as, one by one,
Created ever new, the moments run.

Here his emphasis is not just on physical change of shape but on change as a universal principle. Nothing stands still; no image stays as it is; no moment remains the same. Everything is always different, always new. He applies the idea both to nature (physical phenomena) and to history (*Met.* xv, 215–17):

> nec quod fuimusve sumusve,
> cras erimus; fuit illa dies, qua semina tantum
> spesque hominum primae matrisque habitavimus alvo.

> *Nor tomorrow shall we be*
> *What we have been, and are: there was a day*
> *When housed within our mother's womb we lay.*

But man after all did not stay in the womb; he was born (*natura . . . emisit in oras*), grew up, grew old and died. So also on a larger scale, there is change and development in the *species* of animals and natural things (*nec species sua cuique manet*) and in the civilizations of man (Troy is a ruin, but Rome has risen to take its place).

But Ovid's problem, of course, was to convert the idea of change into the organizing principle of an epic. Unless he could show some *continuity or direction in change*, the principle of change could not in itself help him. But did he in fact see such continuity? What, in other words, was the real plan of his epic? It is curious that, so far as I can discover, this has heretofore eluded the critics and commentators. Or rather, they have all gone on the

tacit assumption that beyond the mere category of metamorphosis, the separate links, the sheer chronology and (though not
all have agreed on this) the more or less uniform epic style, there is
no plan or unifying factor to be found. This is why they have not
really taken Ovid's *carmen perpetuum* or continuous narrative very
seriously. But in point of fact, there is a very definite plan to the
poem, a plan which is, on the whole, both clear and coherent. We
can, of course, miss many of its finer points or, alternatively,
impose upon it a consistency and refinement that it does not
possess, but we can hardly fail to recognize its major outlines once
we actually see them.

The first thing to do is to note the poem's essential divisions.
Despite the 'continuity'—the poet's obvious determination to
heal all gaps by at least the appearance of unbroken narrative—
there are four unmistakable divisions or sections of the work:

Section I   Book I–Book II (end, line 875): The Divine Comedy
Section II Book III–Book VI, 400: The Avenging Gods
Section III Book VI, 401–Book XI (end, line 795): The Pathos of Love
Section IV Book XII–Book XV (end, line 879): Rome and the Deified Ruler

This division can be justified both by content-analysis and by
study of the homologous structures or plans of the separate parts.
The first section deals primarily with the gods and their amours
and constitutes what might well be called (though not in Dante's
sense) *The Divine Comedy*. With Book III, a quite different
subject-matter is emphasized, namely, the gods as *ministers of
vengeance* (hence my title for it). The emphasis is now not (as in
the first section) on the gods themselves but rather on those
mortals on whom their vengeance is executed (that is Cadmus,
Actaeon, Semele, Pentheus, the Minyades, Arachne, Niobe). The
divine-vengeance motif clearly continues through the stories of
Niobe, the Lycian Peasants and Marsyas (Book VI to l. 400). But at
VI, 401 (the Philomela–Procne–Tereus story) a quite new kind of
motif is emphasized: the theme of amatory tragedy (mortals—
especially women—disastrously involved in some sort of sexual
passion). This emphasis continues through the long episodes of

Cephalus–Procris, Scylla, Byblis and Myrrha to the story of Ceyx and Alcyone in Book XI (the Aesacus story that concludes Book XI forms the epilogue to the long succession of amatory disasters). The last section (Books XII–XV) begins with the story of Troy (XII–XIII) and ends with the story of Rome (XIII–XV): it is the properly historical part of the epic that both juxtaposes old Troy to new Rome and develops to a climax the greatest of all metamorphosis themes, deification of the hero.[1]

Each section reveals a very similar kind of balance or symmetry (though the first and last, I and IV, have each unique features). We can briefly indicate their plans here (though these will be, of course, much more fully explained in later chapters):

Section I (Books I–II)

(1) Epic Introductory Panel:
      The Creation and Fall of Man (Flood, Re-creation)   (415 lines)
            Divine *Amor*: Apollo, Daphne
            Divine *Amor*: Jupiter, Io
(2)   Epic Central Panel (Phaethon, Conflagration of
            Universe)   (432 lines)
            Divine *Amor*: Jupiter, Callisto
            Divine *Amor*: Apollo, Coronis
Transitional and Divine *Amor*: Hermes and Herse
concluding   Divine *Amor*: Jupiter, Europa
Amores

Section II (Books III–VI, 400)

(1) Vengeance Episodes (Actaeon, Semele, Narcissus–
      Echo, Pentheus)
      First Amatory Frame: Love Tales of the Minyades
      Epic Central Panel (Perseus–Andromeda–
      Phineus)   (449 lines)
      Second Amatory Frame: Love-tales of the Muses
      (Proserpina)
(2) Vengeance Episodes (Arachne, Niobe, Lycian Peasants,
      Marsyas)

---

[1] The division is of course obscured not only by Ovid's insistence on liaison (the appearance of unbroken narrative, *carmen perpetuum*) but by his preparation for, or anticipation of, one section by another. Yet the vengeance theme only becomes dominant (or isolated from the love theme) in Book III, the amatory *pathos* theme

SECTION III (BOOKS VI, 401–XI, END)

┌ (1) First Amatory *Pathos* (Philomela, Procne, Tereus)
│   A: Miracles of Death and Resurrection (set in
│   amatory frame)
│ ┌ (2) Second Amatory *Pathos* (Scylla)
│ │   ┌ First Epic Panel (Meleager–Althaea)   (287 lines)
│ │   │ Interset contrasting Theodicies (Philemon–
│ │   │   Baucis, Erysichthon)
│ │   └ Second Epic Panel (Hercules–Deianira–
│ │   Apotheosis)   (272 lines)
│ └ (3) Third Amatory *Pathos* (Byblis)
│   B: Miracles of Punishment and Reward (set in
│   amatory frame)
└ ┌ (4) Fourth Amatory *Pathos* (Myrrha)
  └ (5) Fifth Amatory *Pathos* (Ceyx–Alcyone)

SECTION IV (BOOKS XII–XV)

┌ (1) Troy (Lapiths and Centaurs)
│   Judgement of Arms (Rhetorical Panel)
└ (2) Troy (Hecuba)
      ┌ (1) ┌ Aeneas (Aniades)
      │   │   Amatory Story (Galatea, Scylla, Circe)
      │ (2) ┤ Aeneas (Sibyl, Achaemenides)
      │   │   Amatory Story (Circe, Picus, Canens)
      └ (3) └ Aeneas (Deification)
┌ (3) Rome (The Native Gods, Pomona–Vertumnus, Romulus)
│   Pythagoras Soliloquy (Philosophic Panel)
└ (4) Rome (Foreign Gods: Hippolytus, Aesculapius)
         Conclusion: Apotheosis of Caesar

The basic principle of structure here is that of symmetrical correspondence: each section (save the last) has one central panel (differentiated from the other episodes in bulk, content and style) with corresponding episodes on each side. Thus in the first section the long Phaethon panel is much more epic in tone and subject-matter (it is not strictly an amatory story) than the obviously matched *amores* on each side of it. Again, in the second section, the

at VI, 400 or 420 (Philomela–Procne–Tereus), and the strictly historical element (Troy–Rome) at XII. The *Ceyx–Alcyone* of XI is linked to history (Peleus) but it is obviously not in the least historical *per se*. The true meaning or function of the sections only becomes fully apparent when we grasp the design or plan of each.

epic Perseus episode (its 449 lines overlap the two central books,
IV and V) divides both the matching amatory groups (Minyades,
Muses) and the long vengeance episodes (Actaeon, Semele, Pentheus, Arachne, Niobe, etc.). The third part has again its central
epic panel but this is now divided into two distinct halves (Meleager, Hercules) separated by two obviously balancing theodicies
(Philemon–Baucis, Erysichthon). Around this central complex
are placed the main episodes of amatory tragedy and the matching
groups of miracles (death, rebirth, reward and punishment). In
the last section each of the outer portions (*Troy* and *Rome*) has its
own large centrepiece or panel (one in rhetorical and the other in
philosophical style) while the connecting Aeneas story is (for
obvious purposes of contrast) intricately interlaced by the
amatory escapades of Circe.

But what light does such a structural analysis shed on the continuity of the epic? The best short answer that can be made (in
anticipation of the more detailed analysis to come later) is that it
provides the element of stability against which both the necessary
variety and, above all, the unceasing process of motif transformation can be set in relief and given some semblance of continuity.
Each section has its own major theme (even though that, for variety's
sake, is diluted by lesser themes) and thus holds the reader's attention long enough to establish one major impression and set it in
effective contrast with the next impression to come. On the other
hand, each section shows its own development which its own
symmetry brings out: though the episodes after each central panel
correspond to those before it, they also reveal a significant change,
a change which almost insensibly prepares the reader for the next
major section. We may call this the *law of symmetrical progression*:
it is really a 'control' of the poem's restless variety and movement. An original motif, *ab*, never corresponds to an identical *ab*
later on, but instead corresponds to a congruous or similar but
different *ab* (or an *a'b'*).

Thus, in the first section, the chiastic 'correspondence' of the
Apolline and Jovian *amores* is quite unmistakable:

```
┌   Apollo–Daphne (ab)
│ ┌ Jupiter–Io (bc)
│ │ PHAETHON PANEL
│ └ Jupiter–Callisto (b'c')
└   Apollo–Coronis (a'b')
```

But (as we have already seen) the Callisto episode, though it clearly recalls and in part repeats the Io episode, adds to it quite new elements that directly anticipate the later Actaeon, Semele and Ino stories. The Coronis episode is concerned not so much with love as with tattle-tales and the god's jealousy and vengeance. This latter motif and another motif, the rescue of a god's unborn child, of course look ahead to the Semele and Bacchus episode of Section II, as Jupiter's conflict with Juno in the Callisto story looks ahead to it also and indeed to the major theme (the vengeful Juno) of the first half of Section II (up to the Perseus panel). Thus though, in a sense, the main topic of the Callisto and Coronis stories is *love* (the gods in love), they (unlike the preceding Daphne and Io stories) prepare the way for the motifs (especially the divine vengeance motif) of Section II. We can see the same principle at work in Sections II and III. The vengeance stories before the *Perseus* panel are quite different from those after it (Juno and Bacchus are replaced by Minerva and Latona as avenging gods; error and resistance to divine possession are replaced by envious pride as the 'crimes' to be avenged). But this is a new kind of vengeance that particularly brings out the human emotion involved: we are thus prepared for the great emphasis on human *pathos* in the following section (III). So too with the amatory stories before and after the Meleager–Hercules panel of the third section (in the first set, the metamorphoses are due to criminal violence; in the second to unreciprocated or thwarted passion). As we shall see, the type of metamorphosis also shifts with the emotions and actions portrayed. Finally, there is a developmental correspondence between the great epic 'panels' at the centres of each section. We have the *discomfited god* (Phoebus in the Phaethon story), the *triumphant hero* (Perseus), the *defeated* and *deified heroes* (Meleager,

Hercules) and finally (in Section IV) the *Roman deified hero* (Aeneas, Romulus, Caesar).

Again, while minor contrasting motifs within each section are certainly added to provide variety, they also serve quite as much to anticipate future sections. Thus the amatory tales of the Minyades (in Section II) really anticipate the main topic of Section III (amatory tragedy) just as the deification of Hercules in Section III clearly anticipates the deifications of Aeneas, Romulus and Augustus in Section IV. But, on the other hand, there are also *recalls* of former motifs which very effectively measure for the reader the distance (in action, feeling, etc.) that has been covered. Thus the long Ceres–Proserpina–Arethusa tale in Book VI takes us back, so to speak, to the atmosphere of Book I (the amorous god, the fleeing nymph, etc.) and brings out the contrast between amatory and vengeful gods. Again the Philemon–Baucis and Erysichthon legends of Book VIII inevitably recall the Lycaon and Deucalion–Pyrrha stories of the Flood: we are back once more in a world of crystal-clear theodicy, and we thus see with fresh insight its difference from the world of Medea or of Ceyx and Alcyone.

But the rather intricate *symmetrical* progression must not lead us to suppose that the poem has no main line or direction. There is variety and varied correspondence, but there is also a quite simple and impressive unity to each part and to the whole poem. Apart from the Creation scene of the opening, the first section is clearly devoted to the lighter, the amorous side of the gods: even Phaethon's father, the sun-god, is a somewhat ridiculous figure. In the second, the gods are pre-eminently avengers, and this change in their behaviour (the fact that they punish rather than love) carries with it an evident shift of our interest and sympathy. We are now much more concerned with the human beings who suffer than with the gods who make them suffer. This concern ultimately reaches a kind of climax in the Niobe story: she is certainly at fault, but she is mercilessly treated and, in the end, her petrifaction is not punishment, but mere recognition of the sheer insensibility to which she has been reduced. We are thus prepared for mankind itself, mankind without, or at least not mainly preoccupied by, the gods. Here metamorphosis is really an all but inevitable way out of an impossible situation, something that is no longer the punishment for, but the result of, an abnormal passion or an intense grief that can no longer endure human existence. In the Hercules story, however, we see how man can, by heroic and noble action, actually rise to the status of a god. This last theme is then, we need hardly say, developed to its Augustan climax in the final section.

It is only by bearing this structure in mind that we can properly understand the poem in detail. The episodic approach—the attempt to set each separate story against its sources and, on this piecemeal basis, work out a theory of Ovid's 'originality'—has been chiefly responsible for a good deal of scholarly misunderstanding of the *Metamorphoses* both in whole and in part. At times Ovid changes a source, at times prefers one to various alternative versions of a myth, at times adds or subtracts only a few significant details; but all these procedures are dictated by the effect or point he wants to bring out in a special context. In the *Daphne* and *Io* he is, basically, humorous; in the *Actaeon* and *Niobe* he verges on the pathetic; in the *Byblis* and *Ceyx–Alcyone* he is almost exclusively pathetic. In the *Perseus* and *Apotheosis of Caesar* he is deliberately Virgilian. Unless we feel the continuous shifts of mood and motif, of tone and style, the *diminuendo* and *crescendo* of his nominally epic narrative, we shall be quite unable to appreciate his approach to his sources—the way he picks and chooses, alters, revises, or occasionally repeats almost verbatim the material that he drew upon. The *Metamorphoses*, in short, is really a *carmen perpetuum*, a blend of continuity and change, of epic uniformity and un-epic variety, of specious transition and careful progression. It is above all a work of art. For it is the very height of folly to take Ovid's pseudo-Virgilian pretence of 'incompleteness'[1]

---

[1] Cf. *Tristia* I, 7. 11–40, especially 40: *emendaturus, si licuisset, eram.* But the gesture of burning the MS. seems an obvious imitation of Virgil. See Albert Grisart, 'La Publication des "Métamorphoses": une source du récit d'Ovide

too seriously and ignore the intricate plan of the poem. We must now turn from the bare bones of the poem's structure to its actual flesh and blood. The plan of the *Metamorphoses* (as just set forth) can be useful only in so far as it helps us to understand the substance of the poetry.

(*Tristes* I, 7. 11–40)', *Atti* II, pp. 125–55. Ovid admits that, despite his gesture, copies of the poem survived and, in *Tristia* II, he uses the poem's Augustan ending in his plea for mercy from the Emperor.

CHAPTER IV

THE DIVINE COMEDY

THE first section of the poem has an obviously symmetrical structure: two great epic panels (*Creation, Fall of Man and Flood*, I, 1–415; *Phaethon and the Conflagration of the Universe*, I, 747–79; II, 1–400) and pairs of divine *amores* (Apollo–Daphne, Jupiter–Io, Jupiter–Callisto, Apollo–Coronis, Hermes–Herse, Jupiter–Europa), the first four arranged in chiastic balance. The problem is to find out what this means.

It is fairly clear where Ovid got his basic design. In the *Fasti* (IV, 783 f.) he raises a question about the curious use of water and fire at the festival of the *Parilia*. Is it because these are the two great contraries from which all things come (*cunctarum contraria semina rerum*): or is it an allusion to Phaethon's fire and Deucalion's flood (793)?

> sunt qui Phaethonta referri
> credant et nimias Deucalionis aquas.

> *Those there are who think that Phaethon is alluded to and the*
> *superabundant waters of Deucalion.*

These myths (Phaethon, Deucalion) had long been associated with the two great catastrophes or Doomsdays, the Fire and the Flood. In Plato's *Timaeus* (22b) devastations by flood and fire are compared and the myth of Phaethon explained as a symbol of the latter. So also in Lucretius (v, 380 f.). Hyginus[1] tells, and (perhaps wrongly) attributes to Hesiod, a version which makes Deucalion's flood the means of quenching Phaethon's blaze. In any event Ovid saw fit to organize his first two books around the

---

[1] See Rzach, *Hesiodus*, 199. Haupt–Ehwald's suggestion (*ad loc.*) that Ovid found the two themes (flood–fire; Deucalion–Phaethon) coupled together in a mythological συναγωγή can hardly be right. Ovid had already coupled the themes in his *Fasti* (where the reference is obviously not to a συναγωγή).

two catastrophes and their appropriate myths. Jupiter was about
to destroy the world by his thunderbolts (*Met.* 1, 254–61):

> Sed timuit, ne forte *sacer tot ab ignibus aether*
> *conciperet flammas, longusque ardesceret axis.*
> *Esse quoque in fatis reminiscitur, adfore tempus,*
> *quo mare, quo tellus correptaque regia caeli*
> *ardeat* et mundi moles obsessa laboret.
> Tela reponuntur manibus fabricata Cyclopum.
> *Poena placet diversa, genus mortale sub undis*
> *perdere* et ex omni nimbos demittere caelo.

> *Now when about to strike, Jove stayed his hand,*
> *Lest, while his lightnings kindled every land,*
> *Some spark, by this vast conflagration sent,*
> *Should fire the sacred far-spread firmament.*
> *Mindful, moreover, how in fate's decree*
> *A time was doomed to come when land and sea*
> *And heaven's imperial seat, with all the frame*
> *Of the fixed universe, should fall in flame,*
> *The god replaced his fierce incendiaries,*
> *The lightning bolts (the Cyclops' work were these),*
> *And planned to send the rain, fire's opposite,*
> *From all the sky, and drown the race with it.*

The flames, however, that he then deferred almost have their way
in the *Phaethon*: Jupiter there calls the gods to witness that (*Met.* 11,
305):   nisi opem ferat, omnia fato
interitura gravi.
                    did he not lend his aid,
        all things would perish by a grievous fate.

But between the two catastrophes and their mythical accom-
paniments and consequences, intervene the *amores* of Apollo and
Jupiter, *amores* that are resumed after the Phaethon episode to
reach a sort of climax or symbolic finale with the Europa myth.
The Jupiter who began his amatory role in this section by making
Io a cow, ends it by making himself a bull. The association of the

two myths was used by Moschus in his *Europa* to produce an extremely subtle reinforcement of his basic amatory theme. On Europa's basket the story of Io is beautifully carved: she unwittingly carries her fate (or its emblem) with her as she goes to meet the entrancing bull. Ovid was not aiming at quite so delicate or restrained an effect. But we can hardly be wrong in seeing Moschus as another primary source of his plan for this part of his poem.

But what explains his use of such sources? Why this blending of the two catastrophes with the amorous cow and bull? We can understand his aim only by following his plan as he himself put it into execution. It will help, first of all, to reproduce the plan or schema of the section.

	Amores	*Epic Panels*	
Book I		Philosophical Exordium (Creation)	
1–415		Fall of Man (Four Ages)	Creation and
	E I	Flood (Universe inundated)	Flood Epic
		Re-creation of Man (Deucalion–Pyrrha)	
416–567	A 1: Apollo,	Daphne	
568–746	A 2: Jupiter,	Io	
747–774		Transition: Epaphus, Clymene, Phaethon	
Book II		Meeting of Phoebus and Phaethon	
1–400	E 2	Phaethon's Ride	Fire Epic
		Fire (Universe in Flames)	
		Death of Phaethon (Heliades, Cygnus)	
401–530	A 3: Jupiter, Callisto		
531–675	A 4: Apollo, Coronis		
676–832	A 5: Hermes–Herse–Aglauros		
833–875	Coda: Jupiter, Europa		

E I. The initial Creation–Fall–Flood epic is really one continuous, coherent narrative. We can analyse it thus:

(1) I, 1–4 (general introduction to whole poem)
(2) I, 5–88 (from Chaos to the *Creation* of Man) (84 lines)
(3) I, 89–162 (The *Fall* of Man: the Four Ages) (74 lines)
(4) I, 163–252 (The *Concilium Deorum*) (90 lines)
    [Speech of Jupiter: 182–243]
(5) I, 253–312 (The *Flood*) (60 lines)
(6) I, 313–415 (*Re-creation* of Man: Deucalion and Pyrrha) (103 lines)
    [Re-creation of animals: 416–33: *ignis* and *aqua* = *vapor*]

The story starts with the emergence of the world from aboriginal chaos (2) and ends with a partial repetition of the process,
the re-emergence of the world from the chaos of the deluge (6).
The change from creation to re-creation is brought about by the
Fall of Man (3) and by the devastating Punishment (Flood) which
is its consequence (5). Jupiter's speech (in 4), which occupies the
exact centre of the 415 lines, marks the transition between the two
extremes: between the Fall and its punishment; between the
iniquity of Lycaon and the innocence of Deucalion–Pyrrha;
between the old and the new creations. The whole story is told as
a single uninterrupted process of change.

Its tone is deliberately elevated and almost solemnly epic (at
least on the surface). The first eighty-five lines, after the brief introduction (1–4), are didactic and philosophical. Their likeness to
the beginning of Silenus' song in Virgil's sixth Eclogue is very
striking: obviously the proper way to begin a universal epic
of this sort was with the Hesiodic chaos, but in both Virgil and
Ovid an element of Stoic philosophy is added to Hesiod's cos-
mogony. For the time of creation precedes the origin of the
Olympians: there is only a vague, unnamed deity at work: *deus sive
natura, quisquis fuit ille deorum, mundi melioris origo, mundi fabricator,
ille opifex rerum.* A generalized cosmic process of dissociation and
cohesion, not the piquant activity of anthropomorphic gods, is
being described. But we must. not overdo the significance of
the philosophy: Ovid did not want at this point to compose a
theological essay, to justify his myths in philosophical terms,
but simply to write the most exalted and sober exordium in his
power.

With the account of the four ages (the Fall of Man) we pass to a
rather different style. We now enter a truly Hesiodic and mythical
world. But the Age of Gold (its spontaneity and innocence; the
absence of war, private property and agricultural implements; the
wonderful, eternal springtime) recalls the earlier language of
Virgil and Horace (*Eclogue* 4, *Epode* 16, *Georgics* II) and their
longing for the lost paradise. And so also with the decline: the fall

of man is told with something of the accent of Horace describing the sins of his contemporaries (*Odes* III, 6. 45):

> Aetas parentum peior avis tulit
> nos nequiores, mox daturos
> progeniem vitiosiorem.

> *Our fathers' generation—worse than our grandfathers'— brought forth us, worse yet, soon to produce a progeny more vicious still.*

There is a gravamen of moral passion in the lines in which Ovid concludes his description of the iron age (*Met.* I, 141–50):

> Iamque nocens ferrum ferroque nocentius aurum
> prodierat; prodit Bellum, quod pugnat utroque,
> sanguineaque manu crepitantia concutit arma.
> Vivitur ex rapto; non hospes ab hospite tutus,
> non socer a genero; fratrum quoque gratia rara est.
> Imminet exitio vir coniugis, illa mariti:
> lurida terribiles miscent aconita novercae:
> filius ante diem patrios inquirit in annos.
> Victa iacet pietas; et virgo caede madentis
> ultima caelestum terras Astraea reliquit.

> *So iron came, and gold, more hurtful far;*
> *And armed with iron, armed with gold, came war.*
> *(In war's red hand when rattling weapons shake,*
> *Men plunder men, and live by what they take.*
> *In the fierce strife all loyalties expire:*
> *Who weds the daughter, plots against the sire;*
> *Fierce stepdames mix the ghastly aconite;*
> *And wedded love converts to murderous spite;*
> *And friend doubts friend, and brother brother fears;*
> *And sons, impatient, count their father's years.)*
> *Conscience lay crushed; and as the slaughter spread,*
> *Last of the gods, the maiden Justice fled.*

Here the repetitions (*prodierat, prodit, non...non...*), the strong initial verbs (*vivitur, imminet*), the alliteration (*crepitantia, concutit arma*), the emphasis of the baleful epithets (*sanguinea, lurida, terribiles*), the energy of the short sentences—all are designed to produce a shocking, an almost awesome effect, without, however, sensibly diminishing the rapidity of the metre. Then the attack of the giants, still more the additional, secondary creation of *men* from their impious blood, mark the very nadir of moral decline.

All this is needed to prepare us for the *concilium deorum* of lines 163–252 (1, 163–7):

> Quae pater ut *summa vidit* Saturnius *arce,*
> ingemit et, facto nondum vulgata recenti
> foeda Lycaoniae referens convivia mensae,
> ingentes animo et dignas Iove concipit iras
> *conciliumque vocat.*

> *Jove, from his watchtower, saw the crimes of men:*
> *One (known to him alone) was recent then:*
> *Lycaon's loathsome feast: the thought of this*
> *Moved him to wrath—and where is wrath like his?*
> *He called the gods: the gods obeyed his call,*
> *And quickly gathered in the council hall.*

This is obviously Ovid's bow to epic convention and particularly to Virgil. There is even a specific reference to *Aeneid* x (1–4):

> Panditur interea domus omnipotentis Olympi
> *conciliumque vocat* divum pater atque hominum rex
> sideream in sedem, terras unde arduus omnis
> castraque Dardanidum aspectat populosque Latinos

> *Meanwhile the house of omnipotent Olympus is thrown open*
> *and the father of gods and king of men summons a council to*
> *his starry abode—the abode whence he looks down and sees*
> *from on high all the lands below, the camp of the Trojans and*
> *the Latin peoples,*

and perhaps a suggestion of the Jupiter of *Aeneid* I (223–6):

Aethere summo dispiciens mare...
terrasque iacentis...sic vertice caeli
constitit et Libyae defixit lumina regnis.

*Looking down from the heights of aether at the sea...the
earth lying below, he stood on the top of Heaven and fixed his
eyes on the realm of Libya.*

It is almost as if Ovid were insisting on the epic character of his
poem: like Virgil, he is bringing in Jupiter at the start, and, like
Virgil, he is indicating the solemnity of crisis by a formal council
of the gods. *Dignas Iove concipit iras*—here is a proper epic rage;
here is a god whose wrath befits his august power.

But in the next few lines (168–80) Ovid does something very
un-Virgilian. He modernizes the whole scene and brings it right
down to the level of his own, contemporary Rome:

Est via sublimis, caelo manifesta sereno:
lactea nomen habet, candore notabilis ipso.
Hac iter est superis ad magni tecta Tonantis
regalemque domum. Dextra laevaque deorum
atria nobilium valvis celebrantur apertis;
plebs habitat diversa locis; a fronte potentes
caelicolae clarique *suos posuere Penates.*
Hic locus est, quem, *si verbis audacia detur,*
haud timeam magni dixisse Palatia caeli.
Ergo ubi marmoreo superi sedere recessu,
celsior ipse loco sceptroque innixus eburno
terrificam capitis concussit terque quaterque
caesariem, cum qua terram, mare, sidera movit.

High in the firmament with lustrous ray,
Shines heaven's bright thoroughfare, the Milky Way;
And there the palace lies: on either hand
The crowded doors of courted nobles stand.
Elsewhere (to speak so bold) the suburbs lie,
Where dwell the common people of the sky;
But here, where powers and princes make their home,

Heaven has its social summit, much like Rome.
Now when the gods of rank were seated all
Within the marble rondure of the hall,
And Jove, in high authority of place,
Presided, leaning on his ivory mace,
Three times he shook his locks, and caused to quake
The land and sea and sky, and then he spake.

Virgil had wholly avoided such topical description (only the phrase *considunt tectis bipatentibus*, x, 5, indicates the setting of his council). But Ovid is so precise that we can at once identify the details. His *via sublimis* corresponds to what archaeologists refer to as the *Clivus Palatinus*, the narrow street that rises from the *Via Sacra* at about the present Arch of Titus and goes up the Palatine to the house of Augustus (*domus Augustana*). This 'house', at the time of Ovid's writing, was surrounded by the gleaming marble temple of Apollo and by the mansions of the great. Here Cicero had lived and Antony and Agrippa; Augustus had himself appropriated the residence of Hortensius. It was indeed no plebean quarter. In fact, the Senate at this time often did meet in the library of Augustus' house: the *celsior ipse loco* is an apt description of his exalted position as he presided over the *Patres* from his *sella curulis* between the two consuls.[1] Ovid of course goes through the pretence of deprecating his comparison (175–6):

Hic locus est, quem, *si verbis audacia detur,*
haud timeam magni dixisse Palatia caeli

This is the place which—were I to speak audaciously—
I should not shrink from calling high heaven's 'Palatine'

but its shock effect is not thereby diminished. It is as if a modern American were to speak of God's 'White House' and Heaven's 'Pennsylvania Avenue' or a Briton to place the Last Judgement in a celestial Buckingham Palace.

Nor does Ovid stop at this. After Jupiter's introductory words

[1] See Suetonius, *Divus Augustus* 29; Lugli, *Roma Antica, Il Centro Monumentale* (1946), pp. 406–10, 434–40.

on human wickedness and the infamous impudence of Lycaon, the gods' horror is compared to that of the *human race* at the assassination of Caesar (199–205):

> Confremuere omnes studiisque ardentibus ausum
> talia deposcunt. Sic, cum manus impia saevit
> sanguine Caesareo Romanum extinguere nomen,
> attonitum tanto subitae terrore ruinae
> humanum genus est totusque perhorruit orbis:
> nec tibi grata minus pietas, Auguste, tuorum est,
> quam fuit illa Iovi.

> *His hearers shuddered, and the council room*
> *Rang loud with clamour for the sinner's doom.*
> *So, when a lawless hand took frenzied aim*
> *To drown in Caesar's blood the Roman name,*
> *The race of men was struck with quick alarm,*
> *And all earth shuddered, fearing mortal harm;*
> *And not less dear thy people's loyal love*
> *To thee, Augustus, than the gods' to Jove.*

We need not try to mitigate the shock of this comparison by insisting on the difference between Ovid's age and our own. Ovid's procedure is the very reverse of that of Virgil, who clearly realized the necessity of maintaining the dignity and symbolic efficacy of his divine machinery. It is only by way of prophecy or through elaborately staged prophetic devices (the show of Heroes, the Shield) that Virgil brings in Augustus, and even then at a level far below Jupiter, the supreme Fate figure. Even Neptune calming the storm (*Aeneid* I, 148–56) is not directly compared to Augustus but only to a man *pietate gravis ac meritis* assuaging *seditio* in a great people. Greater precision would have assuredly spoiled the force of the simile and removed all its impressive suggestiveness, its delicate indication of symbolic meaning without obtrusive detail. Virgil well knew the thin line that separated his epic conventions, above all his divine machinery, from sheer bathos and grotesque flattery.

Does this then mean that Ovid was simply guilty of bad taste and incompetence—inadvertently exposing, as it were, his inferiority to Virgil? This is hard to believe since it is in fact rather evident that he is here consciously imitating Virgil: his *concilium deorum* is certainly indebted to Virgil's and his comparison of Jupiter with Augustus is very likely suggested by Virgil's comparison of Neptune and the statesman (compare Ovid's *manus impia saevit* with Virgil's *saevitque animis ignobile vulgus*). It is much more probable that Ovid saw quite well what Virgil had done and deliberately set out to 'go him one better': his vulgarization of Virgil even carries a slight nuance of malice.

On the surface, however, the *maiestas* and solemnity of the narrative is kept up. The wickedness of Lycaon and his fitting punishment (metamorphosis into a wolf) is a kind of little theodicy, preluding and symbolizing the more terrible and universal punishment to come with the Flood. Jupiter's hesitation as to the method of destroying the wicked human race (253 ff.)—whether by fire or by water—is slightly ridiculous (he rather resembles a cautious engineer: *timuit ne forte sacer tot ab ignibus aether conciperet flammas*) but, on the whole, he maintains his majestic façade.

The Flood allows Ovid to relax to some degree. He permits himself to point out the paradoxes involved: men catching fish from the top of an elm-tree or anchoring their boats in a once green meadow; ugly seals changing places with the graceful goats. But such comments are very restrained. With the pious Deucalion and Pyrrha we embark on another theodicy (the counter-theodicy to Lycaon): innocence saved and rewarded. The re-creation of mankind from the stones they throw over their shoulders is a fitting conclusion to the long narrative: man is now meant to be a hard race (*durum genus*) designed for harsh toil (*experiens laborum*).[1] The old days of innocent spontaneity and relaxed wickedness are gone beyond recovery.

Thus though the epic *maiestas* has been as it were illuminated by

[1] Cf. Virgil, *Georgics* I, 145–6.

a few hints of the incongruity to come, the tone has been pretty well maintained up to this point. The gods are solemn and moral: vice is punished; virtue rewarded. Metamorphosis is but the means of divine justice; divine dignity is never let down; Jupiter's indignation is as righteous as it is majestic. His council and speech constitute the centre of a real epic that, in structure and mood, is rather obviously indebted to the *Aeneid*.

A1 But then there is an abrupt change. Content, style, point of view—all are altered or, rather, transformed into almost a carica-ture of what they had just been. There is a short transitional pas-sage (lines 416–33 or eighteen lines) in which the re-creation of the animals is described (it is the joint work of fire and water, that *discors concordia*: again we see the motif of the two elements whose respective predominances constitute the two great narratives of this section of the poem). But this is put in only to introduce the new monster Python and his defeat by the god Apollo. Apollo celebrates his victory by establishing the *Pythian* games but only with oak, not laurel, crowns for the victors. The laurel is as yet unknown. Phoebus has no laurel for his own hair. The laurel, in fact, is a quite unforeseen consequence of Phoebus' rather exces-sive pride in his great Pythian victory. By unwisely showing his contempt for Cupid whose arms cannot hit Pythons but only nondescript lovers (459–62),

> modo pestifero tot iugera ventre prementem
> stravimus innumeris tumidum Pythona sagittis.
> Tu face nescio quos esto contentus amores
> inritare tua, nec laudes adsere nostras

> *By shafts of mine the snake that pressed the plain,*
> *Acre on acre, like a blight, was slain.*
> *You, with your torch, set hearts on fire, and be*
> *Content with that, and leave my fame to me,*

Apollo finds himself, in fact, love's victim and the cause of Daphne's impromptu metamorphosis into a laurel tree.

This transition is, of course, an obvious *jeu d'esprit*. But it has a certain symbolic point. The gods had so far been solemn, serious and moral, soberly Virgilian in both action and *ethos*. The other and lower level of ancient mythology had as yet been ignored. Apollo now brings it into play by his own self-esteem and self-righteousness: he insists on a dignity that he cannot keep. In ceasing to be the great warrior and protector of mankind, he becomes only the fatuous lover. The majesty of the gods and of the epic code of behaviour, and of the epic style itself, is now sub-jected to the unbearable strain of the ridiculous. Even the effort to maintain it increases the comedy, the classic comedy of the pompous deflated and abased.

The incongruity of the god and the lover is emphasized from the first. He speaks to Cupid with epic amplitude (456–60):

> 'Quid'que 'tibi, lascive puer, cum fortibus armis?'
> dixerat: 'ista decent umeros gestamina nostros,
> qui dare certa ferae, dare vulnera possumus hosti,
> qui modo pestifero tot iugera ventre prementem
> stravimus innumeris tumidum Pythona sagittis.'

> *'Is this', said he, 'a playful boy's affair?*
> *Such deadly weapons are for me to wear.*
> *When I with aim unerring shoot my dart,*
> *What foe, what fearsome beast, but feels the smart?*
> *By shafts of mine the snake that pressed the plain,*
> *Acre on acre, like a blight, was slain.'*

The solemn repetitions (especially the double *qui* clause), the elaborate description of the Python (459–60), the editorial 'we', the sonorous periods, the climactic piling of the *cola*—all reflect the self-important god. How different a figure he cuts only a few lines later (495–503)!

> *Sic* deus in flammas abiit, *sic* pectore toto
> *uritur* et sterilem sperando nutrit amorem.
> Spectat inornatos collo pendere capillos,
> et *'quid, si comantur?'* ait. *Videt* igne micantes

sideribus similes oculos; *videt* oscula, *quae non
est vidisse satis*; laudat digitosque manusque
bracchiaque et nudos media plus parte lacertos;
si qua latent, meliora putat. Fugit ocior aura
illa levi.

*So love consumed the god: he turned to fire,
And fed with hope his ill-conceived desire.
Upon her neck he saw the tumbled hair:
What would it be, he thought, with proper care?
He saw her eyes: no stars could gleam so bright;
He saw her lips, and wanted more than sight;
Approved her fingers, arms, and shoulders bare;
And what he did not see, surmised more fair.
The maiden fled light as the wind away.*

Here there is no time or inclination for elaborate oratory. Instead, we have the staccato sentences (the two swift *sic*'s), the revealing comment (*quid si comantur?*), the impassioned *videt*'s (we catch the lover's eye devouring the girl), the undignified desire to see more, finally his pursuit—off after her like the wind. Ovid now sees through the pompous façade and easily reads the lover's very human thoughts and feelings.

Apollo's situation is the most ridiculous possible. Ovid presumably altered his source[1] (possibly Calvus' *Io*) to give Cupid not one but two arrows (the gold point that induces love; the lead point that repels it) and thus provide Apollo with a passion both undignified and hopeless. He is not only made to love but to love in vain! Daphne is really nothing but the determined virgin whose single role is to thwart the infatuated lover. It is on him that our attention is focused: his thoughts and words that we share. The climax of the absurdity is, of course, the chase itself and this is accentuated by the god's desperate attempt to combine it with his courtship. His address to the girl (lines 504-24) is an absurd blend of dignity and passion: there is the situation itself (he is trying to convey a sense of his decorum and rank even while he is running

[1] See Appendix, pp. 379 f.

her down); there is the curious blending of love with solicitude (she may get scratched by the brambles: he will run more slowly if she does); there is the incongruity of his feelings with his enounced respectability (he assures Daphne he is no uncouth shepherd or rustic but an extremely well-connected personage). The final metamorphosis, of course, is necessary to complete the comedy: the god cannot even catch the girl; she turns into a laurel before he can get his hands on her. All she will consent to is to be his tree! As the frustrated Apollo remarks (557–8):

> at quoniam coniunx mea non potes esse,
> arbor eris certe...mea.

> *'Since then', he said, 'my wife you may not be,*
> *I take you, lovely Daphne, for my tree.'*

Ovid's purpose is obvious. The divine majesty or dignity, with which we have been so much concerned, is deflated at the first touch of love. The epic style of life simply cannot maintain itself under erotic stress. The mere attempt to do so is high comedy. Love is not 'funny' *per se*, but divine majesty is not set up to include love. Homer, of course, had no difficulty in handling the amorous dealings of the gods, but Ovid's comedy is not Homeric. His gods, though they may act like Homer's, are nevertheless measured by a Virgilian standard.[1] The resultant incongruity is what makes them ridiculous.

A2   But all this has been only a sort of preview of a still mightier fall from majesty. We now see Jupiter himself in the same situation as Apollo (Io episode, 568–746). It is quite evident why Ovid wanted these two stories to follow in this order: one such episode was not enough to make his full point and, obviously, he wanted Jupiter to come as a sort of climax to Apollo. In fact the actual liaison is of the flimsiest sort. After Daphne's metamorphosis all the streams come to Tempe to condole with or to congratulate (they are a little uncertain) her father, the river Peneus. Inachus

[1] See pp. 124 f. and 341-2.

only is absent, for Inachus is also extremely unhappy; he too has just lost his daughter, Io. It is evident that Ovid has only the slightest interest in this convocation of the streams. What he is really concerned with is the similarity of the stories themselves, the way in which the *Io* develops and carries out the ideas of the *Daphne*.

The *Io*[1] starts with a situation all but identical with that of the *Daphne* (the main differences are that there is no Cupid and no arrow, and no metamorphosis to keep the pursuing Jupiter from his prize; he is not a god to put up with a virgin's notions). But Jupiter woos Io very much as Apollo wooed Daphne. He is not, he explains to her, a plebean (595–7):

> 'Nec de plebe deo, sed qui caelestia magna
> sceptra manu teneo, sed qui vaga fulmina mitto.
> Ne fuge me!' Fugiebat enim.

> '*No god of lowly birth: enthroned on high*
> *I dart the lightnings, and I rule the sky.*
> *Ah, fly me not*', he cries, but Io flees.

But all this phase of the story is disposed of in thirteen lines (588–600) out of the episode's total of 159. Ovid obviously wants to make the connection (to repeat the same motif in brief) but he is now concerned with quite another aspect of the divine *eros*. Jupiter is ridiculous because he is a henpecked husband; Juno, because she is an extremely possessive wife. Juno's suspicions are aroused by the clouds with which Jupiter has surrounded his amour. She is too experienced not to suspect what this means (605–9):

> Atque, suus coniunx ubi sit, circumspicit, ut quae
> deprensi totiens iam nosset furta mariti.
> Quem postquam caelo non repperit, 'aut ego fallor,
> aut ego laedor' ait, delapsaque ab aethere summo
> constitit in terris nebulasque recedere iussit.

[1] See Appendix, pp. 379 f.

And looking round for Jove (for oft had she
Exposed her husband's amorous larceny)
She cried, as heaven revealed no Jove to view,
'He plays me false, if what I think be true.'
Then gliding down from heaven, she set her feet
On earth below, and bade the mists retreat.

The humour here is hardly subtle, but the repetition and rhyme of 'aut ego fallor, aut ego laedor', and the promptness of Juno's reactions, are nevertheless extremely amusing. Jupiter, however, has sensed her approach and turned Io into a cow, a handsome cow (*bos quoque formosa est*). Juno, of course, asks all about the beast and Jupiter tries to conceal his responsibility by pretending that the cow is only a product of the Earth. But Juno sees through him: she now asks for the cow as an outright gift. Jupiter's dilemma is then truly comic (617–21):

Quid faciat? Crudele, suos addicere amores:
non dare, suspectum est. Pudor est qui suadeat illinc,
hinc dissuadet amor. Victus pudor esset amore:
sed, leve si munus sociae generisque torique
vacca negaretur, poterat non vacca videri.

And what could Jove do, trapped by his own lie?
'I give her', was a cruel word to say:
Refusing, he would give himself away.
Bad conscience on the one side bade him yield,
And love in opposition took the field.
Conscience it would have been that took a fall,
But that the heifer, as a gift so small,
Might well have seemed no heifer, if denied
To one by blood and bed so near allied.

The essence of the comedy is, of course, the application of this particular motif to Jupiter (of all people!): the well-worn theme of *pudor* v. *amor*—the typical conflict of love-stricken women like Medea or Dido—is grotesquely incongruous when applied to this wielder of the thunderbolts who is also the very prince of philanderers. Furthermore, the easy familiarity with which Ovid makes himself free of Jupiter's mind and psyche—all epic distance between men and gods has now utterly disappeared—marks the extent to which we have descended from the solemnity of the *concilium*, from the Jupiter who (166) *ingentes animo et dignas Iove concipit iras* (His heart conceives a rage, mighty and fit for Jove) to the Jupiter who lies and shuffles before the irate Juno and displays a motivation as transparent as that of any other husband in difficulty. The *pretty* cow is the crowning point of the absurdity: no other beast into which Io could possibly have been turned could have made Jupiter or Juno look quite so foolish.[1] And it is, of course, the very commonplaceness of the metamorphosis that puts Jupiter in such difficulty: *si vacca. . .negaretur, poterat non vacca videri!*

All this (who can doubt it?) is eminently Ovidian. Ovid certainly knew and even paraphrased Calvus' *Io*, but he could hardly have derived this kind of humour from a neoteric *epyllion*. We need not describe more particularly the rest of this very amusing story: the trickery of Argus, the pursuit of Io across Asia, her eventual restoration of shape. Two details are especially piquant and Ovidian: the emotions of the bovine Io and the putting to sleep of the hundred-eyed Argus. Io's metamorphosis is quite distinct from the later, tragically coloured metamorphoses of the love-lorn women of Section III. She does not lose her human mentality or, except in shape, descend to the animal level. Instead, she is afraid of her own lowing (637–8); she reveals herself to her father by *writing* on the sand with her hoof (649–50); even when restored to her original humanity, she is still too scared to speak (745):

> metuit. . .loqui ne more iuvencae
mugiat.

And shy of speech at first, for fear she moo.

The effect of the cow on the woman is highly comic.

[1] See Appendix, p. 386.

Again, the use of the Syrinx story—it is only a thinly disguised version of the *Daphne*—as a quick soporific, is a most subtle and amusing commentary on the intrinsic absurdity of the motif. Argus' hundred eyes are closed before Hermes can even get to Pan's first addresses to his *inamorata*. There is nobody in the whole episode (save the mischievous Hermes) who really knows what he is doing. Argus, Jupiter and Io may struggle to maintain appearances and to act as if decorum were still possible: they are nonetheless ignominiously defeated.

E2   Ovid had now deflated his divine prologue. Apollo's pursuit of Daphne, Jupiter's affair with Io, had not left the gods with much of the majesty that they had so conspicuously showed in the *concilium deorum* and the Flood epic. Ovid could not, therefore, start his next great epic—the *Conflagration* that balances and rivals the *Flood*—on the same solemn note. Here the epic mood and style are from the very beginning, subjected to the strain of most un-epic forces and passions. Here the grandeur and universality of the catastrophe—the Fire threatens to be quite as destructive as the Flood—is grotesquely contrasted with the petty motives and feelings of its unwitting agents. Here Epic and Comedy are finally at grips with each other. The length and style of the *Phaethon* (it is not only the longest single episode of the poem but one of the most epically conceived) assuredly indicate its importance: it is at once the centre of its section (I) and an answer to the majestic introduction.

Here the liaison is crucial since it sets the tone, determines the plot, of the whole epic to come. Jupiter's affair with Io had a consequence, the child Epaphus. He is brought up in Egypt and quite naturally has an Egyptian playmate, Phaethon, who is himself the 'consequence' of the god Phoebus' affair with Clymene (now married to the Ethiopian king, Merops). So the whole episode starts in a boyish quarrel: the two lads boast of their divine fathers; Epaphus, obviously the more sophisticated of the pair, doubts the vaunted paternity of Phaethon. Clymene, he suggests, may only be giving a respectable excuse for a very disreputable past (753–4):

> 'matri'que ait 'omnia demens
> credis et es tumidus genitoris imagine falsi.'

And said at last, provoked: 'The crazier you,
To take whate'er your mother says for true,
And, falsely fathered, swell with pointless pride.'

It is thus Phaethon's boyish embarrassment and shame that initiate all the action. He takes his problem to his mother and she—either touched by his plight or angered at the slur on her own reputation: her motive is ambiguous (*ambiguum*) according to Ovid— sends him off to the Sun-god for the confirmation or proof of her word (771–2):

> si ficta loquor, neget ipse videndum
> se mihi, sitque oculis lux ista novissima nostris!

May he himself, if I speak falsely, cast
My light in shade, and make this day my last.

All the ensuing events—Phoebus' hasty oath, his consequent inability to retrieve the situation, and the following catastrophe— depend on such beginnings: a typically boyish quarrel, a weak mother's embarrassment, and a weak father's unthinking attempt to allay a child's incredulity. It is the emotion of Phaethon that reacts on Clymene and in turn reacts on Phoebus: under its stress he commits himself to an impromptu decision that might have entailed and almost did entail the ruin of the whole universe.

Here Ovid obviously altered his sources to secure exactly the motivation he wanted.[1] The myth had come down to him in two principal versions: one (partially reproduced in the thirty-eighth Book of Nonnus' *Dionysiaka* and in the twenty-fifth of Lucian's *Dialogues of the Gods*) contained no promise or oath and represented the sun-god as moved solely by the prolonged supplications of Phaethon and Clymene; the other (that of Euripides'

[1] See Appendix, pp. 389 f.

Phaethon) traced the promise back to Phaethon's very conception and thus left no place for the sequence of events we find in Ovid. In Euripides, Phaethon knew in advance both of the promise that had been made him and the use he would make of it (i.e. the loan of the sun-chariot). In Ovid the promise *and* oath are solely the impromptu workings of a harassed father's emotions. The wish (for the loan of the chariot) expresses the spontaneous reaction of the boy. It is all done on the spur of the moment (II, 42–6):

> 'nec tu meus esse negari
> dignus es, et Clymene veros' ait 'edidit ortus,
> quoque minus dubites, quodvis pete munus, ut illud
> me tribuente feras! Promissi testis adesto
> dis iuranda palus, oculis incognita nostris!'

> *With truth has Clymene declared your birth,*
> *Nor does your blood', said he, 'surpass your worth.*
> *For more assurance ask what gift you will:*
> *A father's bounty shall your wish fulfil;*
> *And let that water, never seen by me,*
> *The pledge of oaths divine, my witness be.'*

So speaks the unthinking god. It is only after Phaethon gets out his wish with such speed that Phoebus cannot stop him (the event comes in the next line, 47: *vix bene* (Phoebus) *desierat, currus rogat ille paternos*), that the god sees what he has done. But he is then quite helpless. His wits have been completely worsted by his emotions. His divine decorum and power are quite unsuited to both his paternal and his erotic feelings. On this incongruity, indeed, the comic force of the whole epic depends.

But the deliberately epic style of the episode makes possible a far more sustained and effective use of incongruity than was the case in the shorter and much less epic *amores* with which we have just been concerned. First we see the sun-god's gorgeous epic setting, his resplendent palace (II, 1–2):

> Regia solis erat sublimibus alta columnis,
> clara micante auro flammasque imitante pyropo.

The sun-god's palace soars on pillars bright
Of bronze and gold, a thing of flame and light.

We see the wonderfully sculptured doors (II, 5–18). We see the full glory of Phoebus' court and regal state (23–7):

> purpurea velatus veste sedebat
> in solio Phoebus claris lucente smaragdis.
> A dextra laevaque Dies et Mensis et Annus
> Saeculaque et positae spatiis aequalibus Horae
> Verque novum stabat cinctum florente corona.

> *With lustrous emeralds shone the chair of state,*
> *Where Phoebus, robed in regal crimson, sate;*
> *And Days, Months, Years, and Centuries had place*
> *To left and right, with Hours of equal space;*
> *And youthful Spring, with flowery garland bound.*

Phaethon's first words to Phoebus are in the best epic diction (35–6):

> o lux immensi publica mundi,
> Phoebe, pater, si das huius mihi nominis usum,

> *The boy replied: 'O Phoebus, chartered light*
> *Of heaven and earth—O father, if by right*
> *I name you.'*

But what follows is, as we have seen, the immediate conversion of epic reassurance into un-epic disaster. The next line after Phoebus' promise (47), *vix bene desierat, currus rogat ille paternos*, sets the solemnity of his oath (*promissi testis adesto | dis iuranda palus, oculis incognita nostris!*) against the curt request that follows: the *vix bene desierat* (he'd scarcely stopped) gives us a picture of the eager boy getting out his wish even before his illustrious but epically long-winded father had quite finished speaking. But Phoebus' repentance is now too late: he has sworn by the Styx, an unalterable oath. All he can do is dissuade. And his epical but paternally excited oratory is grotesquely ill-adapted to its object, the irresponsible and inexperienced Phaethon (49–55):

Paenituit iurasse patrem. Qui terque quaterque
concutiens inlustre caput 'temeraria' dixit
'vox mea facta tua est. Utinam promissa liceret
non dare! Confiteor, solum hoc tibi, nate, negarem;
dissuadere licet. Non est tua tuta voluntas;
magna petis, Phaethon, et quae nec viribus istis
munera conveniant nec tam puerilibus annis.'

The god, repenting, shook his radiant head:
'Too rash my words, in light of yours,' he said;
'Were't lawful, what I promised, not to pay,
In this alone I would my son gainsay.
Let me dissuade: unsafe the boon you seek,
Too great a task for years and strength so weak.'

The eloquent speech that follows is so much waste of words. The
dangers mentioned do not touch the boy. The paternal emotion
(91–2),

Pignora certa petis? Do pignora certa timendo,
et patrio pater esse metu probor

A sign you seek, to prove you surely mine?
My fear is proof: there needs no surer sign.
None but a father feels a father's fear,

has no effect whatsoever. All that Phaethon cares for is the
promise; all he dreads is its revocation, as Phoebus bitterly
perceives (100–2):

Quid mea colla tenes blandis, ignare, lacertis?
Ne dubita; dabitur—Stygias iuravimus undas—
quodcumque optaris: sed tu sapientius opta.

Nay, cling not so with coaxing arms, my son;
It seems you know not that your suit is won.
'Tis true, 'tis yours; the Styx has heard my voice,
Whate'er you choose; but make a wiser choice.

But *sapientia* is precisely what Phaethon lacks. He holds to his *idée*
fixe (*propositum premit flagratque cupidine currus*) though Phoebus

tries, to the very last moment (146–9), to change his mind. The dignity of the god has almost completely succumbed to the solicitude of the father, but even the father can make no impression.

The description of the ride that follows sets the rapid disillusionment and panic of Phaethon against the cataclysmic shattering of the whole universe. Ovid successively sees the various events from a number of viewpoints (that of the horses, the constellations, Earth, Neptune, Jupiter, Phaethon himself). But the underlying theme throughout is the incongruity of the cause with the result, the difference in scale between Phaethon and the cosmos. We first see the horses and how they sense the change of charioteers (161–2):

> Sed leve pondus erat, nec *quod cognoscere possent*
> Solis equi.   *and, feeling not their freight,*
> *Wonder to miss the yoke's accustomed weight.*

Then we grasp the feelings of the constellations (171–7):

> Tum primum radiis gelidi caluere triones,
> et vetito *frustra temptarunt* aequore tingi,
> quaeque polo posita est glaciali proxima serpens,
> frigore pigra prius nec formidabilis ulli,
> incaluit *sumpsitque novas fervoribus iras.*
> *Te quoque turbatum* memorant fugisse, Boote,
> *quamvis tardus eras et te tua plaustra tenebant.*
>
> *Then first the Bears felt heat, and tried in vain*
> *To pass their bounds, and plunge beneath the main;*
> *And near the pole the numbed innocuous Snake*
> *Felt, with the warmth, his wicked passions wake.*
> *Boötes too, they say, made off in dread,*
> *Though with slow steps his lagging wain he led.*

Finally we turn to Phaethon (183–8):

> Iam *cognosse genus piget et valuisse rogando:*
> *iam Meropis dici cupiens* ita fertur, ut acta
> praecipiti pinus borea, cui victa remisit

frena suus rector, quam dis votisque reliquit.
Quid faciat? Multum caeli post terga relictum,
ante oculos plus est. *Animo metitur utrumque.*

He wished his father's team well left alone,
His prayer unanswered, and his birth unknown;
Wished Merops for his sire (ambition new)
As like a ship before a storm he flew,
Whose helmsman, pressed too hard, resigns his care,
And leaves the craft to providence and prayer.
What now? He scans the sky with measuring mind;
Much heaven before him lies, no less behind.

The humour of the contrasts is evident: the overheating of Draco
and the flight of the slow-moving Bootes are of course comic in
themselves, but even more comic is the collocation of forces: on
the one side the frightened, helpless boy anxiously measuring the
distances covered and to be covered; on the other, the stars in or
rather *out* of their courses. Characteristically it is the sight of the
terrible Scorpion which causes Phaethon (now only a very frightened child) to abandon the reins and bring on the culminating
disaster (*mentis inops gelida formidine lora remisit*, line 200).

Then indeed (210 ff.) the damage becomes truly cosmic in
scope. Forests, cities, mountains go up in flames; the earth-orb
itself catches fire; the Ethiopians are turned black from the heat; the
rivers and springs dry up; the light penetrates Tartarus; the sea-level
sinks and all creatures on its surface die. Even Neptune cannot bear
the heat long enough to lift his head from the waves. We have
at last returned to a truly cosmic scene like that of the Flood or the
Creation itself. Earth herself now speaks to Jupiter. Her first point
concerns the author of the catastrophe. What does Jupiter want? If
to destroy the world, then why not do it with his own thunderbolts?
At least he might lend his *auctoritas* to the deed (279–81)!

Si placet hoc, meruique, quid o tua fulmina cessant,
summe deum? Liceat periturae viribus ignis
igne perire tuo *clademque auctore levare*!

'By fire', said she,
'If 'tis my due to fall, and thy decree,
Why lag thy lightnings? Let me fall, most high,
By fire of thine, consoled, by whom I die.'

The implication of Earth's remark is only too clear. It at once
shows up the absurdity of Jupiter's plight: he has let a thoughtless
boy endanger the whole universe. For quite apart from the earth
itself, the sky, the very poles, are in danger (293 ff.). This is indeed
just the possibility that Jupiter foresaw when he originally preferred the flood to his thunderbolts (I, 253–5):

> Iamque erat in totas sparsurus fulmina terras:
> sed timuit, ne forte sacer tot ab ignibus aether
> conciperet flammas, longusque ardesceret axis.
>
> *Now when about to strike, Jove stayed his hand,*
> *Lest, while his lightnings kindled every land,*
> *Some sparks, by this vast conflagration sent,*
> *Should fire the sacred far-spread firmament.*

He is thus forced into hasty action but not without a brief and
absurdly unnecessary explanation of his purpose (II, 304–6):

> At pater omnipotens, superos testatus et ipsum
> qui dederat currus, nisi opem ferat, omnia fato
> interitura gravi...
>
> *Now Jove almighty made the gods attest*
> *(Him that had lent the car among the rest)*
> *·What choice remained: to use his instant aid,*
> *Or see the worlds in grievous ruin laid.*

The obsequies of Phaethon are appropriately anticlimactic. His
sisters literally grieve themselves into trees, his relative and friend
Cygnus becomes a swan (thus even as a bird avoiding the heat and
sticking to the water), and Phoebus himself goes into deep mourn-
ing. But even in grief he remains the fatuous father. Jupiter, he
exclaims, should have driven the sun-chariot himself before
brandishing his 'father-bereaving' thunderbolts (390–3):

Ipse agat, ut saltem, dum nostras temptat habenas,
orbatura patres aliquando *fulmina* ponat.
Tum sciet, ignipedum vires expertus equorum,
non meruisse necem, qui non bene rexerit illos.

Let Jove with his own hands attempt the feat,
That so, for some short space well-occupied,
He lay his bolts, that strike our sons, aside,
And try the steeds, and what their strength can do,
And learn by proof if death be failure's due.

If the Flood was due to human wickedness, this disaster was due only to divine folly. It was Phoebus' amatory and paternal sentiments, his ridiculous promise and oath, that had caused all the trouble. A god had put himself entirely at the mercy of an irresponsible boy. Nor had Jupiter played an especially dignified role in the episode: only at the very last gasp, in the very nick of time, had he finally intervened. All the gods had, in fact, been humiliated and the whole universe put in extreme danger for the most absurd and insignificant reasons: a sly love-affair, a boy's pique, a mother's threatened reputation, a father's fatuous precipitancy and a sadly misplaced bit of juvenile curiosity. But was not this the behaviour that might have been expected of the amatory and intriguing gods of the *Daphne* and *Io* episodes? The major impression is that of a general loss of dignity all around. Earth had summed up the true issue when she remarked that if such a disaster were deserved, it should have been the work of Jupiter himself (279–81). But, unlike the flood, this is no theodicy but sheer accident and irresponsible folly. We have described, as it were, the full circle that goes from the sublime to the ridiculous.

A3   The Callisto episode[1] (401–530) now harks back to and obviously corresponds with the Io episode that had just preceded the long Phaethon panel. In one sense the motifs are remarkably similar: the amorous god, the resisting virgin, Juno's jealous intervention, the transformation of the nymph into an animal (a

---

[1] See Appendix, pp. 379 f.

bear this time, not a cow) and the final resolution of the nymph's suffering with Juno's reluctant consent. But we find also differences that clearly point ahead to motifs of the next section (II). Juno's jealousy is now much less comic: it reveals something of the sheer malevolence that is to come out in the Semele and Ino episodes ahead. It is she who now performs the metamorphosis as an act of spite and vengeance; the shape is now that of an uncouth bear, no pretty cow.[1] Above all, however, the Callisto story prefigures that of Actaeon: here we find Diana bathing with her nymphs and suggesting, by her harshly puritanical attitude toward Callisto, her future treatment of Actaeon; here also we find the Actaeon motif of a transformed human being (Callisto as she-bear) exposed to destruction from unsuspecting kindred or friends. The difference is that here the ultimate disasters are avoided: Callisto is only driven from Diana's company (not cruelly punished by her); she is not after all killed by her son, Arcas, since Jupiter in the nick of time transports her to heaven. In short, the Callisto story is an exceedingly skilful piece of motif-transformation: the older amatory theme persists but is definitely yielding place to the Diana, vengeance and tragic error themes. Yet the story's mood is still, in the main, amatory and comic.

The comedy is quite in the vein of the *Daphne* or the *Io*. Jupiter comments on his prospective deed (423-4):

'Hoc certe furtum coniunx mea nesciet' inquit:
'aut si rescierit,—sunt o sunt iurgia tanti.'

And this time hoped to hide his escapade
From his stern spouse: 'or if she learns,' he thought,
'And scolds me, still the pleasure's cheaply bought.'

Callisto is definitely worth a quarrel. But the deception of Callisto (Jupiter in the shape of the virginal Diana) and the absurd courtship are more than simple variations of the amorous god-determined virgin motif. The fact that Jupiter changes his shape in order to win the girl suggests, of course, his much more radical

[1] See Appendix, pp. 379 f.

117

and comical transformation in the Europa episode. The introduction of the false Diana points ahead to the later appearance of the true one.

But the accounts of Callisto's shame, and of the revelation of it in the bathing scene, are not merely humorous. Ovid's sly reference to Diana's virginal naïveté (451–2),

> Et, nisi quod virgo est, poterat sentire Diana
> mille notis culpam; nymphae sensisse feruntur
>
> *Were Dian not a maid, by many a clue*
> *She well had known what all the others knew,*

does not really lessen our sympathy with the poor girl—shamed, desolate and pregnant—whose nakedness is exposed, in spite of herself, to Diana's unpitying eyes (463–5):

> Attonitae manibusque uterum celare volenti
> 'i procul hinc,' dixit 'nec sacros pollue fontes'
> Cynthia, deque suo iussit secedere coetu.
>
> *She stood abashed, and with her arms she tried*
> *To hide her state. 'Begone,' the goddess cried;*
> *'Begone, I say: be banished from our train;*
> *Take from our sacred founts so foul a stain.'*

And it is just because Callisto does thus arouse our sympathy that we also see the cruelty as well as the comic possessiveness of Juno. In Juno's eyes, Callisto's forced motherhood only aggravates her offence. There is, of course, a certain comedy in this and in Callisto's new ursine shape (she does not dare to stay at home though alarmed by the other bears), but there is none in her encounter with her young son, Arcas (500–4):

> Incidit in matrem, quae restitit Arcade viso
> et cognoscenti similis fuit. Ille refugit
> immotosque oculos in se sine fine tenentem
> nescius extimuit, propiusque accedere aventi
> vulnifico fuerat fixurus pectora telo.

They meet; his mother sees him, stops, and shows
By gestures almost human that she knows;
And while the boy shrinks back, caught unaware,
She eyes him with a long unwavering stare;
Then lumbers forward, while her son in fear
Levels, to strike her heart, the deadly spear.

Callisto is throughout the innocent victim of the gods: it is only by a hair's-breadth that her story escapes a tragical end. Yet Juno's final remarks are quite amusing. Jupiter, she complains, has restored Io's shape and made Callisto a goddess: why not complete the job and take her into his celestial bedroom, formally accepting the infamous Lycaon (Callisto's father) as his father-in-law? The only satisfaction Juno finally gets is to keep the two Bears from setting in the ocean. The story thus ends with a most comically motivated *aition*.

A4   The next tale—Coronis and Apollo[1]—is clearly also an offset to the previous Apollo episode (Apollo–Daphne) but here the original motif is not only transformed but elliptically reduced to a mere shadow of itself. Coronis is no determined virgin but a girl who even allows another lover to share her favours with the god. But the emphasis of the episode is not at all on the love but on the tell-tale crow who informs Apollo of Coronis' infidelity and thus causes the god's hasty vengeance and unavailing repentance. The idea of the talking crow was doubtless taken from Callimachus' *Hecale*[2] but Ovid certainly used it in a most original manner. The garrulous raven tries to keep the crow from tattling by telling of her own sad experience: *her* only reward for tattling was to take second place to the infamous Nyctimene (the incestuous girl turned owl). But the crow nevertheless persists and is finally turned black for his pains. The result of his tattling is indeed to ruin everything—to destroy Coronis and reduce Apollo to misery. Only the unborn child—the future Aesculapius—is saved from the general catastrophe. Here we have a prefiguration of the Semele

---

[1] See Appendix, pp. 379 f.   [2] See Appendix, p. 388.

theme (the birth of Bacchus) and, more important, of a motif very dear to Ovid (it is specifically repeated in the later Leucothoe and Ascalaphus stories), the futility of tattling, especially in amatory matters. The busybodies work nothing but havoc and themselves suffer for their officiousness. The anguish they provoke is much worse than any amount of deception or ignorance.

A 5   It is indeed with the corruption of love, with its defamation by jealousy and envy, that Ovid is now mainly concerned. There is nothing of the comic character of Juno's jealousy (Io, Callisto) in Apollo's anger at Coronis.[1] It is only the chattering raven and stupid crow who keep the element of comedy going in this episode. Similarly with the ensuing Hermes–Herse–Aglauros episode. The thieving Hermes is merely comic (the double-deception of the Battus story is very amusing) and his wooing of Herse is not without its humour (he combs his hair and shines his sandals like any courting gallant, lines 731–86), but the grisly invocation of Envy by Minerva and Envy's horrible infection of Aglauros (Herse's sister) are meant to excite a kind of melodramatic *frisson* in the reader. Ovid was here indebted to Virgilian figures like Fama and, especially, Allecto, but he greatly accentuated the visual and plastic detail (Invidia is a kind of preview of Tisiphone in the Ino episode and of Fames in the *Erysichthon*): the result is hardly convincing save as a piece of ingenious make-believe.

But the metamorphosis of Aglauros—she is turned into a stone when she enviously refuses to let Hermes pass into the house— points ahead to a much more important idea: the use of the metamorphosis as a means of divine vengeance (not simply spite as with Juno) adapted to the situation and conduct of the victim. The emphasis is no longer on the god, but on the human object of the god's wrath. It is Aglauros and Envy, not Hermes, who bulk so large in this episode. To be sure, Lycaon's metamorphosis into a wolf had prefigured this type of change, but only in a premonitory and paradigmatic way. Ovid wanted at the start of his epic to set

[1] See Appendix, p. 388.

forth both the good and bad types of metamorphoses: the degradation of the human (Lycaon into wolf) and the elevation of the
non-human (stones into men). But these metamorphoses were
obviously not meant to set the tone for the *Divine Comedy* as a
whole. Battus also had been punished and turned into a stone, but
this was but a brief and largely comic interlude: with Aglauros, however, a much more important phase of Ovid's epic was prefigured.

Coda Ovid had now called up the major and some of the minor
motifs of Section II: divine vengeance, Junonian spite, grisly
personification, jealousy, envy, tale-telling. The amatory and
comic element of the Daphne and Io episodes had insensibly made
way for other themes and another mood. Yet the general correspondence of the post- with the pre-Phaethon episodes had been
maintained: Jupiter and Apollo are still in love and to them
another amorous god, Hermes, is added; the comedy, though more
muted and varied, still persists.[1] Now with Europa[2] (833–75) we
come to a brief coda that ends and sums up the whole of Section I,
while also, according to the convention of the *carmen perpetuum*,
preparing the transition to Cadmus and the next section. But the
episode is not primarily liaison: it is in effect a seal or *sphragis* that
points the moral of the whole *Divine Comedy*.

Hermes is now, on his return from Athens (the locale of the
Herse–Aglauros story), given a bucolic commission (his connection with cattle had already been established in the Battus
incident). Jupiter tells him to drive the royal herd of Tyre from
the mountains to the sea-shore, to the exact spot, in fact, where the
Tyrian Europa was accustomed to play with her companions.

We are thus prepared for the most startling of all the metamorphoses of the *Divine Comedy*: that of Jupiter into a handsome
bull. The lines by which this scene is introduced express the
leitmotiv of the whole first section (846–51):

[1] It is thus clear that Section I (Books I–II) is a whole with symmetrically
matching *amores* and epic pieces. But because the *Metamorphoses* is a *carmen
perpetuum*, each section is *also* anticipated by its predecessor. Cf. pp. 86 f. above.
[2] Cf. Appendix, p. 395.

Non bene conveniunt nec in una sede morantur
maiestas et amor: sceptri gravitate relicta
ille pater rectorque deum, cui dextra trisulcis
ignibus armata est, qui nutu concutit orbem,
induitur faciem tauri mixtusque iuvencis
mugit et in teneris formosus obambulat herbis!

'Tis ill when love and lordship in one mind
Together dwell. His sceptred state resigned,
The king of gods, by whose right hand is hurled
The three-forked fire, whose nods convulse the world,
Among the herd, transformed in voice and mien,
Treading the sward, a comely bull was seen.

This is, indeed, the exact antithesis to the Jupiter of the divine
council and the Flood. The god whose royal gravity awed the
assembled divinities (*clamor pressus gravitate regentis,* I, 207) is now
not only an amorous but a peaceful and pretty bull (*nullae in
fronte minae, nec formidabile lumen:* | *pacem vultus habet,* 857–8). The
contrast of images is striking and intentional: in the one is
maiestas; in the other is *amor*; and the two do not agree.

The primary reference here, as we have already pointed out, is
to the Io episode. There the girl became a cow: now the god
becomes a bull. In Moschus' *Europa*, the one transformation preceded and suggested the other. And so with Ovid. But in the *Io*,
Jove's struggle is between his *pudor* and his *amor* (I, 618–19); he is
ashamed to be caught by his wife and yet determined to keep his
love. But more than shame has been overthrown for the sake of
Europa. What began with the protective metamorphosis of the
seduced has now reached its climax in the aggressive metamorphosis
of the seducer. Love had at last reached the substance of Jove's
divine majesty.

Maiestas, indeed, has a much loftier connotation than *pudor*. It
conveys, in Cicero's words (*De Or.* II, 164), the *amplitudo ac
dignitas civitatis*. It means even more than *imperium, dignitas*, or
auctoritas, for it clearly excites also *reverentia, honor* and *obsequium*.

In the only other place where it is used in the *Metamorphoses* (IV, 540) it signifies the divine glory of the newly deified Ino and Melicertes. Neptune took away what was mortal and imposed on them *maiestatem verendam* instead. In the *Fasti* (V, 11–52) *maiestas* signifies the new order of Saturn which was threatened by the revolt of the giants and finally re-established by Jupiter. The anarchy (under which even plebean gods could sit on Saturn's throne) was replaced by the awe—the *maiestas*—of Jove. *Maiestas* was thus originally divine and only reached earth at the time of Romulus and Numa when it became the great protector of the Roman state. So though *Pudor* and *Metus* (Shame and Fear) sit with *Maiestas* on the throne, they are clearly not the same: rather, Shame and Fear are the qualities which *Maiestas* excites; they indicate its power, not its essence. *Maiestas* itself can only be defined as the supreme authority which excites supreme respect and reverence. It excludes everything which is not consistent with such respect: ignorance, foreign necessity, passion and love (Cicero, *De Natura Deorum*, II, 28, 30–77). It was certainly such a conception of the word that induced Augustus to give a new content to the crime of *laesa maiestas* by applying it to such sexual derelictions as those of the two Julias and Silanus (Tacitus, *Annals*, III, 24).

Hence when Jupiter himself takes on the shape of an amorous and attractive bull, he violates far more than conjugal *pudor*: he sets at naught the very authority of his office, of his divine supremacy. All the dignity and gravity of the *concilium deorum* have now yielded to his thoroughly undignified passion. *Amor* and *maiestas* simply do not agree.

This is a conception which has but little to do with Homeric or Hellenistic ideas. The Homeric Zeus could make love without seriously compromising his power or authority: the Aphrodite of Apollonius' *Argonautica* is hardly very conscious of her divine dignity. The gods of Callimachus and Theocritus are deliberately modernized or brought down to very human dimensions (we think, for example, of Callimachus' Artemis or Zeus, of Theocritus' Heracles or Polydeuces). But the *maiestas* of Ovid's *concilium deorum* is not Greek but Roman; his gods, when they are majestic, are majestic in a Roman and Virgilian way. The contrast of *maiestas* and *amor* is, to some extent, therefore, one between Roman and Greek theologies. But Ovid is not simply contrasting Greek and Roman ideas. He has cast all his material—whether Roman–Virgilian or Hellenic–Hellenistic in its sources—into much the same mould and style. Just as he sees Jupiter's residence as a *Palatia caeli* or Palatine, so he also sees Jupiter's *amor* in the full context of his Roman *maiestas*. To put it another way: Ovid's Jupiter is not Roman when he presides over the gods and Greek when he seduces Europa. One episode may come from a Roman and the other from a Greek source, but the Jupiter who causes the Flood is the same god who has his way with Io, Callisto and other helpless virgins.

For it is not inconsistency that marks Ovid's *Divine Comedy*, but a very different thing, incongruity. To apply a Virgilian epic style to the very mixed content of Greek myth and literature was *per se* nothing but an experiment in incongruity. No such result, of course, could arise from a merely elegiac treatment of Greek material, for Latin elegy, as we have seen,[1] had changed neither the content nor the style of its Greek models. There was no *maiestas* in either the *Amores* or the *Fasti*. What is new in the Divine Comedy of the *Metamorphoses* is the addition of *maiestas* to *amor*.

Here the difference between Virgil and Ovid as well as between both and Greek epic is very significant. Virgil was not 'objective' as Homer or even Apollonius was. A very large part of his narrative is in fact both empathetic and subjective: he both shares his characters' feelings and makes moral comments on them. But this subjective style, which in Greek poetry is largely confined to lyric and elegiac verse, and even there is quite embryonic (compared to the lyric or narrative verse of Romans), only heightens Virgil's epic *maiestas* because in fact Virgil is writing of characters that are predominantly majestic and because he himself is greatly concerned to enhance their *maiestas*. Even Dido, for example, is

---

[1] Cf. pp. 24 f. above.

far from being just another amatory heroine: she is also in large part a queen, an *alter Aeneas*, and the conflict of her *amor* with her queenly dignity or *maiestas* is a tragic one in every sense of the word. For this reason also, Virgil never writes of the gods in their relaxed or 'off' moments. There are some awkwardly Homeric scenes (especially the Venus–Vulcan scene of *Aeneid* VIII), but even these are much toned down from their Homeric originals. His Venus and Juno, of course, are set on a level much below Jupiter, but neither goddess descends to anything like the manner of Ovid's Juno in the *Io* or of his Venus in other places (notably with Adonis). As for Virgil's Jupiter, he is the lofty equivalent of *fatum*: the majestic god who holds all the threads in his hands. But Ovid employed Virgil's subjectivity in a wholly different way and to a wholly different end.

We can best define the difference by saying that he united three things that no one before him had ever thought of combining: epic continuity, style and elevation; Virgilian subjectivity; and an amatory, un-epic subject-matter. What really fused the epic with the un-epic and amatory elements was the subjectivity—the fact that Ovid empathetically shared the feelings of his characters and personally reacted to them. But this very subjectivity forced him to account to himself for the behaviour of his gods and finally to discriminate between appearance and reality—between what his gods pretended to be and what they really were. Presumably, neither he nor Virgil believed in the factual existence of Jupiter, Juno, Apollo, and the others. But whereas Virgil did certainly believe in their symbolic reality—their relation to universal forces and ideas—Ovid seems to have humanized them simply. He saw them, in other words, as quite ordinary men and women of his own time. Apollo speculating on what was and what was not visible of the original Daphne, Jupiter caught between Io and his wife, Juno enraged at Callisto's pregnancy—these are surely but projections of Ovid's own contemporaries or of 'human nature' as he saw it. His empathetic picture of Jupiter when his 'bull-game' is just upon the verge of success (862–3),

Gaudet amans et, dum veniat sperata voluptas,
oscula dat manibus (vix iam, vix cetera differt)

*He loves and rejoices and, till the hoped-for consummation of
his bliss, kisses her hands (scarce now can he put off the rest of
love),*

is assuredly not very divine.

All this is obvious: what is not perhaps so obvious is its corollary
that Ovid could only see *maiestas* in similar terms; that is, as something which also applied to his contemporaries, as something also
'human' that he had to account for. It is here most relevant to
recall how he described the Jupiter of the *concilium deorum*: he
dwelt in a sort of Palatine; his words excited the same kind of
response as those of Augustus at the assassination of Caesar. But
whereas Ovid can believe in the lover, he cannot believe in the
maiestas. He could see the majestic façade: the reality was quite a
different matter. At the first touch of genuine emotion, Jupiter
leaves his sceptre (*sceptri gravitate relicta*) and, *pater rectorque deum*
though he may be, moves and walks like a bull; Phoebus descends
from his exalted state and pleads tearfully with his embarrassing
but beloved child. The Flood, with all its accompaniment of god-
like anger and god-like punishment, is discounted by Phaethon's
most un-godlike conflagration.

Does this mean that we are to read a political meaning into the
Divine Comedy? Was the majestic Augustus who presided over
the Senate also an undignified lover (the ribald party-goer of
Suetonian gossip)?[1] Is Ovid saying that the Augustan *maiestas* is
only a sham and that the 'gods' of Rome are, after all, as amorous
and comically human as anybody else—as himself for example?
We cannot perhaps rule out the possibility of at least an innuendo
to this effect. But Ovid's main point does not seem to be a political
one: such an explanation is not only too simple but false to the
spirit of the poem. He is anti-Augustan not in his politics but in
his distaste for moralism and moral propaganda. Men of his age

[1] Cf. Suetonius, *Divus Augustus*, 68–70.

could not, like Homer, take Jovian majesty and Jovian sensuality
as parts of one simple picture. Either they tried, like Virgil, to
invest the gods with the dignity of the Roman state, or, like Ovid,
they more or less cynically accepted the incompatibility of
maiestas and *amor*. After all, official pretence has always concealed
a very human reality. From this point of view, the exalted
Augustanism of Virgil and Horace must have been very uncongenial to Ovid. Why try for a dignity that is above one's capacity?
Why punish the real present in one's regret for a mythical innocence? Why attempt to reform an essentially irreformable
human nature? Why pretend that rustic morality is so much better
than urban civilization? Why be the stern moralist who rejects his
own age?

> Prisca iuvent alios, ego me nunc denique natum
> gratulor: haec aetas moribus apta meis.
>
> (Ars III, 121–2)

> *Let others delight in the things of old: I glory in my modernity.*
> *This is the age that suits my character.*

This sentiment of the *Ars Amatoria* (repeated also in the *Fasti*)
expressed the view of a man who was reacting against what he
thought to be hypocrisy. The *Divine Comedy* says much the same
thing. *Maiestas* is all very well—so we might put Ovid's feelings in
our own words—if one remembers that *amor* will always have its
way. Beside Jove's sceptre we must set the beautiful and amorous
bull.

CHAPTER V

THE AVENGING GODS

THE Europa story is not only the epilogue of the *Divine Comedy*: it is also a bridge to the next section. With the wanderings of Europa's brother, Cadmus, and his foundation of Thebes (III, 1–137), we embark on a series of heroic myths that are grimly different from the amatory tales that have preceded. Here Ovid is certainly piloting his *carmen perpetuum* on the historical course that leads from the gods of the Creation through the royal family of Thebes, to Athens, Calydon, Troy and Rome. But he is not primarily concerned with heroic descent or local legend: it is the motifs, the concatenation of ideas and tones that control and order the poem, here as in Section I.

The dominant motif is that of divine vengeance; divine vengeance where the mortal, not the god, is accented and where the problem of theodicy is seen, largely, from the human side. Against this major motif, however, a subsidiary one is set: love; mortal love on one side of the section's central 'panel' and divine love (a 'recall' of the *Divine Comedy* theme) on the other side. The central panel itself deals with a heroic episode (the story of Perseus' fight to free and keep Andromeda) that is not of 'divine' vengeance, though it partly maintains the vengeance motif and something of the tone of the other vengeance narratives. So also the love-stories of the Minyades and Muses are brought within the 'vengeance' framework since they are narrated by the principal characters of divine vengeance episodes (Minyades, Muses). The structure of this section (II) is therefore quite clear and very symmetrical.

Thus this chapter falls logically into three distinct topics: the main (divine) vengeance theme; the 'epic' of the central panel; and the minor, love theme that forms the contrast to both.

VENGEANCE EPISODES	AMATORY CONTRAST EPISODES	EPIC CENTRAL PANELS

Book III

1–137	[Introductory: Cadmus, foundation of Thebes]	
138–252	Actaeon	
253–315	Semele	
316–338	[Tiresias]	
339–510	Narcissus–Echo	
511–733	Pentheus (Tyrrhene Sailors)	

Book IV

1– 42	⎧ Minyades (introductory)	
43–166	⎪ ⎧ First Sister's Tale: Pyramus, Thisbe	
167–273	First Frame ⎨ Tales of Minyades ⎨ Leuconoe's Tale: Leucothoe–Clytie	
274–388	⎪ ⎩ Alcithoe's Tale: Salmacis	
389–415	⎩ Minyades (metamorphosis)	
415–562	Ino	
563–603	[Cadmus, Harmonia, Snakes]	
604–803		PERSEUS–ANDROMEDA

CENTRE OF SECTION

Book V

1–249		PERSEUS–PHINEUS
250–340	⎧ Muses–Pieriae (Minerva)	
341–661	⎪ ⎧ Ceres–Proserpina with sub-tales	
	Second Frame ⎨ Tales of Muses ⎨ (Ascalabus, Ascalaphus, Arethusa, Triptolemus)	
662–678	⎩ Metamorphosis of Pieriae	

Book VI

1–145	Arachne	
146–312	Niobe	
313–381	Lycian Peasants	
382–400	Marsyas	

I (THE VENGEANCE THEME)

The great problem of Section II is that of understanding Ovid's apparently total shift of tone and purpose from the preceding *Divine Comedy*. What, apart from a mere desire to 'cover' this material and include it in his epic, was he aiming at? What do these lengthy vengeance stories, this abundance of tragic and violently epic material, really add to his previous pictures of amorous gods or do to prepare us for the succeeding pictures of amorous mortals?

One thing is clear: he has not followed the order of any genealogy or mythological compendium. Though he treats a single house and family (Cadmean Thebes) at considerable length (most of Books III–IV), he decidedly rearranges the usual order. Actaeon (Semele's nephew) is put first before Semele herself; Pentheus (Ino's nephew) is put third (after the quite extraneous Narcissus–Echo story) and again before the story of his aunt (Ino). Here the divergence between Ovid and Apollodorus' *Bibliotheca* (that almost certainly follows the normal order of Theban chronology) reflects a clear design on Ovid's part.[1] He quite obviously put Actaeon first (after the Cadmus introduction) in order to provide a proper introduction for Juno. The excessive vengeance of Diana is calculated to arouse her implacable sister. Juno, unlike the other gods, is not concerned with the justice of Diana's act but only with its lesson for herself. She rejoices in the suffering of Actaeon because he is, after all, a descendant of the Theban line to which Europa (her avowed enemy) belonged. But his 'punishment' only reminds Juno of a yet unpunished Theban successor of Europa—the 'trollop' Semele. Thus the cruelty of Diana is made to motivate the jealousy and spitefulness of Juno. But from Semele, of course, is born Bacchus and from him comes another and greater spur to Juno's spite. Bacchus, that 'wanton's offspring' (*de paelice natus*), can punish Pentheus, the Tyrrhene sailors and the

---

[1] The difference between Apollodorus (III, 2–4; 21–39) and Ovid is well shown by W. Klimmer (*Die Anordnung des Stoffes in den ersten vier Büchern von O's Met.* p. 46), who here supplemented the earlier work of Hermann Kienzle (*Ovidius qua ratione compendium mythologicum ad metamorphoses componendas adhibuerit*, Diss. Basel, 1903), esp. pp. 17–20. The order in Apollodorus is: Europa, Cadmus, Semele, Ino, Actaeon, Pentheus, Tyrrhene sailors, Cadmus and Harmonia. That of Ovid is: Europa, Cadmus, Actaeon, Semele, Pentheus (with Tyrrhene sailors inset), Ino, Cadmus and Harmonia. It must also be noted that the tales of the Minyades (inserted between the *Pentheus* and *Ino*) are quite as much novelties of Ovid as his rearrangement of Theban genealogy.

Minyades, while Juno herself is seemingly unable to punish anybody. But Bacchus, like Diana, has now shown her the way (*ipse
docet quid agam*) and this time the imitation (Ino episode) is very
circumstantial indeed, a horrible parody of the Pentheus episode.
The last act of Juno's revenge is completed by the metamorphosis
of Cadmus and Harmonia. We can then look back and see the
meaning of Ovid's prophetic words about the newly founded
Thebes (III, 131-7):

> Iam stabant Thebae, poteras iam, Cadme, videri
> exilio felix: soceri tibi Marsque Venusque
> contigerant: huc adde genus de coniuge tanta,
> tot natas natosque et, pignora cara, nepotes,
> hos quoque iam iuvenes; sed scilicet ultima semper
> exspectanda dies homini est, dicique beatus
> ante obitum nemo supremaque funera debet.

> *When Thebes at length stood firm, one might have guessed*
> *That Cadmus in his banishment was blessed:*
> *Happy, with child of Mars and Venus wed;*
> *Happy, with children of such mother bred:*
> *In sons and daughters did his race endure,*
> *With grandsons tall to make succession sure.*
> *But wise the word: 'Await the end: let none*
> *Be counted happy till his days are done.'*

Ovid's arrangement of the Theban stories thus has a dramatic
logic that quite surpasses the logic of genealogy.

The Juno of this section, it is plain, is based on that of the
Aeneid. Juno's vengeful soliloquies (III, 256 ff.; IV, 416 ff.) clearly
re-echo those of *Aeneid* I, 37 ff. and VII, 293 ff. Furthermore, the
Tisiphone scene of the Ino episode (IV, 432 ff.) is plainly suggested
by the *Allecto* of *Aeneid* VII. Just after this, the Perseus episode
(Books IV–V) carries on the Virgilian theme to a kind of climax:
Andromeda, Phineus and Cepheus are the obvious Ovidian
equivalents of Lavinia, Turnus and Latinus. The battle scenes are
meant to recall those of the Iliadic *Aeneid*. Finally the epic and

warlike note is continued in the successive death-scenes of the *Niobe*, the last major episode of this whole section.

Thus there are two partial schemata that account for much of the order of the vengeance episodes. They can even be roughly set out as follows:

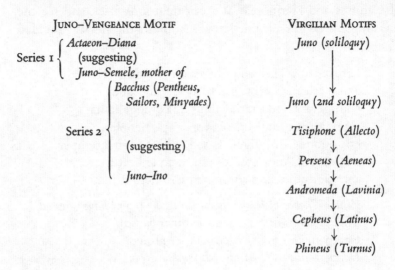

JUNO–VENGEANCE MOTIF   VIRGILIAN MOTIFS

Series 1 ⎰ *Actaeon–Diana*   *Juno (soliloquy)*
      ⎱ (suggesting)
        Juno–Semele, mother of

Bacchus (Pentheus, Sailors, Minyades)   *Juno (2nd soliloquy)*

Series 2   *Tisiphone (Allecto)*

(suggesting)   *Perseus (Aeneas)*

Juno–Ino   *Andromeda (Lavinia)*

Cepheus (Latinus)

Phineus (Turnus)

It is not, however, the similarity to, but the difference from, Virgil that is here significant. Virgil's Juno is a symbol of counter-fate, the element that deliberately tries to thwart both Aeneas and his *fatum*. In Virgil, moreover, it is not Jupiter's philandering—his affairs with nymphs or mortal women—that motivates Juno but her thwarted love for Carthage and, in the later books, her devotion to Turnus. Juno's hatred not only has a proper and dignified cause but is carefully subordinated to a beneficent fate. She never succeeds in undermining either the justice or the authority of Jupiter and, hence, never quite negates the effective theodicy that is really at the heart of the *Aeneid*'s divine machinery. Ovid, on the other hand, discards every element that can restrain Juno's spite or lend it dignity. Her emotions are almost despicably human but her power is still divine. The victims of her wrath, accordingly, produce more than an effect of pathos: they put in question the whole moral status of the gods. Here Ovid seemed to be doing much the same thing that Euripides did in his *Hippolytus* or *Mad Heracles*. But, in fact, the Virgilian coloration of Ovid's narrative gives his vengeance stories a quite un-Euripidean effect. What he writes is not simply a comic but a cuttingly bitter 'parody' of Virgil: his gods are no longer ridiculous but repulsively cruel. The 'cruelty' is never simple or unrelieved: at times Ovid reduces his divine machinery to a kind of phantasmagoria in which all that really impresses the reader is the grotesquely amusing detail. But Ovid's evident concern with the vengeance motif is far from conventional or topical: his avenging gods are to an appreciable extent images of arbitrary power very like that which he saw in the Augustan state.

The Actaeon episode sets the tone of the whole vengeance series. Actaeon is represented as the 'first' calamity of the flourishing Theban dynasty founded by Cadmus. He blundered into the naked Diana at her bath, was immediately turned by her into a stag and then died miserably under the onslaught of his unwitting dogs and hunting companions. But his fate was due only to an *error*. The real crime is not his, but Fortune's (III, 141):

> At bene si quaeras, fortunae crimen in illo,
> non scelus invenies: quod enim scelus error habebat?

> *Who weighs his deed will find no crime therein,*
> *But fate made error pay the price of sin.*

There can be no doubt that Ovid emphasized both Actaeon's innocence and Diana's cruelty or *severa virginitas* far beyond anything in his sources. Of the authors[1] that attribute Actaeon's fate to his glimpse of the naked Diana, some (Nonnus, Hyginus) say that he was sexually desirous of the goddess: some (for example, Apollodorus and presumably the Alexandrian epic he quotes) simply indicate the goddess' wrath at being surprised without her clothes. Ovid seems to have had both versions of the story in mind.

[1] See Appendix, pp. 396 f.

133

Callimachus in his *Baths of Pallas* (*Hymn* v) mentions the Actaeon story as a negative parallel to the similar (but differently ending) story of Athene and Tiresias. Athene explains to Tiresias' mother, Chariclo, that she takes no pleasure in punishing a 'child' like Tiresias (he is made blind after he inadvertently looks at the naked goddess) but that she is bound by an unbreakable law of Chronos. Athene even adds that Tiresias is much more lucky than the unfortunate Actaeon, for Tiresias will be compensated for his blindness by the gift of prophecy. Clearly Callimachus is concerned not with the innocence of the victim but only with the benevolence of the goddess: she has to keep the tabus that surround her sacred presence (no one can see what is not permitted, τὰ μὴ θεμιτά) but she does her utmost to soften the blow and demonstrate her deep and sensitive sympathy for the poor mother. Ovid, however, emphasizes only the cruelty of Diana. The 'punishment' is altogether out of proportion to the 'error'.

Callimachus' Athene is a masterpiece of delicate feeling, a most successful attempt to combine the awfulness and the humanity of a goddess.[1] Ovid's Diana is human in a very different way. She is, in effect, an instance of outraged female propriety with obviously Roman characteristics. Her bath reminds us of the toilet of a wealthy Roman virgin or matron: each maid has a particular duty —one to hold her hunting equipment, another to take her clothes, two to unlace her shoes; the most expert (*doctior*) of all, Crocale, is the hairdresser who (III, 169-70)

> sparsos per colla capillos
> colligit in nodum, quamvis erat ipsa solutis

With art more expert, knots the straying hair.
Her own hangs loose.

Finally the remaining maids—Nephele, Hyale, etc.—pour the

---

[1] See the discussion in Appendix, pp. 396-400. It seems most probable that Ovid combined two versions of the story: one that attributed Actaeon's disaster to righteous punishment for his indecent behaviour; another that upheld his innocence.

bath water from capacious urns (at this point Ovid seems almost to have forgotten the beautiful natural fountain!). When Actaeon appears, the same maids respond with all the proper ululations (*ululatibus*) and form themselves at once into an impromptu screen. Diana's words have the true accent of outraged respectability (III, 192–3):

> Nunc tibi me posito visam velamine narres,
> si poteris narrare, licet.
>
> *Now go, and say you saw Diana nude,*
> *If say you can.*

The contrast with the corresponding words of Callimachus' Athene:[1]

What, Euērideus' son, what daimon has brought you to us—
  Brought you on journey so harsh, sightlessly home to return?

is very illuminating: the sarcasm of Ovid's Diana—'now go talk about me undressed, if talk you can!'—is that of an irate lady with a reputation to lose; the mingled pity and mysterious foreboding of Callimachus' Athene are quite un-Ovidian.

This is, of course, the same Diana who was so shocked at the pregnancy of poor Callisto. Indeed Ovid has subtly prepared us for this by the earlier episode. Thus the misadventure of Callisto (when she in her ursine disguise was almost killed by her huntsman son) is repeated, on a much more pathetic level, in the death of Actaeon. The essence of his tragedy is that he combines an animal form with a human mind (*mens tantum pristina mansit*, line 203). He tries to communicate his identity to his dogs and his friends (III, 229–41):

> Heu, *famulos fugit ipse suos*! Clamare libebat
> 'Actaeon ego sum, dominum cognoscite vestrum!'
> *Verba animo desunt*: resonat latratibus aether.
> Prima Melanchaetes in tergo vulnera fecit,
> proxima Therodamas: Oresitrophus haesit in armo

---

[1] *Hymn* v, 80–1.

OVID AS AN EPIC POET

(tardius exierant, sed per compendia montis
anticipata via est); dominum retinentibus illis
cetera turba coit confertque in corpore dentes.
Iam loca vulneribus desunt. Gemit ille, *sonumque*
etsi non hominis, quem non tamen edere possit
cervus, habet maestisque replet iuga nota querellis;
et genibus pronis *supplex similisque roganti*
circumfert tacitos tamquam sua bracchia vultus

Their luckless prey, where once he followed, fled:
Fled his own hounds: the words he would have said:
'Know me, your master', came not when he willed;
With noise of baying hounds the air was filled.
*   Blackhair bit first, who on his neck had sprung*
With Killer; Hill-bred to his shoulder clung:
Late starters these, but following o'er the crest
A shorter track, they closed before the rest,
And held him, till the pack collected round,
And fleshed their fangs, and left no place to wound.
He groans, a noise 'twixt deer and man, and fills
With cries of pain the well-remembered hills;
And kneels within the pitiless ring, to raise
Instead of arms a mute beseeching gaze,

and thereby only intensifies the agony of his terrible death. But
Diana exacts the last ounce of vengeance (III, 251-2):

Nec nisi finita per plurima vulnera vita
ira pharetratae fertur satiata Dianae.

And when by countless wounds Actaeon died,
Diana's wrath at last was satisfied.

The curious mixture of moods in this episode (the satirical
realism of the bathing scene—the maids, hairdresser, urns, etc.;
the grotesque plight of the man-stag that looks like an animal and
really is a human being, and the sharp pathos of the ending) is as
thoroughly Ovidian as the straight comedy of the Io and Daphne
episodes. But here humour has become melodrama: Ovid here

136

passes the border-line that he had not really overstepped in the Callisto story. The human animal's inability to communicate with his fellow-humans now leads to sharp pathos and death; the shocked respectability of Diana is now allowed to produce its full effect. The result is a quite moving contrast between inhumanly rigid propriety and intensely human suffering. The whole question of theodicy is raised. Even the gods—even the powers that be—are divided on the justice of Diana's act (III, 253–5):

> Rumor in ambiguo est: aliis violentior aequo
> visa dea est, alii laudant *dignamque severa*
> *virginitate* vocant: pars invenit utraque causas.

> *Opinions differed, when the tale went round,*
> *And two contending schools of thought were found:*
> *A harsh vindictive goddess, some would cry;*
> *Some praised her justice, strict as chastity.*

Only Juno is completely indifferent to the ethics involved (255 ff.). She merely rejoices in the event, for her hatred extends from the 'Tyrian trollop', Europa, to the whole Agenorid (Cadmean) clan (*in generis socios*). But this reminds her: Semele has now duplicated Europa's offence and become pregnant to boot! Juno's soliloquy here is a bitter parody of Virgil (*Aen.* I, 46–8):

> Ast ego, quae divum incedo regina Iovisque
> et soror et coniunx, una cum gente tot annos
> bella gero.

> *But I who take my place as queen of the gods, Jove's sister and*
> *wife—for all these years I wage a war with one sole people.*

(*Met.* III, 265–8):

> si sum regina Iovisque
> et soror et coniunx, certe soror. At, puto, furto est
> contenta [i.e. Semele], et thalami brevis est iniuria nostri:
> Concipit! Id deerat!

> *Jove's wife and sister, as I claim to be—*
> *Sister, at least. And yet I think that she,*

137

> *Content with stolen pleasures, does me wrong*
> *As lawful wedded wife—but not for long.*
> *Yet, pregnant, she (last insult!)—thus she shows*
> *Her crime to all.*

Juno has not lost an acrid humour (*certe soror!*) but she is not the comic figure of the *Divine Comedy*. The plot against Semele is another bitter 'parody', this time of a motif (the over-hasty wish motif) of the *Phaethon*. Here, as Phoebus before him, Jupiter commits himself (even to the point of swearing the unbreakable Stygian oath) before he can know what the wish really is (Semele coyly asks first for an unnamed wish, *sine nomine munus*). And Jupiter, exactly like Phoebus, is caught unawares by the wish itself (III, 295–6):

> voluit deus ora loquentis
> opprimere: exierat iam vox properata sub auras.

He would have stopped her, but the words had fled.

But here the event is not due to a child's immaturity and a father's indulgence. It was premeditated by Juno and Jupiter only springs the trap that she has laid; but he is just as helpless as ever Phoebus was. He can save Semele's unborn child (the future Bacchus) but he cannot save Semele, even though he fatuously tries to mitigate his divine splendour by assuming his 'second-best' thunderbolts and his inferior regalia. But the effect, unlike that of the *Phaethon*, is not comic. Juno is too malevolent to be simply amusing. Even poor Tiresias is penalized for deciding the famous *argumentum amoris* against her: *gravius Saturnia iusto nec pro materia fertur doluisse*. And it is Jupiter, not (as in Callimachus) the aggrieved goddess, who compensates Tiresias by making him a prophet.

But the real horror of Juno's *ira* has as yet been masked by its grotesque and comic accompaniments. It is the Pentheus episode that raises the vengeance theme to a tragic height and works, by suggestion, to produce the horrendous Juno of the *Ino*. Here the Semele motif (the impact on Juno of another god's successful vengeance) is repeated and at the same time intensified. Bacchus not only sets Juno an example (as did Diana) but is himself a living reminder of his mother, Semele, and of Juno's partially frustrated vengeance on her (she could destroy the pregnant mother but not the unborn son). But, more important still, Bacchus is represented (at least at first) as the opposite of Juno (he is himself the innocent object of her wrath) and as the worker of righteous and justified punishment rather than mere spite or revenge. Therefore, Juno's horrible parody of Bacchus' vengeance on Pentheus (in her own vengeance on Ino, the nurse and foster-mother of Bacchus) has a climactic force that makes it the proper conclusion of the first half of the section (before the central panel). Here at last we see the true *ira deum* in all its irresponsible inhumanity.

The distinctive feature of Ovid's *Pentheus* (the Theban king destroyed by his mother in a moment of Bacchic madness) is the interpolated story of the Tyrrhene sailors. This is told by the mysterious Acoetes (probably an alias for the god himself) in answer to Pentheus' threatening questions. He explains why he is a votary of the god by recalling his strange experience on ship-board—how he saw sailors made into dolphins because they impiously refused to acknowledge the god and took advantage of the inexperienced 'youth' they supposed him to be. It is hard to say where Ovid got the idea of combining the two episodes (the sailors and the Pentheus story).[1] Pacuvius wrote a *Pentheus* that may contain an Acoetes narrative though we are not told so in Servius' brief summary. Nonnus attributes the story to Tiresias and makes it part of that prophet's warning to Pentheus. It is possible that Pacuvius, Nonnus and Ovid all go back to a Hellenistic 'short epic' which had already made the combination. But it is more likely that Nonnus' version (as well as that of the mytho-grapher Hyginus) is a more or less garbled copy of Ovid. It is evident that Ovid would, in any event, have been strongly tempted to work this episode into the Pentheus story, thus giving a meta-morphosis to a legend that is not one in itself. The *effect* of

[1] See Appendix, pp. 400 f.

Acoetes' tale as it stands in Ovid is to enhance our sympathy for Bacchus and increase our sense of the justice of Bacchus' vengeance.

The contrast between the brutal sailors and the apparently defenceless, drunken 'youth' (III, 654–5):

> Quae gloria vestra est,
> si puerum iuvenes, si multi fallitis unum?

> *Or is it sport for men*
> *To cheat a boy, when he is one to ten?*

as well as the contrast between the poor but pious seaman (whose only inheritance is his 'art' of helmsmanship) and the headstrong Pentheus (*acrior admonitu*), are well calculated to direct our sympathy towards the god. Bacchus, the orphaned child of Semele, who always appears in the most innocent and unprovocative of disguises but is also a truly present god to all who have any religious sensitivity, is the perfect foil to crass ignorance, brutality and pride. And yet the horrible death of Pentheus—the rending of his body by his aunts and mother—recalls most pathetically the death of his cousin Actaeon. Like him, Pentheus is unable to communicate with his human assailants and, like him also, he is forced to beg for mercy without the human means to do so (III, 723–5):

> *Non habet infelix, quae matri bracchia tendat:*
> trunca sed ostendens disiectis vulnera membris,
> 'adspice, mater!' ait.

> *No suppliant arms were by his mother seen:*
> *He showed the gaping wounds where arms had been:*
> *'See, mother, see!'*

And though Pentheus is not in fact an animal—this is no actual metamorphosis—he appears as such to the frenzied women (III, 714–15):

> Ille aper, in nostris errat qui maximus agris,
> ille *mihi feriendus aper.*

Yon monstrous boar that roams our countryside—
Come, see the kill!

He himself grasps the terrible parallelism (III, 719–20):

'fer opem, matertera' dixit
'Autonoë! moveant animos *Actaeonis umbrae*'

'Give aid, dear aunt,' said he,
'And let Actaeon's memory plead for me.'

But it is too late for mercy: the gruesome scene reaches its logical
conclusion and even points a moral (III, 732–3):

Talibus exemplis monitae nova sacra frequentant
turaque dant sanctasque colunt Ismenides aras.

The Theban wives, awed by the new god's might,
Honour his altars, and attend his rite.

Ovid here shows the ambivalence of his feelings. The god is in
one sense right: Pentheus deserves to be punished. But the
punishment is surely excessive! Indeed Pentheus' recall of
Actaeon—and thus of another divine act of inhumanity and cruelty
—seems to be Ovid's own invention. He is deliberately setting the
two episodes in parallel. He wants to show that the justice of
Bacchus has now given place to his cruelty. It is now evident that
the only alternative to 'piety' is the terrible wrath of the god, as
the priest-seer (presumably Tiresias) warns the women of Thebes
(IV, 8–9):

saevam *laesi* fore *numinis* iram
vaticinatus erat.

Fierce, he forewarned them, would the anger be
Of Bacchus, should they slight his majesty.

For this is, after all, a religion of terror. The Minyades (the next
victims of Bacchus' wrath) are but one more illustration of his
divine *ira*, though their main function is to provide a frame for
quite different stories, stories that mark a deliberate contrast to the

vengeance theme. But the Minyades at any rate maintain the tension—maintain our sense of divine cruelty and ferocity—until Juno herself can return.

Now she soliloquizes once again on her supposed inferiority to other gods, but now she is no longer ironic or humorous (IV, 422–31):

> potuit de paelice natus
> vertere Maeonios pelagoque immergere nautas,
> et laceranda suae nati dare viscera matri
> et triplices operire novis Minyeidas alis:
> nil poterit Iuno nisi inultos flere dolores?
> Idque mihi satis est? Haec una potentia nostra est?
> Ipse docet, quid agam (fas est et ab hoste doceri),
> quidque *furor* valeat, Penthea caede *satisque*
> *ac super* ostendit: cur non stimuletur eatque
> per cognata suis exempla furoribus Ino?

> *My rival's son had might*
> *To change the Tuscan sailors, and to send*
> *Them under sea; to make a mother rend*
> *Her son in pieces; and to give the three*
> *Daughters of Minyas pinions strange to see.*
> *Shall it be said, to Juno naught belongs*
> *Save leave to weep her unrequited wrongs;*
> *My threats so feeble, and my powers so few?*
> *My foe himself instructs me what to do,*
> *Who did by Pentheus' death too well display*
> *Delirium's power, and point me out the way.*
> *The lesson's learnt: let Ino feel the goad,*
> *And like her kinsfolk, tread the madman's road.*

So we revert once more to divine revenge or spite as distinguished from divine punishment. Ino (the aunt, nurse and foster-mother of Bacchus) is happy and prosperous with her husband Athamas and her two children, Learchus and Melicertes. This is what Juno cannot bear (420 ff.). The notion that gods should punish only an offence, a positive crime or misdeed, is quite remote from her thoughts. But she fully sees the infernal possibilities of such *furor*

as Bacchus had sent upon Agave and her sisters: it is even enough
for such spite as her own (*quid furor valeat...satis superque...
[Bacchus] ostendit*). Thus the Ino story is Juno's supreme act of
tragic parody—a parody that horribly repeats the cruelty but quite
lacks the justice of the Pentheus story. There is no overruling
power, no fate, that can put these two acts of divine vengeance into
any comprehensive theodicy or any morally intelligible relation
to each other. Now the 'justice' of Bacchus is wholly offset by
the injustice of Juno; the mood of the Ino episode brings us back
to the beginning of the vengeance series, to the cruelty and heartless indifference with which Diana disposed of Actaeon.

Here Juno's wrath finally takes on a truly hellish character. She
uses the Fury, Tisiphone, to infuse a pseudo-Bacchic, child-
destroying madness in Ino and Athamas. As in the seventh book
of Virgil's *Aeneid* (Ovid's imitation is close and deliberate)[1] Juno
draws on the underworld to compensate the deficiencies of
heaven (IV, 447–8):

> Sustinet ire illuc caelesti sede relicta—
> tantum odiis iraeque dabat—*Saturnia* Iuno.
>
> *Hither did Juno from her bright abode,*
> *To serve her hate and anger, take the road.*

But Ovid makes Juno herself walk through the vast recesses of
Hades in order to find Tisiphone with her sisters in the wretched
House of Crime (*Sedes Scelerata*). The details of the visit are
piquantly grotesque: Cerberus' three barks, the three sisters
combing their snaky hair, the horrible exhibits of the place
(Tantalus, Ixion, Sisyphus, so many more examples of punishment
for Juno to follow), the way in which Tisiphone brushes a snake
from her face—all is concrete, precise, even amusing, nothing in
the least like Virgil. But the actual operation of Ovid's Tisiphone
—the spreading of her venom by means of the snakes—is very
similar to that of Allecto, though again more precisely and
pictorially conceived.

[1] See Appendix, pp. 401–3.

The Bacchic madness of Ino and Athamas and the parents' destruction or attempted destruction of the children (Athamas tears the little Learchus from his mother's arms, rotates it like a sling and dashes it to death on the rocks: Ino leaps into the sea with the little Melicertes at her bosom) are deliberate repetitions of the Pentheus–Agave scene (IV, 519-24):

> tum denique concita mater,
> seu dolor hoc fecit seu sparsi causa veneni,
> exululat passisque fugit male sana capillis
> teque ferens parvum nudis, Melicerta, lacertis
> 'euhoe Bacche' sonat: Bacchi sub nomine Iuno
> risit et 'hos usus praestet tibi' dixit 'alumnus.'

> *The mother shrieking fled, with grief distraught,*
> *Or madness that the sprinkled poison wrought.*
> *Her hair flew wild, and with bare arms she pressed*
> *The infant Melicertes to her breast.*
> *She called on Bacchus: Juno grimly smiled,*
> *And wished her profit of her foster-child.*

At the end, however, pitying Venus calls on Neptune's aid and transforms both Ino and Melicertes into divinities of the sea. As in Virgil, Venus is used to counter Juno but there is no higher God, Fate or Justice at hand. The horror of the episode is thus only slightly softened. Juno is left to complete her grim task by turning Ino's grieving attendants into statues and birds, and, last of all, Cadmus and Harmonia into snakes.

These episodes leave us with a number of mixed and rather bewildering impressions. Ovid never seems to omit pictorial detail or amusing comment; but he is not mainly amusing; he also conveys his distaste for his gods and their almost diabolical cruelty. It is all, of course, make-believe, a retelling of old tales for whose primary content Ovid is not himself responsible. But here, as in the *Divine Comedy*, the motives of his gods are too 'human' or too 'inhuman' not to convey their own comment on life.

From one point of view, the Virgilian touches—the jealous Juno, the snaky Tisiphone—are satirical and even comic. But there is more here than satire. There is also a deliberate refusal to take theodicy seriously, to acknowledge the reality of divine justice and goodness. Ovid does not deny that some men are foolish, wicked or deserving of punishment: he does deny that the powers in fictitious or actual control of men are just and merciful. Whether it is Diana's severe virginity, Juno's sexual jealousy or Bacchus' ambiguous blend of outraged innocence and diabolical revenge, the motive is not worthy of its divine origin. The first section had shown us gods whose divine majesty could not contain their very human feelings. We have now seen gods whose human feelings frightfully abused their divine power. But such 'gods', after all, are only thinly-disguised men and women, especially such men and women as hold positions of power and authority. There is no overt criticism of Augustus and his court (even Actaeon's *error* has probably nothing to do with the *error* that led to Ovid's banishment[1]), but there is certainly an implicit criticism of Augustan ideology and practice. What repels Ovid is the mercilessness of absolute power. When the gods are only hypocritical, they are comic. When they are also cruel, they are actually revolting.

The long Perseus–Phineus panel now intervenes (in the exact centre of Section II) to separate the vengeance stories into two portions. The *Perseus* is not about divine vengeance; it is in a quite different genre altogether; it is, in fact, a heroic epic with a human hero and an essentially human subject-matter even though it contains the normal epic equipment of an aiding goddess and a terrible monster. It thus provides both relief and effective demarcation to the Divine Vengeance episodes that surround it.

---

[1] The mention of Actaeon in *Tristia* II, 105 as an analogue of Ovid's own crime (*imprudenti cognita culpa*, 104) is of course suggestive. M. Pohlenz (*Hermes* 48 (1913), pp. 1–13) therefore suggested that Ovid gives a personal nuance to *Met.* III, 141–2 (Fortunae crimen *in illo, non* scelus *invenies*). But the chronology is uncertain: Ovid could have thought of Actaeon as he did without a personal reason.

After it, we find not Diana, Bacchus or Juno in control but the
Muses, Minerva and Latona. With the change of gods goes a
change of human motive: it is no longer error, mischance or a
distaste for religious enthusiasm that cause the trouble, but positive
impiety, deliberate *hybris*. There is some likeness between the
opponents of Bacchus and the opponents of the Muses or Minerva
(the parallelism between the Minyades and Pieriae is close) but
there is also a difference: the insolence or pride of the Pieriae or
Arachne is far more explicit and perverse. The Pieriae shock the
Muses by preferring the impious giants to the Olympian gods and,
above all, by attempting to show the gods at their worst: they are
cowards who run to animal cover (Jupiter, of course, to that of a
bull). Arachne actually weaves a tapestry out of the story of
Europa and supplements it by other examples of philandering
deities in animal disguise. Niobe publicly boasts of her own
superiority to Latona. The Lycian peasants are actively cruel as
well as insolent. In short, these later episodes of vengeance are
quite clear-cut theodicies in which obviously perverse pride is
humbled by obviously just and noble goddesses—Minerva, the
Muses and Latona.

Yet we can also observe a new development that points the way
toward the mood and theme of the third section. In the *Arachne*,
Minerva punishes the unfortunate girl by striking her three times
on the forehead, after which Arachne in her wretchedness tries to
hang herself. Then Minerva (VI, 135–8)

> pendentem...miserata levavit
> atque ita 'vive quidem, pende tamen, improba' dixit:
> 'lexque eadem poenae, ne sis secura futuri,
> dicta tuo generi serisque nepotibus esto.'

> ...*who observed her, and conceived*
> *Some pity, raised her up, and thus reprieved:*
> '*Live, Mischief, live and hang: this sentence be*
> *On you and yours to far posterity*
> *Without remission.*'

The metamorphosis (Arachne becomes a spider) is thus a consequence of Arachne's misery, not of her crime (which has already been punished). Actually it is an act of pity, even though of curiously limited pity. Furthermore, this metamorphosis (unlike the metamorphoses of Io, Callisto, Actaeon or Cadmus) starts a new animal species and seems to involve a complete loss of human mentality and consciousness. But the important point is the motive of the metamorphosis: the anguish that is both perpetuated and assuaged by the change of shape.

This becomes very much clearer in the considerable Niobe story, the last major episode of divine vengeance (167 lines). The interesting thing about it is its development from a quite clear-cut and simple vengeance tale into a truly remarkable study of human suffering. But the connection of the *Niobe* with the preceding narrative clearly shows its parallelism with the Muses–Pieriae and Arachne episodes. Minerva, on leaving Perseus (v, 250), visits the Muses in order to see the new fountain at Helicon. The Muses are full of their troubles with the impious daughters of Pieros and tell Minerva the whole story. Their 'just wrath' then excites Minerva (the parallel with Juno is obvious) and makes her recall and fittingly punish the analogously impious Arachne. Then the Phrygian queen, Niobe, hears of Arachne (she is the talk of all Lydia and nearby Phrygia) but does not heed the moral of her story (*nec tamen admonita est poena popularis Arachnes*). Her own story thus comes as the appropriate climax of the series.

The *Niobe* falls into three distinct parts:
  (1) The Haughty Mother (vi, 146–203)
  (2) The Killing of the Sons (204–66)
  (3) The Killing of the Daughters and Niobe's Metamorphosis (267–312)

The first shows the crime or *hybris*; the second, the punishment; the third, the *pathos* of Niobe. Each is very different, yet all together form a single line of development from Niobe's initial *hybris* to her final metamorphosis. The real interest of the episode lies in the contrast of its beginning with its end.

Ludwig Voit, in an excellent discussion of the sources,[1] has pointed out that the truly Ovidian feature of the story is the motivation of the metamorphosis. Aeschylus and Sophocles had each written a *Niobe* and Ovid was almost certainly familiar with at least Sophocles' play. But Ovid achieved a concentration of plot lacking in the dramatists; he all but eliminated Niobe's husband, Amphion; unlike Sophocles, he preserved the unity of place and time (the deaths of the children, in Ovid, immediately precede the metamorphosis). But his essential divergence from these dramatists (to which, indeed, his other divergences contributed) was his removal of the gods from the metamorphosis. Niobe's petrifaction, as Ovid describes it, is neither divine punishment nor divine mercy but an almost natural phenomenon, an all but inevitable consequence of her *pathos*.

Niobe begins as an obvious *contemptor deum* like Pentheus or Arachne. Like Pentheus, she disdains the pious warning of the prophet (this time Tiresias' daughter, Manto) and tries to put an end to popular worship of Latona. But she goes even further than Pentheus and sets herself up as a preferable object of veneration (VI, 170–3):[2]

> 'Quis furor, auditos' inquit 'praeponere visis
> caelestes? aut cur colitur Latona per aras,
> *numen adhuc sine ture meum est?*

> '*What craze is this, to spurn the gods you see,*
> *And take a wandering voice for deity?*
> *Why thus should worship Leto's altars fill,*
> *While I, no less divine, lack incense still?*'

She tempts fate by boasting of her *felicity* (VI, 193–4):

> Sum felix: quis enim neget hoc? felixque manebo
> (hoc quoque quis dubitet?): tutam me copia fecit.

[1] Cf. Appendix, pp. 404–5.

[2] It is important to note that Ovid here ignores the tradition of Niobe's divine origin. Her claim to equality with Latona is represented solely as *hybris* of the worst sort (a mortal's claim to be a god). The ancestors of ll. 172 f. prove nothing.

My bliss who doubts? That this will long endure,
Who questions? Wealth has made my lot secure.

And she even suggests the extent and manner of her calamity by insisting that with but half of her fourteen children, she would still be superior to Latona and her two.

Such *hybris* is enough for the two divine children in question (Apollo and Diana): they go into immediate action (204–17) even before their mother can properly voice her grievance. The successive deaths of the seven sons (who fall separately to Phoebus' arrows) are described in a series of statuesque vignettes. The whole passage shows Ovid's great skill at producing variations on a single theme. But, much more important, it brings out the rapidity of the action. All is so quick that the victims cannot realize their plight; they are dead before they can properly react. Ismenus, quite unconscious of any danger, is hit in full motion and falls off his horse with the reins still in his hand. Sipylus hears the sound of the god's quiver but is struck before he can come to a stop. Phaedimus and Tantalus are caught wrestling together and are both transfixed by a single arrow. Alphenor is killed as he runs to their aid. Damasichthon is finished by a second arrow as he tries to extract the first. Ilioneus has time to pray for mercy and even move the god to pity, but not time enough to stop the 'irrevocable' weapon that still kills him, though with the 'least possible' of wounds. What therefore stands out in this somewhat macabre series of death scenes, is the speed of the vengeance. The sons are dead before they really know what has happened. The god acts so quickly that even he has no opportunity for remorse. It is all done before anyone can grasp more than the physical occurrence.

We now (Part 3, line 267) turn back to Niobe (who in addition to the loss of her sons has experienced also that of her husband Amphion). How different she now is from the proud queen who had just scorned Latona: *quantum haec Niobe, Niobe distabat ab illa, quae modo Latois populum submoverat aris.* Her pride is now only a gesture of defiance. She kisses her dead sons and bids the *triumphant*

Latona feast her cruel eyes on her grief. But the very word triumphant (*victrix*) suggests the fatal comment (283-5):

> exsulta *victrixque* inimica triumpha!
> Cur autem *victrix*? Miserae mihi plura supersunt
> quam tibi felici; post tot quoque funera vinco!

> *Feed full your heart, and boast your victory,*
> *For in the death of these my seven I die.*
> *Victory, I say: why victory? Joy is thine*
> *And triumph, true, and loss and mourning mine;*
> *Yet in my remnant still I number more,*
> *And with my losses hold the winning score.*

Though not *felix*, as she had originally called herself (*sum felix*, 195), but *misera*, she will not submit. But her response is now not so much *hybris* as impotent rage. She quite fails in her emotional stress to see the ominous suggestiveness of her second claim to superiority. She thus sets up the second act of the tragedy: it is not only an accelerated but also an emotionally heightened version of the first. The killing of the sons had been too swift and unexpected for immediate response; now it is very different. Now Niobe is prepared to take and to feel the final, crushing blow, disposed of in eleven verses (286-96) in contrast to the forty-eight devoted to the sons. The effect is one of massive, undifferentiated and anonymous tragedy (295-6):

> Haec frustra fugiens collabitur, illa sorori
> inmoritur; latet haec, illam trepidare videres.

> *One fleeing fell; on her another died;*
> *One made for cover; one stood terrified.*

Finally, but one daughter is left: we come to the last phase of the last act—Niobe's plea for the poor girl, the latter's death, Niobe's own metamorphosis (298-305).

> Ultima restabat: quam toto corpore mater,
> tota veste tegens 'unam minimamque relinque!

de multis minimam posco' clamavit 'et unam.'
Dumque rogat, pro qua rogat, occidit. Orba resedit
exanimes inter natos natasque virumque
deriguitque malis: nullos movet aura capillos,
in vultu color est sine sanguine, lumina maestis
stant inmota genis; nihil est in imagine vivum.

At last the mother saw but one remain;
Whose body with her own she covered o'er,
Screening her wholly with the robe she wore.
'Ah, leave my youngest' (so her pleadings run),
'I ask but one, my youngest—leave me one!'
But while she asked, the one she asked for bled:
Husband, and sons, and daughters—all were dead.
In uttermost bereavement, sitting lone
Amid her griefs, she turned, with grief, to stone.
No breeze that blew disturbed her chiselled hair;
Her cheeks had colour, but no blood was there;
Eyes fixed and staring in the grief-lined face;
All as in life—of life itself no trace.

Thus the metamorphosis is not punishment at all, not even an
act of divine pity, but the very image of Niobe's final condition.
The last set of killings has a cumulative horror that is overwhelming and unendurable. The death of the last daughter represents the limit beyond which maternal emotion cannot be pushed.
Niobe had by this time become in spirit what she now became in
body, unfeeling stone. Her petrifaction is only the consequence of
a calamity that had already stunned her to the point of absolute
insensibility. At last vengeance had given way to *pathos* (the
pathos of the bereaved mother). The *Niobe* thus marks the transition from the story of divine vengeance to the quite different story
of human *pathos*: from metamorphosis as an act of divine punishment to metamorphosis as a natural phenomenon. Here, as with
Arachne, it is *pathos*, not theodicy, that motivates the change; but
here it is not divine pity so much as nature itself that seems to work
the change.

From another standpoint, it is important to note the line that runs from the simple story of human innocence and divine cruelty (Actaeon) through the tangled web of divine spite and punishment (Semele, Pentheus, Ino) to the theodicy that in its extensiveness (its inclusion of the innocent with the guilty) and its extremism (its disregard of any limit or check) exceeds all mercy or pity. But such a conclusion is revolting! The *Niobe* (by its ending) has at last shown us that there can be a different relation between man and nature (a different conception of metamorphosis) than that which has prevailed up to this point.

II (THE MINOR AND CONTRASTING LOVE THEME)

But Ovid prepared for the next section (III) not only by shift of tone and motif within his vengeance episodes but by the amatory *pathos* of the stories attributed to the Minyades. Here he killed, so to speak, two birds with one stone: he achieved a needed variety and anticipated the amatory emphasis to come. The tales of the Minyades, like the corresponding tales of the Muses (Ceres and Proserpina with the inset stories of Ascalaphus, Arethusa, etc.), are clearly designed to make a strong contrast with both the prevailing vengeance theme and the epically styled Perseus panel in the centre. Furthermore, the *Narcissus–Echo*, though it is nominally a vengeance story (Juno revenges herself on Echo, Echo on Narcissus), is also very like the tales of the Minyades. But the *Ceres–Proserpina* is unlike the *Pyramus–Thisbe*, *Leucothoe* or *Salmacis* in that it refers back to the *Divine Comedy* rather than ahead to the *Pathos of Love*. Logically speaking, Ovid should have put it before the Perseus panel, rather than later in the second half of the section. But Ovid's order is far more satisfactory from an aesthetic point of view. First, he did not want to over-emphasize continuity with the *Divine Comedy* in the first half of this section (II) where, as we have seen, motifs of the *Divine Comedy* are continued in the Actaeon and Semele episodes. Furthermore, it is only after we have been through the rather sombre *Actaeon*, *Pentheus*, and *Ino*, the sad tales of the Minyades, and the massive epic of Perseus, that we are really ready for Comedy once again.

The *Ceres–Proserpina* is sung to Minerva by the Muse Calliope (v, 339).[1] It was the piece that the Muses had originally used in their contest with the impious Pieriae. Just as Minerva later opposed a tapestry of the birth of the Olive to Arachne's scornful depiction of gods debased and made ridiculous by love (Jupiter as the Bull, etc.), so here the Muses opposed the story of Proserpina to the blasphemous Gigantomachy of the Pieriae. The tale of Proserpina is thus meant to be favourable to the gods; the Muses are obviously on their side. But actually, of course, Arachne and the Pieriae were no greater detractors of the gods than had been Ovid himself in his *Divine Comedy*. The repeated reference to the bull-shape of Jupiter by both the Pieriae and Arachne is surely an indirect recall of the *maiestas–amor* theme of Book II. Still, the context is different: the blasphemous intention of the Pieriae and Arachne is emphasized by inclusion of their narratives within the frame of their own vengeance stories. But it is rather disconcerting to witness the respectable Muses relating to the respectable Minerva the story of Pluto's unpremeditated *amor*. Ovid, of course, preserves appearances by an epic tone and decorum (it is this which Heinze took so seriously), but he certainly brings out the humour of the action: the gods who are at such pains to punish criticism are, in fact, only too vulnerable to it. The story of Proserpina is far more akin to the impious stories of the Pieriae than the somewhat unsophisticated Muses can readily understand. Furthermore, the *properatus amor* of Pluto is accentuated by the Daphne-like flight of Arethusa, the matronly grief of Cyane and the tale bearing of Ascalaphus. Altogether the brilliance of this bit of *Divine Comedy* is enhanced by its setting of vengeance stories (especially the vengeance of the Muses themselves), and stands strongly in relief against the multiple killings and petrifactions of the *Perseus*. It is indeed a contrast; perhaps more of a

[1] On this story cf. p. 50, n. 1.

contrast than Ovid really intended, for the *Ceres–Proserpina* is an Ovidian masterpiece in a sense that the *Perseus* is not. It provides, at any rate, the comedy that brings out the full tragedy of Niobe.

The stories of the Minyades are contrast of an altogether different sort. They not only provide relief from the divine vengeance theme; they also suggest the main theme (amatory *pathos*) of Section III. Though they contain many comic touches, they are fundamentally serious and pathetic. The one divine amour (Phoebus and Leucothoe) is not really anything like those of the *Divine Comedy*: its emphasis is on Clytie's jealousy and hopeless passion; her metamorphosis is the result not of a god's vengeance (as with the jealous Aglauros) but of her own emotion. The stories of Pyramus–Thisbe and Salmacis, on the other hand, are wholly without divine motivation: in the first, the metamorphosis (the change of colour in the mulberry) is quite incidental to the main plot; in the second it is a direct result of the nymph's uncontrollable eroticism. The major events are quite human, even though verging on the pathological; Salmacis is both literally and clinically a nymphomaniac. At any rate, the plight of these lovers—of Pyramus, Thisbe, Clytie and Salmacis—is due wholly to their own passion. Together they comprise the three main types of amatory *pathos* with which Ovid was to be concerned throughout Section III: the fatal separation of lovers by death and catastrophe; the grief of frustrated and abandoned lovers; and the uncontrollable *libido* of lovers who cannot win the desired response.

The *Pyramus–Thisbe* (IV, 55–166: the first of the Minyades' tales) is obviously not an ordinary story (53 *hoc placet, haec quoniam vulgaris fabula non est*): it is in every respect unlike the *Pentheus* which has just preceded it and unlike, also, all the divine *amores* of the first section. Here we have no gods or nymphs or even kings and heroes, but a boy and girl living in contiguous houses on a city street. The tiny crack in the intervening wall is their only means of communication. Yet from this humble, idyllic beginning we proceed to a finale that rivals that of *Romeo and Juliet* in its intensity of passion. It is the emotions of the girl that are most particularly

emphasized: Pyramus' suicide speech (108–16) is but prelude to
that of his beloved Thisbe (141–4):

> gelidis in vultibus oscula figens
> 'Pyrame,' clamavit 'quis te mihi casus ademit?
> Pyrame, responde! Tua te, carissime, Thisbe
> nominat: exaudi vultusque attolle iacentis!'

> *and kissed the ice-cold face.*
> '*O Pyramus, what fortune*', *was her cry,*
> '*Has snatched you from me? Pyramus, reply.*
> *Your Thisbe I; 'tis Thisbe calls,' she said;*
> '*O hear my voice, and raise your sunken head.*'

Here, indeed, we have an anticipation of the *Cephalus–Procris* and,
above all, of the *Ceyx–Alcyone* of the next section. Though the
metamorphosis is slight and inconsequential, the theme of mutual
love (love too strong to endure separation) is fully developed.
Under its stress the woman feels all the courage and tragic resolution of a man (148–50):

> 'tua te manus' inquit 'amorque
> perdidit, infelix! Est et mihi fortis in unum
> hoc manus, est et amor: dabit hic in vulnera vires.'

> '*Unhappy one,*
> *By your own hand, and by your love, undone.*
> *Courage for this my own true hand can show,*
> *And love is mine, to nerve it for the blow.*'

The next story (Leucothoe, Clytie) starts with a divine amour:
the capture and indecent exposure of Mars and Venus. But Ovid
does not make much of this episode, as he did, for example, in the
Ars Amatoria and as Homer had done in the *Odyssey*—even the
jocular god of the occasion is referred to anonymously as *aliquis de
dis non tristibus*—but uses it only as an introduction to the story of
Phoebus and Leucothoe: Phoebus' love is Venus' punishment for
his tattling to Vulcan. But Leucothoe's story is itself a means of
transition to the story of her sister's (Clytie's) jealousy. Here (line

255) the plot follows the pattern of the *Coronis* or *Herse–Aglauros*: yet Clytie, the jealous cause of Leucothoe's death and Phoebus' sorrow, is not punished by the god (as we might have expected) but simply allowed to waste away in frustrated love. She can do nothing but look at her beloved (the sun) and turns, almost by dint of her own persistence, into a heliotrope: *vertitur ad solem mutataque servat amorem.* Here the metamorphosis of *pathos*—the metamorphosis that has nothing to do with courtship or revenge and has no obvious divine motivation—is fully prefigured. We shall meet it again, in Section III, with Byblis, Myrrha and Alcyone.

The third story—that of Salmacis or the Hermaphrodite—is also told for its novelty (*novitas*, 284); its preference to the tales that Alcithoe (the third of the Minyades) passes by (Daphnis' transformation into stone by a jealous nymph, the amatory metamorphoses of Crocus and Smilax, the sexual changes of Sithon) is determined by the plan of the epic. The stories of Daphnis, Crocus, etc. are really repetitions of what has gone before (e.g. Narcissus, Aglauros) and add no such pivotal motif as that of the *libido* represented by Salmacis. Salmacis is, in fact, the prototype of the *furiosa libido* that, as the *Ars Amatoria* (I, 296 f.) had declared, is peculiarly female.

Thus Salmacis is (after the doubtful case of Echo) the first instance of a passionate female who takes the initiative. She plays, in fact, the same role as the amorous gods of the *Divine Comedy*. Her sexual impatience is expressed in almost the exact words attributed to the Jupiter of the Europa episode:
IV, 350 (of Salmacis):

> Vixque moram patitur, *vix iam sua gaudia differt*
>
> *She scarce could brook delay, or bear the pain*
> *Of joys deferred;*

II, 863 (of Jupiter):

> Oscula dat manibus; *vix iam, vix cetera differt*

He kissed her hands, as earnest of the sum
Of hoped-for joys, scarce waiting what's to come.

But here, male and female roles are reversed: the woman takes the
initiative; the boy shows all the *pudor* that a virgin could want.
Salmacis is bald and blunt in her desires; the other can only blush
(329–30):

> Nais ab his [i.e. her crudely literal proposals] tacuit.
> Pueri rubor ora notavit
> (nescit enim, quid amor), sed et erubuisse decebat.

So she; but what love was, he did not know:
He blushed to hear her, seeming prettier so.

His bashfulness has very much the same charm as that of Daphne
herself.[1] But the difference of sex produces a wholly different
effect! The tale is not at all tragic or pathetic—its prevailing tone is a
unique mixture of the humorous and the grotesque—but it indicates
the motif that was to be developed in the later stories of Byblis and
Myrrha. Just as in the *Pyramus–Thisbe* and *Leucothoe–Clytie*, Ovid
suggests but does not fully anticipate the themes of Section III.
Thisbe is no Alcyone but a young girl in her first love; Clytie is no
Scylla but a woman thwarted by a god; Salmacis' energetic *eros* is
not quite the unnatural *libido* of Byblis or Myrrha. But the similarities are greater than the differences.

Another, though fainter, premonition of amatory *pathos* is to be
found in the *Echo–Narcissus* (III, 339–510), the earlier story that
immediately followed the *Semele* and preceded the *Pentheus*. This
is in form a divine vengeance tale: it is introduced (like the
Pentheus) by a comminatory prophecy of Tiresias, and its two
metamorphoses (Echo's into a voice, Narcissus' into a flower) are
described as partial acts of vengeance. Echo earned Juno's vengeance by detaining her in conversation and making her lose an
opportunity to catch Jupiter with some nymphs. Narcissus in
turn earned Echo's vengeance by scorning her advances: *sic amet*

[1] Cf. *Met.* I, 526–7 *fugit...tum quoque visa decens...auctaque forma fuga est.*

ipse licet, sic non potiatur amato! (III, 405). But the vengeances are not really integral to the story: both Echo's and Narcissus' passions could have had the same result without them. Actually, the main emphasis of the plot is on Echo's frustrated passion and Narcissus' futile self-love. Yet it is not, in the final analysis, the sufferings of either Echo or Narcissus that impress us so much as the piquancy of their situations: Echo's inability to woo Narcissus except by catching and using his own words; Narcissus' strange incapacity to satisfy a love of which he had, in one sense, full possession (*inopem me copia fecit*). The whole story is a curious blend of vengeance and amatory motifs and is in the main an ingenious exercise in paradox. Where it definitely goes beyond the simple vengeance metamorphosis is in its careful adaptation of the changes in Echo and Narcissus to their pathetic plights: Echo becomes a mere voice because she literally wastes away from love; Narcissus becomes a water-flower because he cannot humanly achieve the self-immersion for which he strives. Thus the story prefigures but in no sense anticipates the tales of the Minyades.

We can now set forth the basic relation of this section (II) to the sections (I, III) that surround it as follows:

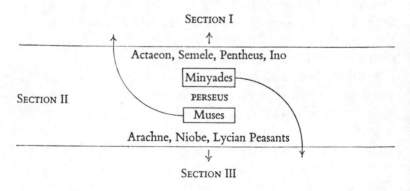

The first set of vengeance stories repeat and develop motifs already set forth in Section I (Callisto, Coronis, Aglauros) and the second set anticipate motifs to be set forth in Section III (Scylla, Myrrha, etc.). The contrast sections (Minyades, Pieriae) look ahead and back in a chiastic manner (the former ahead, the latter back). But what of the Perseus panel itself? What is its role beyond that of a mere centre around which the general symmetry turns?

III (THE CENTRAL PANEL)

Considered by itself, the *Perseus* exhibits a great deal of Ovidian ingenuity but remains, when all is said and done, a decidedly unfortunate performance. Beside such masterpieces of mock-epic as the *Phaethon* or *Ceres–Proserpina*, it is at once cold and factitious, a kind of bravura piece or little *Aeneid* that does not come off. Here we have an Aeneas (Perseus) who makes, like his Virgilian prototype, a matrimonial treaty with a hard-pressed father; the marriage is his price for rescuing the fair Andromeda from the terrible dragon (IV, 691–705):

> Conclamat virgo; genitor lugubris et una
> mater adest, ambo miseri, sed iustius illa,
> nec secum auxilium, sed dignos tempore fletus
> plangoremque ferunt vinctoque in corpore adhaerent,
> cum sic hospes ait: 'Lacrimarum longa manere
> tempora vos poterunt, ad opem brevis hora ferendam est.
> Hanc ego si peterem Perseus Iove natus et illa,
> quam clausam inplevit fecundo Iuppiter auro,
> Gorgonis anguicomae Perseus superator et alis
> aetherias ausus iactatis ire per auras,
> *praeferrer cunctis certe gener*; addere tantis
> dotibus et meritum, faveant modo numina, tempto:
> *ut mea sit servata mea virtute paciscor.*'
> *Accipiunt legem* (quis enim dubitaret?) et orant
> *promittuntque super regnum dotale parentes.*

> *She screams; her mother and her sire draw nigh,*
> *Both sad, but she with juster cause to sigh;*
> *Their tears, well-timed, they bring, but bring no aid;*
> *They beat their breasts, and clasp the fettered maid.*
> *Said Perseus: 'Years enough for tears and grief*
> *Await you, but for rescue, time is brief.*

If I should seek this maid in marriage, none
Could rival me, being Perseus, and the son
Of her, whom walls could not from Jove withhold,
And Jove, who filled her with the fecund gold—
Perseus, who laid the snake-haired Gorgon low,
And braved the winds, on beating wings to go.
Yet I, with gifts so great, will add to these
Some service also, if the Powers so please.
Then seal the bargain, and the contract sign,
That if my valour save her, she be mine.'
They yield—as who would not?—and beg his aid,
And pledge, for dower, their kingdom with the maid.

So Perseus' superior right *vis-à-vis* that of Phineus (the former
fiancé of Andromeda) is clearly established: he wins Andromeda
by his heroic victory over the dragon. But Phineus denies the
right (v, 10):

en adsum *praereptae coniugis* ultor.

> '*See, I come,*' he cried,
> '*To wreak revenge on him who stole my bride.*'

And Cepheus, Andromeda's father, can only yield, reluctantly, to
his violence (v, 41–5):

Tum vero indomitas ardescit vulgus in iras
telaque coniciunt et sunt, qui Cephea dicunt
cum genero debere mori. Sed limine tecti
exierat Cepheus testatus iusque fidemque
hospitiique deos, ea se prohibente moveri.

Then rank and file with rising heat engaged,
And weapons flew, and stubborn fury raged.
The king himself, when some now raised the cry
That Cepheus with his son-in-law must die,
Had quit the hall, but ere he passed the door,
By gods of hospitality he swore,
Who cherish faith and right, that those who wrought
Such lawless riot set his will at naught.

We are inevitably reminded of Virgil's Turnus and Latinus (*Aen.* IX, 136–8):

> sunt et mea [i.e. Turnus] contra
> fata mihi, ferro sceleratam exscindere gentem,
> *coniuge praerepta*

I have my own opposite destiny: to blot out with the sword the wicked race that has snatched my rightful bride away from me;

(VII, 593 ff.):

> Multa *deos aurasque pater* [i.e. Latinus] *testatus inanes*

★ ★ ★ ★ ★ ★ ★ ★ ★

> nec plura locutus
> saepsit se tectis, rerumque reliquit habenas

After many a vain protestation to the gods and the empty winds, Latinus spoke no more but shut himself in his palace and abandoned the reins of power.

And the ensuing struggle between Perseus and Phineus is obviously meant to recall the Iliadic *Aeneid* and, more generally, the *aristeiai* of epic.

The death scenes are only grotesque. Ovid strives for an ingenious variety that falls short of either pathos or humour. Emathion's tongue continues to mutter *verba exsecrantia* even after his head has been severed from his body (105); the musician Lampetides inadvertently strikes a lugubrious chord with his dying fingers (*casuque fuit miserabile carmen*, 118); Echemmon's neck is pierced by a rebounding sliver of his own broken sword.

But the petrifaction of Phineus and his men (Perseus uses the Medusa-head upon them) provides Ovid with an opportunity for scenes even more *outré*. We see the incongruous postures that each takes as he turns into stone (V, 187–200):

> At Nileus, qui se genitum septemplice Nilo
> ementitus erat, clipeo quoque flumina septem
> argento partim, partim caelaverat auro,
> 'adspice,' ait 'Perseu, nostrae primordia gentis!

Magna feres tacitas solacia mortis ad umbras,
a tanto cecidisse viro'; *pars ultima vocis*
in medio suppressa sono est, adapertaque velle
ora loqui credas, nec sunt ea pervia verbis.
Increpat hos 'vitio'que 'animi, non viribus' inquit
Gorgoneis torpetis,' Eryx: 'incurrite mecum
et prosternite humi iuvenem magica arma moventem!'
Incursurus erat: *tenuit vestigia tellus,*
inmotusque silex armataque mansit imago.

Then Nileus, who (believe his lies!) could claim
From sevenfold Nile himself descent and name,
And bore the boastful blazon on his shield,
Seven streams of silver on a golden field,
Cried out to Perseus: 'Look, my lineage know;
And take for comfort to the shades below
The thought that such a champion dealt the blow.'
He broke off short: his parted lips, you'd say,
Still strove to speak, but gave the words no way.
Then Eryx cried: 'If palsied thus you stand,
'Tis not Medusa's might, but hearts unmanned.
Rush in with me, and lay the sorcerer low,
Before his wondrous weapons deal their blow.'
Rush could he not; the earth his steps delayed;
And there, a warrior cast in stone, he stayed.

Phineus' petrifaction is of course the climax. He pleads with
Perseus exactly as Virgil's Turnus had pleaded with Aeneas. But
Perseus' reply is very un-Virgilian (v, 223–35):

Talia dicenti neque eum, quem voce rogabat,
respicere audenti 'quod,' ait 'timidissime Phineu,
et possum tribuisse et magnum est munus inerti,
(*pone metum!*) *tribuam*: nullo violabere ferro;
quin etiam mansura dabo monimenta per aevum,
inque domo soceri semper spectabere nostri,
ut mea se sponsi soletur imagine coniunx.'
Dixit et in partem Phorcynida transtulit illam,

ad quam se trepido Phineus obverterat ore.
Tum quoque conanti sua vertere lumina cervix
deriguit, saxoque oculorum induruit umor;
sed tamen os timidum vultusque in marmore supplex
submissaeque manus faciesque obnoxia mansit.

He dared not look at him to whom he prayed.
'Faint-hearted Phineus' (Perseus thus replies),
'One thing I grant that in my granting lies,
No small concession to a craven soul—
Relax your fear: your skin shall still be whole.
Yes, this I grant, and more: by my command,
As monument from age to age shall stand,
To cheer my wife, within her father's house,
The deathless likeness of her would-be spouse.'
With that, while Phineus' eyes still shrank in dread,
Full in his face he swung Medusa's head;
His neck grew stark; and in his eyes, which tried
Evasion still, the tears were petrified;
And fixed in stone, his craven looks appear,
His pleading hands and eyes, and abject fear.

Yes, Phineus is to be spared—spared to be a statue and to stand
in Perseus' mansion for his wife's amused contemplation, a quite
unique souvenir of her old fiancé!

All this is clever but decidedly malapropos. Here Ovid's
ingenuity is not so much amusing as gauche and repellent. Perseus
is after all no god but a man, and the curious vengeance he takes
strikes a decidedly discordant note among the amatory, comic or
pathetically human tones of the other episodes of this part of the
poem. Ovid had no taste for heroes and, certainly, no capacity for
creating them. His imitation of Virgil is for once without the
excuse of parody or of deliberately designed incongruity. Unlike
the Virgilian bits of Books XII–XV (Galatea, Achaemenides, the
Sibyl, etc.), the *Phineus* is mitigated by neither humour nor brevity; it cannot be taken as anything but a hollow pretence of epic
that, despite and indeed because of its ingenuities, degenerates into

mere bathos. Here Ovid is at his worst and his worst is very bad indeed.

But we can see why Ovid wanted a hero and heroic *aristeiai* at this point in his poem. Perseus is meant to correspond to the central panel (Meleager and Hercules) of the next section (III), just as these are meant to prepare the way for Aeneas, Romulus and Caesar, the heroes of Rome, in the final section (IV). Perseus, to be sure, is not deified, but his deeds, nevertheless, prefigure those of Hercules and the great Romans. Above all, he prefigures Aeneas in both the legitimacy of his claim (he deserves Andromeda)—*ut mea sit servata mea virtute*—and the impiety of his opponent. Thus Ovid's Virgilian epic is clearly designed to be an integral part of his poem. For all that, the 'heroic' strain which Perseus introduces is a result not of Ovid's own feeling and inspiration but, on the contrary, of a quite external factor—the necessity of preparing an Augustan conclusion to his *carmen perpetuum*. We shall see this more particularly when we come to the concluding section (IV) of the epic. It is enough for the moment to recognize that Ovid wrote the *Perseus–Phineus* against the very grain of his native genius for political, not poetic, reasons. It is surely not the centre-piece that he would have adopted had he been left to his own devices and desires.

As a whole this section (II) is much more ambiguous, much more uncertain, than those that precede and follow it (I, III). Perhaps the major function of the Vengeance theme is to effect the transition from the *Divine Comedy* to the *Pathos of Love*. It does this both because it shifts the poem's emphasis from gods to men and because it largely abandons comedy for the more serious topics of suffering and tragedy. On one side (Section I) was Homeric farce; on the other (III), Hellenistic realism. One was humorous—the incongruity of *maiestas* and *amor*; the other was pathological and romantic—the havoc that sex could make of weak and very unheroic human beings and the triumph of love over defeat. Both were fit subjects for Ovid's exceedingly droll, yet sympathetically amorous, personality. But they had to be connected even though the connecting link, the theme of crime and punishment, of avenging *maiestas*, was clearly repugnant to him. When this repugnance could be expressed, when he could depict his avenging gods as types of puritanical severity, unbridled jealousy, or merciless power, he could produce an effective, if distorted, commentary on human nature and perhaps even on his own times. Something of the sort is surely to be found in the Actaeon, Pentheus, Ino and Niobe stories.

But divine vengeance was, like the heroic *aristeia*, not a theme that really spoke to his poetic genius. The death scenes of Niobe's sons are like so many statues or reliefs: it is only when the grief-stricken mother passes beyond vengeance into sheer *pathos* that Ovid comes to life and feels the full force of the subject.

When for purposes of contrast and anticipation he passes to a different theme (the erotic tales of the Minyades and Muses) he returns as it were to his natural element. Yet these are skilfully kept in their place: they do make a contrast, but they do not displace the major vengeance motif. What most seriously mars the effectiveness and unity of the whole section is the tediously Virgilian Perseus panel: here there is neither sympathy nor sincere repugnance but sheer bathos and bathos increased rather than mitigated by a perverse ingenuity. But here Ovid was vainly trying to be an Augustan *malgré lui*. Still, the Perseus panel does serve to divide the section into symmetrical halves that, by correspondence and difference, give balance and continuity to the whole.

CHAPTER VI

THE PATHOS OF LOVE: I

WE now reach the very heart of the *Metamorphoses*: the third section (VI, 401–XI end) is not only the longest but, obviously, the most complete and finished of the poem. Here Ovid was engaged on his preferred theme, amatory *pathos*, and here at last metamorphosis became an intrinsic part of his plot. It is no more with the incongruities of divine behaviour but with the anguish of human passion that he is concerned. His human beings no longer stand against comic or vengeful gods but against the far more impersonal and enigmatic forces of nature. He is no longer dealing with the conventional mythology of divine comedy or divine vengeance but with the modernized and 'humanized' mythology of neoteric and Alexandrian poetry, with types and situations whose origin can in most cases be traced to Euripides.

This is at least true of the dominant element of the section: the five long episodes of amatory catastrophe (the *Tereus–Philomela*, *Scylla*, *Byblis*, *Myrrha* and *Ceyx–Alcyone*). But these, like the major episodes of the previous section, are arranged around a massive central panel of quite different style (VIII, 260–IX, 272), and are contrasted with equally different subsidiary episodes (miracles of death and resurrection, miracles of reward for piety and punishment for sacrilege and folly). The passion depicted in the major episodes is (with one crucial exception) degrading or catastrophic: metamorphosis comes to it as sheer release from the pain of human existence. But the deification of Hercules that climactically concludes the epic central panel shows human passion converted into divine happiness. Hercules does not become an animal but a god. The subsidiary episodes (Myrmidons, Iphis, Pygmalion) also reverse the trend of the dominant amatory tales:

here ants become men, a statue becomes a living woman, a girl becomes a virile husband. Metamorphosis is human, not animal; up, not down. The way is prepared for the triumphant apotheoses of the last part—Aeneas, Romulus, and Caesar.

But here also lies the problem or mystery of this section of the poem. Ovid's imagination was not primarily on the side of Hercules or the great Romans to come. It is in the neoteric episodes far more than in his epic panel or in his preparations for an Augustan finale that he is most himself and most successful. There is in fact a decided incongruity between his obvious plan (the designed shape of his *carmen perpetuum*) and his actual execution of it. He took pleasure in telling the stories of Iphis and Pygmalion—even the pious idyll of Philemon and Baucis—but he certainly did not enjoy the heroics of his *Meleager* and *Hercules*. It is the climactic *Ceyx–Alcyone* that really shows what he could do. There can be little doubt that if he had been left to himself, if by some miracle he had been relieved of his Augustan responsibilities, he would have given a very different course to his perpetual song. Nevertheless, this section in its entirety (its symmetries and contrasts, its restless progression of motifs) is an exceedingly complicated work of art that well repays careful study. We can hardly embrace all its subtleties in a diagram but we can at least show something of its formal structure (plan on p. 168).

There are here five stories of amatory *pathos* (*Tereus–Philomela, Scylla, Byblis, Myrrha, Ceyx–Alcyone*) varying from 151 lines (*Scylla*) to 339 (*Ceyx–Alcyone*) with a median length of about 240 (*Byblis*, 219; *Myrrha*, 205; *Tereus–Philomela*, 273). The only other episodes of equivalent length are those of Cephalus and Procris (208 lines) and the epic *Meleager* (287 lines) and *Hercules* (272 lines). The two latter are prolonged by their martial not their amatory content, and obviously fit the generally *epic* category of the central panel: they thus correspond to the Perseus–Phineus panel of Books IV–V. The *Cephalus–Procris*, though certainly a story of erotic misadventure, is quite different from the type represented by *Philomela, Byblis, Myrrha*, etc. There is no metamorphosis

PLAN OF SECTION III (VI, 401–XI, 795)

	Episodes of Amatory Pathos	Contrast Episodes	Central Panel
		Miracles in an Amatory Frame	

Bk. VI
401–674   Philomela–Procne–Tereus
                (Introductory 401–23)
675–721   (Transition to Argonauts: Pandion, Cephalus, Procris, Orithyia–Boreas)

Bk. VII
1–158 ⎫
159–296 ⎪ Medea frame ⎧ Medea (love, winning the fleece)
297–349 ⎬   ⎨ Human miracles ⎧ Aeson (the successful miracle of rejuvenation)
350–403 ⎭   ⎩   ⎩ Daughters of Pelias (the false and treacherous rejuvenation)
                        Medea (wanderings)

404–504 ⎫   ⎧ Theseus–Aegeus–Minos–Aeacus–Cephalus (Aegina)
505–613 ⎪ Cephalus ⎨ Divine miracles ⎧ Pestilentia (men destroyed by plague)
614–660 ⎬ frame   ⎩   ⎩ Myrmidons (men created out of ants)
661–868 ⎭   ⎩ Cephalus and Procris (Amatory *Pathos* without metamorphosis)

Bk. VIII
1–151   Scylla
152–182   (Cretan interlude: Minotaur, Ariadne)
183–235   Daedalus–Icarus (Paternal Grief)
236–259   (Perdix)
260–546   ⎧ MELEAGER–ALTHAEA
547–615   ⎪ (Interlude: Achelous, etc.)
616–724   Central Panel   ⎨ Theodicy I (Philemon–Baucis)
725–878   ⎪ Theodicy II (Erysichthon)
878–883   ⎩ (Interlude: Achelous, etc.)

Bk. IX
1–272   HERCULES–DEIANIRA–DEIFICATION
273–323   (Galanthis)
324–446   Dryope (Maternal Grief)   (Iolaus, Callirhoes filii 394–446)
447–665   Byblis
666–797   ⎧ Iphis

Bk. X
1– 77   ⎫   ⎧   ⎧ Orpheus–Eurydice (Separation from wife: rejection of wo
78–105 ⎪ Miracles of ⎨ Amatory insets ⎨ Arbores, etc.
106–154 ⎬ Piety   ⎩ (Homosexual) ⎨ Cyparissus   GODS AND BOYS
155–161 ⎪   ⎪ Ganymede
162–242 ⎭   ⎩ Hyacinthus (Cerastae–Propoetides, 220–42)
243–297   ⎩ Pygmalion
298–502   Myrrha
503–559   ⎧ Adonis   GODDESS AND BOY
560–707   ⎧ Atalanta
708–738   Miracles of ⎨ Amatory insets   Death of Adonis   GODDESS AND BOY
          Impiety   ⎩ (Heterosexual)
Bk. XI
1– 84   ⎩ Death of Orpheus (reunion with wife)
85–193   ⎩ Midas
194–409   Peleus–Thetis ⎫
410–748   Ceyx–Alcyone   ⎬ End pieces for Ceyx–Alcyone
749–795   Aesacus   ⎭

of the major characters (there is only the inserted metamorphosis of the dog and his prey) and the catastrophe is survived and described by the lover, Cephalus.

In contrast, the five tales just mentioned are obviously similar in content and mood: all describe extreme instances of erotic passion; all terminate in catastrophe and metamorphosis; all represent the metamorphosis as the solution and natural sequel of the catastrophe. But there is also much overlap of motif (as the *Cephalus–Procris* illustrates): each of the subsidiary or contrast episodes either possesses amatory-pathetic characteristics of its own or is framed within another tale that possesses them. In the first half of the section, Medea dominates one series of tales; Cephalus another. In the second half (after the central panel), Orpheus and Venus perform a similar function: they not only engage themselves in amatory misadventures; they introduce other amatory episodes (the paederastic series; the love-affair of Atalanta and Hippomenes). Nevertheless all these subsidiary tales of love are clearly distinct from both the dominant five and the central epic panel: they are not only shorter but quite different in amatory content. Neither Medea nor Cephalus–Procris undergoes metamorphosis (Medea's love-story is also elliptically curtailed); the loves of the gods and of Venus in the latter half of the section have little in common with the human passions of Philomela, Scylla, Alcyone, etc., while Atalanta's amour is quite devoid of *pathos* (the metamorphosis is simply punishment for her sacrilege). The difference is also one of style and tone. Ovid always distinguishes between *major* and *minor*, between dominant and subsidiary episodes. The main motif of the section is tragic or catastrophic *pathos* (though, as we shall see, the final effect is not pathetic). The minor tales are much less serious or, conversely, much more moral and pious: without them, the pathological and criminal *amores* of the big scenes would only oppress, if not overwhelm, the rapid reader for whom Ovid designed his *carmen perpetuum*. We must now study each group of episodes (the minor, the major and the central panel) by itself. But we must also bear in mind that it is the whole (the symmetrical whole) that finally counts and puts everything in proper proportion.

I (THE MINOR, CONTRAST EPISODES)

It is perhaps advisable to discuss the minor or 'contrast' stories before embarking on the major elements—the central panel and the five principal amatory episodes. Here the obvious line of demarcation is fixed by the panel:

Part I { (a) Medea frame (Aeson, Daughters of Pelias)
{ (b) Cephalus–Aeacus frame (Pestilence, Myrmidons)
(Daedalus–Icarus)
CENTRAL PANEL
(Dryope)
Part II { (c) Orpheus frame with loves of boys and gods
{ (Miracles in reward of Piety: Iphis, Pygmalion)
{ (d) Venus–Adonis frame, love of boy by goddess
(Miracles of Punishment: Atalanta, Midas)

Parts I and II are roughly equal in length though the *entire* second half of the whole section (IX, 273–XI end) exceeds the first (VI, 401–VIII, 259). Also the separate parts of both I and II (*a, b, c, d*) are approximately equal (*a* = 450 lines; *b* = 465 lines; *c* = 429 lines; *d* = 429 lines). More important, I, II and *a, b, c, d* obviously correspond in a contrapuntal way. The magical *rejuvenation* and treacherous *pseudo-rejuvenation* of *a* (Aeson, Pelias) chiastically correspond to the divinely motivated *destruction* and *resurrection* of *b* (Pestilence, Myrmidons). The beneficent Miracles of *c* (Iphis, Pygmalion) correspond to the punitive Miracles of *d* (Atalanta, Midas). And so also with the amatory motifs: the fierce and baleful Medea (*a*) is opposed to the devoted and pathetic Procris (*b*); the boy-love of the *gods* in *c* to the boy-love (Adonis) of the *goddess* (Venus) in *d*. Finally there is an obvious correspondence of I and II: each describes a miraculous reversal or a disastrous contretemps of the metamorphosis process at work in the five major amatory episodes. The Aegina pestilence and the deceitful murder of Pelias are as much interruptions of the usual man-to-animal sequence as are the rejuvenation of Aeson and the humanization of the ants. The same is true of the miracles of Pygmalion and Iphis (good) or of Atalanta and Midas (bad). They have nothing to do with that pathetic collapse of humanity which in the great amatory tales makes metamorphosis the only alternative to catastrophe.

But there is much more here than counterpoint or symmetry. Ovid's *carmen perpetuum* is also proceeding on its evolutionary way. The ambivalent magic of Medea is succeeded by the divine events that happened to Aeacus at Aegina where the wrath of Juno's pestilence is countered by the beneficence of Jupiter's re-population of the country out of ants. This prepares us for the explicit theodicy and piety of the central panel where the sceptic Pirithous (he refuses to believe that the gods can produce meta-morphoses) is refuted by the pious Lelex: the tales of Philemon-Baucis and Erysichthon are deliberately introduced as instances of divine might and justice; they show us that the gods have power to reward piety and punish impious arrogance. These two theo-dicies then reinforce (as we shall see) the mood of the epic episodes (Meleager, Hercules) between which they are inserted: Meleager died for his own sin as well as by Althaea's fury, but the good Hercules will be deified despite the destructive jealousy of Deianira. We are thus put in a mood to appreciate the miraculous responses of Isis, Venus and Apollo to the piety of Iphis and Pygmalion or to the folly of Atalanta and Midas. What we may call the pious or moralistic theme thus grows in prominence through these episodes and presents an obvious contrast to the ambivalent theology of the great amatory tales.

But, as we have just seen, the moral theme is also mixed with an amatory one. Thus there is a further counterpoint at work. Medea and Procris or Orpheus and Venus (and the *amores* associ-ated with them) are contrasted with both the five central amatory tales and the subsidiary miracles and theodicies. Nor must we think of contrast only: all phases of the *carmen perpetuum* in fact interfuse as one motif suggests, reinforces or counters another. The contrapuntal symmetry of the whole makes a brilliant tapestry of moods in transition.

Medea is introduced *via* the Argonauts. Two of these, the winged Zetes and Calais, are children of the North Wind Boreas by Orithyia, daughter of Erechtheus, successor of Pandion as king of Athens. It had been Pandion's daughters, Procne and Philomela, whom Thracian Tereus had so mistreated. Hence the genealogical transition from the Tereus–Philomela episode to the Argonauts (end of Book VI) and Medea. Ovid is here paying some lip-service to history: his *carmen perpetuum* is getting well into the Heroic Age. But it is also plain that this transition is a transparently specious method of introducing Medea at the exact point where Ovid needs her. He assuredly does not want to retell her tragedy (the child-killing motif of the *Tereus–Philomela* would hardly bear immediate repetition) but he wants to reproduce both the classical love monologue with which she was associated (Apollonius and Euripides had established her undisputed right to it) and the magic by which she could rejuvenate as well as kill. She was brought in, in other words, to play the double role of inaugurating the primary theme of amatory passion (original virtue overcome by erotic impulse) and the subsidiary theme of counter-metamorphosis (the usual course of nature turned back so that the old can become young; the animal, human; the image, the reality it reflects).

Medea's soliloquy in VII, 11–71 strikes a quite new note in the poem. We have already witnessed the *amores* of such women as Thisbe, Salmacis and Leucothoe and such gods as Apollo, Jupiter and Pluto. The terrible passion of Tereus has just preceded. But, as yet, we have had no true account of the genesis of love and certainly not any of woman's love. Thisbe had succumbed to love before her story had really begun, and Leucothoe, Salmacis and Echo had no need to mark the beginning of the passion that overmastered them. Daphne, Io, Proserpina and Philomela were, of course, only reluctant victims of a male *eros* that hardly required psychological description. It is with Medea that the famous duel of *amor* and *pudor* enters the *Metamorphoses* (the *pudor–amor* conflict of Jupiter had been only by-play) and points the way for Scylla, Byblis, Myrrha and Atalanta. Ovid obviously wanted to present the classic or standard amatory *suasoria* (the soliloquy in which the girl analyses her *eros* and persuades herself to yield to it) before introducing the individual *variations* of it that were to come later on. Since he had no intention of retelling Medea's whole story, he was all the freer to isolate her *suasoria*. Nor did he wish, at just this juncture, to over-emphasize the pathetic or tragic note (the *Tereus–Philomela* had just preceded); hence the rather facile ingenuity of the monologue and the unmistakable humour of its Virgilian parody (see pp. 59–62 above).

We need not dwell on the Aeson and Pelias episodes (the first set of 'miracles' or 'counter-metamorphoses'). The fact that even Medea is moved by Jason's *pietas* toward his father (VII, 169–70)— improbable as this may seem—gives Aeson's rejuvenation a moral colour that is obviously laid on for contrast with the impious pseudo-rejuvenation and murder of Pelias. The rather lengthy account of Medea's wanderings (VII, 350–403) that closes the sub-section (I. *a*) is quite uninspired. It at least finishes off this part of the poem and by its elliptical allusions to the Euripidean Medea (VII, 396–7),

> Sanguine natorum perfunditur inpius ensis,
> ultaque se male mater Iasonis effugit arma

> *and when the life*
> *Of her own sons had stained her lawless knife,*
> *Unchilded but avenged, in wholesome dread*
> *Of Jason's sword, the inhuman mother fled,*

suggests (once more) the major motif of the whole section—the *libido* that can so quickly and easily overcome all ethical restraint.

The Aeacus–Cephalus sub-section that begins at VII, 404 (I. *b*) is dominated by a very different kind of love and by a new type of 'miracle' or counter-metamorphosis. Reversing the plan of the Medea sub-section, it presents the *Miracles* first, in a thoroughly heroic and moral setting (the noble old Aeacus, the beneficent Theseus, the loyalty of Aegina to Athens) and the love story only at the end.

The emphasis is now not on an evil woman and her witchcraft, but on heroes (Theseus, Aeacus, Cephalus) of both piety and true nobility of feeling. Amatory jealousy is no longer an unnatural and amoral perversion (as in Medea) but the tragic affliction of a love that even in death retains its power and purity. Furthermore, the love itself is not a present passion but a sad and beautiful memory. It increases the human interest without diminishing the heroic status of the lover.

This is why Ovid deals so cavalierly with the usual order of his myths. In Apollodorus (III, 193-9) the story of Procne and Philomela (Pandion's daughters) is immediately followed by stories of the next generation, the grandchildren of Pandion or children of Erechtheus (Procris and Orithyia). But Ovid only mentions Orithyia at the end of Book VI (right after the Tereus–Philomela story) and puts the story of Procris at the end of Book VII after both the Medea section and Aeacus' stories of the Pestilence and the Myrmidons. His arrangement, as Alfred Rohde has seen,[1] is an aesthetic one, designed to set the Medea episodes against the Cephalus–Aeacus tales and to use the Cephalus–Procris story as the climax of Book VII. But it is also much more than this: it is part of the elaborate symmetry and counterpoint of his whole poem.

The Athenian theme had been introduced with Pandion (VI, 421). Then after telling the story of Pandion's daughters, Procne and Philomela, Ovid had momentarily reverted to Athens so as to mention Pandion's successor, Erechtheus, and Erechtheus' children (the daughters Orithyia and Procris and their respective husbands, Boreas and Cephalus). But Athens was immediately swept out of sight by Medea. Then Medea herself takes Ovid back to Athens (VII, 402 ff.) when she finds an asylum there with a king of another generation, Aegeus. Her plot against Aegeus' son

[1] Rohde, pp. 30–3. It is surely obvious that Ovid is not here *primarily* concerned with *Athens* any more than he was with *Thebes* in Section II. See p. 128 above.

(Theseus) not only introduces that hero but provides a natural transition to the Athenian alliance with Aegina. Theseus is only a transitional figure: he is brought in merely to suggest the type of beneficent hero that is later to be more fully depicted by Hercules and his Roman successors. His eulogy (VII, 433–50) is a bare catalogue of his great deeds, but it still sounds the note of beneficent heroism: the contrast with Medea, whose malice and passion he has just escaped, is made very evident. Ovid then uses the device (almost certainly his own invention) of Cephalus' embassy to Aegina in order to unite Cephalus' love story with the Aeginetan 'miracles' (Pestilence, Myrmidons) that Aeacus (the king of Aegina) tells. He thus invests both narratives with the *ethos* of their heroic narrators. The moment is historically placed: Athens needs Aegina as an ally against Minos; Minos, in fact, is represented as leaving Aegina in bitter disillusion (since his own proposal for an alliance against Athens has been rejected) just before the Athenian legation of Cephalus can arrive (VII, 490–3):

> Classis ab Oenopiis etiamnum Lyctia muris
> spectari poterat, cum pleno concita velo
> Attica puppis adest in portusque intrat amicos,
> quae Cephalum patriaeque simul mandata ferebat.

> *Aegina's walls still held his fleet in view,*
> *When into port with sails full set there flew*
> *An Attic ship, with Cephalus, who bore*
> *His country's greetings to the friendly shore.*

Aeacus and Cephalus are aged heroes who have each undergone a great sorrow. But these sorrows are mitigated by their distance in time and their sequels: the terrible Aegina pestilence was overcome by the metamorphosis of the ant-men; the tragedy of Procris' death by her final awareness of Cephalus' fidelity. In both the metamorphosis and the fidelity we see the very reverse of Medea's witchery and passion, i.e. the miracle that comes to true piety and the love that only noble character can feel.

Though Aeacus attributes the Aegina pestilence (VII, 503–613) to

Juno, he actually minimizes its divine origin and tells his tale in a manner that recalls the didactic plague passages of Virgil, Lucretius or Thucydides. But the total effect is not really didactic and scientific or, as in Virgil, pathetic and sombre. Ovid emphasizes only the paradoxical suddenness and topsy-turviness of the plague: the animals forget their old enemies; the suppliant father dies with the incense still in his hand. It is really a miracle that prepares us for the succeeding miracle of the ant-men. The population of Aegina is lost almost as miraculously as it is recovered. Aeacus himself is the unexpected victim as well as the unexpected beneficiary of divine attention. He lives in a world that has been paradoxically destroyed and re-created.

The stage is thus set for the much more pathetic paradox of loss and recovery in the Cephalus–Procris story.[1] What distinguishes this story, however, from the five major stories of amatory *pathos* is its dignity and restraint. Cephalus the narrator is a true gentleman who tries to glorify and excuse his dead wife by taking on himself the major share of blame. The impression that his story conveys is not so much one of violent emotion and pathos as of respect and continuing affection. The love of which he tells was strong enough to overcome a terrible misunderstanding and to outlast even death. But Cephalus is bereaved, not prostrated: his grief is really a romantic halo that gives him colour and piquancy without in any way diminishing his heroic status. He is both a lover and a gentleman.

Viktor Pöschl[2] is surely correct when he says that what distinguishes Ovid from his sources for this episode is his emphasis on the mutual love of Cephalus and Procris. All the mishaps of the pair come from this single fact. The versions of Hyginus, Pherecydes, Nicander and Apollodorus, as well as Ovid's prior elegiac version of part of the story (the error and death of Procris), do not do this at all. Probably Ovid had a source something like the Hyginus fable (189) or, save for the ending, like Nicander. We find a similar treatment of the same theme in Ariosto's *Orlando*.

---

[1] See Appendix, pp. 410-13.   [2] See Appendix, p. 410.

In Hyginus and Nicander, the parallelism between Procris and Cephalus is almost exact and there is no question about the guilt of either. Cephalus was seduced by the dawn goddess, Aurora; whether he actually submitted to (Nicander) or resisted (Hyginus) her advances, he was at any rate prepared by them to suspect the virtue of his Procris. If *he* could fall or at least be tempted, what about her? He thus conceived the idea of testing her fidelity by arousing her cupidity. He disguised himself (or was disguised by Aurora) and deliberately bribed her to be unfaithful to her supposedly distant husband. He then 'threw off the mask' or resumed his natural form, thus earning a costly triumph over his 'unfaithful' Procris. She thereupon left him and her own country to pass the time with either Minos (Nicander, Apollodorus) or Diana (Hyginus). At length, however, she returned bringing with her the marvellous dog and spear. She could now turn the tables on Cephalus. Disguised as a young hunter, she joined him in the chase and of course easily excelled him. Nothing could beat the dog and spear. They now naturally aroused his own cupidity: in order to possess them he consented to be seduced (homosexually) by the apparently male Procris. But this time discovery led to reunion. Each spouse was now, so to speak, 'even' with the other. Yet jealousy was once again to prove the couple's undoing: Procris heard of Cephalus' addresses to a *Nephele* (cloud) or breeze (Aura) and foolishly supposed the 'Cloud' or 'Breeze' to be a woman. She tracked him to the woods and watched him from the bushes. When they moved, he mistook her for a deer and so killed her with her own gift, the unerring spear.

What Ovid did to his sources is thus clear enough[1] even though we cannot establish all the differences of detail. Ovid's Cephalus greatly tones down the guilt of Procris: she merely wavers at his reiterated bribes; she does not actually submit (VII, 740–1):

> Muneraque augendo tandem dubitare coegi.
> Exclamo, male fictor, 'adest, male fictus adulter!'

---

[1] See Appendix, pp. 410–13.

By adding gift to gift, I made her hesitate. Then, poor dis-
sembler, I exclaim: 'He's here, your unfeigned-lover's here!'

On the other hand, his repentance and desire to recover his lost
bride are wholly animated by love (VII, 747–50):

> Tum mihi deserto violentior ignis ad ossa
> pervenit: orabam veniam et peccasse fatebar
> et potuisse datis simili succumbere culpae
> me quoque muneribus, si munera tanta darentur.

> *Left thus, I felt my love with fiercer flame*
> *Burn to the bone, and soon repentance came.*
> *I owned my fault, confessed I might have made*
> *Like trespass, if by like temptations swayed.*

Later on in the story Procris' shameful proposal is deliberately
obscured and glossed over. Their renewed love is said to be as
strong and beautiful as ever (VII, 800):

> Mutua cura duos et amor socialis habebat.

It is, indeed, this mutual love that makes Procris, as Cephalus
before her, so susceptible to the promptings of jealousy. Yet she is
not the impetuous, uncontrolled Procris of the *Ars Amatoria*. She
hesitates to believe the report of his infidelity and defers all action
to the following day. The episode ends in a death-scene that shows
once again the recovered confidence of each in the faithfulness of
the other (VII, 860–2):

> Dumque aliquid spectare potest, me spectat et in me
> infelicem animam nostroque exhalat in ore;
> sed vultu meliore mori secura videtur.

> *yet looked at me while sight remained;*
> *Then on my lips her luckless life was spent,*
> *But yet she smiled, and seemed to die content.*

Thus Pöschl is quite right[1] when he says that Ovid has trans-

---

[1] See Appendix, p. 410.

formed a *novella*, a game of masks and transformations and magical devices, into a true love story. The sheer cupidity of Nicander's characters as well as their overt eroticism (the heterosexual and homosexual adulteries) are eliminated or greatly toned down. In Ovid their jealousy is a form of love; it is the passion that tries to destroy, even though it does not succeed in destroying, the mutuality on which it insists. He has, in short, wholly changed the motivation. He shows us how Aurora instils the fatal doubt in Cephalus by playing on the very source of his confidence (VII, 716–19):

> facies aetasque iubebat
> credere adulterium, prohibebant credere mores;
> sed tamen afueram, sed et haec erat, unde redibam,
> criminis exemplum, sed cuncta timemus amantes!

> *My wife, whose youth and beauty gave some cause*
> *For question—was she false to wedlock's laws?*
> *And though her virtue gave this thought the lie,*
> *An absent lover, full of fears, was I;*
> *And she from whom I took my homeward way*
> *Herself was instance how a wife could stray.*

He shows the fatal urge that pushes Cephalus toward his own ruin, making him redouble the temptation (VII, 738–9):

> non sum contentus et in mea pugno
> vulnera!

> *To wound myself, I pressed the fight anew.*

He shows the repentance of Cephalus (*et peccasse fatebar*, etc.) and he finally shows the same insidious suspicion at work upon Procris (826 ff.). Here each tries to wound 'the thing it loves'; indeed the 'poetic justice' of Procris' death from her own gift symbolizes the self-destructiveness of love: it destroys its own object and wounds its very self.

But Pöschl has not correctly appreciated the point of view of the narrating Cephalus. What Cephalus tells is not really the true or full story but an edited version of it, a version chastened and corrected by his respect for Procris' memory and by his continuing devotion. For Ovid knew, and knew that Cephalus knew, the actual vengeance of Procris that we find in Hyginus and Nicander. His story starts with the natural curiosity of Aeacus' son, Phocus. Phocus asks about the origin of Cephalus' wonderful spear (*quis tanti muneris auctor?*). His curiosity cannot, however, be satisfied, as Ovid immediately indicates (VII, 687–8):

> Quae patitur pudor, ille [i.e. Cephalus] refert et cetera narrat;
> qua tulerit mercede, silet.[1]

> *And Cephalus answered truly all the rest,*
> *But what the weapon cost him, shame suppressed.*

Cephalus is ashamed to tell the true price for which he got or thought to get the spear; i.e. his compliance with the disguised Procris' homosexual request. In the ensuing narrative he suggests but does not explicitly say the same thing (VII, 751–2):

> Hoc mihi confesso [i.e. after Cephalus has confessed his
>   own fault] laesum prius ulta [i.e. Procris] pudorem,
> redditur et dulces concorditer exigit annos.

> *She first avenged the wound her honour bore;*
> *Then, sweetly reconciled, was mine once more.*

The phrase *laesum prius ulta pudorem* can (as the narrating Cephalus intends) be taken as a reference to Cephalus' pathetic apology for his past mistrust: this was sufficient 'vengeance' for Procris. But in fact the terms 'vengeance' and 'price' (*merces*) can only refer to the indecent proposal we actually find in Hyginus and Nicander. Cephalus lightly passes over both Procris' and his own shame. So too Procris' 'hesitation' (when first pressed by the disguised Cephalus) is only the generous meiosis of the narrating Cephalus who is above all concerned to defend Procris' memory

---

[1] Here I follow the reading of the MSS. Ne² and the Heinsius MSS. (cf. Magnus, *ad loc.*) but it was also known to the scribes of the MSS. M and F (see Magnus' apparatus) at least in part.

and the dignity of his own grief. The harsh cupidity and indecency
of Ovid's sources are softened not so much by Ovid speaking *in
propria persona* as by his narrator, Cephalus.[1]

The plan of the whole Aeacus–Cephalus sequence (VII, 404–868)
should now be clear. Its symmetry can be indicated in a diagram:

	INTRODUCTORY and TRANSITIONAL, VII, 350–504	

L O S S	Cephalus' Question (505–17)	Phocus' Question (661–89)	L O S S
	MEN | PESTILENCE (518–613) ↓ CORPSES	First Loss of Procris (690–758)	R E C O V E R Y
R E C O V E R Y	Response and Prayer of Aeacus, 614–21	The Miraculous Gifts— Miracle of Dog, 759–93	
	ANTS | Miracle of Ants–Men (622–60) ↓ MEN	Second Loss of Procris (794–862)	L O S S
	MIRACLE I	LOVE II	

each of the two parts of the episode has a similar structure.[2]
Each, first of all, is introduced by a question: Cephalus misses and
so asks about the old faces he had once known on his former visit
to Aegina (515–16); Phocus (Aeacus' son) wants to know the

[1] On the significance of the *Procris–Cephalus* for Ovid's whole conception of
love, see ch. VII below (pp. 268–73).
[2] Note also that *this* structure (Aeacus, Cephalus–Procris) corresponds chiastically to the similarly balanced structure of VI, 675–VII, 349 (Medea, Aeson, Pelias)
with the sequence *Love* (Medea, VII, 1–158) + *Miracle* (Aeson, Peliades, VII, 159–
349).

story of Cephalus' wonderful spear (685–6). Each subject of
course arouses a bitter recollection (*Aeacus ingemuit*, 517; *lacrimis
fatur* [Cephalus] *obortis*, 689). In each case the thing observed (the
spear, the replacement of the population of Aegina) has been
gained at the cost of a terrible loss. In each part two complete
episodes (the Pestilence and the Miracle of the Ant-Men; the two
separations of the lovers, by Cephalus' folly and Procris' death)
are joined by an intervening section (the grief and prayer of
Aeacus; the miraculous spear and dog) that prepares the final
dénouement (the new population of Aegina; Procris' death by the
magic spear). But the balance is one of difference as well as of
similarity: the metamorphosis is integral to the Myrmidon episode; it is really quite extraneous to the love story. Ovid, however, altered his source (Nicander) to centre the metamorphosis
(petrifaction of the dog and his prey) between the two sections of
the love story, and thus to establish the symmetry just noticed.[1]
The effect of the whole plan is to relate Aeacus and Cephalus
(each is a hero with a terrible past: each has a present tangible
reminder of this past), to co-ordinate the love story with the rather
impersonal *Pestilence–Myrmidons*, and to merge, as it were, two
quite different topics and atmospheres in one ensemble.

The contrast-episodes that come after the central panel (see
diagram, p. 170) are dissimilar in both structure and tone to the
Medea–Cephalus sequence (the whole of Book vii) just considered.
The most obvious difference is that they are not concentrated
in one book but are instead spread over three books (ix–xi) and
are inserted between three major *pathos*-episodes (Byblis, Myrrha,
Ceyx–Alcyone). But just like the contrast-episodes of Book vii,
they fall into two groups or ensembles, each of exactly the same
length (429 lines). It is useful at this point to reproduce (in somewhat greater detail) the plan of their arrangement.

Here, just as in Book vii, there are two sets of miracles (favourable and unfavourable) which belong to two quite different
frames (Orpheus and Venus) that contain two different kinds of

---

[1] See Appendix, p. 413.

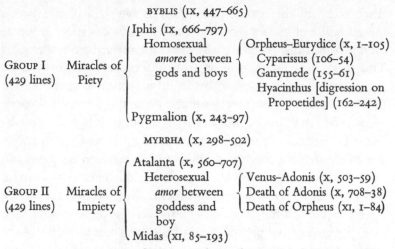

BYBLIS (IX, 447–665)

GROUP I (429 lines)	Miracles of Piety	Iphis (IX, 666–797)		
		Homosexual *amores* between gods and boys	Orpheus–Eurydice (X, 1–105) Cyparissus (106–54) Ganymede (155–61) Hyacinthus [digression on Propoetides] (162–242)	
		Pygmalion (X, 243–97)		

MYRRHA (X, 298–502)

GROUP II (429 lines)	Miracles of Impiety	Atalanta (X, 560–707)	
		Heterosexual *amor* between goddess and boy	Venus–Adonis (X, 503–59) Death of Adonis (X, 708–38) Death of Orpheus (XI, 1–84)
		Midas (XI, 85–193)	

CEYX-ALCYONE with transitional introduction (XI, 194–748)

episodes: homosexual *v.* heterosexual love. But the arrangements are rather different. In Book VII the Medea and Aeacus–Cephalus frames are tight and inclusive; in Books IX–XI the miracles (Iphis, Pygmalion, Atalanta, Midas) stand quite outside the inserted boy–god or boy–goddess affairs and are in an altogether different mood. Furthermore, the links between the tales are of no special significance to the ensembles: the story of Myrrha is obviously quite different from either the Pygmalion or the Venus–Adonis episodes, but all three are put in the mouth of Orpheus. Again Orpheus is also a link between each of the two large groups, since his love story is introduced at X, 1 and his death is not related until XI, 1. But the separation of his love and death scenes is really quite appropriate since, as a result of his parting with Eurydice (related in X, 1 ff.), he eschews women and turns to men (X, 79–80) while, as a result of his death, he rejoins his Eurydice again. Thus each part of his career fits the proper amatory group (homosexual and heterosexual loves). In fact, therefore, the long Myrrha episode effectively separates these contrast-episodes (i.e. all those after the central panel) into two distinct groups.

The general design of both groups really goes back to the

'theodicies' of the central panel (which we shall discuss later). Here Ovid had introduced clear-cut instances of crime or virtue each accompanied by an equally clear-cut reward from the gods. This was a very different thing from the moral ambiguity of his major amatory episodes or his contrast-episodes in Book VII. (There is certainly no moral simplicity in the Cephalus–Procris story.) But this kind of moral simplicity, once it had been established in the central panel, was continued in the two groups with which we are now concerned. Iphis and Pygmalion are pious and innocent and get their reward; Atalanta and Midas are ungrateful and impious and get their punishment. In each case the divine action is just and the miracle is clear-cut. Furthermore, in each case, the violent and pathological note—the sheer passion—of the *Byblis*, *Myrrha*, *Ceyx*, etc. is quite absent: neither Atalanta nor Midas is a tragic figure. The boy–god episodes and the *Venus–Adonis* are, of course, quite different from the four 'miracle' stories. Here we have a series of pretty tales in which the emotion is all one way and not particularly intense: the gods are never involved in passion to anything like the degree of the human characters. And the Orpheus story is obviously not a serious composition.

We need not, in fact, linger over these minor love tales. Ovid's imitation of Virgil's *Orpheus* (*Georgics* IV) is clearly meant to amuse.[1] He had no intention of rivalling Virgil's *ethos* or *pathos*. What he wrote was parody and comedy, not tragedy. Orpheus' long speech to Pluto and Proserpina (x, 17–39) is the kind of amusing *suasoria* that Ovid thoroughly enjoyed. Orpheus explains that he has not come on a sight-seeing tour (*non huc ut opaca viderem | Tartara descendi*) and that he wants Eurydice only as a 'temporary loan' (*pro munere poscimus usum*). The effect of his speech is of course comically exaggerated (the vultures stop eating Tityus' liver, the Danaids stop filling their urns, etc.). Eurydice comes with a limp, for her wound is quite recent. Ovid even corrects

---

[1] Compare this with Ovid's imitation of Virgil's *Achaemenides*; discussion on pp. 73–4, 290.

Virgil and denies that she made any complaint about her lover's fatal glance (*quid enim nisi se quereretur amatam?*). Finally Orpheus' numbed sensibility after the tragedy is likened to the petrifaction of three persons whom Ovid cannot resist mentioning at this point.

All this is an appropriately frivolous introduction to the story of the trees that followed Orpheus, among which of course were Attis and Cyparissus. The latter's story is thus told by Ovid *in propria persona*, but Ganymede's (since he was not a tree) is put in the mouth of Orpheus. The paederastic theme (the love of boys and gods) is then continued through the pretty but jejune Hyacinthus episode. But the corresponding heterosexual, or Venus-Adonis, sub-episode in Group II (see plan, p. 183) has much more merit than the homosexual tales just mentioned. Venus' solicitude for the pretty Adonis is very amusing (*non movet aetas | nec facies nec quae Venerem movere, leones*). We have already mentioned in passing the extremely clever (but deliberately comic) death of Orpheus: Ovid's expansion of Virgil's rather unfortunate account of Orpheus' dissevered head is amusingly grotesque, though his most masterful touch is the description of the reunion in Hades where he tells of how Orpheus deliberately indulged in any number of the glances that had once been so disastrous (XI, 65–6):

> Nunc praecedentem sequitur, nunc praevius anteit
> Eurydicenque suam iam tutus respicit Orpheus.
>
> *And sometimes Orpheus follows, sometimes leads;*
> *And when he leads, looks backward, forfeit-free,*
> *Upon his quite regained Eurydice.*

The fact is that these minor love tales (Orpheus, paederastic amours) are for the most part light relief to the sombre content of the *Byblis* and *Myrrha* as well as to the longer Midas and Atalanta narratives and the far more serious *Iphis* and *Pygmalion*.

In these last two tales Ovid achieved something quite unique. Here human passion receives the sanction of the gods; the harsh world of sin and vengeance recedes and makes way for quite another one; metamorphosis is now very different from the destructive reduction of man to beast, tree or fountain. Here, in short, we have a complete contrast to the crime and pathological passion of Tereus, Scylla, Byblis or Myrrha. Here, in fact, Ovid comes closest to true religious feeling, or at least shows some appreciation of simple piety and innocent credulity.

The story of Iphis was probably taken from the Galateia-Leukippos episode of the second book of Nicander's *Heteroiou-mena*.[1] At any rate, Nicander's version can give us some idea of what Ovid added to his source. In Nicander, the miraculous change of sex (girl to boy) is not connected with an earlier divine revelation. The girl's mother had reared her against the father's express veto: he was very poor and would bring up a boy but not a girl. The mother had relied on some vague dreams and oracles, but had no direct revelation or explicit divine sanction for her act. It was only when the false girl (she had been passed off as a boy to deceive the father) grew old enough and pretty enough to make further concealment of her sex impossible, that the mother turned for help to the goddess Leto: the sex change was necessary to keep the father from realizing that he had been deceived. This is Nicander's version: Ovid changed the motivation completely. In his version, the goddess Isis, in her full splendour, appears to the pregnant mother (Telethusa) and charges her to preserve and bring up the expected child. The father is represented sympatheti-cally (he regrets the necessity for exposing a girl) but is not told of the vision. He is, in fact, deceived by the mother according to Isis' express direction. Telethusa calls the child Iphis (an ambiguous name applicable to either sex) and disguises her as a boy. But it is not, primarily, fear of the father that forces the crisis when the girl grows up. In Ovid, Iphis' coming of age entails her betrothal (the deceived father of course arranges it), and this arrangement is much more than formal: Iphis and her fiancée Ianthe are violently in love with each other. And it is just this romantic and apparently hopeless passion that the miracle fulfils. Isis, by changing Iphis' sex, both rewards the mother's piety and consummates the girl's love.

The really interesting thing in Ovid's version is the contrast between the rather sophisticated scepticism of the daughter, Iphis, and the simple piety of the mother, Telethusa. Ovid is quite aware that the love of Iphis and Ianthe has decided overtones of sexual abnormality. Iphis herself is fully conscious of the unnatural character of her passion. In her monologue (IX, 726–63) she puts her situation clearly (726–8):

> 'quis me manet exitus,' inquit
> 'cognita quam nulli, quam prodigiosa novaeque
> cura tenet Veneris?'

> *'What end awaits me? Oh, what form unknown*
> *Of monstrous passion claims me for its own?'*

If the gods really wanted to spare her, they should have at least given her a *natural* passion (730):

> Naturale malum saltem et de more dedissent!

> *At least some known disease, some natural ill.*

Homosexuality violates the laws of nature. Even Pasiphae's strange love for the bull was not abnormal in this sense. But Iphis absolutely dismisses the possibility of consummating such a love. She wants what no man and no god, even, can give, for she wants something unnatural (756–9):

> Dique mihi faciles, quidquid valuere, dederunt;
> quodque ego, vult genitor, vult ipsa socerque futurus;
> at non vult natura, potentior omnibus istis,
> quae mihi sola nocet!

> *All that they could, indulgent gods have given.*
> *What though my father's wishes, joined with mine,*
> *And with her sire's Ianthe's, all combine,*
> *If nature, stronger far than these, says no,*
> *And does me wrong, my solitary foe?*

But what makes this episode so different from the pathological stories of Byblis, Myrrha, Scylla or Procne is precisely its religious setting, the fact that it is, in origin and genre, a simple miracle tale. The mother, Telethusa, remains, all through, the trusting believer who expects Isis to resolve the dilemma for which the goddess was responsible. To be sure, she tries for a while to gain time and defer the wedding (766 ff.) but in the end she reverts to her original piety (IX, 776–81):

> Te, dea, te quondam tuaque haec insignia vidi
> cunctaque cognovi, sonitum comitesque facesque...
> sistrorum memorique animo tua iussa notavi.
> Quod videt haec lucem, quod non ego punior, ecce
> consilium munusque tuum est: miserere duarum
> auxilioque iuva!

> *Give aid, and cure my fear, thee, thee, erewhile,*
> *Goddess, I saw, as now, with every sign*
> *Of godhead clad, and knew them all for thine:*
> *The brands, the timbrels, and the attendant train;*
> *And fixed thy precepts firmly in my brain.*
> *That Iphis lives, that I unpunished go,*
> *This did thy counsel and thy gift bestow.*
> *Now grant thy aid, and pity me and mine.*

Finally, therefore, nature is subordinated to the divine will: Iphis actually becomes a man; supernatural power gives legitimacy to unnatural desire by wholly removing its unnatural basis. This metamorphosis, therefore, is utterly different from those of Myrrha, Byblis, Scylla, etc., where the human merely reverts to the animal and finds its quietus in a loss of human consciousness that is the partial equivalent of death. Of course the miracle is extremely hard to believe, but Ovid's attitude toward it is quite sympathetic. He shows us the dilemma of Iphis, as Iphis herself understood it, in order to show us also the necessity and rightness of the divine action. Isis is, in a sense, confronting the cruelty of a society that practises infanticide; in assuming final responsibility for her initial humanity (her advice to let the girl live) she shows that justice and benevolence can after all be expected from the divine powers. She thus prevents the kind of catastrophe that ruined Byblis and Myrrha and performs an act of both individual and social justice. Ovid, in other words, altered his sources to establish a point-for-point contrast between the *Iphis* and the *Byblis*.[1]

The story which balances and corresponds to the *Iphis* is, of course, that of Pygmalion, though Pygmalion is also balanced by or contrasted with Midas, as we shall presently see. Here Ovid reversed the procedure of the *Iphis*. He did not introduce an amatory motif into a simple miracle story but, instead, added a miracle (very much along the lines of the Iphis miracle and almost certainly suggested by it) to a purely erotic legend. The original story of Pygmalion was told in the *Kypriaka* of Philostephanus, a work known to us from the Christian authors Clement of Alexandria and Arnobius. It is one of a number of tales of sexual intercourse between men and statues (in this case, it is the statue of Aphrodite) or of erotic objects used for sexual stimulation. Clement and Arnobius cite also Posidippus' story of the young man and the Cnidian Aphrodite; Aristaenetus tells of an artist in love with the picture he painted. All these, like the original Pygmalion, are instances of sexual perversion and are avowedly pathological.[2]

It is all but certain that it was Ovid himself who altered the original legend recorded by Philostephanus. He introduces the story immediately after that of the infamous Propoetides. It seems clear that Ovid wanted to use these particular Cypriot stories (Propoetides, Cerastae, Pygmalion) for his transition from Hyacinthus (and the series of god–boy amours) to Myrrha. Myrrha was not really a Cypriot but an Asiatic figure and, although Ovid connects her with Cyprus (she is said to be Pygmalion's descendant), he indicates in several places (e.g. ll. 307 ff., 316, 478, 480) that he is thinking of Asia as her proper milieu. On

[1] See the further discussion of the Iphis episode in ch. vii (pp. 268–73) below.
[2] See Appendix, p. 418.

the other hand, the transition from Hyacinthus to the Propoetides is specious and artificial in the manner of other liaisons where Ovid had to resort to a *tour de force* in order to place his legends where his schema demanded. Sparta, he tells us, was not ashamed to celebrate Hyacinthus as its native son (*nec genuisse pudet Sparten Hyacinthon*, x, 217) but (l. 220) Cyprus would have preferred to do without the Propoetides or Cerastae. Here the unnatural or evil character of the amatory passion is absolutely undeniable. Whatever we may think of Hyacinth, we can have but one opinion of the Cyprian monstrosities.

But Ovid is not particularly concerned with the Cerastae and Propoetides as such (both take up but eighteen lines, x, 220–37). They are just a means of introducing or re-introducing (for Procne, Philomela and Scylla had already preceded) the theme of the wicked or unnatural woman. Orpheus, to whom all this section of the poem is nominally attributed, had already stated his general theme (x, 152–4):

> puerosque canamus
> dilectos superis, inconcessisque puellas
> ignibus attonitas meruisse libidine poenam.

> *Of boys beloved by gods it falls to sing;*
> *To tell how maidens, crazed with lawless fires,*
> *Suffered for uninhibited desires.*

In other words, he proposed to relate a series of homosexual amours followed by tales of illegitimate or unnatural female passion. But in fact this latter section (which obviously begins at line 220 with the Propoetides) is interrupted by the quite different Pygmalion episode which actually separates the *Propoetides* from the Myrrha episode. Their only bond of unity is their Cypriot origin (Philostephanus). It seems therefore obvious that Philostephanus (or his source) had grouped together in one place a number of indecent Cypriot legends from which Ovid selected the *Cerastae*, *Propoetides* and *Pygmalion*. Thus Ovid changed the original plot of the *Pygmalion* in order to establish a strong

contrast with *Myrrha*. The Cerastae and Propoetides were simply
his point of departure for Pygmalion (x, 243–6):

> Quas [i.e. the Propoetides] quia Pygmalion aevum per
> crimen agentis
> viderat, offensus vitiis, quae plurima menti
> femineae natura dedit, sine coniuge caelebs
> vivebat.

> *And thanks to them Pygmalion, who beheld*
> *Their life of sin, by female faults repelled*
> *(Nature's too numerous gifts to woman's mind),*
> *Lived without wife, to single state resigned.*

And the Pygmalion story itself, as Hermann Fränkel points out,[1] is
a point-by-point contrast to the *Propoetides*. They were the first
prostitutes—the first women to vulgarize their bodies. And their
loss of shame, the bloodlessness of their unblushing faces, was the
appropriate prelude to their actual metamorphosis into bloodless
stone: *in rigidum parvo silicem discrimine versae*. In short, Pygmalion
is their complete moral antithesis: it is his acute sense of shame, his
moral revulsion from the Propoetides, that makes him withdraw
from actual women and devise his own ideal woman (the ivory
statue). And when he falls in love with the ivory statue, he still
retains his piety and modest timidity. He hardly dares to utter his
wish (x, 274–6):

> Constitit et timide 'si, di, dare cuncta potestis,
> sit coniunx, opto' (non ausus 'eburnea virgo'
> dicere) Pygmalion 'similis mea' dixit 'eburnae.'

> *Pygmalion thus with timid utterance prayed:*
> *'O gods, if gods have power unlimited,*
> *This only is my prayer, that I may wed'—*
> *To say: 'my ivory maid', he did not dare;*
> *But turned it thus: 'my maiden ivory-fair'.*

The miracle is thus the direct opposite of the metamorphosis of

---

[1] See Appendix, pp. 418 f.

the Propoetides: modesty and shame are rewarded, not punished. The transformation of the statue is not only the triumph of art over nature but also of piety over moral failure and crime. The parallelism with Iphis is clear. What moves the two goddesses (Isis, Venus) in each case is a respect for virtuous love. Both Iphis and Pygmalion oppose an evil reality; so the divine powers reward them with the ideal, the miracle.

We need not linger over the obviously contrapuntal Atalanta and Midas episodes. Each is an instance of righteous punishment for an evident crime or folly (the ingratitude and sacrilege of Hippomenes and Atalanta; the stupidity and folly of Midas). In each the metamorphosis is deliberate punishment, not, as in the major episodes of amatory passion, the 'natural' consequence of a prior catastrophe or impasse. But the moral is not really the major concern of either story. Atalanta is a naive virgin whose love story is only amusing; her neglect of Venus and act of sacrilege (the crimes that justify the metamorphosis into lions) have no necessary relation to the rest of the tale. Midas is represented as a thick-witted oaf whose misfortunes are in no sense fatal and arise from stupidity rather than positive wrong-doing. Formally considered, both tales are theodicies (punishment metamorphoses) that are obviously meant to stand in contrast to the Iphis and Pygmalion miracles. In fact, they are very different in tone: the story of Atalanta is piquant and sentimental; what amuses us is the contrast between her beauty and her athleticism. Ovid made the most of the golden apples and their devastating effect on the girl who was already half divided between her desire to win the race and her reluctance to lose her lover. The sad fate of her other lover-victims is brought out only to enhance the cleverness of Hippomenes and her own amorous emotions. The Midas story is obviously a prime example of Ovidian humour: he delights in the grotesque details of Midas' golden cuisine, the vivid contrast of Pan and Apollo and the terrible secret of the ass's ears.

But there is one feature of the Midas episode that lifts it above the level of mere wit or humour. It is the story not just of folly but of aesthetic insensitivity; its metamorphosis is thus the exact reverse of that in the corresponding *Pygmalion*. Pygmalion is the artist rewarded; Midas is the philistine punished or stigmatized. The stupidity that prompted his wish for the golden touch had not been overcome by his bitter experience: *pingue . . . ingenium mansit* (XI, 148). He cannot distinguish between the song of Pan and the song of Apollo. When the arbiter of the singing contest, the mountain Tmolus, awards the victory to Apollo, only Midas objects to the decision (XI, 172–5):

> Iudicium sanctique placet sententia montis
> omnibus; arguitur tamen atque iniusta vocatur
> unius sermone Midae. Nec Delius aures
> *humanam* stolidas *patitur retinere figuram.*

> *And with the sacred mountain all agree,*
> *Save Midas; he contests the verdict, he*
> *Disputes the justice of the court's decree.*
> *Then Phoebus bade from those dull ears be gone*
> *The* human shape *they cast discredit on.*

So Midas is made to lose the perfect *humana figura* which Pygmalion's art (*ars adeo latet arte sua*, X, 252) and piety had gained for his ivory image. The true artist has true *ingenium* and does not want to turn his world into gold: on the contrary, his imitation of nature is a humanizing process; he has the ear of Apollo or Venus because his art is inspired by an ideal of human perfection. This is the aesthetic miracle: its converse is the miracle of greed and stupidity.

Taken together, the little miracles reveal a poetic intention. Ovid, at this point in his poem, did not need sombre theodicies of crime and justice so much as delicately modulated tales that would relieve the darker tones of the preceding *Myrrha* and the succeeding *Ceyx–Alcyone*. This partly explains the difference in tone between the little miracles and the large *pathos* episodes. But there is also more than simple contrast or search for variety. The *Iphis*, *Pygmalion*, *Atalanta* and *Midas* are his protests against the grim abnormalities and crimes he elsewhere describes at such length.

They express his hankering for divinities that are neither comic nor cruel, for love that is neither pathological nor perverse, and (in the *Pygmalion* at least) for the ideal, for the coming of perfection to an imperfect and rather frightening world.

II (THE CENTRAL PANEL)

The central panel of this section (III: The Pathos of Love) is not a single episode (like that of Section I: The Phaethon Story) or a double episode (as that of Section II: *Perseus–Andromeda* and *Perseus–Phineus*) but a much more complex arrangement of two contrasted episodes in heroic or epic vein that together enclose two shorter episodes in another vein. The arrangement is as follows:

> First Epic Part of Central Panel: MELEAGER–ALTHAEA (VIII, 260–546)
> Interlude: Theseus in cave of Achelous (VIII, 547–615)
> Philemon–Baucis (616–724)
> Erysichthon (725–78)
> Interlude: VIII, 878–83; IX, 1–3
> Second Epic Part of Central Panel: HERCULES (IX, 4–272)

The whole thus occupies the exact centre of the section and stretches across the two middle books, VIII and IX. There are 1448 lines before, 2058 after it, but the greater length of the second half of the section (some 600 lines longer than the first) does not disturb the over-all symmetry. Ovid certainly intended the Byblis, Myrrha and Ceyx–Alcyone episodes (763 lines) to outweigh the Procne–Tereus and Scylla episodes (425 lines); the subsidiary contrast episodes of Iphis, Pygmalion, etc. to outweigh the preceding contrast episodes of Medea and Cephalus. But there is enough of both types of episodes in each half to maintain the general equilibrium of the whole section.

The major episodes of the panel (*Meleager* and *Hercules*) are of very similar construction. Though the general style and content is epic, each is also based on a combination of epic and tragic sources: the *Meleager* on some sort of Hellenistic *epos* and the Euripidean play of that name (first latinized by Accius); and the *Hercules* on some epic account of his labours and battles (the episode in question is his battle with the stream-god Achelous) and on Sophocles' *Trachiniae*. There is no reason to suppose that it was not Ovid himself who united the epic and tragic sources.

The versions of the Meleager story in Homer (*Iliad* IX, 529–99), Bacchylides (*Epinikoi* 5), Nicander[1] and Apollodorus,[2] all stress the heroic or epic aspect of the legend. In Homer, Bacchylides, Nicander[1] and an alternative version given by Apollodorus,[2] the killing of the sons of Thestios (brothers of Althaea, Meleager's mother) is part of a general battle between the Calydonians and Curetes. Apollodorus,[2] in his main version, closely resembles Ovid (there is no warfare or siege; simply Meleager's homicidal attack on the sons of Thestios) but obviously reproduces an epic original: he gives, for example, an epic catalogue of the heroes engaged in the hunt. On the other hand, the romantic attachment of Meleager to Atalanta and the passionate monologue of Althaea (as she alternates between sisterly and maternal feelings) seem to go back to Euripides and Accius. Ovid's transitions between the epic and the tragic (or romantic) portions of the episode are quite well marked. Thus he adds after his brief account of the first meeting of Atalanta with Meleager (VIII, 327–8):

> nec plura sinit tempusque pudorque
> dicere: *maius opus* magni certaminis urget.

> *Nor time nor conscience lets him further speak: a 'mightier task'—the great contest—presses upon him.*

The phrase *maius opus* seems a clear allusion to the seventh book of the *Aeneid* (45) and Virgil's transition to the greater and more strictly epic theme of war and battle in *Aeneid* VII to XII. Ovid, like Virgil, is engaged on a greater task than the narrating of a love story. Clearly also the account of Althaea's terrible revenge in lines 445 ff.,

> Dona deum templis nato victore ferebat,
> cum videt extinctos fratres Althaea referri, etc.

---

[1] Antoninus Liberalis II (Μελεαγρίδες = Martini, ed., pp. 68–70). [2] *Bibl.* I, 8. 1–4.

Now while Althaea thanked the gods for aid,
And offerings for her son's achievement made,
She saw the sad procession pass the fane,
Her brothers brought back lifeless home again,

marks a new portion of the story. Not only does the scene shift from the embattled heroes to Althaea, but the style shifts also. The long and obviously tragic soliloquy of the mother-sister (481–511) is preceded by a vividly empathetic description of her feelings (445–80) that is in marked contrast to the relatively objective hunt and quarrel that occupied the first part of the episode (260–444).

The division of the *Hercules* is unmistakable: indeed its epic and tragic portions fall into two quite distinct sections: (1) the struggle with the stream-god, Achelous (IX, 4–88); (2) the death and apotheosis (101–272). The former is told by Achelous himself in the first person; the latter is told by Ovid in the third person after the conclusion of the whole Achelous episode (which had started at VIII, 547 and had been the frame of the ensuing Philemon-Baucis and Erysichthon stories). Achelous had been Hercules' rival for Deianira's hand. His consequent battle with Hercules had left him short of one horn. But this was better than the fate of another lover of Deianira, the centaur Nessus! The transition thus comes in the lines (IX, 101–2):

> At te, Nesse ferox, eiusdem virginis ardor
> perdiderat volucri traiectum terga sagitta.
>
> *Less well, wild Nessus, did it fare with you,*
> *Whom passion for the selfsame damsel slew,*
> *When through your spine Alcides' arrow flew.*

But Nessus is only a preliminary to the tragedy proper which starts at IX, 134:

> Longa fuit medii mora temporis, actaque magni
> Herculis implerant terras odiumque novercae.
> Victor ab Oechalia Cenaeo sacra parabat
> vota Iovi, cum fama loquax praecessit ad aures,
> Deianira, tuas.

Years passed: the hero's deeds had won renown
World-wide, and worn his stepdame's malice down;
And at Cenaeum, for Oechalia won,
Thanksgivings, vowed to Jove, had now begun.
Rumour reached Deianira.

We are then, so to speak, *in mediis rebus,* in the dramatic present of Deianira and her soliloquy, and the style is appropriately dramatic and empathetic, exactly like the Althaea portion of the Meleager episode.

But the parallelism of the arrangement is only an index of the parallelism of ideas. Each hero is ruined by the grief or resentment of a woman. The tale of his heroic exploits is followed by that of his terrible doom; the epic career by the tragic dénouement. Yet there is also a difference: Meleager's fate is in some sense deserved; his attachment to Atalanta belied his obvious obligation to his kindred; his anger was recklessly homicidal. Hercules is, on the other hand (quite unlike the hero of Sophocles' *Trachiniae*), represented as the victim of a false rumour. Gossip had exaggerated the matter of Iole, and Deianira had believed the gossip (Fama) (IX, 138–9):

> quae veris addere falsa
> gaudet et e minimo sua per mendacia crescit

> *that talks, and, mixing truth with lies,*
> *From nothing grows, self-fed with falsities.*

Hercules' sufferings are thus represented as a gratuitous calamity which the gods have to avert or change if there is to be any theodicy left in the world. No wonder that Hercules verges on cynical disbelief (203–4):

> At valet Eurystheus! Et sunt, qui credere possint
> esse deos!

> *Eurystheus prospers well; yet those there be,*
> *Who think the gods are more than fantasy.*

His deification is thus represented as an act of justice, a rewarding of services which had long been recognized as divine. No one can truly object (256–8):

> si quis tamen Hercule, si quis
> forte deo doliturus erit, data praemia nolet,
> sed meruisse dari sciet invitusque probabit.
>
> *And if there be, who grudge the gift, aggrieved*
> *To see the hero as a god received,*
> *Yet shall they own it for a just award,*
> *And even although they like it not, applaud.*

The relation of the episodes to each other is thus carefully designed. It is quite possible that it was suggested to Ovid by the wonderful ode of Bacchylides (*Epinikoi* 5) in which Hercules meets the shade of Meleager in the underworld. Here Hercules is so much impressed by Meleager's beauty that he longs for a bride who looks like him: this is, of course, Meleager's sister, the fatal Deianira. But whereas Bacchylides but suggests, with delicate ellipsis, the terrible calamity of Hercules' marriage and the basic similarity of each hero's fate, Ovid stresses the difference. Meleager is, so to speak, a hero whose nobility is flawed and rightly given over to tragedy. Hercules can survive tragedy because he is more than a hero: he is also a divine man—one of the very few whose destiny is with the gods. He is, in the end, invulnerable to the fatal fury that destroys Meleager.

The two episodes thus form a unity and together bridge the gap between destructive passion—the passion that leads to death or loss of humanity—and triumphant achievement, the achievement that leads to immortality and divinity. Thus they are both like and unlike the terrible *pathē* that surround them: the passions and degenerative transformations of Medea, Byblis, Scylla and Myrrha. The kinship between these women and Althaea or Deianira is unmistakable. Deianira cries, in recollection of Meleager and Althaea (IX, 149–51):

> Quid *si me, Meleagre, tuam memor esse sororem*
> forte paro facinus, quantumque iniuria possit
> femineusque dolor, iugulata paelice testor?

What if, remembering that I am your sister, Meleager, I
attempt bold crime and kill the trollop and thus give proof of
what a man's unfaithfulness and female rage *can do?'*

But the accent is not on the *femineus dolor* but on the dying hero.
If he be enough of a hero, if his hands be sufficiently clean, he can
overcome the catastrophe of such passion and leave only what is
mortal to be burned away at the end: as Jupiter declares (IX, 250):
omnia qui vicit, vincet, quos cernitis, ignis.

The combination of epic and tragic elements in the *Meleager* and
Hercules is thus justified by Ovid's purpose: to relate these heroic
episodes to his major theme of erotic passion and to show their
difference from it—their epic quality, the transcendence of erotic
passion and catastrophe by heroic merit and deserved apotheosis.
Hercules here, as in the eighth book of the *Aeneid*, prefigures and
anticipates the later apotheoses of Aeneas, Romulus and Augustus
and paves the way for the Roman dénouement of the whole poem.
Furthermore, Ovid here, as in the preceding Perseus panel, wanted
to fortify the centre of the longest section of his poem by the
weight and grandeur of epic material.

But here also, just as in the *Perseus*, the epic material does not suit
Ovid's style or temperament. The boar-hunt is not designed to
enhance the romantic charms of Atalanta (Ovid thus curtly disposes of her in order to deal with his *maius opus*, VIII, 328). Its
heroic incidents are both tedious and grotesque. Ovid seems, so
far as we can tell, to have introduced Nestor into the usual gallery
of hunters, only to show the old man's escape from the boar by a
sort of 'spear-vault' into a tree (VIII, 365 ff.). This is just the kind of
misplaced grotesquerie that set our teeth on edge in the *Perseus*.
That Telamon should have tripped on a root (379) and Atalanta
have nicked the animal's ear (382) are incidents scarcely worthy of
epic narration even if the 'ear-nicking' gives Meleager a chance to
glorify his beloved (VIII, 386–7):

> Et primus sociis visum ostendisse cruorem
> et 'meritum' dixisse 'feres virtutis honorem!'

It seems that he first saw the blood—that he
First made it seen by all the company.
'The prize for manly valour' (thus he speaks)
'Is yours, fair maid.'

This is, perhaps, an apt illustration of Meleager's infatuation, but it belies the epic tone and gravity that Ovid seems so intent upon.

The curious duel of Hercules and the stream-god Achelous is even less edifying. Instead of one of Hercules' authentic labours, Ovid only tells us of how Achelous lost one of his horns. When Achelous gives up the attempt to fight *in propria persona* and transforms himself into a snake, Hercules regales him with a speech (IX, 67 ff.) on his own prowess as snake-killer: *Cunarum labor est angues superare mearum.* 'That's baby-stuff for me', we might, perhaps not so inappropriately, translate. One cannot resist such truly Ovidian humour, but it is surely fatal to the epic pretensions of the episode.

But it is the tragic parts of the two episodes which most signally fail to convince. The meditations and soliloquies of Althaea and Deianira are skilful enough (Ovid tactfully shortens those of Deianira since he had already devoted a good deal of space to the similar sentiments of Althaea) but very incongruous with their setting. Althaea's version of the 'soliloquy of conflicting impulses' (it goes back to the Medea soliloquies of Apollonius and Euripides which Ovid had partially reproduced at the beginning of Book VII), even though it is changed from a struggle between *pudor* and *amor* to one between maternal and sisterly love, is not sufficiently prepared for by the preceding narrative: we cannot really sympathize with her as either mother or sister. More disastrous is Ovid's version of the *Trachiniae*. The long speech of Hercules (IX, 176–204) that precedes his apotheosis is altogether too rhetorical for its agonized setting. Above all, the shift from a tragic to a happy ending (especially the joy and self-congratulation of Jupiter when he sees that the gods are actually alarmed at Hercules' misery, 242 ff.) is utterly unconvincing.[1]

[1] Cf. pp. 349 f. below.

Ovid's alterations of Sophocles are necessary for his purpose (he wants to end on an auspicious and Augustan note: the apotheosis of merit) but fatal to the emotional unity of his episode. This is a tragedy that altogether misfires.

Why did Ovid break the continuity of the main panels (Meleager, Hercules) by the two theodicies (Philemon–Baucis, Erysichthon)? It is clear, first of all, that he needed to separate the two panels by some intervening material: otherwise the total effect would have been repetitious and monotonous. The parallelism of the two episodes required a similarity of design (e.g. the union of epic and tragic, or erotic and heroic motifs) that would have cloyed and satiated the reader if the material had not been properly spaced. But of course Ovid planned it this way only because he also wanted the space for another purpose. The panel as a whole (including the theodicies) is a deliberate contrast to the eroticism and passion that surround it. In it, the merely pathological meta-morphoses of Tereus, Scylla, Byblis, etc. are countered by their opposites: apotheosis, reward of piety, clear-cut punishment. Not only the pious miracles of Iphis and Pygmalion in the second half of the section but, far more important, the Roman apotheoses of the last section of the poem (IV) are here adumbrated and sketched. In another sense, we revert to the initial theodicies of the Creation time (Book I): the pious Deucalion and Pyrrha, the impious Lycaon. In other words, this is the true centre of the whole poem, the place in which the beginning is recalled, the end anticipated and the major theme of the entire epic—the power and justice of the gods—explicitly emphasized.

This is made clear at the introduction of the first theodicy, the *Philemon and Baucis*. Achelous (VIII, 575 ff.) points out to the visiting Theseus some islands (the Echinades) that were once nymphs or naiads. This *factum mirabile* excites the interest of the other guests of the stream-god. One of them, the wicked son of Ixion (*deorum spretor*), scoffs at such credulity (VIII, 614–15):

> 'Ficta refers nimiumque putas, Acheloe, potentes
> esse deos,' dixit 'si dant adimuntque figuras.'

' Tales, Acheloüs! Gods that make and mar,
Shape and reshape—you stretch their powers too far.'

The ensuing consternation of Achelous' guests (VIII, 616),

Obstipuere omnes nec talia dicta probarunt

All present listened with affronted ears,

recalls that of the gods in council when Jupiter related the crime of
Lycaon (I, 199–201):

Confremuere omnes studiisque ardentibus ausum
talia deposcunt: sic, cum manus impia saevit
sanguine Caesareo Romanum extinguere nomen...

His hearers shuddered and the council room
Rang loud with clamour for the sinner's doom.
So, when a lawless hand took frenzied aim
To drown in Caesar's blood the Roman name,
The race of men was struck with quick alarm.

It is now the pious Lelex (*animo maturus et aevo*) who undertakes to
answer the son of Ixion. The gods' power, he asserts, is boundless
and irresistible (VIII, 618–19):

immensa est finemque potentia caeli
non habet et, quidquid superi voluere, peractum est.

To power celestial end or bound is none,
And whatsoe'er the gods have willed, is done.

And, to illustrate it, he tells the story of Philemon and Baucis,
whose moral is carefully pointed at its end. Lelex himself sums
it all up in the words (VIII, 724): *Cura deum di sint, et qui coluere,
colantur* or *piety maketh gods.*

But the *Philemon and Baucis* is capped by the stream-god, who
tries to satisfy the pious desire of Theseus to hear more such edifying
tales: *facta audire volentem | mira deum* (726). The *Erysichthon* is
thus introduced as the proper pendant to its pious predecessor.
Appropriately of course, the tale of wickedness punished (Ery-

sichthon is almost an incarnation of impiety) follows the tale of piety rewarded. At the end, the gods' power and morality seem impressively re-established. The way has been fully prepared for the apotheosis of Hercules.

The inspiration of the two tales seems to be in large part Callimachean.[1] The account of the reception of the gods (Jupiter and Hermes) by the poor couple in their humble cottage is obviously indebted in some degree to Callimachus' *Hecale*. Nor is it at all likely that Ovid could have used this famous bit of Callimachus in his *Philemon and Baucis* and failed to recall the story of Callimachus' Demeter Hymn in the immediately following *Erysichthon*. He also, of course, had other sources for both stories. There is, for example, no mention of a daughter of Erysichthon in Callimachus and there was obviously some sort of Phrygian legend behind the *Philemon–Baucis*: it is to one striking incident, not the main plot of the *Hecale*, that Ovid refers, but he was surely aware that it was Callimachus, not some relatively obscure legend, that his readers would think of first. This perhaps explains the strange fact that the style and mood of the two stories are so un-Callimachean. Ovid was diverging from Callimachus precisely because he had Callimachus so definitely in mind. He was showing how he could raise the Callimachean material to epic dimensions.

We have already seen how very unlike Callimachus the deliberately epic and rhetorical *Erysichthon* of Ovid is.[2] Ovid's Erysichthon is no child or juvenile, the impact of whose catastrophe falls primarily on his prestige-conscious parents and rural-bourgeois household. Ovid wholly avoided the kind of modernization, above all the piquant detail, that we find in Callimachus. He gives us only a picture of Impiety personified, an elaborate piece of divine machinery, a detailed allegory—in short, a bravura epic utterly denuded of concrete substance and environment.

In the *Philemon–Baucis* he certainly dwells upon the humble details of the couch, the unsteady table, the vegetables and meat, the

---

[1] See Appendix, pp. 413 f.
[2] See above, pp. 65 f. and below, p. 416.

earthenware dishes, etc. But these details do not set us in a live environment, do not bring real characters into a true social relation as do the details of Callimachus. Indeed, they illustrate only the piety of the old couple, who are really just another Deucalion and Pyrrha. They are the opposite of the inhospitable people who reject the visiting gods (VIII, 628–30):

> Mille domos adiere locum requiemque petentes,
> mille domos clausere serae; tamen una recepit,
> parva quidem stipulis et canna tecta palustri.

> *At doors a thousand rest and room they crave:*
> *A thousand doors refused; one only gave,*
> *A reed- and straw-thatched cottage, small but dear.*

The *canna tecta palustri*, etc.—in short, all the specific aspects of poverty—are but rhetorical contrast to the generality of evil (*mille . . . mille*, etc.). The episode of the goose (it is *unicus*, their one watchman, yet they try to catch and kill even it in their unexampled hospitality) does not produce an effect of humour or realism so much as of laborious exaggeration. Ovid heaps on the detail in order to force the antithesis—divine wealth *v.* poverty—to a climax that will permit the obvious moral or theodicy to be articulated (VIII, 689–91):

> 'Di'que 'sumus, meritasque luet vicinia poenas
> impia' dixerunt; 'vobis immunibus huius
> esse mali dabitur!'

> *'High gods are we, and by our just command,*
> *Stern punishment shall strike this impious land.*
> *Yourselves alone shall scape the destined end.'*

The marble temple into which the cottage is finally transformed (caelataeque *fores adopertaque* marmore *tellus*) illustrates Ovid's subordination of realism to formal theodicy. The cottage has no value in itself: it is only a device for producing an effect. The subsequent obliteration of the cottage and its whole environment does not bother Ovid because he has not been interested in them at all.

The main value of the final metamorphosis of the aged couple (into trees) is that it establishes the tree-shrine on which Lelex finally pins his offering and pronounces his moral epigram.

But it would be a gross error, as we have already seen, to condemn Ovid by stressing his inferiority to Callimachus in these two episodes. He did not want Callimachean realism (the piquant modernization of myth) for his reciprocal theodicies, set, so carefully, between the reciprocal epics of Meleager and Hercules. The whole central panel is both an offset to the major erotic episodes of the section, and a carefully planned precursor of the Roman apotheoses to come in the next section. The interset theodicies or 'pious legends' add exactly the note of pious credulity and divine justice that Ovid here wanted.

Nevertheless, it must be admitted that Ovid was not 'at home' with moralism and theodicy in anything like the sense that he was at home with the erotic passions and Euripidean motifs of his episodes of *pathos*. This central section has a coldness and formality that belie its message. But because Ovid was always, to at least some degree, himself, it contains many Ovidian touches: the clever paradoxes, the humour of the Mestra episode in the *Erysichthon*; the vividness of the meal in the *Philemon–Baucis*; the skilful rhetoric of Althaea's monologue; even (taken by itself) the amusing 'spear-vault' of Nestor. But it is not what Ovid would have written had he not felt it necessary to make some obeisance to Augustan morality and Virgilian seriousness. There is ingenuity in his plan of concentrating theodicies and epic *aristeiai* at the pivot or centre of his poem. What was lacking was the conviction that could bring the plan to life. Ovid was neither a moralist nor an Augustan at heart.

III (THE MAJOR PATHOS EPISODES)

The five major episodes of amatory *pathos* (*Tereus–Procne, Scylla, Byblis, Myrrha* and *Ceyx–Alcyone*) have, obviously, a number of points in common that distinguish them from the episodes of either the central panel or the contrast sections considered in

Part I of this chapter. Each of the five stories (with the exception noted at (2)) has four major characteristics:

(1) It is an essentially tragic story.

(2) The love involved (with the crucial exception of the *Ceyx–Alcyone*) is pathological or unnatural.

(3) The metamorphosis is the solution of an otherwise unendurable anguish, the only possible alternative being death by suicide or external violence.

(4) The metamorphosis itself involves a loss of human consciousness and is a true reversion to animal existence. It is not (as in, e.g., the Actaeon and Io episodes) a mere preservation of human identity in an animal exterior.

These are the salient points: but there are also a number of other common features. All these episodes (save for the *Scylla*) are longer than any others of the section excepting of course the epic pieces of the central panel (Meleager, Hercules). They are all subjects specially preferred by the writers of neoteric short epics or *epyllia*. Myrrha was the subject of the most famous of such poems, Cinna's *Zmyrna*. The *Scylla* and *Tereus–Procne* are specifically mentioned in Virgil's neoteric list in Eclogue 6. *Byblis* is one of the subjects that Parthenius suggested to Gallus, the 'neoteric' friend of Virgil. Cicero had written a short epic on the Alcyone theme, presumably under the influence of the very *neoterici* whom he so slightingly labelled. More generally, the subjects show a Euripidean ancestry common to many Greek poets of the late Hellenistic era: Euripides' Medea and Phaedra are certainly the ultimate ancestresses of Ovid's Scylla, Byblis, Myrrha and Procne. In short, Ovid was here dealing with a central topic of Hellenistic and neoteric poetry—a topic that he had already treated at length in his *Heroides*.

But, though the general provenience of these episodes is evident, there can be no doubt of the individuality of Ovid's treatment of them. In the first place, as we have seen in our analysis of his *Scylla*, he maintains a narrative continuity that is quite lacking in the *Ciris* or in such a typically neoteric *epyllion* as Catullus'

Peleus and Thetis. The narrative is not stopped by the heroines' monologues, or by a Euripidean debate (as in the *Ciris* and *Zmyrna*), and is not asymmetrically restricted to moments of *pathos.* Ovid does emphasize the fatal decision of Scylla, the struggle of Byblis and Myrrha with their terrible *libidines*, the anguish of Procne and Alcyone, but he carefully preserves at least the illusion of movement and narrative progression. Everything proceeds toward the final metamorphosis which is intimately connected with the foregoing action and is indeed its almost inevitable dénouement. Furthermore, Ovid's narrative quite lacks the obscurity and Hellenistic learning or preciosity of the *Zmyrna*, the *Peleus and Thetis* or, almost certainly, of Parthenius' and Euphorion's little epics.[1] These stories, in short, are part of his *carmen perpetuum* and preserve the movement, symmetry and continuity of his general epic style.

They are also related to his whole scheme, and by their similarities and dissimilarities maintain the emphasis as well as the variety, the progression of motif and tone, that he wanted in this section of his poem. The development is from positive crime (the cruel rape of Philomela by Tereus, the child-murder of Procne, the parricide of Scylla) to unnatural or pathological passion (Byblis, Myrrha) and, finally, to a kind of resolution in the metamorphosis of the concluding *Ceyx–Alcyone.* This is paralleled by the shift of plot-structure: the *Tereus–Procne* obviously reproduces, at least in part, a tragedy that brings husband and wife into fatally destructive conflict. The succeeding *Scylla*, *Byblis* and *Myrrha* are each concentrated on one female character; she affects the other characters (and is in turn affected by them), but does not really enter into dramatic conflict with them. Finally the *Ceyx–Alcyone* wholly transcends the neoteric framework of its three predecessors and rises, in both its style and its content, to an epic plane that almost permits the two main characters to impose their love—the mutuality of their affection—upon nature itself. It is an answer to the tragic conflict of Tereus and Procne and to the pathological

[1] See above, pp. 62–73 and below, pp. 221–5. See also my *Virgil*, pp. 27 f.

isolation of Scylla, Byblis and Myrrha. We can represent the progression somewhat as follows:

Criminal		Tereus–Procne:	a *Tragedy* of criminal conflict
		Scylla:	Pathological Eros with criminal sequel
	Neoteric		CENTRAL PANEL
Pathological	Epylliac	Byblis:	Pathological Eros with pathetic sequel
	in type	Myrrha:	Byblis theme heightened and sharpened
Cosmic		Ceyx–Alcyone:	an *Epic* of catastrophic separation resolved in metamorphosis

In each case the metamorphosis is a solution or resolution of a catastrophic situation. This is why it is also a reduction of the human being to an animal level. This kind of metamorphosis was, as we have seen, prefigured in the Arachne and Niobe episodes, but it is now wholly divorced from any suggestion of divine vengeance. What destroys these characters (the *Ceyx–Alcyone* is the great exception) is the perversion of their own *eros* or the destruction and loss of the erotic object. The gods play no role at all or at best a role of belated pity that does not truly motivate the metamorphosis. The passion and the catastrophe are fully human: this is what clearly distinguishes these episodes from the preceding vengeance episodes of Section II (the Avenging Gods).

But we cannot, of course, take the five episodes in isolation from the context of the whole section. As we have already seen, both the subsidiary or contrast episodes (the Medea–Cephalus sequence of Book VII; the four miracles and god–boy or goddess–boy *amores* of Books IX–XI) and the central panel (Althaea, Deianira) contain erotic elements that either carry on the amatory theme or form an intricate counterpoint with it. We must bear in mind that the ordinary reader could hardly visualize the schema that we, for purposes of critical analysis, have set forth at the head of this chapter. Furthermore, Ovid would have been quite false to his concept of *carmen perpetuum* if he had separated the three basic elements of the scheme (major *pathos* episodes, contrast episodes, central panel) by watertight divisions that excluded mutual penetration and influence. This does not mean, however, that the scheme did not actually exist in Ovid's mind. Like all good artists, he kept his plot or plan discreetly hidden; carefully concealing the breaks by artful liaison; cleverly covering his real sequence by various artificial ones. Yet he did not really mean to deceive; he only wanted to maintain a superficial appearance of unity. And he certainly produced the intended effects: the contrast or variation of tone and motif that keeps the reader alert and interested and the constant repetition that allows impressions to sink in. Above all, the perpetual movement—the development of one motif out of another, the law of symmetrical progression to which we have already referred—produces the sense of climax, of accomplished progress that justifies and gives meaning to the *carmen perpetuum.*

The *Tereus–Procne* clearly marks the emergence of the theme of human amatory *pathos* from the previous divine-vengeance theme of Section II. Niobe's fate had produced much discussion and concern in the surrounding towns (VI, 401 ff.). All the neighbouring states sent their rulers to Thebes on missions of consolation and sympathy (*ad solacia*). Only Athens did not send a representative (*solae cessastis Athenae*, 421) because Athens was engaged in a desperate war. It was then that Thracian Tereus came to her aid, dispelled her enemies, and rightfully gained the Athenian princess, Procne, for his wife. Yet this apparently auspicious event is the cause of terrible woe; to this marriage (VI, 429–31)

> Non Hymenaeus adest, non illi Gratia lecto:
> Eumenides tenuere faces de funere raptas,
> Eumenides stravere torum.

> *No Grace, no Hymen, stood beside the bed.*
> *For nuptial flares the furies robbed the pyres,*
> *And lit the wedding feast with funeral fires;*
> *The furies spread the couch.*

But this is only the formal introduction of a *human* tragedy. The cause of the trouble is not divine spite or vengeance but Tereus' innate *libido*: even Philomela's beauty is but the agent that provokes it (VI, 458–60):

> Digna quidem facies, sed et hunc *innata libido*
> exstimulat, pronumque genus regionibus illis
> in Venerem est: flagrat *vitio gentisque suoque.*
>
> *Well might that face inflame him, and beside*
> *Inherent lust a secret spur applied;*
> *For Thracian blood runs hot, to passion prone,*
> *And racial fires were added to his own.*

Tereus' terrible *libido* is what uses and perverts the strong sisterly affection of Procne and Philomela as well as the goodwill of their father, King Pandion. In consequence Procne and Philomela are transformed and degraded into mere incarnations of vengeance. All they can do is to express their inhuman hostility to Tereus. The internecine conflict is thus appropriately perpetuated in an animal form (VI, 666–73):

> Nunc sequitur [i.e. Tereus] nudo genitas Pandione ferro.
> *Corpora Cecropidum pennis pendere putares:*
> *Pendebant pennis.* Quarum petit altera silvas,
> altera tecta subit; *neque adhuc de pectore caedis*
> *excessere notae, signataque sanguine pluma est.*
> Ille *dolore suo poenaeque cupidine velox*
> *vertitur in volucrem,* cui stant in vertice cristae,
> prominet immodicum pro longa cuspide rostrum.
>
> *Last, on the sisters with a sword he sprang:*
> *Their forms in air on pinions seemed to hang;*
> *And hang they did: one seeks the woodland leaves,*
> *The other makes her mansion in the eaves.*
> *The plumage of their breasts, which still retain*
> *The marks of murder, shows a crimson stain.*
> *Tereus, by grief and lust of vengeance spurred,*
> *In mid-pursuit became a crested bird,*
> *Hoopoe by name, that, with his freakish bill,*
> *So long and slender, looks the swordsman still.*

It is difficult to reconstruct exactly what Ovid did to the original tragedy he used for this episode: it is certainly Sophocles' *Tereus* or some later version of it.[1] But Sophocles himself was, in all probability, influenced by Euripides' *Medea* (the *Tereus* is almost surely posterior to 431 B.C.). In any event, the Euripidean inspiration of Ovid is clear (especially in the child-killing scene). Ignazio Cazzaniga has ably discussed the source problem and has reached the conclusion that Ovid's *Tereus* reveals two styles: that of the *novella* or Hellenistic *epyllion* in VI, 424–586; and that of tragedy in the final portion (587–674). But this is to measure a highly wrought and unified work of art by a quite external standard which takes no account of Ovid's artistic purpose. In the first part of the *Tereus* (424–586) Procne appears only for a moment at the beginning; it is almost wholly the story of Tereus' *libido* and Philomela's agony. In the second part, Procne dominates the scene: it is she who frees Philomela, plots the revenge, murders the little Itys, and prepares the terrible meal. But the reason for the shift of emphasis as well as of scene is perfectly clear: the transformation of Procne's character (the turning of her love into implacable hate; the souring of her maternal feelings) is solely due to the fatal *libido* of Tereus. It is this that destroys her humanity. The final tragedy would be both unintelligible and grotesque without an explanation of its cause. It is the love of the two sisters, the horror of Tereus' *libido*, the callous brutality of the rape, that explain the murder of Itys and the terrible banquet.

The story starts (424 ff.) with the self-deception of all the major characters. Tereus and Procne are happy in their marriage and in their new son, Itys. To such a degree is reality hidden by appearance: *usque adeo latet utilitas* (438). What sets the tragedy in motion is Procne's affection for her sister, Philomela. She cozens her husband (*blandita viro*) to let Philomela pay her a visit. This will be his great gift to her (VI, 443–4):

> magni mihi muneris instar
> germanam vidisse dabis.

[1] See Appendix, pp. 406 f.

Husband, I want no gift, but grant instead
My fondest wish, to see my sister dear.

Tereus complies at once: everything indicates the perfect confidence of husband and wife in each other. But the first sight of Philomela (*ecce venit...Philomela*, 451) awakens his innate *libido*. This is represented as a fatal and overmastering force that breaks out at once and can only with great difficulty be concealed. It takes at first the ironical form of husbandly consideration: Tereus piously pretends to abet his wife's affection for her sister (473–4):

> ipso sceleris molimine Tereus
> creditur esse pius laudemque a crimine sumit.

> *Tereus draws credit from his guilt, and seems*
> *True husband, while he lays his treacherous schemes.*

Ovid is here both empathetic (he reads Tereus' feelings and thoughts) and disapproving: he implicitly condemns the cruel *libido* in almost every turn of phrase; and he condemns it also in the most explicit language. Tereus even envisages Philomela's pleading endearments to her aged father as lustfully transferred to himself (481–2):

> et quotiens amplectitur illa parentem
> esse parens vellet; *neque enim minus impius esset.*

> *and every time she embraces her father, the father would he be!*
> *And had he been her father, he would have been no less*
> *persistent in his impious design.*

He would have felt no differently if he had been her father! Such is the shamelessness of his passion. The moving plea of the father himself (496 ff.) heightens the irony.

The actual rape—its delay, its secrecy, its union of brutal violence with defenceless innocence (the lamb and the dog, the dove and the eagle, 527 ff.)—is told in such a way as to emphasize the difference between Tereus' complete destruction of everybody's security (*omnia turbasti* is what the ravaged Philomela tells him,

536) and his futile attempt to hide the fact. The *glossotomia* or tongue-cutting (Tereus severs Philomela's tongue with forceps and sword) is in itself grotesque, but it is necessary for the future tragedy: Procne must learn the truth while Tereus still thinks that his cruel stratagem has kept it hidden. Philomela's web is the symbol, as it were, of dumb innocence made articulate.

The action now (587) mounts rapidly to the tragic dénouement. The bacchic revel by which Procne finds and frees the imprisoned Philomela recalls the Pentheus-motif, but it echoes even more directly the Ino-motif: a counterfeit bacchic madness with a child-murder. But here all the characters are human and the vengeance is both human and conscious: Procne kills the little Itys in cold blood. The motivation of the murder is brilliantly conceived and seems, so far as we can tell, an invention of Ovid himself. Procne's feelings, just like those of Medea (Ovid certainly had Euripides in mind), are divided between desire for revenge and maternal love for the child. But it is not Tereus' unfaithfulness; it is his cruelly libidinous nature, so horribly and suddenly revealed, that disgusts Procne with the very thought of their former relations and thus completely sours her feelings for her and *his* child. Itys resembles his father!

> Ad matrem veniebat Itys. Quid possit, ab illo
> admonita est oculisque tuens immitibus '*a, quam
> es similis patri!*' dixit (620–2).

> *Hard on her speech came Itys, and she drew*
> *Suggestion from the child, what she might do.*
> *She looked with eyes unsoftened. 'Ah,' said she,*
> *'How well the father in the son I see.'*

It is the fact that Itys can speak and the tongueless Philomela cannot which finally decides Procne (632 ff.). Everything in Itys reminds her of his father's lust and brutality. Her pity is thus stopped at its source. Here the importance of the first part of the episode is manifest: had we not been apprised of Tereus' *libido*, the extent to which it had abused every human obligation and feeling and severed every emotional tie with the past, we could scarcely account for Procne's action at all. The cogency of this child-murder seems far superior to that of Euripides' *Medea*.

But Procne has now herself descended to a sub-human level. Her vengeance shows deterioration of character to a far greater degree than that of Euripides' Hecuba. She no longer cares for Itys' cry of 'mater, mater'; she even strikes him as he tries to embrace her and does not hide her face from the blow (641–2):

> Ense ferit Procne, lateri qua pectus adhaeret,
> nec vultum vertit. *The sword she coldly eyed,*
> *And struck 'twixt rib and breastbone, through his side.*

In the end she becomes a virtual fiend like Tereus himself. Just as he could hardly contain his *libido* (467, *iamque moras male fert*, etc.), so she cannot dissimulate her savage exultation at the horrible meal (653–4):

> Dissimulare nequit crudelia gaudia Procne:
> iamque suae cupiens existere nuntia cladis...

Procne cannot contain her cruel joy—hot now to burst forth with the announcement of her crime.

Philomela is much the same (658–60):

> Prosiluit Ityosque caput Philomela cruentum
> misit in ora patris nec tempore maluit ullo
> posse loqui et mentis testari gaudia dictis.

> *Philomela sprang, and sped*
> *Full in his face the infant's bleeding head.*
> *If e'er she craved the common speech of men*
> *To put her joy in words, she craved it then.*

There could be but one ending for this dehumanized trio: the metamorphosis that in effect ratified the animality to which they had already descended. It is a solution of their catastrophe as well as a perpetuation of it. The eternal enmity of Tereus to Procne and

Philomela is transferred to the eternal enmity of the birds they became.

Ovid had now fully launched the motif of erotic *pathos*. This motif had been anticipated in the previous sections, but the emphasis there had been on the *gods'* amours or vengeances. The more or less human stories put in by way of contrast were but premonitions of the true *pathos* to come. Pyramus and Thisbe were only youthful victims of an accident; Salmacis a somewhat unusual nymph; Echo and Narcissus a little beneath or above the level of ordinary humanity; Niobe had undergone a metamorphosis that resembled those of this episode, but the story of Niobe as a whole is of divine, not human, vengeance. The *Tereus–Procne*, however, combines *eros*, *pathos* and metamorphosis in one unified *human* action. This is the true amatory-*pathos* that we have defined above (p. 206). Ovid's problem now was to vary and develop it: to transfer the *libido* from the man to the woman; to change the tragic-dramatic form into neoteric-epylliac and epic forms; to give a quite different nuance to the *libido* itself. It is most instructive to see how he did this.

The *Tereus–Procne* is the last important episode of Book VI. The brief forty-seven lines that remain in the book take us from Pandion's Athens to the Argonauts. Book VII almost immediately (9 ff.) introduces Medea. But, as we have seen, Ovid had no intention of retelling the tragedy of Medea (the child-murder, etc.). He had told it before (elliptically in the *Heroides*, fully in his own dramatic version) and, in any event, had no intention of immediately repeating a motif (the child-murder) almost identical with that of the preceding *Tereus–Procne*. Nevertheless, he surely counted on his readers' perceiving the identity. Indeed, he refers to the child-murder in a brief sentence later on (396–7). This enabled him to make a transition from the male to the female *libido* and from one type of tragic motivation to another. It is by emphasizing the *difference in similarity* (here the *different* motives of the *similar* child-murders) that he effected a major variation of his dominant theme.

Procne was once the loving wife of Tereus as we are explicitly told. But Ovid's emphasis is wholly on the cruel, disruptive *libido* of Tereus and on Procne's affection for her sister. It is not sexual jealousy but resentment of Tereus' brutal assault on Philomela that makes Procne avenge herself by the child-murder. In the Medea story the motivation is the other way around: she is the 'woman scorned'; her great passion has been flouted; her devotion callously ignored. It is not what Jason had done to another woman, but what he has done to her which motivates her vengeance. This is why the love itself—especially its inception and conquest of all countervailing forces—is so essential to the story. With Medea, in other words, the *libido* shifts from the man to the woman, and the vengeance is a direct outgrowth of the *libido*, not an external reaction to it as with Procne. By repeating the Euripidean soliloquy in which Medea persuades herself to yield her *pudor* to her *amor*, her better part to her worse, Ovid prepares the reader for later instances of female *libido* triumphant over all ordinary morality and custom. But, as we have seen above, he only prepares or *suggests*. He cuts off the tragedy before it has really begun and he diminishes the tragic note by introducing an element of parody and humour. Medea directly introduces not another erotic episode but a series of magical rejuvenations which are meant to stand in contrast with the major amatory-pathetic theme.

But the amatory theme recurs with the Cephalus–Procris episode at the end of Book VII. Here the major emphasis is again on the woman (Procris), though the man (Cephalus) is also prominent. The *pathos* is, of course, muted (Procris dies but only after being reassured of Cephalus' constancy) and the metamorphosis is omitted. Cephalus, who survives, can speak of the sad event as something in the past: he still has his own heroic role to play. The episode is thus not at all comparable to the five major stories of *pathos*. But it still carries on the amatory motif (in its muted way) and introduces a new variation of it: the theme of *frustrated mutual love*. This was not present in the *Tereus–Procne*: it will only emerge fully in the concluding *Ceyx–Alcyone*.

With the beginning of Book VIII, however, we are introduced to Scylla.[1] This episode is very close to the form of a neoteric *epyllion*, though greatly abbreviated (151 lines). Ovid clearly wished to defer a complete or rounded example of the genre until the later *Byblis* and *Myrrha*. He knew he could not repeat his effects too often and that Scylla was too commonplace, too familiar, for lengthy treatment. But her story, nevertheless, marked an intermediate stage of the motif-transformation which his *Medea* had begun. The Euripidean monologue (an 'auto-*suasoria*' much like that of his *Heroides*) is now completed by a criminal act: the act in turn necessitates the metamorphosis. Both Scylla and her ruined father, Nisus, perpetuate their hostility in animal form. Furthermore a new motif (merely hinted at with Medea)—that of the frustrated female *libido*—is now introduced.

The pathetic and amatory themes are kept alive in the *Althaea* and *Deianira* portions of the central panel which almost immediately follows the Scylla episode (after the brief interlude of Daedalus and Icarus) and takes up the second half of Book VIII and the first half of Book IX. But the amatory theme is muted, since Ovid was still saving it for the major episodes to come. He wanted an epic, not an amatory, subject-matter at this point in the poem. Althaea is Meleager's mother and she is not torn between erotic *amor* and *pudor* but between maternal and fraternal love, while the description of Deianira's sexual jealousy (so directly akin to that of Medea) is greatly abbreviated.

It is only after the central panel (the long description of Hercules' apotheosis and the brief Dryope episode which in some sense corresponds to the Icarus story of the first half of the section) that Ovid finally relates *at full length* (219 lines) an amatory *pathos* in which a frustrated female *libido* dominates the narrative. But the *Byblis* is also an extremely subtle variation of the theme. The principal change that Ovid seems to have made in his sources is the omission of Byblis' suicide or attempted suicide.[2]

[1] See the discussion of this episode (Scylla) on pp. 62 f. above.
[2] See Appendix, p. 415.

The metamorphosis is represented as the *direct* consequence of her sexual frustration. This in turn is related to the Euripidean–Apollonian *pudor–amor* motif in a thoroughly novel manner that is certainly Ovid's own invention.

Byblis is represented at the beginning as prey to an emotion (her *libido* toward her brother Caunus) that she does not consciously realize (IX, 464–5):

> Sed nondum manifesta sibi est nullumque sub illo
> igne facit votum: verum tamen aestuat intus.

> *Yet, ignorant of herself, repressed her fires,*
> *And let no prayers express her real desires.*

The truth is not very deeply hidden: she shows it when she urges her brother to call her *Byblis* rather than *soror* (497). But as long as she is awake (*vigilans*), her conscious mind refuses to entertain the *spes obscenas*. Sleep, however, lets down her guard: she emerges from a vivid sexual dream into full awareness of her condition.

Ovid now gives us her thoughts in a very significant variation of the usual Euripidean 'auto-*suasoria*'. What weight should Byblis attach to her dream?

> Quid mihi significant ergo mea visa? Quod autem
> somnia pondus habent? An habent et somnia pondus?
> (495–6)

> *Yet, if so,*
> *What mean my dreams? Are dreams of weight, or no?*

The obvious moral answer, of course, is to deny any veracity to such incestuous images: *Di melius!* But the word 'gods' (*Di*) at once suggests that gods were not subject to such scruples with their own sisters: *di nempe suas habuere sorores.* But the proper answer again is that gods have their own laws which are quite different from those of mortals. The only right choice for Byblis is between self-denial and suicide. But she immediately proceeds to the reflection that this is really a matter for the two of them (herself and her brother) to decide. Yet this is a faint hope: she knows that her brother will probably look on her desire as a crime (*scelus*). But then, examples of other sisters who loved their brothers come immediately to mind. This thought, however, makes her once more turn back on herself: where did she get it? (*unde sed hos novi?*). Where are her desires actually taking her? A slight renewal of moral resistance at this point is nevertheless once more dissipated by the thought of her brother: would she *resist* his advances if *he* were shaken by love as she is? She knows she would not. Why then should she not actively seek what she would passively grant? It is only at this moment that the familiar duel of *pudor* with *amor* is mentioned. She now knows what she wants; she wants to bend her brother's will to hers. But can she actually dare broach the subject to him? She communes with herself (IX, 514–16):

> poterisne loqui? Poterisne fateri?
> Coget *amor*: potero. Vel, si *pudor* ora tenebit,
> littera celatos arcana fatebitur ignis.

> *But can you make confession? Dare you speak?—*
> *Love will compel: if shame my lips repress,*
> *A letter shall my secret fires confess.*

Her *pudor*, in other words, is to be satisfied by a procedure that will soften the shock of its violation. A question of morality has quickly become only a question of strategy. The fluid sophistry of this monologue—it is one of the cleverest in Ovid—contains, however, ominous elements: the ease with which Byblis has persuaded herself, her actual blindness to reality. She has concealed from herself the true meaning of her letter: it is not *pudor* at all but only a fatal facsimile of it.

The letter itself is, in fact, the second step in her downfall. The *pudor* is now strangely mixed with audacity: *in vultu est audacia mixta pudori* (527). And what she writes is not (like her monologue) a mixture of *libido* and moral reluctance but an artful piece of special pleading. She dwells on her scruples and her terrible struggle with her feelings (which is, of course, the exact opposite of the truth). She mentions once more the example of the gods, but now without any moral qualification. She advocates enticingly the recklessness appropriate to youth even though she quite inconsistently dwells on the *safety* of the proposed *liaison* (after all they are brother and sister and have so many opportunities to get together!). She leaves her strongest argument, a very commonplace one, for the close: she must die if he refuses! The sophistry of all this is equalled only by its folly: Byblis has blinded herself to the true character of both her brother and her action. Her precipitancy and cleverness have made her flippant as well as immoral.

The actual transmission of the letter, however, is a difficult moment. She can hardly bring herself to tell the slave that it must be carried to her—brother. But her *pudor* is now rapidly ebbing. Even the evil omen of the tablet's fall (it slips from her hands as she gives it to the slave) does not deter her: *misit tamen.*

Ovid does not describe the brother's character, but he is obviously meant to be a kind of Hippolytus, the very last person to sympathize with Byblis' desires or arguments. The ferocity of his reaction to the letter stuns her and finally forces her to recognize her folly (moralizing of 585 ff.). But it also provides her with one more excuse. She recognizes that she should not have begun, only to draw the corollary that she cannot turn back (IX, 618–19):

> Nam primum, si facta mihi revocare liceret,
> non coepisse fuit: coepta expugnare secundum est.

> *Best not begin, could I the past undo;*
> *But once begun, best see the contest through.*

Thus she sets in motion the last act of her tragedy: *cum pigeat temptasse, libet temptare.* She gradually abandons all restraint and finally makes herself such a nuisance that her brother, in self-defence, has to flee his own home and country (633, *mox ubi finis abest, patriam fugit ille nefasque*). This brings on the dénouement. In her madness she publicly admits her love and shamelessly tries to track her brother down, howling and shrieking like a wild bacchante. Finally exhausted by her fruitless pursuit, she comes,

220

at the autumn leaf-fall, to a strange country: there she collapses in tears on the ground and refuses to move, to listen to the words by which the kindly local nymphs try to keep her alive. She literally dissolves—like ice in the spring sun—and instead of a weeping woman becomes the fountain that still retains her name.

Ovid has thus depicted the relentless process of self-deception in a rather weak, if clever, woman. The sophistries, in effect, grow with their lack of success: each failure is an argument for another attempt. Finally there is nothing left but physical pursuit and its necessary end. It has all the aspects of a true drama. One step leads fatally to the next. But the materials of which the drama is made are quite commonplace and rather trite: the Euripidean monologue, the seduction letter (a *suasoria* like many of the *Heroides*), the Hippolytus motif, the very ordinary metamorphosis. Yet Ovid has used them in a quite original way. His effective separation of the two initial *suasoriae* (Byblis' monologue and the letter) and his employment of the *amor–pudor* motif as the means of introducing the letter, his treatment of the effect of failure on Byblis' *libido* (especially in her second monologue) and his transformation of a quite ordinary suicide–metamorphosis sequence into a metamorphosis that grows with some inevitability out of Byblis' plight and condition—all compose a smoothly continuous narrative of great psychological cogency and finesse. Furthermore, Ovid has made the three *suasoriae* (Byblis' two soliloquies and the letter) actually contribute to the action of the story: for it is here Byblis, not Ovid himself, who is too clever. The ingenuity with which she convinces herself is the very means by which she brings about the tragedy. In the *Heroides*, the *suasoriae* are static and cloying: here they are integral to a constantly moving drama.

No other episode of the *Metamorphoses* indicates so clearly the long way that Ovid had come from elegiac and neoteric narrative: most of the *Byblis*' components are to be found in his amatory poems, but the thing that makes it move, makes it a true narrative and drama, is precisely its non-elegiac or epic continuity, the fitting of the neoteric motifs into an 'empathetic continuum' that is essentially dramatic. The *suasoriae* and the stock motifs are not isolated but are related to each other within the ongoing consciousness of Byblis herself. The narrative proper reveals exactly the same subjectivity as the soliloquies. In the lines that intervene between the soliloquy (in which she finally decides to approach Caunus by letter) and the letter itself (IX, 517–34),

Hoc placet, *haec dubiam vicit sententia mentem.*
In latus erigitur, cubitoque innixa sinistro
'viderit: insanos' inquit 'fateamur amores.
Ei mihi! Quo labor? Quem mens mea concipit ignem?'
Et meditata manu componit verba trementi.
Dextra tenet ferrum, vacuam tenet altera ceram.
Incipit, et dubitat: scribit, damnatque tabellas:
et notat, et delet: mutat *culpatque probatque:*
inque vicem sumptas ponit positasque resumit.
Quid velit, ignorat; quicquid factura videtur,
displicet: in vultu est *audacia mixta pudori.*
Scripta 'soror' fuerat: *visum est delere sororem*
verbaque correctis incidere talia ceris:
'Quam, nisi tu dederis, non est habitura salutem,
hanc tibi mittit amans: pudet, a! pudet edere nomen.
Et si, quid cupiam, quaeris, sine nomine vellem
posset agi mea causa meo, nec cognita Byblis
ante forem, quam spes votorum certa fuisset', etc.

There came decision: there her waverings fled;
And, rising on one elbow, thus she said:
'Yes, he shall judge: let this my love be writ—
This madness rather. Woe is me, what pit
Is at my feet, what fire is in my brain!'
With this resolve she sinks in thought again;
Puts word to word, with hands that shake the while
(Her left the wax, her right hand holds the style);
Begins, and pauses; writes, and then rejects;
Marks, and erases; likes, dislikes, corrects;
Lays down her tablets, takes them up anew;

What's in her mind can scarce herself construe;
About to act, abandons her intent;
Shame in her face appears with boldness blent.
She writes: 'Your sister'; then scores out the words,
And on the amended wax these lines records:
'One sends you health, who loves you—health that she,
Save by your gift, herself shall never see.
To tell you who I am, is shame on shame:
Ah, could my suit be heard without my name!
A stranger still, not Byblis, would I be,
Till prayers have proof, and hopes are certainty',

there is no break between what Ovid says about Byblis' feelings
and the feelings themselves. We see exactly how the troubled
mind of her previous soliloquy is brought to the point of composing the difficult message. The same thing is true of the transition
between the dream and the soliloquy (IX, 468–75):

Spes tamen obscenas animo demittere non est
ausa suo vigilans: placida resoluta quiete
saepe videt, quod amat. Visa est quoque iungere fratri
corpus; et erubuit, quamvis sopita iacebat.
Somnus abit. Silet illa diu repetitque quietis
ipsa suae speciem *dubiaque ita mente profatur:*
'Me miseram! Tacitae quid vult sibi noctis imago?
Quam nolim rata sit! Cur haec ego somnia vidi?'

She watched her waking thoughts, and did not dare
To let unlawful hopes have entrance there;
But, when relaxed in sleep's passivity,
The object of her love would often see,
And dream she clasped him too, and, as she lay
In sleep, she blushed; then, waking, long would stay
In silent thought, conning her dream; then sighed,
Perplexed in mind, and, 'Woe is me!' she cried;
'What means this dream? Why was it given to me,
Who ne'er would wish it true, this dream to see?'

Again, just as in the *Scylla*, the action continues through the soliloquies into the third-personal narrative: there is no real difference between the poet's empathetic penetration of Byblis' mind and his direct reproduction of it in her own words. From the dream to the soliloquy and the soliloquy to the letter, from the letter to the dispatch of the letter, etc. there runs an empathetic continuum which is not broken. It is only at the end that we see Byblis, as it were, from without, but this is because there is now no distinction between her internal emotions and her external acts: she has reached a stage of passion in which she does not care who knows what she is or what she does (IX, 635-44):

> Tum vero maestam tota Miletida mente
> *defecisse* ferunt, tum vero a pectore vestem
> diripuit planxitque suos furibunda lacertos.
> *Iamque palam est demens inconcessamque fatetur*
> *spem Veneris*; sine qua patriam invisosque Penates
> deserit et profugi sequitur vestigia fratris;
> utque tuo motae, proles Semeleia, thyrso
> Ismariae celebrant repetita triennia bacchae:
> Byblida non aliter latos *ululasse* per agros
> Bubasides *videre* nurus.[1]

> *Ah, then did Byblis, wholly dispossessed*
> *Of reason, tear her clothes and beat her breast;*
> *And raving now with madness unconcealed*
> *To all the world her lawless love revealed.*
> *From native land and hateful home she fled,*
> *And followed where her brother's footsteps led.*
> *Like bacchants whom the mystic wand excites,*
> *When each third year brings round the Thracian rites,*
> *Shrieking she ran, and where Bubassus lies*
> *Amid broad fields, amazed the women's eyes.*

She is now to be seen and judged by the whole countryside as is

---

[1] *Sine qua* in l. 639 is the reading of all the MSS. (including the originals of N and possibly M) and is clearly correct: without the prospect of love, her home is hateful.

shown by the indirect discourse (*maestam...defecisse* ferunt) and the reference to external observers (*Bubasides* videre *nurus*). The difference of all this from the 'jerky' discontinuity of elegy or the immobilized *pathos* of the neoteric *epyllion* (*Ciris, Peleus–Thetis*) is striking indeed.

But the *Byblis* must also be seen in the context of the whole section. It is clearly a step in Ovid's transition from *Scylla* to *Myrrha*. Unlike the *Scylla*, there is no overt crime: her incestuous desire is fatal to herself, but she neither commits an act like Scylla's parricide nor actually consummates her incestuous *libido*. The darkest shades, the worst horrors, of incest are reserved for the *Myrrha* episode to come.

The interval between the *Byblis* and the *Myrrha* is occupied by the two miracles, *Iphis* and *Pygmalion*, and the homosexual amours of Cyparissus, Ganymede and Hyacinth, along with the framing and introductory *Orpheus–Eurydice*. We can set down the succession of motifs somewhat as follows:

(1) *Iphis* (direct contrast to Byblis: Iphis expressly rejects an unnatural *amor*).

(2) *Orpheus and Eurydice* (the theme of *thwarted mutual love* is re-introduced: this of course recalls the *Procris and Cephalus* and anti-cipates the coming *Ceyx–Alcyone*).

(3) *The Homosexual Amores* (Cyparissus, etc.) revert to the theme of unnatural love but in a quite beneficent or neutral con-text (for the gods are different: neither human passion nor morality is involved). This is an obvious 'contrast' to the sombre *Byblis, Myrrha*, etc.

(4) *Pygmalion*. He, as we have seen, is deliberately contrasted with the impure Propoetides (just as was Iphis with Byblis). We are thus ready for the much greater and more explicit contrast with *Myrrha*.

The diagram on p. 226 illustrates the whole sequence.

Thus, though these intervening stories are mainly put in for contrast with the major theme, they also suggest and anticipate its development. We are now ready for a climactic expression of the general motif (unnatural female *libido*) of the *Medea, Scylla* and *Byblis* and for a final and extreme statement of the particular *Byblis* motif (incest).

(1) Byblis (guilty and incestuous love leading to destructive metamorphosis)

(2) *Contrast:* Iphis (innocent but unnatural love miraculously justified by metamorphosis)

(3) Orpheus, Cyparissus, Ganymede, Hyacinthus (unnatural love justified by the special privilege of the gods and saved by metamorphosis)

(4) Propoetides (guilty unnatural love punished by metamorphosis)

(5) *Contrast:* Pygmalion (innocent but unnatural love miraculously justified by metamorphosis)

(6) *Myrrha* (guilty and incestuous love leading to destructive metamorphosis)

We can to some extent reconstruct the sources Ovid used for his *Myrrha*.[1] The tale is related by Antoninus Liberalis (34) and may go back to Nicander, though Antoninus does not explicitly attribute it to him. But Ovid certainly had Cinna's famous *Zmyrna* in mind. The plan of the *Zmyrna* (as we can see most especially from the *Ciris* which in part recalls the *Zmyrna*) also included a dialogue between Myrrha and her nurse. It is ultimately, of course, a reminiscence of the similar dialogue in the *Hippolytus* of Euripides. But Ovid's style was assuredly very different from that of Cinna: furthermore, the one thing he would not do was copy Cinna in a literal or slavish fashion. Thus it is certain that Ovid greatly reduced the extensive dialogue of the *Zmyrna*. Cinna, like the author of the *Ciris*, had built his *epyllion* around a single *pathos*-scene (Myrrha's long conversation with the nurse following her attempted suicide) that must have taken up a very large part of his poem. Ovid confines the scene to a relatively brief episode of his strictly continuous narrative. His emphasis is on the *horror* of Myrrha's *act* (after all Myrrha consummated her incestuous desire as Byblis did not) and on the special nuance which this gave to her metamorphosis. The episode as a whole is meant to complete and lend climax to the female *libido* and incest motifs. The *libido*,

[1] See Appendix, p. 420.

the consummation of the *libido* and the metamorphosis-solution, all reach their most extreme and, in this sense, definitive form.

Ovid strikes, at once, the proper note of horror, of sacrilege (x, 300–3):

Dira canam: procul hinc natae, procul este parentes!
aut, mea si vestras mulcebunt carmina mentes,
desit in hac mihi parte fides, nec credite factum:
vel, si credetis, facti quoque credite poenam.

A dreadful theme is mine: ye daughters, fly;
Fathers, avert your gaze, and come not nigh.
Or, if my art beguiles, let credence fail;
And think that here I tell a truthless tale;
Or, if you take the tale of guilt for true,
Believe the tale of retribution too.

He protests, perhaps, too much. Obviously he finds in such a topic a quite fair field for his poetical skill. But the difference between Byblis and Myrrha is carefully underlined. Myrrha's soliloquy (x, 320–55) does not end in the easy victory of her *libido*. She finally sees through her own self-deception (345 f.) and, though she still longs for a similar *furor* in her pious father, she knows that the longing is futile (351–5). After the usual hesitation she actually puts the rope to her neck. It is the nurse who stops the attempted suicide and then, in a scene heavily indebted to Euripides' *Hippolytus* (where the nurse is likewise the chief culprit), discovers and undertakes to abet her charge's incestuous desire. The clandestine amour between Myrrha and her unwitting father is, of course, invested with all the stock accompaniments of fatality and horror (452–4):

Ter pedis offensi signo est revocata, ter omen
funereus bubo letali carmine fecit:
it tamen.

Three times did Myrrha stumble: thrice, in vain,
That adverse omen bade her turn again;
And graveyard owls gave forth their boding strain.
Yet on she went.

The discovery of Myrrha's identity by her father leaves Myrrha no alternative but flight: she instinctively escapes her enraged father's sword. And she finally sees that her death would, in fact, pollute another realm with her accursed presence. She must abandon both the dead and the living (x, 485–7):

> sed ne violem vivosque superstes
> mortuaque exstinctos, ambobus pellite regnis,
> mutataeque mihi vitamque necemque negate.

> *But lest, if living still, a curse I shed*
> *On living men, or dying, on the dead,*
> *Ban me from both the worlds, and bidding fly*
> *My human shape, both life and death deny.*

This prayer appears also in Antoninus Liberalis and may go back to Nicander, but Ovid changed the sequence of events in Liberalis (there the father discovers the identity of his secret paramour only after the birth of her child) to show the gradual development of Myrrha's despair and *taedium vitae*. She wanders, after her discovery and escape, through the Arabian fields; it is only toward the end of her term of pregnancy that she has recourse to the desperate prayer (x, 481–3):

> tum nescia voti
> atque inter mortisque metus et taedia vitae
> est tales complexa preces.

> *in blind appeal did cry*
> *(Being tired of life, and yet afraid to die).*

Furthermore, the metamorphosis is explicitly declared to be a kind of death, a real loss of human consciousness and identity (x, 498–500):

> subsedit mersitque suos in cortice vultus.
> Quae quamquam *amisit veteres cum corpore sensus,*
> flet tamen.

> *Then in she sank, drowning her face within the bark. Though*
> *human consciousness and human body both were lost, yet still*
> *she weeps.*

Myrrha, in short, is the extreme instance of human degradation to a sub-human form. The fact that Ovid insists on her loss of consciousness, of all her self except its grief, is especially significant. He had now reached the lowest point in his narrative of unnatural *libido* and perverted desire.

But so far we have seen but one side of human passion. Tereus, Procne, Scylla, Byblis and Myrrha had been contrasted with the sad but hardly tragic Procris and Cephalus (that for this very reason lacked a metamorphosis) or with the pious Iphis and Pygmalion. But these latter stories were short 'miracles' or theodicies that hardly impinged on the real world of love and passion. The following episodes of Venus and Adonis, Atalanta and Midas were, as we have already seen, set in quite another key. In order to right the balance, to end his series of *pathē* on a more benevolent note, Ovid needed a more benevolent *amor*, one that would not separate the lovers but actually unite them in the final metamorphosis. So far, the husbands and wives of this section (Tereus–Procne, Cephalus–Procris, Orpheus–Eurydice, Atalanta–Hippomenes) had met tragic or disagreeable fates; the amorous heroines of the *libido* episodes had been unable to gain, still less to marry, the lovers they coveted. Metamorphosis simply removed their degraded humanity from an impossible existence. In short, the horrible finale of the *Myrrha*, and indeed the whole *libido* section that it brings to a climax, required a corrective or antidote: both love and metamorphosis had a deeper and greater meaning for Ovid than could be expressed by the quite negative episodes of Tereus, Scylla, Byblis and Myrrha.

Furthermore, the arrangement of the second half of the section (after the central panel) indicates clearly the necessity of a quite considerable erotic episode at its end. Here we have:

Central Panel

Byblis

Iphis–Homosexual Amores–Pygmalion Sequence

Myrrha

Atalanta–Venus–Adonis–Midas Sequence

The two sequences, each of exactly the same length (429 lines), are obviously designed as contrast to the central panel and the two *pathos* episodes of Byblis and Myrrha. But Ovid would hardly have *ended* with a contrast section. Just as the Avenging Gods section began with the Actaeon story and ended with Niobe and the Lycian Peasants, so here also the initial episode of *pathos* (Tereus–Procne) required a comparable ending in the same style. Furthermore, the relative length of the two contrast-sequences (858 lines) demanded that the final *pathos* episode be of considerable size and prominence: the balance of the whole section had to be maintained.

Nor could Ovid end the section on a feeble or uncertain note. The *Europa* episode of the first and the *Niobe* of the second sections had set, as it were, their seal on all that had gone before: they occupied the final or climactic positions because they were in fact the climaxes of their sections. Hence the obvious importance of the episode that was designed to conclude the longest and most pivotal of all the sections. The *Ceyx–Alcyone* is, in fact, so significant that we must devote a whole chapter to its elucidation.

CHAPTER VII

THE PATHOS OF LOVE: II

THE *Ceyx and Alcyone* comes at the very end of Book XI almost as part of the transition to Troy and to the 'historical' events of the last four books. But neither the story of Peleus that immediately precedes it nor the story of Aesacus that immediately follows it (and ends the book) is in the least heroic or historical. They concern primarily the love of Peleus for Thetis; the love of Aesacus for the nymph Hesperie. Each nicely balances the other: the violent courtship of Peleus is successful; that of Aesacus is catastrophic. They constitute, in short, a pair of end-pieces that are meant to set off the mighty epic that lies between them. Their brief reversion to the themes of the *Divine Comedy* (the love of gods and mortals, the pursuit of a timorous nymph) provides the appropriate contrast to the *Ceyx–Alcyone*. The ensemble (the *Ceyx–Alcyone* with the framing *Peleus and Thetis* and *Aesacus*) immediately follows the long Atalanta–Venus–Adonis–Midas sequence. It thus in effect 'corresponds' to the *Myrrha* episode that had in its turn followed the exactly parallel Iphis–Orpheus–Pygmalion sequence. Both the position (at the end of the section) and the elaborate framing of the *Ceyx–Alcyone* indicate its relative importance. This is also shown by its mere length (338 lines), for it is, after the *Phaethon*, the longest single episode of the poem.

Ovid really gives us the major clue to its meaning in the preliminary liaison that connects it with the brief *Peleus–Thetis* episode. Peleus, an exile polluted by the murder of his brother Phocus, comes to Trachis, Ceyx's kingdom, for asylum. There Ceyx receives him with great politeness but also explains that he cannot entertain him as he would like. For a great sorrow has come to the land of Trachis: the sad fate of Ceyx's niece, Chione, and of her father, his own brother, Daedalion. Chione (Ceyx tells the story) had abused her relation to Apollo and even boasted of her own superiority to the goddess Diana (*quae se praeferre Dianae | sustinuit*). Her consequent death (from Diana's arrow in her impious tongue) then provoked Daedalion's attempted suicide and metamorphosis into a hawk. The attribution of the Chione-narrative to Ceyx, as well as some of its details, are obvious inventions of Ovid. He makes Ceyx express grief and shock over Chione's behaviour in order to indicate clearly that he is *not* attributing a like behaviour to Ceyx himself. In short, Ovid here emphasizes his quite deliberate divergence from his source or from the usual Ceyx–Alcyone legend heretofore known.

We know that Nicander included the story in his *Heteroioumena*.[1] The version he presumably followed can be found in Apollodorus, Eustathius and the Homeric scholia: it makes Ceyx and Alcyone jointly guilty of an impiety very like that of Chione. They call each other Zeus and Hera and altogether display a most improper pride which is then punished by their metamorphosis into sea-birds or halcyons. But another version exists (we find it in pseudo-Lucian's *Halkyon*, Theocritus and Dionysius Paraphrastor) that makes the metamorphosis a direct result of Alcyone's *grief* over Ceyx's accidental drowning in a sea-storm. Actually, however, it seems most likely that the version which Ovid had in mind and which, very likely, Cicero had used in his *Alcyones*, united the impiety with the drowning as they are in fact united in a scholium on the *Birds* of Aristophanes (l. 250). Here the couple's impiety is punished by the sea-storm that drowns Ceyx, but the metamorphosis itself is represented as an act of divine pity for the inconsolable Alcyone. That Ovid knew of the impiety (and deliberately omitted it) is shown not only by the way he attributes the Chione narrative to Ceyx but by his special emphasis, in the story proper, on Alcyone's *piety* toward Hera or Juno (XI, 578 ff.):

> *Ante tamen cunctos Iunonis templa colebat*
> proque viro, qui nullus erat, veniebat ad aras,

[1] See Appendix, p. 421 for a discussion of the sources of this episode.

utque foret sospes coniunx suus utque rediret,
optabat, etc.

She worshipped most of all at Juno's shrine,
And for her husband (now no more) would pray
That he might live, and find the homeward way.

Juno, in Ovid's version, is moved only by the religious 'uncleanness' of Alcyone's prayers for the dead: she has no enmity whatever toward Alcyone herself. Ovid obviously takes special pains
to make this clear. Thus it seems quite evident that Ovid deliberately changed a more or less typical legend of divine vengeance
into a quite different tale of human bereavement and sorrow. The
gods, in Ovid's version, have nothing to do with the tragedy.
Despite the facts that Alcyone is the daughter of the wind-god
Aeolus and that Ceyx is the son of Lucifer, neither god shows the
least interest in his disastrous death. It is only at the end of the story
that the gods show any pity at all for the unfortunate couple.

The importance of Ovid's elimination of the divine-vengeance
motif is, however, only apparent when we consider the form and
style of the whole episode. It is essentially an epic: its vocabulary,
set speeches and descriptions or *ekphraseis*, as well as its very
amplitude and symmetry, all make this plain. Furthermore, the
epic gods are still on hand: but they are not what they were in
Ovid's epic models. The great storm, so obviously based on those
of the *Aeneid* and *Odyssey*, is not attributed to some deity; the
metamorphosis is only divine by 'courtesy', so to speak. In the
final analysis, it is nature, the inanimate powers of nature, that
destroy and heal. And the 'epic' as a whole is concerned with the
cosmic sympathy or antipathy that exists between man and nature.
The contrast with Virgil and Homer is therefore sharp and
deliberate. The gods are neither naively accepted nor symbolically
transformed: they are mentioned only to be discounted. All this
makes Ovid's *Ceyx and Alcyone* a quite new creation.

The structure of the episode is obviously symmetrical and of
considerable relevance to its meaning. It falls into four parts:

The principle of balance is very clear: the *Departure* balances the *Return*; the long *storm* (Ceyx) passage balances the long *sleep-dream* (Alcyone) *ekphrasis*. But the effect and meaning of the balance will not be apparent until we have considered each part in some detail.

I   *THE DEPARTURE OF CEYX* (410–73)

The character of Alcyone is revealed to us even before the episode proper begins. When Ceyx prepares to hunt the terrible wolf with Peleus and his men, Alcyone (XI, 384–8)

> excita tumultu
> prosilit et, nondum totos ornata capillos,
> disicit hos ipsos, colloque infusa mariti,
> *mittat ut auxilium sine se*, verbisque precatur
> et lacrimis, *animasque duas ut servet in una.*

> *Alcyone rushed wildly on the scene,*
> *With hair not wholly dressed; and from the strands*
> *Already tied, she tore away the bands;*
> *And clung about her husband's neck, and so*
> *With words and weeping begged him not to go;*
> *To send without himself the needed aid,*
> *And save two lives in one.*

Her conjugal love takes the form of an excessive concern for her husband's safety. She cannot in fact disentangle her own personality from his; any physical separation is to her a premonition of death. Her affection is from the start coloured by a sense of impending tragedy.

When he decides to go overseas to consult the oracle at Delos (Delphi was then inaccessible), she re-enacts the earlier scene with an emphasis derived from her own peculiar knowledge of the winds and sea: she is the daughter of the wind-god Aeolus; she knows from personal experience (*nam novi et saepe paterna | parva domo vidi*) the nature of Ceyx's danger. Even so it is not the danger itself but the separation that she fears; death itself will be bearable in his company (XI, 441–3):

> certe iactabimur *una*,
> nec, nisi quae patiar, metuam; *pariter*que feremus,
> quidquid erit.

> *At least, while tossing with you on the brine,*
> *To present ills I shall my fears confine;*
> *At least we'll face the dangers side by side.*

But Ceyx, out of his own love for her, cannot let her run the risk: *nec vult Alcyonen in partem adhibere pericli* (447).

The three elements of the impending tragedy are thus established at its very start: Alcyone, Ceyx, and the winds and waves. She knows that her father, Aeolus, can control the winds and calm the waters if he will, but she knows also that neither she nor Ceyx can rely on him to do so (XI, 430–2):

> Neve tuum fallax animum fiducia tangat,
> quod socer Hippotades tibi sit, qui carcere fortes
> contineat ventos et, cum velit, aequora placet!

> *Let not false confidence your soul inspire,*
> *Because I call Hippotades my sire,*
> *Thinking he keeps the blasts in jail confined,*
> *And calms the surges when he has the mind.*

The debris of wrecked ships, the nameless tombs of drowned men, all indicate the pitiless inhumanity of the forces to which Ceyx is about to entrust himself (426–9). From the very start, Alcyone dismisses the possibility of any personal influence on the powers of nature: her mythological status (as Aeolus' daughter) only supplies a better reason for her terror. Thus the tension between the mythical and the natural components of the story is clear at its very beginning. Alcyone will not trust in the gods (even a father-god) but only in her own love; it is on this that she relies to prevent or at least share the calamity she foresees.

The departure of Ceyx is interesting not just because it skilfully prepares us for his future tragic return but also because it measures for us the difference between Ovid's epic and elegiac styles. Ovid had already depicted an all but identical episode (a wife's despairing witness of the gradual disappearance of a departing husband's ship) in the elegiac 'letter' of Laodamia to Protesilaus (*Heroides* 13). But Laodamia's farewell is quite commonplace: she watches the ship sail away, then falls into a heavy swoon from which it takes plenty of cold water to revive her; on coming to herself, she is so grief-stricken that she loses all interest in her coiffure or her gold-lamé dress (17–32). Alcyone, on the contrary, collapses before the ship sails (460). But she immediately revives, for she cannot allow her weakness to make her lose the last possible glimpses of her beloved: *sustulit illa | umentes oculos*. She exchanges signs with her retreating husband and, after he is no longer visible, watches the ship and, last of all, its white sails until even these have faded into the horizon. Only then does she go to her couch which of course once more revives all her emotions (XI, 472–3):

> renovat lectusque locusque
> Alcyonae lacrimas et, quae pars, admonet, absit.

Both room and couch renew Alcyone's tears and remind her how precious a part of herself is gone.

In short, Alcyone acts like the devoted wife that she is. Her feelings are, after all, *controlled* by her love. Each separate impression—Ceyx himself, the ship, the sails, the marriage couch—finds its mark in her heart. Laodamia by contrast is only histrionic: her collapse—after all her careful farewells—is obviously contrived. The specific detail is lost in a conventional pattern. Compare the lines about Alcyone (XI, 465–71),

> concussaque manu dantem sibi signa maritum
> prima videt, redditque notas; ubi terra recessit
> longius, atque oculi nequeunt cognoscere vultus,
> dum licet, insequitur fugientem lumine pinum.

Haec quoque ut haud poterat, spatio submota, videri,
vela tamen spectat summo fluitantia malo:
ut nec vela videt, vacuum petit anxia lectum

> *'twas she who first descried*
> *His signals and with waving hand replied.*
> *She watched him from the fast receding shore,*
> *Till eyes could trace the lineaments no more;*
> *Then watched the hull till that with distance fails;*
> *Then watched the masthead with its flapping sails;*
> *When sails as well were gone, she sought her bed,*

with those of Laodamia (*Heroides* 13. 17–24),

> Dum potui spectare virum, spectare iuvabat,
>   sumque tuos oculos usque secuta meis;
> ut te non poteram, poteram tua vela videre,
>   vela diu vultus detinuere meos;
> at postquam nec te nec vela fugacia vidi,
>   et quod spectarem, nil nisi pontus erat,
> lux quoque tecum abiit, tenebrisque exanguis obortis
>   succiduo dicor procubuisse genu

> *While I could watch my man, to watch you I rejoiced,*
> *following your eyes with mine to the very last. When I could*
> *see you no more, your sails I still could see; long did your sails*
> *detain my gaze. But after I saw neither you nor flying sail and*
> *nothing was left to see but ocean, the light itself went with*
> *you, my blood stopped running, darkness came upon me, my*
> *knees gave way, as they tell me, and I collapsed.*

Here the otiose pentameters correspond to the light and generic
description: Laodamia is composing an affecting farewell-scene
for Protesilaus' perusal. Alcyone preserves the dignity of true
grief which the dignity of the style (the continuous hexameters
above all) effectively reproduces.

   The function of the parting scene (the gradual disappearance of
Ceyx's ship into the ocean and Alcyone's growing consciousness
of separation from him) is of course to prepare the tragedy to

come. The winds and waves are, as Alcyone foresees, the chief
threats to both Ceyx and herself, the real third party—the main
opposition—in their drama. (The gods, for all their kinship, do
not count at all.) This parting is a faint symbol of the terrible
drama to come. It is also a forecast of Ceyx's even more terrible
return.

II THE STORM (474–572)

The emotional tone of the farewell (the dramatic crescendo) is
continued in this part of the story. No sooner have they fairly
put to sea, than the waves begin to rise and the winds to blow (XI,
480–1):

> Cum mare sub noctem tumidis albescere coepit
> fluctibus, et praeceps spirare valentius eurus.

> *The night came on; the waves grew rough and white;*
> *The wild southeaster blew with greater might.*

The continuity between Alcyone on her desolate couch and Ceyx
on his ship is expressed in the sequence (XI, 472 ff.):

> *renovat* lectusque locusque
> Alcyonae lacrimas et, quae pars, *admonet*, absit.
> Portibus *exierant*, et *moverat* aura rudentes:
> *obvertit* lateri pendentes navita remos
> cornuaque in summa *locat* arbore totaque malo, etc.

> *But lonely room, and place untenanted,*
> *Reminded her, while tears again flowed on,*
> *What precious portion of herself was gone.*
>   *The harbour cleared, a puff of wind had sprung*
> *To stir the shrouds, and soon the oars were slung.*
> *They set the yards mast-high.*

The sequence from present tense (*renovat, admonet*) to the pluperfect (*exierant, moverat*) and back to the present (*obvertit, locat*)
tells the whole story: while Alcyone weeps, Ceyx and his men
(for they *had* now put to sea) unfurl the sails: they *were already
cleaving the waves* at midpoint between land and land (*secabatur*),

when the storm *began* (*coepit*) to arrive. The succession of tenses carries us without a break from Alcyone to the storm.

But the storm is not described from the point of view of Ceyx. It is rather the captain, the sailors and above all the winds and waves that take our attention. The captain vainly tries to give orders; the sailors vainly try to trim the ship; but the forces of the storm are irresistible (XI, 484 ff.):

> Hic [the captain] *iubet: impediunt* adversae iussa *procellae,*
> *nec sinit audiri vocem fragor* aequoris ullam.
> Sponte tamen properant *alii* subducere remos,
>
> *   *   *   *   *   *   *   *   *
>
> aspera crescit hiems, omnique e parte feroces
> *bella gerunt venti.*

> *but wind and water made*
> *His orders futile, and his voice unheard;*
> *Yet all the seamen haste, and need no word.*
>
> *   *   *   *   *   *   *   *
>
> *while the tempest grew,*
> *And warring winds from every quarter blew.*

From l. 492 to l. 534 (forty-four lines) there is no mention of anything but waves, winds and sky.

The *leitmotiv* or 'key' of the storm-description is contained in the initial phrase (491): *bella gerunt venti.* This is clearly a reminiscence of Virgil's storm-winds (*Aen.* I, 82 ff.):

> *ac venti velut agmine facto,*
> qua data porta, ruunt, etc.

> *And the winds, just like an army making a sortie, rush out*
> *wherever they find a way.*

And the war of the winds is conceived (after Virgil) as a siege. Ovid's main model for the siege is, however, Homeric. In the *Battle of the Ships* (*Iliad* XV) Homer compares the Trojan assault on the banked Greek ships with that of wind-driven waves on a ship at sea (381-4) or he likens the Greek resistance to a rock against which the waves beat (617-29) or Hector's leap among the Greek defenders to a wave leaping on a storm-tossed ship while the wind thunders against the mast (623-9). This is a quite ordinary simile (we find it, for example, in Apollonius and in the seventh book of the *Aeneid*)[1] but Ovid changes its whole force and meaning by reversing its application: instead of comparing men to waves and winds he compares waves and winds to men. In fact the waves and winds are themselves the besiegers. By this shift in the simile's incidence (its reversed application and its gradual transformation into true metaphor), he literally animates the inanimate and reveals the malicious intention of the sea-storm. The prophetic suggestion of Alcyone thus becomes a reality: the true enemy is unmasked.

The whole storm-*ekphrasis* is in fact built 'around' this simile-metaphor, as the following analysis indicates:

(1) (lines 474-81). Departure and beginning of storm: *cum mare...tumidis* albescere coepit...*fluctibus et praeceps spirare valentius eurus.* (The waves and winds are not as yet invested with any true personality: the description is still quite conventional.)

(2) (lines 482-489 middle). Reaction of captain and sailors. This suggests (though still very faintly) a kind of *siege: pars* munire *latus,* etc. But the point of view is still that of the sailors.

(3) (lines 489 middle-491). As the storm rises (*aspera crescit hiems*) the *personal animus* of waves and winds is first clearly suggested: feroces | bella gerunt *venti fretaque* indignantia *miscent.*

(4) (lines 492-4). The helplessness of captain and crew: *tanta mali moles, tantoque* potentior *arte est.*

(5) (lines 495-506). Generic description of storm based largely on *Aeneid* 1: the noise (creak of ropes, shouts of men, thunder), the alternate lifting and sinking of the ship as it goes from crest to trough of each wave.

(6) (lines 507-13). The *siege* simile is now explicitly developed at some length. The simile-form, however, is still carefully preserved: the waves are only *like* battering rams, etc. (507-9):

---

[1] Cf. Apollonius, *Argonautica* II, 70 ff. and *Aeneid* VII, 586 ff.

Saepe dat ingentem fluctu latus icta fragorem:
nec levius pulsata sonat, quam ferreus olim
cum laceras aries ballistave concutit arces

The timbers, as the waves struck blow on blow,
Boomed loud—the noise of battle thunders so,
When iron rams and hurling engines pound
The fortress wall, and beat it to the ground,

and the wave-simile is, following Homer (*Iliad* xv, 630–7),
doubled by that of a lion (510):

Utque solent sumptis incursu viribus ire
pectore in arma feri protentaque tela leones

As, gathering strength for onset, lions go
Breasting the levelled lances of the foe.

But Ovid's lions, unlike Homer's, attack armed *men*, not cattle:
Ovid, in fact, seems also to recall Virgil at this point (*Aen.* ix,
551 ff.):

Ut fera, quae densa venantum saepta corona
contra tela furit, etc.

as a wild beast which a dense ring of hunters envelops, lashes
out against their weapons.

As yet, it is clear, the waves are not unalterably identified with
human besiegers. They are like besiegers *or* lions: they are,
in short, malevolent and ferocious but not fully humanized
enemies.

(7) (lines 514–23). Continuation of generic description of
storm (after Virgil and Pacuvius): the ship begins to crack and
admit the water; the rain falls in torrents; the sea rages; the sails
are drenched; total darkness alternates with vivid lightning. Here
it is the *intensification* of the storm (as compared to section 5 (lines
495–506)) that is emphasized.

(8) (lines 524–36). Now the siege-simile is much more explicitly applied and, at the end, merged into a metaphor: the
waves are now actually besiegers in their own right. Ovid starts
with the simile (524–30):

Dat...saltus intra cava texta carinae
fluctus; et *ut miles* numero praestantior omni,
cum saepe adsiluit defensae moenibus urbis,
spe potitur tandem laudisque accensus amore
inter mille viros murum tamen occupat unus:
sic ubi pulsarunt noviens latera ardua *fluctus,*
vastius insurgens *decimae* ruit *impetus undae*

Now leaping waves within the fabric fall;
And as a soldier tries, outdaring all,
Time and again to scale the guarded wall;
And then succeeding, and on glory bent,
One in a thousand, wins the battlement,
So, when nine waves against the sides were cast,
The tenth made onslaught with a surge more vast,

but then insensibly relapses into metaphor (531–2):

Nec prius *absistit fessam oppugnare carinam,*
quam *velut* in captae descendat moenia navis.

Nor stayed the assault, till, all defence worn down,
It swept the vessel like a taken town.

The *velut* is obviously an afterthought, a sort of belated concession to the simile-form. But the ensuing lines (533–4),

Pars igitur *temptabat* adhuc *invadere pinum,*
pars maris intus erat

And half the sea still strove to force a way,
And half within the hold already lay,

abandon the struggle to keep the simile: the waves are now fairly personalized. The next lines (534–6),

trepidant haud segnius *omnes,*
quam solet urbs...
atque aliis murum, trepidare, tenentibus intus

All quake, as quakes a city, when the mines
Are dug without, and foes are in the lines,

take us back to the crew (*omnes*): the *haud segnius quam* still recalls the simile-form but at the same time intensifies the *personal* character of the struggle.

(9) (lines 537–50). We now turn to the members of the crew and to Ceyx. Each, at this moment of hopelessness and despair, thinks of what is dearest to him. To Ceyx this is of course Alcyone: *Alcyone Ceyca movet, Ceycis in ore | nulla nisi Alcyone est.*

(10) (lines 551–557 middle). The victory of the besiegers is now accomplished (551–3):

> Frangitur incursu nimbosi turbinis arbor,
> frangitur et regimen, spoliisque animosa superstes
> unda, velut victrix, sinuataque despicit undas.

> *With fiercer onset now the rain-soaked blast*
> *Wrested the rudder off, and snapped the mast,*
> *And flushed with spoils the wave, which reared its crown,*
> *And, curling over, looked in triumph down.*

The wave falls on the ship like an uprooted Athos or Pindus.

(11) (lines 557 middle–569). The crew and Ceyx now meet their deaths in the water. But the waves' personality is still apparent: in default of all other auditors, Ceyx murmurs Alcyone's name to them (*ipsisque immurmurat undis*) and begs them to waft his body back to her (564):

> illius ante oculos ut agant sua corpora fluctus.

The great skill of the whole *ekphrasis* is shown principally in Ovid's fusion of three motifs (the crew, the generalized storm, the waves–wind–siege). The succession is:

(1) Introductory: crew and waves–wind before the storm (though it is clearly foreshadowed)

I
- (2) Crew (the first reaction as to a siege)
- (3) Waves–winds (the war declared)
- (4) Crew (helpless but not yet overwhelmed)

II
- (5) Storm (fully developed but not yet at peak)
- (6) Waves–winds (the great attack of the besiegers)
- (7) Storm (at peak)
- (8) Waves–winds (the final onslaught)

III
- (9) Crew (utter despair)
- (10) Waves–winds (victory)
- (11) Crew and Ceyx (final catastrophe: the plea for mercy)

After the introductory section (1), the piece falls into three main parts: the antiphonal trilogies (2, 3, 4 and 9, 10, 11) which measure the two extremes (beginning and end of the catastrophe) and the central part composed of two doublets, the second doublet accentuating and heightening the first. The action and emotion rise throughout to a climax in the last line (569):

> Frangitur et rupta mersum caput obruit unda.

It breaks and breaking overwhelms his head submerged.

The Virgilian storm passages (5, 7) give weight and body as well as setting to the duel between the *crew* and the *waves–winds*. The simile-metaphor of the siege is the primary means by which the duel is made vivid and dramatic. For Ovid, the real struggle is that of men against waves and winds; the gods are not involved. Aeolus is Ceyx's father-in-law, but he does not appear at all; as for his own father, Lucifer, he simply hides his head. This fact is significantly mentioned in a three-line epilogue that closes the whole episode (570–2):

> Lucifer obscurus, nec quem cognoscere posses,
> illa luce fuit; quoniamque excedere caelo
> non licuit, densis texit sua nubibus ora.

> *The Morning-Star [i.e. Lucifer] was dimmed, and might have gone*
> *Unrecognized, when that drear dawn came on:*
> *Forbid to leave the sky and speed his flight,*
> *He massed the clouds, and hid his face from sight.*

The contrast with Virgil's storm (*Aeneid* 1, 34–156) is marked and is surely intentional. There the sequence goes:

> (1) 34–49: Juno's motivation
> (2) 50–80: Juno summons Aeolus to release the winds
> (3) 81–91: Storm, outbreak
> (4) 92–101: Aeneas' reaction to the storm
> (5) 102–123: Storm at peak and overthrow of the ships
> (6) 124–156: Neptune intervenes and calms the winds

Virgil's emphasis is on the divine causation of the storm (Juno–

Aeolus) and its divine cessation (Neptune). The two storm-passages (3, 5) are designed to enclose Aeneas' famous speech (4) of weariness and despair (O *terque quaterque beati*, etc.). They are, so to speak, the setting for his first appearance in the poem. The symbolic significance of the storm is, as in Ovid, indicated also by a reversed Homeric simile: the comparison (148–53) of the storm to a civic riot (*seditio*) which a pious statesman proceeds (like Neptune) to calm. (In Homer, *Iliad* II, 144 ff., it is the riot that is compared to the storm.) The storm, in other words, is only meant to prevail for a moment: like all other instances of *furor* in the *Aeneid*, it is fated to disappear before divine *fatum* and human *pietas*. There can, in the nature of the case, be nothing like Ovid's sustained crescendo and catastrophic climax.[1]

The difference is clear: Virgil's storm is part of a divine–human action sequence and reflects or symbolizes the deeper forces of *pietas* and *furor* in which Aeneas is involved. The storm is raised by Juno and Aeolus only to be calmed by Neptune (just as civic and human *furor* is ultimately to be calmed by the pious Aeneas and the gods who aid him). It is all part of a scheme which is designed not so much to endanger as to test the hero's *pietas* and *virtus*. There is therefore no attempt to animate the actual winds or waves; no duel between man and the blind malevolence of nature. The real forces at work are Juno and Neptune: Aeolus and the winds (Eurus, Zephyrus, etc.) are simply their servants.

What Ovid has done, therefore, is to remove the gods from the scene. But this is not because he is writing a more or less realistic storm-piece in which the gods would be out of place, but because, on the contrary, he wants to emphasize their absence as strongly as possible. The obvious indebtedness of his Storm to Virgil's (and ultimately to Homer's)—the very fact that it is a quite deliberate epic *ekphrasis*—and the obviously intentional references to Aeolus and Lucifer (the gods are there but do not deign to appear), make his purpose quite plain. Ceyx is forsaken by the gods and abandoned to nature itself. The winds, in fact, are not represented by

[1] Cf. my *Virgil*, pp. 233 ff.

Ovid as epic personalities (like Eurus and Zephyrus in Virgil: Virgil's Neptune actually addresses them in a reproving speech, 130 ff.) but as inanimate forces (*venti, freta, fluctus, pars maris,* etc.) that take on, as it were, malevolent personal purpose (hence the inverted Homeric simile). This is obviously meant to be a surprise, a sort of paradox. Knowing Virgil, we expect a theodicy of some sort. And this in fact is precisely what Ovid found in his sources (the Aristophanes scholium): there, as we have just seen, the storm is divine punishment for Ceyx's impiety.[1] But Ovid only uses Virgil to emphasize his own very different point of view. Ceyx and Alcyone may be related to Aeolus and Lucifer: for all that, they stand quite alone against cruel forces that recognize no divine justice or law. Nothing in fact seems more hopeless and wasted than poor Ceyx's prayer, his pathetic murmuring of Alcyone's name to the waves that drown him.

III *ALCYONE'S DREAM* (573–709)

This is a typical epic piece: Juno sends Iris to the god of sleep who in turn sends a false dream to Alcyone. The passage is reminiscent of Homer (Hypnos episode of *Iliad* xv; the lying dream of *Iliad* ii), of Virgil (*Aeneid* i and v, 604 ff.) and, doubtless, of many similar scenes in Hellenistic epics. But why should Ovid now introduce the divine machinery he had so pointedly discarded in the Storm? The answer is clear, once one grasps the nature and plan of the episode. It can be analysed as follows:

(1) 573–582: Alcyone's anxiety while she is yet ignorant of Ceyx's death
(2) 583–592: Juno's charge to Iris
(3) 593–632: Iris' visit to Somnus
    (*a*) 593–615: description of Somnus' cave
    (*b*) 616–632: Iris' request
(4) 633–649: Choice and despatch of Morpheus
(5) 650–673: Morpheus' message
(6) 674–709: Alcyone's reaction and grief.

There is a definite movement from anxious ignorance (1) to

---

[1] See Appendix, p. 422.

tragic knowledge (6). But the movement is beautifully balanced around the central Somnus scene. Morpheus' message to Alcyone (5) actually fulfils the request of Juno (2). The mission of Iris (3) is paralleled and completed by the dispatch of Morpheus (4). The indirect method of action (both Juno and Somnus act by intermediaries: they meet neither each other nor Alcyone herself) serves to isolate and give remoteness to the pivotal figure of Somnus as well as to separate Alcyone and her woe from the world of Juno and Somnus. The gods remain cold and indifferent. We see this in the very first word of the episode (573):

> *Aeolis* interea tantorum ignara malorum
>
> *Aeolus' daughter, meanwhile, ignorant of these great woes*

The 'daughter of Aeolus' does not know what havoc her father's winds have wrought: Aeolus has been no help to her. She piously beseeches the gods for Ceyx's safe return—Juno beyond all others —only to incur their disdain for her unwittingly 'unclean' devotions (583 ff.):

> At dea non ultra pro functo morte rogari
> sustinet, utque manus funestas arceat aris,
> 'Iri, meae' dixit, etc.
>
> *But Juno, wearying of this wasted breath,*
> *And altars tainted with the hands of death,*
> *To Iris, trusted courier, thus did say:*

The coldness and unfeeling indifference of Juno are quite evident. Ovid has replaced the 'impiety' of the original Alcyone of his sources by almost its opposite: piety requited by divine indifference.

But this remoteness provides exactly the atmosphere he wants at this point in his narrative. Somnus lives in a deep Cimmerian cave far away from either Juno or Alcyone and from all the emotional tension of the story proper. It is the very epitome or quiet and repose, a place where no light or noise or disturbance of any kind can enter (593–602):

Mons cavus, ignavi domus et penetralia Somni:
quo numquam radiis oriens mediusve cadensve
Phoebus adire potest...

A hollow hill, the home and haunt of Sleep.
Here Phoebus never enters with his ray;

Non vigil ales ibi cristati cantibus oris
evocat Auroram, nec voce silentia rumpunt
sollicitive canes canibusve sagacior anser;
non fera, non pecudes, non moti flamine rami
humanaeve sonum reddunt convicia linguae:
muta quies habitat.

Here is no crested bird, with summons clear,
To wake the dawn; no watchdog, quick of ear,
Nor quicker goose, disturbs the silence here.
No creature, wild or tame; no bough, wind-stirred;
No tongue of man in clamour loud is heard.
Deep silence dwells.

This scene is, in short, the exact opposite of the Storm or of the
anguished and vocal farewell of Alcyone: the contrast is explicit
and carefully designed. To the boisterous rage of the tempest
(495–6):

Quippe sonant clamore viri, stridore rudentes,
undarum incursu gravis unda, tonitribus aether

The cordage creaked; the men were loud with cries,
Mid crash of wave-shocked waves, and thundering skies,

there is counterset the soporific murmur of Lethe (603–4):

Rivus aquae Lethes, per quem cum murmure labens
invitat somnos crepitantibus unda lapillis

And o'er the chattering pebbles as it flows,
The gently murmuring stream invites repose,

and Iris' exquisite invocation of Sleep (623):

Somne, quies rerum, placidissime, Somne, deorum
Sleep, restful sleep, of all the gods most kind.

To the ominous night on the ocean (521):

Caecaque nox premitur tenebris hiemisque suisque

and night was unillumed,
By its own blackness, and the storm's, engloomed;
(549):

inducta piceis e nubibus umbra
omne latet caelum, duplicataque noctis imago est

And pitch-black clouds, to hide the stars from sight,
Draw their dark veil, and night is doubly night,

there is opposed the soothing darkness of the House of Sleep (595):

nebulae caligine mixtae
exhalantur humo, dubiaeque crepuscula lucis

Here fog-soaked vapours from the ground ascend,
And baffling vision, light and darkness blend;
(606):

soporem
Nox legit et spargit per opacas umida terras

with saps of sleepy power,
Which Night collects, and scatters o'er the land.

The harsh sounds (*s, c,* especially) of the storm have been as it were regularized and tamed. Between (496)

undarum incursu gravis unda, tonitribus aether
and (604)

invitat somnos crepitantibus unda lapillis

there is much superficial similarity: each line has two spondees, followed by three dactyls; each line has *c, s, t,* and *r* sounds; each line is onomatopoeic. But the harsh elision (*undarum incursu*), the placing of the polysyllabic words (*incursu, tonitribus*), the

249

irregularity of the pauses, give the first line (496) a violent power; the even spondaic disyllable (*somnos*), the centrally placed *crepitantibus*, and the smooth, liquid dactyls of the second line all produce an effect of soothing fluidity, of soporific regularity.

But the difference of tonality between the two sections (storm and sleep) is more than a matter of sound and metric. In the storm, Ovid's humour is in abeyance: malevolence, fear, violence, tragedy, pathos are there at work. But in the sleep *ekphrasis*, a light and muted, but still indubitable, humour plays over the whole scene. The absence of dogs and the *sagacior anser* is commented upon. The squeak of doors is eliminated by the simple expedient of leaving them off (608-9):

> Ianua nec verso stridores cardine reddit:
> nulla domo tota est.
>
> *No door, lest loud upon the hinge it sound.*

The waking of Somnus is a slow and reluctant process (619-21):

> Vix oculos tollens iterumque iterumque relabens
> summaque percutiens nutanti pectora mento
> excussit tandem sibi se.
>
> *And lifting heavy lids, with toil and pain,*
> *And struggling up, and sinking back again,*
> *With nodding chin a-knocking on his chest,*
> *Shook off himself at last.*

The elaborately allegorical picture of the cave seems carefully designed to take us away from Ceyx's tragedy and Alcyone's grief into a realm of pleasing paradox and unreality.

The whole thing in fact is a trick: Morpheus is chosen by Somnus to bear the message to Alcyone because he alone can imitate men: Icelos' speciality is animal mimicry; Phantasos can only ape the inanimate. It is out of this deceptive sleep-world, however, that awareness comes to Alcyone. The tragedy which was inaugurated as well as foreseen in the fearful parting and which had reached the violent climax of Ceyx's death in the storm, had been for a time muted and pushed out of sight. The reader indeed requires the moment of repose and calm in order to appreciate and feel the concentrated emotions of the finale. The rise and fall of the tension, the rhythmic succession of violence and quiet, is the means by which Ovid achieves his major effect. So too with the contrast between the real and the unreal, the demythologized storm and the mythologized sleep. In the one, the usual divine machinery is omitted and the inanimate forces of nature—winds and waves—are by the use of simile–metaphor invested with a sort of malevolent personality. In the other, the most personal and subjective of events—the lover's dream—is deliberately objectified and clothed in the garments of epic fantasy and myth. Ovid was only able to remove us from the tense and anxious Alcyone by as it were 'depersonalizing' her own emotions and her own dream: he puts her quite outside them, indeed far away from them, until he is ready to bring her back and thus to recommence the tragic emotion that had for this magical moment been stilled.

The speech of Alcyone after the dream (684–707) corresponds of course to the last thoughts and words of Ceyx in the storm (544–69): Ceyx implores the waves to carry his body back to Alcyone; Alcyone laments her inability to join Ceyx in his death and burial. We have now reached at last that point of impasse from which the metamorphosis can logically issue. We are now ready not only for the climax of Alcyone's anguish but for her reunion with Ceyx and for the reconciliation of both with the waves and winds that have as yet revealed only the malice and cruelty of their nature.

IV *RETURN OF CEYX AND
METAMORPHOSIS* (710–48)

The last part of the episode (thirty-nine lines) is appropriately short and concentrated. It is now the morning after the terrible night of her dream: *mane erat*. Alcyone by an overwhelming impulse rushes to the shore, the same shore from which she had witnessed Ceyx's departure. But even while she is recalling this event (712–15):

Dumque moratur ibi, dumque 'hic retinacula solvit,
hoc mihi discedens dedit oscula litore' dicit,
dumque notata locis reminiscitur acta fretumque
prospicit

> *And lingering on the spot, and saying: 'This*
> *Is where he sailed, and gave the parting kiss',*
> *Each place recalling, and each incident,*
> *She saw, with gaze upon the horizon bent,...*

she sees something unexpected and new: *in liquida, spatio distante, tuetur | nescio quid quasi corpus aqua.* Now the process of his departure is ominously reversed; the recall of the earlier scene (463–71)—the gradual withdrawal of Ceyx, his ship and sails from her sight—gives, of course, added poignancy to this one: her sighting first the vague, body-like object, her subsequent recognition (as it comes nearer) that it is indeed a body, and her final knowledge that it is truly Ceyx's body, form a crescendo of rising emotion which passes naturally into action as she herself completes the reunion which Ceyx's ominous 'return' has made possible. At first there is only uncertainty and faint suspicion: *quid illud esset erat dubium.* Then the thought of what it means to be a shipwrecked sailor's wife (720–1):

> 'heu! miser,' inquit
> 'quisquis es, et si qua est coniunx tibi!'

> *'Unhappy one,' she cried, 'whoe'er you be;*
> *And if you have a wife, unhappy she.'*

Then the swift removal of all lingering doubt (722–8):

> Fit propius corpus: quod quo magis illa tuetur,
> hoc minus et minus est mentis. Iam iamque propinquae
> admotum terrae, iam quod cognoscere posset,
> cernit: erat coniunx! 'Ille est!' exclamat et una
> ora comas vestem lacerat, tendensque trementes
> ad Ceyca manus 'sic, o carissime coniunx,
> sic ad me, miserande, redis?' ait.[1]

[1] In line 723 Magnus reads: *minus est mentis sua iamque propinquae* which he thinks to have been the original reading of O (the ancestor of his MSS. M and N). But the fragment τ, F and Magnus' X MSS. (most of the so-called *deteriores*) give

Washed nearer by the tide, and closer viewed,
It caused her more and more disquietude;
Now closer, closer to the land it lies;
Now near enough, at last, to recognize.
She sees it clear: it is, it is her lord.
''Tis he', she cried; and with her nails she scored
Her face, hair, robe; then trembling hands outspread
To Ceÿx. 'Husband, is it thus', she said,
'That you return, most piteous and most dear?'

But the time for long laments and soliloquies has gone. The one brief reproach (her recollection of Ceyx's original promise to return) immediately preludes her frenzied flight to the beloved body (728–31):

'Sic ad me, miserande, redis?' ait. Adiacet undis
facta manu moles, quae primas aequoris undas
frangit et incursus quae praedelassat aquarum.
Insilit huc.

'... That you return, most piteous and most dear?'
 Hard by, a sea-wall rose, erected here
To break the sea's first anger, and withstand
And tire its strength, before it reached the strand;
On this she leapt.

But how could she hope to succeed in reaching her Ceyx? The doubt, however, is raised only to be dissolved (731):

Insilit huc, *mirumque fuit potuisse: volabat.*

On this she leapt; and—how was this?—she flew.

Her passion had, as it were, given her new power. In her grief, her plaintive crying, and her passionate skimming of the water that lies between her and Ceyx, she has taken on a form that expresses her human desire and overcomes the obstacles that had so far thwarted her love.

the text I print above. It seems to me clearly correct, cf. my remarks in *Harvard Studies in Classical Philology* 41 (1936), pp. 131–63.

(731)   volabat;
    percutiensque levem modo natis aëra pennis,
    stringebat summas ales miserabilis undas,
    dumque volat, maesto similem plenumque querellae
    ora dedere sonum tenui crepitantia rostro.

                        she flew,
    Beating the buoyant air with pinions new.
    She seemed to sorrow, as she skimmed the sea,
    And with her slender bill cried piteously.

The moment of metamorphosis defies observation: the wonder of
the bystanders is really a belated perception of the fact. The transition is so smooth, the movement from anguished attempt to
completed act is so natural, so emotionally inevitable, that there
can be no exact demarcation of before and after. We see the same
thing in the metamorphosis of Ceyx: when Alcyone reaches his
body and kisses him with her beak (739–41):

    Senserit hoc Ceyx, an vultum motibus undae
    tollere sit visus, populus *dubitabat*: at ille
    senserat

    If it was this, or movement of the wave,
    That Ceÿx felt, observers could not trace;
    But past all doubt, he seemed to lift his face.
    Ah yes, he felt it,

the moment of change is lost in the swift sequence of emotions
and events. That love should so dare, that love should so respond
to love, is the almost necessary climax of a passion that will not be
thwarted.

But in fact the real turn of events has preceded the metamorphoses. We now realize that Ceyx's request to the waves
illius ante oculos ut agant sua corpora has been in fact fulfilled, that
the malice of the storm has been transformed into sympathetic
obedience to his desire. Now there is indeed a change in the indif-

ference of nature and the gods. At last they show pity (*tandem superis miserantibus*, 741); Aeolus (748) restrains the winds so that the reunited pair can rear their young on an ocean of *halcyon* calm.

Finally, then, the trio of the opening scene (Ceyx, Alcyone and the waves–winds) have been reconciled. The storm has yielded to a blessed peace. The force of love is harmonized with the forces of the sea (743):

> Tunc quoque mansit amor nec coniugiale solutum est
> foedus in alitibus: coeunt fiuntque parentes,
> perque dies placidos hiberno tempore septem
> incubat Alcyone pendentibus aequore nidis.
> Tunc iacet unda maris.

> *Linked by a common fate, their loves still last:*
> *Between the birds the marriage bond holds fast;*
> *And in the winter, when they mate and breed,*
> *Seven days of perfect calm to storms succeed,*
> *While on the nest, amid the billows hung,*
> *Alcyone sits brooding o'er her young.*

It is the mystic moment when the powers of nature achieve a perfect harmony, when humanity finds itself at one with nature in a kind of cosmic sympathy. The idea is beautifully expressed in the *Halcyon* of Pseudo-Lucian:

CHAEREPHON: Is this the Halcyon that you are talking about? I have heard its voice before but it falls on my ear as something really strange. At least the animal emits a truly mournful sound. About how large is it, Socrates?

SOCRATES: Not large. Large however is the honour it has gained from the gods through its love for its mate. For at the birth of its young the cosmos holds the so-called Halcyon days, wonderful for their mid-winter tranquillity: today is a superlative example. Don't you see how clear it is above, how motionless and calm the whole sea is, almost like a mirror?

One can almost describe the halcyon season in the words of *Tintern Abbey*:

> that blessed mood
> In which the burthen of the mystery,
> In which the heavy and the weary weight
> Of all this unintelligible world
> Is lightened.

Here nature seems to take man to itself: the terror and ferocity of things really yield to the power of love.

This effect is accomplished not just by the ending but by the symphonic balance of the whole episode. The harsh introduction (Part I) is countered and transformed by the irenic close (Part IV). The violence of the storm is offset by the quiet in the Cave of Sleep, the malice of the storm-waves by the humanity of the waves that waft Ceyx back to Alcyone; above all the terrible separation of the lovers by their blessed reunion. But it is the theme of metamorphosis which dominates. The change of the lovers into halcyon-birds has a truly cosmic significance: the hostility of man and nature transformed by love; death made into new life; human tragedy converted to cosmic beneficence.

The symphonic rhythm of the episode—the rise and fall of emotional tone—is carefully planned. (We can represent it by the diagram on p. 257.) The two climaxes are obviously the drowning of Ceyx (the victory of the waves–winds) and Alcyone's recognition of Ceyx's body. The sleep *ekphrasis* is the dead centre of calm between them. Its dramatic and aesthetic function in the whole narrative is, as we have already seen, quite obvious. Alcyone's passionate parting from Ceyx starts an emotional crescendo that continues without a break right to the end of the storm section: the prophetic fear of the wife is immediately realized in the fate of the husband. But Alcyone's actual desolation—her conscious response to the *fact* of Ceyx's death—represents quite another emotional crescendo that obviously needed to be separated from the first by some sort of interval.

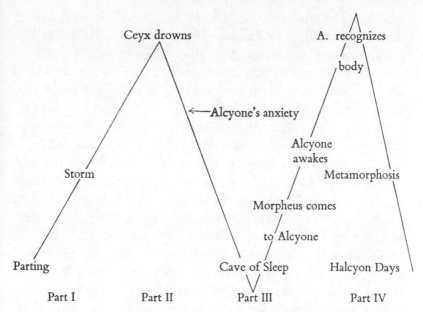

But the sleep *ekphrasis* is much more than an interval or an artful piece of contrast. It is also the one section of the episode in which the divine machinery of epic is almost ostentatiously present. It thus provides a very subtle commentary on the story as a whole. For it is, in fact, nothing but a disguised form of the divine-vengeance motif that Ovid had found in the original legend as well as in the *Aeneid* (the Storm is Juno's vengeance on Aeneas). But Ovid (as we have already seen above) had denied the impiety of Alcyone and deliberately emphasized her special devotion to Juno. Juno's motive is therefore not vengeance (in the usual sense) so much as a cruel punctiliousness (a chilling reaction to the unintended 'uncleanness' of Alcyone's sacrifices). The attitude of Juno and her messenger is clearly brought out in the bald words that Morpheus (in the role of Ceyx) speaks to Alcyone (661): *nil opis, Alcyone, nobis tua vota tulerunt!*

All that Juno wanted Alcyone to do was to stop her tiresome prayers. She shows no sense of the irony of the situation—the fact that she could use the innocent and relaxing sleep—that most placid of gods, that *quies rerum* (623)—to destroy all possibility of sleep or tranquillity for Alcyone. But the pleasantly pictorial and mildly humorous setting of *Somnus* makes a most suggestive contrast to the actual plight and grief of Alcyone. Here Ovid uses the fantasy and charm of his divine machinery to accent the cruelty and bitterness of the human tragedy. The juxtaposition of moods and tones—the violence and destructiveness of the storm, the pathos of the bereaved wife *vis-à-vis* the pretty décor of Sleep, the detached and unhurried action of the gods—brings out admirably the difference between two thought-worlds, two conceptions of the relation between gods and men. The gods do not think of men as men think of them. The Virgilian type of theodicy is suggested only to be reversed and implicitly denied.

For what, in fact, motivate the return of Ceyx and the metamorphosis are quite vague forces. Aeolus and Lucifer are mentioned at the end; the gods (plural) are said finally to have pitied the poor couple (741); but the real emphasis of the story is on the forces of nature—on the winds and the sea. It is because the waves have seemed so human—this is the effect of Ovid's reversal of the Homeric simile—that we half-believe in their change of heart and response to Ceyx's last request and see something more than a coincidence in the return of his body. And it is this that prepares us for the metamorphosis. Ceyx and Alcyone carry on, as it were, their human affection in an animal form: *tunc quoque mansit amor.* What we finally sense is no theodicy, no divine action of the usual epic sort, but a common basis of feeling in all nature. After all, Alcyone is not so much an individual as a type, a personification so to speak of the female's affection for her mate. Besides that, her human identity hardly seems to matter.

This epic, therefore, is essentially one of man in nature, one in which the ferocity (storm) and the gentleness (halcyon calm) of the sea are related to a fundamentally cosmic fact (love) pervading all realms of existence. The one supernatural scene (the Sleep *ekphrasis*) sets this in brilliant relief: we see that the fantasy world of the Olympians is not the true reality. The plastically conceived gods of the deliberately 'epic' sleep episode are indifferent; the others (Aeolus, Lucifer, the *di miserantes*) are but names for the forces of nature. The winds and the sea, the human beings and the birds, are united by a cosmic sympathy that is far more real than the fantasy of myth.

The subjective style of the narrative is, of course, essential to its blending of the human and non-human elements. The author's empathetic identification of himself with Alcyone is established in the first part (415–16):

> Consilii tamen ante sui, *fidissima*, certam
> *te* facit, Alcyone.

> *Yet first he breaks his plan to thee, Alcyone, loyallest of wives!*

It is to Ovid that Alcyone appears *fidissima*: it is *to her* that he caressingly addresses himself. His empathy with Ceyx (444 ff.) is, for obvious reasons, much less close: it is Alcyone who stands at the emotional centre of the drama. The long storm passage (II) pits, as we have seen, the ship and crew against the winds and waves. Ceyx is now lost sight of in the combat of men with the sea. But Ovid empathetically identifies himself with both. We feel the dilemma of the captain (492–3):

> pavet, nec se, qui sit status, ipse fatetur
> scire ratis rector, nec quid iubeatve vetetve[1]

> *Unnerved, the captain swears,*
> *Himself, he knows not how the vessel fares,*
> *Nor what to order,*

and we feel also the intention of the waves (524 ff.):

> *Dat* quoque iam *saltus* intra cava texta carinae
> *fluctus.* Et ut miles numero praestantior omni
> *   *   *   *   *   *   *   *
> spe potitur tandem laudisque accensus amore, etc.

> *Now leaping waves within the fabric fall;*
> *And as a soldier tries, outdaring all,*

---

[1] Here *vetetve*, the reading of the so-called *deteriores* (the Amplonianus and the Heinsius MSS.), is obviously superior to *velitve*, Magnus' O (M, N, etc.). Cf. my remarks on Heinsius and the Amplonianus in *AJP* 81 (1960), pp. 85–91.

> *Time and again to scale the guarded wall;*
> *And then succeeding, and on glory bent...*

It is only at the end of the storm that we revert to Ceyx and once more read his mind (544):

> Ceycis in ore
> nulla nisi Alcyone est; et *cum desideret unam,*
> *gaudet abesse tamen.*

> *No thought has Ceÿx but Alcyone;*
> *Upon the lips of Ceÿx none but she.*

Finally, however, the two *personae* (waves, Ceyx) come together. Because at the end he is actually merged with the waves of the sea, he can murmur to them his request for reunion with Alcyone. We then catch (beginning of Part III) one brief glimpse of Alcyone's feelings (573 ff.) only to start on the Sleep *ekphrasis.* Here, as we have seen, empathy is in abeyance: we observe rather than feel the detached actions of very remote individuals. But when Alcyone wakes, we of course revert to her (674):

> Ingemit Alcyone, etc.

The final part (IV) is intensely empathetic (711–14):

> Maesta locum repetit, de quo spectarat euntem,
> Dumque moratur ibi, dumque 'hic retinacula solvit,
> hoc mihi discedens dedit oscula litore' *dicit*
> dumque *notata locis reminiscitur acta.*

> *She sought upon the shore below*
> *The place where she had stood to watch him go;*
> *And lingering on the spot, and saying: 'This*
> *Is where he sailed, and gave the parting kiss',*
> *Each place recalling, and each incident.*

Alcyone's quoted words are insensibly merged with her thoughts: Ovid empathetically embraces both. But when she flies away as a halcyon bird, it is the watching crowd on the shore (*populus,* 740) whose feelings we share and follow. The final metamorphosis is seen from a distance through the eyes and thoughts of by-standers, for Ceyx and Alcyone have now passed from the realm

of man into the realm of nature. But the bystanders have nevertheless witnessed the unbroken continuity of Alcyone's *pathos*:
she flew *to* Ceyx; Ceyx, at her caresses, had been seen to respond.
It is Ovid's ability to penetrate the *psyche* of all these elements,
human and inhuman, that enables him to unite them in an
emotional continuum.

This episode thus represents a decisive point in Ovid's *carmen
perpetuum* of metamorphoses. He began (in Section I) with a
purely mythical conception of metamorphosis. Daphne's transformation into a laurel is merely part of an amusing story, a device
for preserving her virginity. In the *Io* and *Callisto*, the cow and
bear are but temporary disguises: the discrepancy between their
still subsisting human emotions and their animal shapes is in fact
highly amusing. Ovid does not do more than exploit the
humorous or grotesque possibilities of his myths. Much the same
thing is true of most of the Divine Vengeance episodes of Section
II. The unhappy Actaeon, for example, is a sort of Disneyish
character: his human *psyche* gives a grotesque significance to his
stag-like exterior. The Tyrrhene sailors become rather comic
dolphins. Other vengeance metamorphoses are not so much
comic as grotesque: Ovid delights in the detailed process of the
transformation. But in none does the metamorphosis really
escape its mythical and miraculous setting.

It is only with Arachne and Niobe that a new conception of
metamorphosis emerges: here the change of shape is not simply
a miraculous act of vengeance but a result of human inability to
retain the human condition. Niobe is amply punished before she
turns to stone: her petrifaction was, as we have seen, a recognition
of her incapacity to feel any more emotion. She had, in fact,
become like stone before she became a stone in reality. It is this
conception of metamorphosis (as a sort of validation of the sub-
human condition to which *pathos* has reduced a once human
being) that is fully expressed in the major amatory episodes of
Section III. Tereus, Procne and Philomela had finally sacrificed
everything to lust or to vengeance; their transformation into birds

enabled them in fact to perpetuate the quite animal emotions that dominated the end of their drama. It is much the same with Scylla and Byblis: balked of their desire, they had nothing to live for but their grief. Metamorphosis is here the only alternative to suicide. Myrrha on the other hand had forfeited her right to live or to die: only a third realm, the realm of inanimate nature, could accept her unwelcome presence.

But human love is not only pathological or criminal. In the *Iphis* and *Pygmalion*, Ovid had reversed the degenerative process of the *Scylla*, *Byblis* or *Myrrha* and rewarded the thwarted lover who refused to accept an unnatural or imperfect realization of his desire. In these stories, piety and idealism miraculously gain a normal and human satisfaction. But such miracles obviously belonged to the periphery and not the centre of his poem. The process of metamorphosis, as Ovid conceived it, was essentially one that led from the human to the animal or to the inanimate and not *vice versa*. The only great exception to this rule is that of the deified hero, the man who becomes a god, and this (save for the preparatory Hercules episodes) is reserved for the concluding part of the poem. Man, to be sure, had once emerged from a lower level (there were Deucalion's stones) but could not, in the normal course of things, repeat the process. (The Myrmidons were obviously a very special case.) It can be said, of course, that animals preceded men in the evolutionary timetable, but Ovid's perspective was not evolutionary in this sense. The mythical tradition that he inherited was thoroughly anthropomorphic: the human gave meaning to the non-human and not *vice versa*. It was, however, possible to conceive of human emotions as akin to animal or even inanimate forces. Beyond the usual anthropomorphism of mythology, there lay in fact a much more philosophic anthropomorphism by which nature as such—that is, non-mythologized nature—could be invested with human feeling or sympathy. The idea is usually thought of as Stoic (and cosmic sympathy was in fact a specifically Stoic doctrine) but it had also a general currency that went far beyond the philosophical schools themselves. Ovid, at least, seems to have used it in a poetical rather than an intellectual way. We can best express his point of view by saying that for him cosmic sympathy meant an erosion—almost an elimination—of the barrier between man and nature. The non-human or sub-human was not only a receptacle for abnormal or ruined men and women: it was also a completion or continuation of good human purposes because it shared the beneficence as well as the malice of man. This, it seems to me, is the deeper meaning of the *Ceyx and Alcyone*.

For here, though passion and catastrophe effect a reduction of the human to the animal, there is no perpetuation of hostility or other evil emotion, no mere negation of human feeling, but, instead, a victory of love, a sympathetic co-operation of nature, in the very bestowal of the animal form. The passion of Alcyone is pitted not against a recalcitrant lover, but the sea itself: it is thwarted only to triumph in the very change that seems to end its human character. What we are conscious of in the stories of Tereus and Procne, or of Scylla, Byblis and Myrrha, is a quite negative result or meaning of metamorphosis. What we see in the Pygmalion and Iphis stories is a metamorphosis that reverses nature by *force majeure* from above. In the *Ceyx and Alcyone*, on the contrary, the metamorphosis is positive and beneficent and, for all its mythical substance, a part of the very nature from which it comes. It is thus quite appropriately the climax of the long section that we have entitled *The Pathos of Love*. It marks a decisive stage in the metamorphosis of metamorphosis.

It is now time, therefore, to look back at the whole section (i.e. the whole *Pathos of Love*, Book vi, 401 to the end of Book xi)— it is certainly the heart of the *Metamorphoses*: its length as well as its position are sure indices of the importance Ovid ascribed to it— and reach some conclusions about its broader significance and meaning. Its subject is love and it is surely love that was the central theme of both the poem and the poet. We shall later be much concerned with the Augustan finale and the Augustan elements (such as the central panels of this section) that lead up to it. For the moment, however, we shall neglect the Augustan and look only at the erotic or amatory Ovid. No one, I think, can dispute the fact that it is here—in this third section—that Ovid expresses himself most fully and most decisively upon the subject with which he was most concerned and most imaginatively involved. What then *was* his conception of love and what was there about it that we can call original?

We have already indicated (Chapters II, III) some of the differences between his elegiac and his epic style and content. His release from elegy made possible a quite new kind of narrative: with the change of style and technique went also a change of content and attitude. Ovid's elegiac *amor* was tied to elegiac convention: no one could want to deny all originality to the *Amores*, *Ars* and *Heroides*, but no one can contest their obvious derivativeness. In the *Amores*, Ovid was burlesquing an old theme rather than inventing a new one. The *Ars* is a *tour de force*, a clever reduction of the *Amores* to mock-didactic.

The *Heroides* are more serious: some of them repeat motifs of the earlier poems; others are quite different from anything Ovid had done before. But he is here also treading a very well-worn path. Penelope, Phyllis, Briseis, Oenone, Hypsipyle, Ariadne and Sappho are all lorn females abandoned by or separated from their men. This was a stock motif of Hellenistic and neoteric poetry (the classic example for us is, of course, Catullus 64). Phaedra and Medea, Dido and Hermione are clever retouchings of Euripides and Virgil. Canace is more original, but the love element is there greatly subordinated to the tragedy. As for the double letters, they also add little that is new: there is no real interaction of the lovers. Paris and Helen are clever in the best style of the *Ars Amatoria*; Hero and Leander are like other separated couples, and both bewail their separation in very similar terms.[1]

In short, Ovid's elegiac love poetry is really a clever re-working of convention and tradition: the elegiac *sermo amatorius* reduced to a sort of light-hearted game (*l'amour de coquetterie*) or the Hellen-

[1] No student of Ovid's style can (as I see it) deny the genuineness of the Hero–Leander letters. It seems (at this late date) rather superfluous even to argue the point.

istic–neoteric amour reduced to the form and dimensions of a *suasoria*. There is no attempt to rethink the problem of love in a serious way.

One basic difficulty of the *Heroides* is, of course, the static situation of each heroine: this is reinforced by the letter-form, but is, as we have seen, an essential characteristic of Hellenistic–neoteric narrative. The narrative is static because the feeling it expresses is isolated and generic rather than dramatically concrete. If we dismiss such obviously untypical cases as the coquettish Helen, the faithful Penelope or the 'war widow' Laodamia, we find an essentially identical phenomenon. Euripides and, more directly, Euphorion and the New Poets, had fixed the symptoms, defined the status, of amatory passion. It comes in an instant without warning in full force and fury; it overmasters every other interest or emotion; balked of continued fulfilment, it leads only to death and catastrophe. There is, of course, a difference between the 'heroines', but it is a difference of external situation rather than of intrinsic content. Deianira, Medea and Phaedra are obviously embarked on a more desperate course than the merely despairing Oenone or Ariadne. Sappho is not the simple Canace. But their basic *pathos* is very similar. All are overmastered by love rather than by a lover. What is lacking (and it is not merely the letter-form that produces the lack) is any sense of dramatic relation between two separate personalities. *Amor* is an external, impersonal force (a kind of disease) that prostrates its victims: separation from or abandonment by the lover is itself a consequence of the love—such recklessness, such sacrifice of all else to one emotion, was made for catastrophe.

When we turn from the *Heroides* to the *Metamorphoses* we can see at once what has happened. The love is no longer static: it can still be isolated, but its isolation is now dramatically contrasted with its mutuality. Byblis no longer confines herself to one monologue or letter: both are dramatic elements in a swiftly developing tragedy of frustration. Her *libido* is not noticeably different from that of Medea, Phaedra or Canace, but we now see and feel its isolating effect: she cannot gain her desire and the attempt to do so brings her step by step to catastrophe. But Byblis, Scylla and Myrrha are set apart from Thisbe, Procris, and Alcyone. Here the original emotion—Thisbe's devotion to Pyramus, Procris' love for Cephalus, Alcyone's conjugal passion—is no *nosos* or disease, no impersonal isolating force, but an element in the drama of *two* lovers. Love, in other words, ceases to be external or impersonal in becoming both mutual and dramatic.

Nor is this just a matter of Ovid's progression from elegy to epic, from static to dramatic narrative. His values have also changed. At bottom, the *Ars* is a rather cold guide to sexual success in the *demi-monde*; the *Heroides*, a clever re-setting of Euripides. There is no real concern with the 'ethic' or 'meaning' of the familiar stories. But in the *Metamorphoses* the pathological, isolating *eros* is assessed and deliberately contrasted with the normal, human love of two mutually responsive personalities. It is actually conjugal love—the love of husband and wife—that constitutes the ethical apex of Ovid's amatory scale. And it is just here that Ovid is most original: nobody in classical or Hellenistic or previous Roman literature really anticipated him.

In Homer we have, to be sure, the moving stories of Hector and Andromache or of Odysseus and Penelope. But these are hardly amatory in any developed sense: each woman is in her way the traditional 'good' wife and the husbands, in each case, respond with admiration and affection rather than actual passion. It is only with the morally ambiguous Helen and the witch-like Circe that a strictly erotic element enters the story. Greek amatory lyric—so far as we can judge from the available remains—paid singularly little attention to the mutual passion of a man and a woman, save perhaps in the most limited sexual sense (as for example in the *Palatine Anthology*). Here the *mores* of post-Homeric Greek society must, of course, be taken into account. Of the many remarkable women of fifth-century tragedy, few or none can be said to have been engaged in a truly mutual amour. We have spoken of the pathological heroines (Medea, Phaedra) of Euripides. His good women are either nobly asexual (like Polyxena and Macaria) or nobly dutiful (like Alcestis). He, no more than Aeschylus or Sophocles, seems to have been able to depict a good and at the same time passionate union of the sexes, still less a conjugal amour that is really amorous. And here he certainly prefigured the Hellenistic love literature. We lack by far the greater part of it, but it seems probable that Apollonius' *Medea*, Theocritus' *Simaetha*, and Moschus' *Europa* are reasonably typical (even if artistically superior) instances of the Hellenistic heroine. Woman is here the victim of sexual passion: there is no true mutuality or goodness in the *pathos-nosos* that overcomes her.

The new comedy of Menander and his contemporaries only seems to be an exception. Certainly the *liaison* of some well-born son with a handsome slave-woman is often represented as a good as well as passionate thing, and justified by the discovery that the slave is after all a free, rich and marriageable girl. But the amour proper—the dramatic actuality of the love—is not very prominent. It is the intrigues, the peripeties, that make the plays. More important perhaps is the Greek love romance (which in its sources at least goes quite far back into Hellenistic times), but here also the love is rather static and the actual narrative is of the adventures and mishaps which retard the marriage till the very end of the story. Longus' *Daphnis and Chloe* is, perhaps, an exception, but it is probably very late.

The Romans, by all accounts, were quite unlike the Greeks in their valuation of heterosexual love. Yet it is remarkable how small a part this different valuation plays in Roman literature before Ovid. The New Poets and the Elegists, the lovers in Virgil's Eclogues, are not noticeably engaged in a beneficent, mutual amour. Though there are red-letter days in the amatory careers of Catullus and Propertius, they are conspicuous for their rarity. Love is a bitter fate in the elegiac book; there is no suggestion of marriage. Conjugal love is all but totally absent. The post-mortem letter of Cornelia to her husband Paullus (Prop. IV, 11) is the noble farewell of a truly Roman spouse, but it can hardly be called amatory. Nor can we make too much of Dido: there was certainly mutual passion (despite the commentators who would deny it) but the passion was clearly illicit and destructive.

It is only as we try to comprehend this background of amatory literature that we can really see the originality of Ovid. The best way, perhaps, to deepen our understanding of this is to review the alterations he made in his Hellenistic sources. These are in sum extremely revealing. We can be reasonably sure that he altered his source or sources for the *Cephalus–Procris* so as to eliminate or greatly tone down its intrigue (the game of masks) and above all its purely erotic content (the respective seductions of each spouse by the other). It seems all but certain that he changed the *Ceyx–Alcyone* from what was merely an episode of divine vengeance into a tragedy of innocent, mutual love. In both the *Iphis* and the *Pygmalion*, he seems to have been solely responsible for the idealization of the amatory element. Isis transforms Iphis not simply to protect her from a deceived father (as in the original version that Ovid used) but to consummate and justify a mutual passion that would otherwise have been unnatural or maleficent. Pygmalion is not the perverted iconophile of the Cypriot legend but the idealist who realizes his love by his very refusal to accept a sordid reality. Yet Ovid almost certainly did not make such drastic changes in his sources for the *Procne–Tereus*, *Scylla*, *Byblis* and *Myrrha*. For these, it is evident, were wholly in the Euripidean or Hellenistic–neoteric tradition. He assuredly added many touches of his own—above all the subjective-dramatic narrative—but he did not alter their essential plot or structure. In other words, he altered his plots when he needed an essentially beneficent and, above all, mutual amour; he did not alter them when he wanted the opposite, the bad amour that isolates and destroys its victim.

The reason for this is quite obvious. In the one case his sources were deficient; in the other, they were not. When he wanted a Euripidean or Hellenistic *libido* he had no lack of models to draw upon; when he wanted truly mutual or conjugal love, he had to invent it or at least wrest it from very refractory material. But why did he want such love? Why did he need to depart from his Hellenistic–neoteric originals, particularly in a section (III) cast in a Hellenistic–neoteric mould? Here we must especially consider the reciprocal relations of the amatory episodes in the section as a whole.

We can group the major amatory episodes of the first three sections in the following schema:

(1) The Divine Comedy (Daphne, Io, Europa): here the female role is simply passive; the god's almost purely sexual.

(2) The tales of the Minyades (Pyramus–Thisbe, Salmacis, Leucothoe): here we have one instance of mutual love (tragically cut short); one of sheer *libido* (with no mutuality whatsoever); one of completely isolated passion (Leucothoe wastes away because the sun-god will pay no attention to her).

(3) The Ceres–Proserpina (this is a reversion to the Divine Comedy): virginity and innocence are rudely attacked by sheer lust.

(4) Human Love: the motifs of (2) are now made central and dominant. The basic plan of this part (Section III) is:

(*a*) The Tragedy of *Libido*: a *libido* attacks a whole complex of affectional relations and dehumanizes all of them (Tereus–Procne–Philomela).

(*b*) Mutual love threatened but not finally overcome (Cephalus–Procris).

(*c*) Three neoteric episodes (Scylla, Byblis, Myrrha) in which a perverted *libido* is wholly unable to secure its object and, as a result, becomes isolated and dehumanized.

(*d*) Two contrast (to *c*) episodes (Iphis, Pygmalion) in which an innocent and pure *love* finally wins its object.

(*e*) Mutual love threatened but finally triumphant (Ceyx–Alcyone).

When we examine the correlated motifs here it becomes evident that Ovid is contrasting sheer *libido* and mutual *amor* as the negative and positive poles of his amatory system. Even in the *Ars* he was quite aware that the sexual *libido* (especially the female *libido*) could be immensely destructive (*Ars* I, 280):

> Parcior in nobis [i.e. men] nec tam furiosa libido;
> legitimum finem flamma virilis habet.

> *Our lust is milder and not so furious: masculine passion keeps its allotted bounds.*

He then cites the instances of Byblis, Myrrha, Pasiphae (at some length), Aerope, Scylla, Clytemnestra, Medea, the concubine of Amyntor, Phaedra and Eidothea. But the contrast here is not so much between male and female as between the 'legitimate' or limited goal of sexual satisfaction and the erotic fury that overrides all law and reason. Tereus in the *Metamorphoses* is as much an instance of this as Scylla, Byblis or Myrrha. The *Ars* is primarily concerned with 'gallantry' or the limited sexual *liaison*. But the *furiosa libido* of Tereus, Scylla, etc. in the *Metamorphoses* is bad not so much for its obvious consequences as for its exclusion of true mutuality. There is much more to love, as Ovid sees it, than the blind sexual urge that he depicts in Tereus, Salmacis, Byblis, etc. Tereus' *libido* in fact destroys his family and dehumanizes both himself and his victims. But its obverse in the *Metamorphoses* is not the sophisticated philandering of the *Ars* but the genuine devotion of a man and a woman. It is Pyramus and Thisbe, Procris and Cephalus, Ceyx and Alcyone who represent the Ovidian ideal: their tragedy arouses sympathy and pity, not horror or disgust; and in the *Ceyx–Alcyone* at least, their sheer devotion effects their victorious metamorphosis. To both Iphis and Pygmalion, an unnatural or venal satisfaction (homosexuality, prostitution) is quite incompatible with the mutual heterosexual affection they crave. They are rewarded because, fortunately, they are genuinely 'in love' with a worthy object and (at least in the case of Iphis) the 'object' is itself another person who fully reciprocates the love.

In this sense, indeed, the conjugal love of husband and wife is the most adequate instance of Ovid's amatory ideal. It is, of course, notoriously difficult to make a story out of such love (hence the typically romantic ending at the marriage): the conjugal love must in fact be broken and interrupted in order to retain any narrative significance. But the very interruption accentuates the mutuality. Procris and Cephalus skirt disaster by trying to prove the mutuality beyond any reasonable limit. Yet their story is still one of mutual affection and not a mere *contretemps* —a clever juxtaposition of seductions—as it was in Ovid's source.

Ceyx and Alcyone are separated by a physical mishap (the Storm) but this is, so to speak, the test of their wholly reciprocal devotion. Yet Ovid has not left out the sexual element in such love. It is only because the *libido* of the *Procris–Cephalus* and *Ceyx–Alcyone* is mutual and personal, not isolating and impersonal, that it is love and not lust. When Cephalus 'edits' the real story of Procris in order to express his true affection for her or when Alcyone (unlike Laodamia) controls her feelings at Ceyx's departure and Ceyx refuses to endanger her by the sea-voyage, we see the true nature of the tie that binds them. It is not 'romantic' in the usual sense. There is no idealization or 'spiritualizing' of the relationship. Pygmalion's statue in fact becomes a real woman whom he can and does possess: otherwise the story would revert to its original obscenity. Procris and Alcyone are simplified, yet nevertheless thoroughly human, beings. But there *is* a romantic element in another sense of the word and this is Ovid's high valuation of *love as such*. By and large, other emotions, other goals, mean little to him: Procris and Cephalus are certainly immoderate in their demand for fidelity; Alcyone seems obsessively preoccupied with the physical presence of her husband. But Ovid accepts this as the consequence of love: that love is, so to speak, 'all of life' to his characters is but a reflection of his own view. It is all of life to him. *Maiestas*, heroic glory, religious enthusiasm and all the other motives leave him cold and receive but perfunctory attention.

There can be no doubt that such a conception and valuation of love was a really new thing or, perhaps more accurately, had received from Ovid a quite new emphasis. Hellenistic, neoteric and elegiac literature was in great degree amatory: the classical epic and tragedy that the Maecenas circle tried to revive was obviously not amatory, save, perhaps, for its imitations of Euripides (and the amatory limits of Euripides we have already considered). But when Ovid put love at the centre of an epic, he did not merely combine the neoteric and classical ideals. He of course rejected the Virgilian or Augustan programme according to which the hero must relinquish and transcend love when love was in any danger of competing with his heroic and Roman motivation: but he did not on the other hand maintain the neoteric and elegiac conception of love as an illicit and catastrophic passion. Instead he put the normal, human, heterosexual love of affianced or married lovers at the centre of his poem and the apex of his amatory scale of values. It is certainly not the *libido* of Tereus or the neoteric horrors of Scylla, Byblis and Myrrha but the *Procris–Cephalus*, *Iphis*, *Pygmalion* and, above all, the *Ceyx–Alcyone* that indicate Ovid's positive or 'true' conception of love.

There are two aspects of this conception that demand our attention: its connection with metamorphosis and its characterization of the lover. We have already discussed some major characteristics of the Ovidian metamorphosis. There is, however, one point that deserves further and special notice. Ovid, as we have just seen, made his 'positive' or 'affirmative' episodes (e.g. the *Procris*, *Iphis*, *Pygmalion*, *Ceyx–Alcyone*) out of Hellenistic–neoteric tales of a very different plot and character. On the other hand, his 'negative' or 'pathological' episodes (*Tereus–Procne*, *Scylla*, *Byblis*, *Myrrha*) all end in metamorphoses that, though separately not Ovidian (they were in his sources), are nevertheless incorporated in the general sequence of episodes and metamorphoses set forth just above on p. 269. Here the *tragedy* of the libidinous Tereus is balanced by the following semi-tragedy of Procris and the victorious metamorphosis-ending of Ceyx and Alcyone at the end of the series, while the interset neoteric episodes (*Scylla*, *Byblis*, *Myrrha*) are balanced or counteracted by the 'miracles' of the *Iphis* and *Pygmalion*. *Without the metamorphoses*, the tragedy would be unrelieved: Iphis and Pygmalion would not get their innocent and worthy desires; *Tereus*, *Scylla*, etc. would be unmitigated catastrophes; and death would be the only result of the steadfast devotion of Ceyx to Alcyone and Alcyone to Ceyx. It is, therefore, the metamorphosis that saves the day and validates Ovid's positive estimate of mutual or conjugal love. Metamorphosis, in other words, is the *deus ex machina* that softens the horror of unrestrained sex and rewards the virtue of true love. On a narrative level, it is what makes possible the conversion of a dramatic, even tragic, plot (exactly what Ovid needed to bring out and test the mutuality of his *eros*) into a happy finale of cosmic peace. The *Tereus* is tragedy; the *Procris–Cephalus* near-tragedy; the *Ceyx–Alcyone* melodrama with an irenic, beneficent ending. What unites the wretched birds of the first to the halcyons of the last is a providence that mitigates the bad and rewards the good while setting both in an essentially harmonious, cosmic whole.

But we can hardly forget that such a conception of amatory metamorphosis would have been quite absurd had not Ovid adapted his characters to it. These characters are anything but complex. Each is governed by one simple emotion: vengeance, *libido*, conjugal devotion, the simple desire to marry and possess the beloved. As we have already seen, the gap between man and the animal is never very great: the transformation of Alcyone from one kind of loving mate into another is not disturbing because we have never been allowed to see Alcyone as anything but a loving mate. The metamorphosis, thus, acquires the poetic inevitability which was essential to Ovid's continuity. But this does not mean that his valuation of mutual or conjugal love was therefore wholly unsophisticated. It is not the simple lovers but the poet himself who really creates the value. Or in other words, it is how he feels for his characters rather than any objective presentation of their own feelings that finally counts. The combination of empathy with sympathy in his narrative (which we have already discussed) enables him to give full vent to the horror, pity and approval with which he sees the action and its psychic causes. In the last analysis, it is Ovid, not Tereus or Procne, Ceyx or Alcyone that we encounter. Consider the lines about Alcyone's transformation (XI, 710–35):

> Mane erat, egreditur tectis ad litus et illum
> *maesta* locum repetit, de quo spectarat euntem,
> dumque moratur ibi, dumque 'hic retinacula solvit,
> hoc mihi discedens dedit oscula litore' dicit,
> *dumque notata locis reminiscitur acta* fretumque

273

715 prospicit: in liquida, spatio distante, tuetur
nescio quid quasi corpus aqua, primoque, *quid illud
esset, erat dubium*; postquam paulum appulit unda,
et quamvis aberat, corpus tamen esse liquebat,
qui foret, ignorans, quia naufragus, omine mota est,
720 et tamquam ignoto lacrimam daret, 'heu! miser,' inquit
'quisquis es, et si qua est coniunx tibi!' Fluctibus actum
fit propius corpus: *quod quo magis illa tuetur,
hoc minus et minus est mentis.* Iam iamque propinquae
admotum terrae, *iam quod cognoscere posset,*
725 *cernit: erat coniunx!* 'Ille est!' exclamat et una
ora, comas, vestem lacerat, *tendensque trementes*
ad Ceyca *manus* 'sic, o carissime coniunx,
sic ad me, miserande, redis?' ait. Adiacet undis
facta manu moles, quae primas aequoris undas
730 frangit et incursus quae praedelassat aquarum.
Insilit huc, mirumque fuit potuisse: volabat;
percutiensque levem modo natis aëra pennis,
stringebat summas ales *miserabilis* undas,
dumque volat, maesto similem plenumque querellae
735 ora dedere sonum tenui crepitantia rostro.

*Dawn came: she sought upon the shore below
The place where she had stood to watch him go;
And lingering on the spot, and saying: 'This
Is where he sailed, and gave the parting kiss',
Each place recalling, and each incident,
She saw, with gaze upon the horizon bent,
A shape, perhaps a body, on the brine,
Not easy, at that distance, to define;
Which, washed a little nearer by the sea,
Though still far off, a body proved to be,
A shipwrecked stranger; yet it touched her near,
And as for one unknown, she shed a tear.
'Unhappy one,' she cried, 'whoe'er you be;
And if you have a wife, unhappy she.'
Washed nearer by the tide, and closer viewed,*

It caused her more and more disquietude;
Now closer, closer to the land it lies;
Now near enough, at last, to recognize.
She sees it clear: it is, it is her lord.
''Tis he', she cried; and with her nails she scored
Her face, hair, robe; then trembling hands outspread
To Ceÿx. 'Husband, is it thus', she said,
'That you return, most piteous and most dear?'
Hard by, a sea-wall rose, erected here
To break the sea's first anger, and withstand
And tire its strength, before it reached the strand;
On this she leapt: and—how was this?—she flew,
Beating the buoyant air with pinions new.
She seemed to sorrow, as she skimmed the sea,
And with her slender bill cried piteously.

The words in italic are technically narrative, but are psychically
one with Alcyone's 'quoted' words. We see the whole process by
which despair is converted into suicidal impulse and triumphant
metamorphosis. Ovid puts himself wholly in Alcyone's place:
more than that, he also puts himself in nature's place. The shift of
tenses (*insilit, volabat*) in line 731, the phrase of subjective commentary (*mirumque fuit potuisse*) and the vivid presentness of the now fly-
ing halcyon (*percutiens, stringebat,* 732–3) link the emotion (the love
so charged with the poet's sympathy) and the metamorphosis in
an indissoluble psychic unity. Compare the metamorphosis of
Scylla (VIII, 142–51):

> vix dixerat: insilit undis
> consequiturque rates, *faciente cupidine vires,*
> Gnosiacaeque haeret *comes invidiosa* carinae.
> Quam pater ut vidit—nam iam pendebat in aura,
> et modo factus erat fulvis haliaeëtus alis—
> ibat, ut haerentem rostro laceraret adunco.
> Illa metu puppim dimisit, et aura cadentem
> sustinuisse levis, ne tangeret aequora, visa est.
> Pluma fuit: plumis in avem mutata vocatur
> ciris, et a tonso est hoc nomen adepta capillo.

She said no more, but plunging in the wave
O'ertook the fleet, such strength her passion gave;
And clutched the Cretan's craft, which o'er the blue
With Scylla and her shame hag-ridden flew.
Her father, now transformed, who hung in air,
A tawny-winged sea-eagle, saw her there,
And came to rend her: terror made her weak:
She loosed her hold, to shun the curving beak;
But though she fell, she might not touch the wave:
Some waft of wind—or wing—was there to save:
Yes, winged and plumed was she, a bird in air,
Called Ciris, from the severed lock of hair.

The difference of feeling is apparent. Here the poet's sympathy is minimal: this monstrous victim of *cupido* (her strength comes only from that) is a *comes invidiosa*; her transformation is nothing but her permanent subjection to the father she has made into an implacable enemy. Again, Minos' rejection of Scylla is also associated with the poet's own rejection of her (VIII, 94–7):

> *scelerataque* dextra
> munera porrexit. Minos porrecta refugit,
> *turbatus*que *novi* respondit *imagine facti*:
> 'Di te summoveant, o nostri infamia saecli...'

And then the girl held out her accursed *gift. Minos shrank*
from the offered prize, confounded at the image of this unpre-
cedented deed: 'May the gods remove you from my sight
[he said], infamous blot on all our generation'...

Ovid's conception of true love has certainly no surprises for us. It is, indeed, very close to what we may call the western ideal: the fact remains that it was a novelty for the literature of its time. Nothing was in one sense more normal: it is the opposite of perversion and pathological deviation;[1] the opposite also of the spiritual *eros* of Plato and the Romantics. There is absolutely no

---

[1] Ovid was notably disenchanted with homosexuality (see especially the *Iphis*: IX, 726–63); Tibullus, Propertius and Virgil are, in this respect, very different.

glorification of the *Liebestod*, the union of love with death that bulks so large in Hellenistic and modern literatures. But it is assuredly not an Augustan ideal save in the sense that Ovid lived in the Augustan age. It is not the hero or patriot but the lover that dominates both the epic and the imagination of Ovid.

But the lover of his ideal is not—we must insist once more on this crucial fact—the libidinous monster of neoteric or Hellenistic poetry. The sixth Eclogue of Virgil gives us one list of the preferred neoteric types (Pasiphae, Scylla, Procne–Tereus are specifically mentioned) and Parthenius' *Erotica Pathemata* (note the very title!) another. How different are Pyramus and Thisbe, Procris and Cephalus, Ceyx and Alcyone! Ovid obviously awards them his approbation—and, what is much more, his interest and affection. For the fact must be admitted: the 'naughty' and sophisticated poet of the *Amores* and *Ars*, the cleverly neoteric poet of the *Heroides*, had in the *Metamorphoses* taken his place as the West's first champion of true, normal, even conjugal love. Strange as it may seem, there is a goodness in Ovid that at this point shines through.

Yet the goodness is limited. We cannot help noticing the exclusiveness, the jealous possessiveness, of Procris and Alcyone. This kind of love is far removed from any moral or social purpose. Ovid is not Virgil. But the difference between the sheerly libidinous and the truly mutual and therefore humanly good *amores* is quite real. We shall see it once more in the story of Picus, Canens and Circe (XIV, 320–96): the moving contrast between Circe's heartless lust and Picus' genuine devotion to his loving wife (and hers to him) is, as it were, the swan-song, the last lingering echo of Ovid's amatory ideal.

CHAPTER VIII

TROY AND ROME

THE purpose and function of the fourth and concluding section of the poem are apparent from its very plan:

	THEME	EPISODES	PANELS
Bk. XII, 1–62		[Trojan section: liaison]	
1–145		[Introduction: Trojan War, Fama, Cygnus]	
146–535		⌐Caeneus, Lapiths–Centaurs (epic)	
536–611	TROY	[Periclymenus: Death of Achilles]	
612–Bk. XIII, 398			ARMORUM IUDICIUM
Bk. XIII, 399–575		⌐Hecuba (tragic)	
576–622		[Memnon]	
623–718		[Aniades–Orionides (Aeneas)]	
719–897		Sicily ⌠ Galatea–Cyclops–Acis	
898–Bk. XIV, 74		⌡ Scylla–Glaucus–Circe	
Bk. XIV, 75–153	AENEAS	[Aeneas, Sibyl]	
154–307		Italy ⌠ Ulysses–Cyclops–Circe	
308–440		⌡ Picus–Canens–Circe	
441–608		[Aeneas, Turnus, Apotheosis Aeneae]	
609–771		Native Gods ⌠ Pomona–Vertumnus (Iphis–Anaxarete)	
772–851	ROME	⌡ Apotheosis Romuli	
Bk. XV, 1–478			PYTHAGORAS SOLILOQUY
479–621		Foreign Gods ⌠ Hippolytus	
622–744		⌡ Aesculapius	
745–870		*Apotheosis Caesaris*	

The contrast with the plan of the other three sections (especially II and III) is clear: unlike them, there is no central panel in the epic style; instead, the lighter material (the amours of Galatea and Circe) is set in the middle and the heavier material is put at the beginning and end. The initial and concluding parts of the section have a similar plan: each has as its centre-piece a long episode in a novel style (one is rhetorical, one philosophic) with balancing episodes around it. From the standpoint of content, Trojan and Roman parts surround a central part that describes Aeneas' journey from Troy to Rome. The essential structural elements can be thus schematized:

Troy
- Battle Epic
  - ORATORICAL PIECE
- Tragedy

Aeneas
Troy–Latium
- Aenean frame
  - *Amores* (idyll and epyllion)
- Aenean frame

Rome
- Story of Native Gods (amatory, religio-patriotic)
  - PHILOSOPHICAL PIECE
- Story of Foreign Gods (religio-patriotic)

CONCLUSION: CAESAR'S APOTHEOSIS

The reason for the different structure of the section is almost self-evident. The centre of gravity is, as befits a conclusion, at the end, especially the Julio-Augustan portion of the end. The theme of apotheosis is no longer carried by the central panel (as in Section III and, proleptically, in Section II) but is spread throughout the whole in a crescendo that appropriately reaches a climax at the very end. We have the story of Trojan defeat offset by Aeneas' successful voyage to Latium and apotheosis there, by the founding of Rome and the consequent apotheosis of Romulus and, finally, by its refounding through the apotheosized Julius and his august successor. The general movement toward the final climax is clearly indicated. But Ovid obviously felt the necessity of interrupting the heaviness of the Trojan and Roman portions: hence his reduction of the Aeneas story (he did not, in any event, want to rival Virgil directly) to what is in large part a mere frame for lighter, erotic episodes that break and lighten the intensity of the long epic, tragic, oratorical and philosophical pieces that really carry the main burden of his argument.

In one sense, the section is remarkably well balanced. There is an obvious and pleasing symmetry in the arrangement; an evident continuity of movement and theme is combined with a refreshing variety. Epic, oratory and tragedy at the beginning; idyll and *epyllion* in the middle; religion and philosophy at the end: the shift of moral and tone is both piquant and refreshing. But in another sense the section is contrived and factitious in a way that belies the extraordinarily subtle and natural movement of the preceding section. The gradual development of motifs up to the crowning *Ceyx and Alcyone*, the deft transition from the comedy of the first section to the vengeance of the second and the amatory *pathos* of the third or from the humorous metamorphoses of Daphne and Io to the pathetic metamorphoses of Procne, Byblis, etc.—all this is now suddenly abandoned in favour of a quite artificial pastiche of bravura pieces. The epic contest of Centaurs and Lapiths, the tragedy of Hecuba, the amusingly Theocritean song of Polyphemus, the clever oratory of Ulysses and long-winded philosophy of Pythagoras have only the most formal relation to each other. They are not assimilated to the whole; they have no true reason for being where they are. There is a plan that unites them, but it is, after all, a quite external and superficial one.

The prime reason for this was political necessity. Ovid felt he had to make the section, as the close of his peculiar kind of Augustan epic, end with the deification of Caesar and the reign of Augustus. The deification motif had in fact been already introduced in anticipation of this section. The epic panels of the first three sections form an evident sequence:

(1) The God (Jupiter, Phoebus)
(2) The Victorious Hero (Perseus)
(3) The Hero become God (Hercules),

preparing us for the apotheoses of Aeneas, Romulus and Caesar here. Furthermore this was obviously the section in which the transition from legend to history, from the Heroic-age Greeks to the Romans, had to be accomplished. Like Virgil, Ovid had to connect the Fall of Troy with the founding of Rome, Aeneas with Romulus and Caesar. Such considerations clearly suggested the epic and tragic Trojan episodes and the philosophic 'digression' by which Ovid, like Virgil in *Aeneid* VI, tried to give dignity and solemnity to his patriotic-Augustan ending.

But all this was quite unrelated to the major motif-sequences of the poem. Indeed, the preceding Perseus and Hercules panels, so specifically designed to introduce the motif of the divine-man (the deified hero) also stand out from their contexts in a quite disconcerting way. Ovid could conceivably have written his *continuous poem* so that it would, quite naturally, have terminated in epic battles, philosophic soliloquies and apotheoses. But he certainly did no such thing. His humour and pathos proved fatal to his heroics. The latter, at best, was clever imitation; at worst, a dreadful exercise in the incongruous and grotesque. But here we must be careful to note Ovid's intention: his incongruity and even bathos may not be quite so undeliberate as at first they seem.

In the Trojan portion of the section, Ovid certainly had the *Aeneid* well in mind. The fall of Troy and the founding of Rome represent the two divine decisions that encompass Virgil's *Aeneid*: this is the main burden of the second book (the oracles of Anchises are the offsetting counterpart of those of Laocoon) and of the clearly marked contrast between the second and eighth books. Aeneas leaves the site of Troy in order to reach the site of Rome. Ovid's Aeneas, in fact, repeats the movement of Virgil's (XIII, 623–5):

Non tamen eversam Troiae cum moenibus esse
spem quoque fata sinunt: sacra et, sacra altera, patrem
fert umeris, venerabile onus, Cythereius heros.

The fates withheld their sanction, after all,
That Troy's last hope should with her fabric fall;
And shoulder-high the son of Venus bore
Her gods, and, sacred too, one burden more,
His aged sire.

But Ovid's Trojan section has, nonetheless, no resemblance to Virgil's. It is in fact composed of three episodes none of which has any relation to Aeneas. There is, first, the epic battle of the Lapiths and Centaurs. This is no Trojan episode though it is rather cleverly linked to one. Ovid obviously wanted to introduce the concluding section of his 'epic' with an epic battle-piece, but he quite as obviously did not want to 'rival' Homer or Virgil too directly. He felt differently about Euripides, whose *Hecuba* he imitates in the third of the Trojan episodes. He not only needed a tragedy to balance the epic 'Lapiths and Centaurs' but he had a decided partiality for Euripidean *pathos*. Obviously the middle piece of the Trojan series had to be a relief from the intensity of epic or tragedy: the clever *controversia* between Ajax and Ulysses was thus inserted. It was a stock subject of the rhetorical schools and gave Ovid a fine opportunity to show his *ingenium*. He obviously felt far more sympathy for the clever Ulysses than for the usual epic hero. But the net result of the three pieces thus arranged was to destroy the significance of the Trojan theme. Ovid's viewpoint (save for the *Hecuba*) is far more Greek than Trojan. It is in fact his Ulysses who overshadows everybody else. The ensemble is, all told, very amusing and 'Ovidian' but has no true continuity with either the preceding *pathos* section or the following Roman episodes. Here the superficiality of the liaison conceals no deeper purpose whatsoever, though it may, possibly, conceal a lighter one.

The Virgilian character of the whole section is indicated at the start by the Fama *ekphrasis* (XII, 39–63). This is, of course, absurdly out of any proper context: Ovid's Fama only spreads the news of the approaching Trojan war. It is the first hint to the reader that Ovid's attitude to the Roman world of Virgil is not without its share of paradox and subtle parody.

Ovid displays great skill in treating the Trojan war without really touching any of its major episodes. It is not the contest of Achilles with Hector but that of Achilles and Cygnus (the invulnerable man) at which he begins. Cygnus then becomes a topic of conversation among the Greek heroes and easily sets in motion the encyclopaedic memory of Nestor: Cygnus is like Caeneus, the curious girl-man he remembered from the battle of the Lapiths and Centaurs. But even Caeneus is a rather thin excuse for introducing the battle since he only takes part in a brief episode at its end. The frivolousness with which Ovid finds metamorphoses in this material and the *tours de force* to which he resorts for liaison, display an almost overt indifference or carelessness toward his subject-matter. The epic battle is on the whole tedious and otiose. It reminds us of the *Perseus–Phineus* and the *Meleager* in its succession of *outré* killings; and Ovid, of course, makes the most of the incongruity between the horse and the man in his centaurs. The combustion of Charaxus' hair (XII, 271 ff.) and the sound of his boiling blood (it is likened to the hissing of the smith's hot iron when plunged into water), the insertion of a weapon at the juncture of the equine and human portions of a centaur (298 ff.); above all, perhaps, the delicate manners of the Centaur Cyllarus (who had a human spouse and dressed up for her) are all typically Ovidian additions to the cliché killings of his epic predecessors. These are amusing bits, but there is no consistent parody: the effect of the more ingenious death-scenes is on the whole grotesque, not humorous; most of the description is merely gory; the battle itself has no proper sequence or development. And the ending is perfunctory: the death of Caeneus so rouses the Lapiths that they cannot stop before (XII, 530–1) ... *data pars leto, partem fuga noxque removit.*

But the very exaggeration of this 'epic'—all the spattered blood, brains and furniture—prepares us for the *ingenium* of Ulysses: the exploits of Achilles (his duel with Cygnus and death from Paris' arrow) had constituted, as it were, the setting of the *Lapiths and Centaurs*: now we listen to the debate on his arms. Here the brute force that the Centaurs and Lapiths had so prodigally displayed is set in relief by one man's *ingenium*. Ajax can fight, but his physical prowess is discounted by his stupidity. Ulysses knows and uses his brains: to Ajax's scorn for verbal cleverness Ulysses replies that physical force needs *ingenium* and *facundia*. Many men as strong as himself have yielded to his counsels, for it is only *ingenium* that can make force useful (XIII, 361–6):

tibi dextera bello
utilis: ingenium est, quod eget moderamine nostro;
tu vires sine mente geris, mihi cura futuri;
tu pugnare potes, pugnandi tempora mecum
eligit Atrides; tu tantum corpore prodes,
nos animo.

You give good blows, but when it comes to brain
You need my guiding hand upon the rein.
Strength without understanding marks your deeds:
My province is to care for future needs.
To fight a battle lies within your power:
But I and Agamemnon choose the hour.
You in your body's strength alone can find
The means to serve: but I in powers of mind.

But there is more here than simple defence of brains and intellect.
Ulysses also displays the 'shadiness' or outright mendacity that
Ajax had already held up to scorn. Ulysses' speech is that of a very
clever lawyer who knows every trick of his craft: he even plays his
own 'modesty' against the arrogance of his opponent. He does
not pretend to be above his audience.

Here Ovid strives for an obvious *ethopoeia*, the stupid Ajax contrasted with the clever Ulysses. But the *ethopoeia* is also very
Ovidian. To Ulysses' skill in counsel and resourcefulness in
stratagem, he adds aesthetic capacity. Ulysses can appreciate a work
of art as Ajax cannot (XIII, 290 ff.):

artis opus tantae, rudis et sine pectore miles | indueret?
. . . postulat, ut capiat, quae non intellegit, arma!

Or think you, when the fond sea-mother made
Her influence felt, her hero son to aid,
She meant that arms divine, of art so rare,
A rough and soulless man-at-arms should wear?
. . .
These, which he cannot grasp, he seeks to gain.

Ajax's stupidity is to be scorned for more than utilitarian reasons.

It is also an affront to the artist! The humour of such lines lies in their incongruity with the mood or heroic content of epic. Ulysses' *facundia* and *ingenium* are, at bottom, much like Ovid's own, and Ovid is saying not only that brain is better than brawn but that the traditional respect for brawn—the heroic and epic code in short—is itself rather ridiculous. He can tell of an epic battle—witness his *Lapiths and Centaurs*!—but he deflates it as soon as he has finished. It is not Troy, Aeneas or the *aristeiai* of heroes that engage his imagination: it is the shrewdness and sophistication of the man of words and letters.

After this clever debate, the immediately following tragedy of Hecuba seems shockingly incongruous. Here Ovid imitated Euripides very closely but with little sense of his model's peculiar excellences. The sacrifice of Polyxena loses all the specificity and freshness of its original. Euripides' heroine speaks simply and her heroic behaviour is as convincing as the tears that it excites: Ovid's Polyxena is stagey and rhetorical. The accounts of Polyxena's death are a good place to see the difference (*Hecuba* 568 ff.):

ἣ δὲ καὶ θνῄσκουσ' ὅμως
πολλὴν πρόνοιαν εἶχεν εὐσχήμων πεσεῖν
κρύπτουσ' ἃ κρύπτειν ὄμματ' ἀρσένων χρέων.

> *And she though dying, yet*
> *Took care, great care, all decorously to fall,*
> *Hiding what should be hidden from men's eyes.*

Ovid, *Met.* XIII, 479–80:

> Tunc quoque cura fuit partes velare tegendas,
> cum caderet, castique decus servare pudoris.
>
> *And even in falling scrupulous was she*
> *To cloak her form, and guard her modesty.*

Here the phrase *casti decus servare pudoris* wholly spoils the fresh directness of Euripides' πρόνοιαν εἶχεν εὐσχήμων πεσεῖν. Ovid's narrative of Hecuba's vengeance on Polymestor is too brief to show the dreadful degeneration of Hecuba's character that most readers find so arresting in Euripides. Her actual metamorphosis into a dog (which is of course non-Euripidean) lacks the 'inevitableness' of that of Alcyone or Byblis and seems oddly ill-adapted to the preceding narrative. The whole is a smooth abbreviation of Euripides (it is only 146 lines in length) that suffers from this very fact: in condensing, Ovid had to generalize and thus to lose almost all the concreteness and actuality of his source.

This Trojan section is now followed by the intermediary Aeneas section. But Ovid passes over the voyage and Italian career of Aeneas in the minimum of space. Obviously he did not want to repeat or copy Virgil: but his use of the *Aeneid* (as a frame for rather light, erotic episodes or for unmistakable parodies) is a sure indication of his perfunctoriness, his indifference to his ostensibly serious Augustan purpose. He 'covers' most of the material of *Aeneid* I–III in thirteen lines (XIII, 623–35) and, after the briefly told metamorphosis of the daughters of Anius and Orion, abruptly brings Aeneas and his company to Sicily. Their passage of the straits of Scylla and Charybdis provides the link for the stories of Scylla, Galatea, Polyphemus and Glaucus (XIII, 730–XIV, 74), the Sicilian portion of the section.

There are really two stories here, though they are linked through the character of Scylla (Ovid here gives another version of her story from that of Section III above). The plan of the stories is quite symmetrical:

Link with Aeneas (XIII, 719–29)
  Introduction: Scylla and Galatea (730–49)
  (1) { Galatea, Acis, Cyclops (750–88)
       Song of Cyclops (789–869)
       Death and Metamorphosis of Acis (870–97)
  (2) { Scylla and Glaucus (898–916)
       Narrative of Glaucus (917–65)
       Glaucus and Circe (XIV, 1–40)
       Metamorphosis of Scylla (41–74)

The Galatea story is recounted at one remove: she herself tells it to Scylla. Scylla can reject her lovers with impunity; but Galatea

could not reject the love of Polyphemus without real suffering
(XIII, 744-5):

> Non nisi per luctus licuit Cyclopis amorem
> effugere.   *suffered bitter woe,*
> *Before my Cyclops lover let me go.*

Her story is thus ostensibly tragic: actually it is Ovid's version of
the comic courtship of Polyphemus in Theocritus' eleventh and
sixth idylls, a subject that Virgil had partially imitated in his
second and seventh Eclogues. The heart of it is the Cyclops' own
song that Galatea repeats verbatim after a preliminary recital of his
principal amatory symptoms.

Ovid has here converted the light comedy of Theocritus into
farce. Polyphemus does not merely comb his hair; he goes at it
with a rake. Telemus the seer had, in Theocritus, warned the
Cyclops about his eye: in Ovid, the warning is made a joke.
Galatea, says Polyphemus, already has his eye (*altera iam rapuit*):
why should he worry about Ulysses? His actual song exaggerates
the Theocritean and Virgilian motifs to the point of absurdity.
Galatea is not merely *thymo dulcior...candidior cycnis* and *hedera
formosior alba* as in Virgil (Eclogue 7. 38-9) but also *floridior pratis,
procerior alno, splendidior vitro, lascivior haedo, levior...detractis
conchis, gratior umbra, nobilior palmis*, etc. (XIII, 789 ff.) as well as
saevior iuvencis, durior quercu, fallacior undis, inmobilior scopulis and
so on for seven lines. Polyphemus boasts of his size (*adspice, sim
quantus*), of his hairy body (what horse or goat or sheep would not
be ugly without hair?) and his single eye (the sun himself has only
one!). In the end, of course, Polyphemus acts like the brute that
he is and overwhelms Acis with part of a mountain. But the
tragedy is averted by Acis' timely metamorphosis into a fountain.

Galatea's story should have warned Scylla, but Scylla was not to
be warned. Glaucus, the fisherman so miraculously turned into a
sea god with a proper fish-tail, courts her and tells her his story but
cannot hold her attention long enough to finish his remarkable
narrative (XIII, 966-7):

Talia dicentem, dicturum plura, reliquit
Scylla deum.

Here Scylla left him, having heard enough.

He approaches Circe for help in his love-affair, but Circe will not help him to anything but herself: he scorns her, but she sees to it that he does not get the handsome Scylla who now receives, thanks to Circe's magical herbs, a most unpleasant addition to her beautiful physique. She becomes the sea monster who threatened Ulysses and finally ends her chequered existence as a rock. We can hardly take either Galatea or Scylla very seriously, but Circe introduces a slightly more sombre note. Her baneful magic now dominates the second half of the Aeneas section.

The plan of this half is obviously contrapuntal to the first and the relationship can be seen from the following synopsis:

I.   Introduction of Aeneas (Aniades, Orionides), XIII, 623–718
  (1) Galatea, Acis and the Cyclops, 719-897
  (2) Scylla, Glaucus, Circe, 898–XIV, 74
II.   Aeneas *en route* to Caieta (Sibyl), 75–222
  (3) Adventures of Ulysses' men, 75–319
  (4) Circe, Picus, Canens, 320–440
III.   Conclusion of Aeneas story (War in Italy, *Deification of Aeneas*), 441–608

Here four episodes are framed within the Aeneas story. The first two are basically Sicilian: the transition from Sicily to Italy occurs when Glaucus (XIV, 1 ff.), the sea god, swims across the Tuscan sea to Circe's home in Italian Circeii. Hence Episodes (1) and (2) are basically Sicilian; (3) and (4) Italian. There is also an obvious correspondence between (1) and (3) and between (2) and (4). The first episode (1) describes the Cyclops (Polyphemus) before the visit of Ulysses; the third (3) describes the visit and its effect. Ulysses is still the great instance of *ingenium* victorious over brute strength. His ability to withstand Circe's magic (the story immediately follows that of his blinding of the Cyclops) is but another illustration of his quality: neither force nor witchcraft finds him at a loss. The story of Picus–Canens (4) is, of course, the complement of *Glaucus–Scylla* (2): in both, Circe is balked of her desire (for Glaucus and Picus) and, in both, exercises her vengeance on the woman preferred to her (Scylla, Canens). But the *Picus–Canens* also advances the movement of the poem by bringing in a Roman site at its close: Canens becomes a Roman spring, the famous Camenae near the Porta Capena.

Ovid displayed considerable skill in varying the tone of the four episodes. The first (Galatea and the Cyclops) is comedy or farce for the most part; the second (Glaucus and Scylla) is a rather exotic sea-piece which certainly contains no serious emotion (our sympathy with Scylla is minimal) but quite lacks the burlesque or frivolous quality of the Cyclops' song. The stories of Achaemenides and Macareus (to line 319: the Cyclops and Circe–Ulysses episodes) are direct imitations or recalls of the *Aeneid* and *Odyssey*.

But Ovid, for this very reason, avoids the epic style or tone. The Cyclops and Circe stories are not told by Ulysses or some dignified hero but by two common sailors of Ulysses' crew. Achaemenides had been left behind with the Cyclopes and was thus ignorant of the further adventures of his companions. After telling his own story of abandonment and rescue, he naturally tries to get all the information he can from his mate Macareus. It seems certain that the encounter of Achaemenides and Macareus at Caieta (a very unimportant place in the *Aeneid*) is Ovid's own invention. It enabled him not only to introduce the two episodes together but to give them just the right coloration and style: they are, so to speak, the plebeian, the man-in-the-street's view of the marvels of Virgil and Homer. The light parody or, better, designed vulgarization of epic originals, is a most significant clue to Ovid's intention in this part of the poem.

The very name Macareus is Ovid's contribution; he had used it for one of the Lapiths before (XIII, 711); it is not in Homer or any other source. The clue to its importation here is its association with that of Achaemenides: the latter is a Virgilian innovation (as is Virgil's variation of Homer's and Dionysius' Cyclopean episodes) and Ovid thus shows he can go one better than Virgil by bringing in another unknown as well. The sequence of events is as follows:

(1) Aeneas, after leaving Cumae, reaches Caieta, not yet of course so named though his old nurse Caieta is soon to die there (*litora...nondum nutricis habentia nomen*) and give her name to the place (XIV, 154–9).

(2) Here an old comrade (*comes*) of Ulysses, Macareus, meets Achaemenides, the shipmate who had been left behind at Polyphemus' cave and later rescued by Aeneas. Macareus naturally asks for the story (160–4).

(3) Achaemenides' story of his abandonment and rescue (165–222).

(4) Macareus in his turn satisfies Achaemenides' curiosity as to his adventures with the Laestrygonians and Circe (223–319).

(5) Macareus adds, *at second hand* (his source is one of Circe's handmaidens), the tale of Picus and Canens (320–440). Though the once-removed narrator is the same, the Picus–Canens story obviously falls into quite a different category from the others. The intended scheme of correspondence is indicated on p. 288.

We have commented above (Chapter III) on Ovid's transformation of Virgil's Achaemenides episode (*Aeneid* III, 588–691). The eerie effects and pathetic colouring of Virgil are conspicuously absent. Achaemenides is now a spruce and nattily dressed person (*iam non hirsutus amictu*) who tells of a long-past event in the manner of a sailor spinning a good yarn. It is the cannibalism, not the unearthly horror of Polyphemus, that he emphasizes. Ovid in fact gives the whole show away when he makes Polyphemus deliver a cannibalistic speech of the 'fee-fi-fo-fum' variety. It is Aeneas that Achaemenides has to thank for his narrow escape from the monster's teeth and stomach! Ovid's Achaemenides is in fact a quite ordinary sailor who could not possibly dwell in the high-poetical world of his Virgilian original. The parody is obvious and very amusing.

The tale of Macareus is an equally clever and equally 'down-to-earth' variation on Homer. What Macareus dwells on is the actual process of becoming a pig—the swelling of the bristles, the first grunts, the nose made into a snout (XIV, 279–82):

> (Et pudet et referam)—saetis horrescere coepi
> nec iam posse loqui, pro verbis edere raucum
> murmur et in terram toto procumbere vultu:
> osque meum sensi pando occallescere rostro.

> *I blush to tell the tale, but then and there*
> *The change began: stiff bristles clothed me o'er;*
> *My speech was grunts, I uttered words no more;*
> *Face down I dropped; I felt my neck bulge out*
> *With muscle; and my nose became a snout.*

The process is also reversed in similar detail.

The story of Picus and Canens is obviously meant to rise above such delightful parody: it is, indeed, as the immediate precursor of Aeneas' Italian war and deification, more serious than even the 'corresponding' Glaucus–Scylla episode (see plan on p. 288). Here Circe is a much more malicious sorceress than she was in the Glaucus–Scylla episode. We cannot waste much sympathy on Scylla, and the god Glaucus is not represented as particularly grieved, but Picus is a faithful husband and Canens a devoted wife: Circe's malicious vengeance on the happy pair is as cruel as it is undeserved. Nevertheless the tale is too brief and truncated—it is a sort of rapid summary of very familiar motifs: we think of Procris–Cephalus, Salmacis and particularly Byblis—to move us very much.

The conclusion of the Aeneas section (XIV, 441–608) illustrates again the 'perfunctoriness' which is so manifest in Ovid's use of Virgil. The brief Achaemenides narrative was all that he could allow himself of direct parody: for the rest he cuts his Virgilian material ruthlessly and introduces all the piquant details and incidental metamorphoses he can. Juno's hostility and Venus' protection of Aeneas, Evander, Lavinia, etc. are briefly dismissed, but a number of lines are devoted to the rather extraneous metamorphoses of Diomedes' crew and of Aeneas' ships. The twelfth book of the *Aeneid* is thus summarized (XIV, 572–3):

Bella gerunt, tandemque Venus victricia nati
arma videt, Turnusque cadit.

[they] fight on for victory's sake;
Till Venus, at long last, saw victory crown
Aeneas' arms, and Turnus stricken down,

and the emphasis is put on the odd metamorphosis of Turnus' city
into an Ardea-bird! But we are, of course, on the way to another
and more important transformation. The apotheosis of Aeneas is,
as Venus urges Jupiter, fully deserved by his past suffering. It was
surely enough to see the Styx once! (*satis est inamabile regnum* |
aspexisse semel, Stygios semel isse per amnes, XIV, 590–1). The actual
change of man into god is described in language that, for obvious
reasons, re-echoes the lines in which Hercules underwent the same
process (XIV, 600–4):

Hunc iubet Aeneae *quaecumque obnoxia morti*
abluere et tacito deferre sub aequora cursu.
Corniger exsequitur Veneris mandata, suisque,
quidquid in Aenea fuerat mortale, repurgat
et respersit aquis. *Pars optima restitit illi*

All in Aeneas that could be the prey
Of death, she bade this river wash away,
And carry with its noiseless current down
To sea, and in the depths of ocean drown.
The hornèd god obeyed, and washed him free
From all admixture of mortality;
All imperfections by his cleansing shower
Were purged: the finer part withstood his power;

(IX, 262):

quodcumque fuit populabile flammae,
Mulciber *abstulerat*; nec cognoscenda remansit
Herculis effigies, nec quicquam ab imagine ductum
matris habet, tantumque Iovis vestigia servat.
Utque novus serpens, posita cum pelle senecta,

luxuriare solet squamaque nitere recenti:
sic ubi *mortales Tirynthius exuit artus*
parte sui meliore viget, maiorque videri
coepit et augusta fieri gravitate verendus

Meanwhile, whate'er in Hercules was clay,
Which fire could ravage, Vulcan swept away.
His mother's likeness vanished, and his own:
He kept the traces of his sire alone.
The snake, which sheds its age with weeds outworn,
In mail new-burnished thrills with life reborn:
So, stripped of what was mortal, Hercules
Felt, in the finer part, his strength increase.
He grew in stature, and, before the eye,
Was clothed with awe-inspiring majesty.

We now come to the third and last part of the final section. Its detailed plan is as follows:

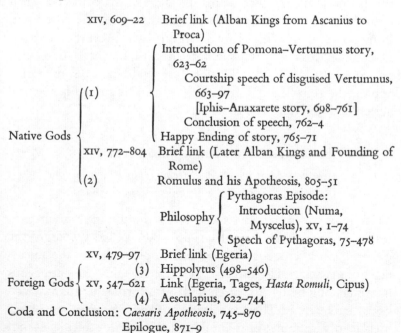

	XIV, 609–22	Brief link (Alban Kings from Ascanius to Proca)	
Native Gods	(1)	Introduction of Pomona–Vertumnus story, 623–62 Courtship speech of disguised Vertumnus, 663–97 [Iphis–Anaxarete story, 698–761] Conclusion of speech, 762–4 Happy Ending of story, 765–71	
	XIV, 772–804	Brief link (Later Alban Kings and Founding of Rome)	
	(2)	Romulus and his Apotheosis, 805–51	
	Philosophy	Pythagoras Episode: Introduction (Numa, Myscelus), XV, 1–74 Speech of Pythagoras, 75–478	
	XV, 479–97	Brief link (Egeria)	
Foreign Gods	(3)	Hippolytus (498–546)	
	XV, 547–621	Link (Egeria, Tages, *Hasta Romuli*, Cipus)	
	(4)	Aesculapius, 622–744	

Coda and Conclusion: *Caesaris Apotheosis,* 745–870
Epilogue, 871–9

It is easy to see that, save for the concluding apotheosis of Caesar, the plan corresponds to that of the first part of this section: balancing episodes on each side of an elaborate 'panel'. Also the two panels, oratorical and philosophical, obviously balance each other. On the other hand, the surrounding episodes of this part are not at all like those of the Trojan part. They are, in fact, rather slight, in both size and style: the love-tale of Vertumnus–Pomona and the long voyage of the Aesculapian serpent are not meant to be major pieces. The Pythagoras section is so huge and ponderous (almost 500 lines) as to equal by itself all the preceding and succeeding episodes (509 lines as against 478; or 243 lines before and 266 after, excluding the Apotheosis of Caesar). As we shall see, the Pythagoras episode points toward and prepares the way for the Julio-Augustan finale. The tales of native and foreign gods that encompass it are not meant to compete with it but, rather, to set it in appropriate relief.

The wooing of Pomona by the local god Vertumnus is one of the better pieces of the poem. It suggests, of course, a great number of preceding episodes in a similar vein. At first sight, Pomona seems only one more determined virgin on the model of Daphne or Arethusa. But she is decidedly one with a difference: her concern is not with wild woods or wild beasts but utilitarian apples; she is in fact a Roman girl at heart, a girl with practical agricultural interests (XIV, 626–7):

> non silvas illa nec amnes,
> rus amat et ramos felicia poma ferentes.
>
> *She loved not woods and streams, but garden-ground,*
> *Where laden boughs with smiling fruits abound.*

Vertumnus woos her by successively disguising himself as a reaper, a pruner or, better still, an apple-picker! His wooing in the guise of an old crone is not confined to platitudes on the advantages of marriage. He adds to it a cautionary tale—the outrageous treatment of Iphis by Anaxarete and the unfortunate ends to which both thereby came. There is a little irony in Vertumnus' use of this melancholy example: he is anything but ready for suicide, even if

Pomona refuses his offer. But all is well: in a piquant reversal of pattern, Pomona does not act the determined virgin but gives in at once (XIV, 770-1):

> Vimque parat: sed vi non est opus, inque figura
> capta dei nymphe est et mutua vulnera sensit.
>
> *His looks prevailed: no need his power to prove;*
> *And won thereby, she ached with answering love.*

The Latin colouring of this episode is rather faint and, at that, diminished by an inserted tale that is not Latin at all. But it is Latin enough to fit the sequence of Roman history. Ovid pays only the scantest attention to the founding of Rome, but he adds enough historical or legendary incidents (e.g. the miraculous heating of the water at the gate of Janus) to preserve a decent distance between the apotheoses of Aeneas and of Romulus. In his account of the latter, he varies the theme by introducing the preparatory conversation of Mars and Jupiter,[1] and by accenting the mysteriousness of Romulus' disappearance from the eyes of men and Iris' reassuring message to his wife Hersilie. By the end of Book XIV, therefore, the Roman and apotheosis motifs had been properly sounded. The *carmen perpetuum* was now ready for its Augustan conclusion. But this would have been horribly anticlimactic had it not been given a prelude, and proper weight and solemnity, by a massive 'introduction' in an appropriately dignified style: the Pythagoras speech is, in fact, the real climax of the poem; the actual apotheosis of Caesar is only its formal pendant and ratification.

The Hippolytus and Aesculapius episodes that separate the Pythagoras episode from its 'pendant' or *Apotheosis of Caesar* are, of course, an essential interlude as well as a proper balance to the preceding *Vertumnus* and *Romulus*. Ovid had to let the Helenus prophecy in Pythagoras' speech remain unfulfilled for at least enough space to give the illusion of some passage of time between the prediction and its fulfilment. This the episodes of the two foreign gods do well enough under the circumstances. Ovid

[1] Here Ovid certainly had Ennius in mind.

could not, in the interest of the big scenes that surround them, make too much of them, but they convey fairly well the impression of important events and maintain the note of solemn religiosity. The tragic, Euripidean character of Hippolytus' story (his transformation into the Roman god Virbius is but a footnote to the story) is followed by the epic majesty of Aesculapius' progress to Rome. The introduction of Aesculapius (xv, 622–5),

> Pandite nunc, Musae, praesentia numina vatum
> (scitis enim, nec vos fallit spatiosa vetustas),
> unde Coroniden circumflua Thybridis alti
> insula Romuleae sacris adiecerit urbis
>
> *O Muses, goddesses of song, who see*
> *Undimmed the vistas of antiquity,*
> *Say how Asclepius left his distant home,*
> *To join on Tiber's isle the gods of Rome,*

achieves at once the epic dignity that Ovid wants here. The journey of the god from Epidaurus to Rome is conceived as a geographical crescendo—a climactic series of revered names and connotations—that reaches its high point at the divine snake's entrance into the city (xv, 736):

> Iamque, caput rerum, Romanam intraverat urbem
>
> *Had entered Rome, the head of things, at last,*

and proud possession of his island in the Tiber.

But it is the Pythagoras episode and its completion in the Augustan ending which form the intended climax of the section and the poem. It is important to note carefully the structure of this long (479-line) 'digression' and its quite ingenious plan:

(1) Introduction: the curiosity of Numa and its gratification by Pythagoras (xv, 1–74). Numa is not satisfied with a knowledge of Sabine rites (xv, 5–6):

> animo maiora capaci
> concipit et, *quae sit rerum natura*, requirit.
>
> *With deep receptive mind still grasped at more,*
> *And sought to learn, by study, nature's laws.*

This desire is fulfilled when he visits Croton and learns from one of its elders (*e senioribus unus...indigenis*) of the divinely motivated foundation of the city by Myscelus and of its later reception of the divinely inspired Pythagoras. It is Pythagoras' public discourse on the *magni primordia mundi et rerum causas* that the old man retells to Numa.

(2) The Discourse of Pythagoras (75–478)
    (*a*) The impiety of animal food (75–175)
    (*b*) The Law of Universal flux (176–452)
       (i) The Law defined (176–85)
       (ii) Heavenly changes, the seasons (186–213)
       (iii) Changes of bodies and elements (214–51)
       (iv) Changes of species (252–417)
       (v) Historical changes, Rome (418–52)
          [Helenus prophecy, 439–49]
    (*c*) Reversion to impiety of animal food (453–78)

(3) Return of Numa and his successful application of the wisdom of Pythagoras (479–84) (xv, 483–4):

> Sacrificos docuit ritus, *gentemque feroci*
> *adsuetam bello pacis traduxit ad artes.*

> *He taught the forms of worship, and led o'er*
> *A people, prone to bitter strife before,*
> *To practices of peace.*

The connection of the Pythagoras episode with Rome is more than formal. The wisdom that Numa learns at Croton is related to Rome in that it sets Rome in a universal perspective. The small city over whose cultural beginnings Numa presides is destined (434 f.) to become the *immensi caput orbis* under the rule of Augustus (447 f.). The historical development between Numa and Augustus is, however, set in the context of all the ages that have run since the very beginning of the universe (*magni primordia mundi*). Hence the Pythagoras discourse embraces the entirety of Ovid's *carmen perpetuum* and represents metamorphosis as the universal key to the secrets of both nature and history. It is evident that Ovid, just like Virgil in the philosophic portion of the sixth book of the *Aeneid*, uses philosophy to lend weight and solemnity to his Roman-Augustan conclusion. But there are questions that cannot be answered solely in terms of Ovid's desire to introduce Augustus at the end of his epic. How far did he intend the philosophy to 'explain' the metamorphoses of the whole poem? How far did he envisage Rome as a 'natural phenomenon' wholly subject to the law of change? How far, in short, is he really philosophic and to what extent is the philosophy to be read into the preceding mythology?

One thing seems clear enough: the exhortations to vegetarianism at the beginning and end of the speech (*a* and *c*) are no part of the message with which Ovid is really concerned. These are typical transition passages, designed to characterize the historical Pythagoras and thus to 'frame' his central philosophy. Ovid was not pleading for Pythagoras' special doctrine but only providing a suitable *ethopoeia*. We already know, from the prelude to the speech, that Pythagoras' teaching is looked upon as an answer to Numa's general curiosity about nature as such (*quae sit rerum natura, requirit*, 6) and that the speech is, in fact, repeated to Numa precisely because it satisfies that curiosity (*et rerum causas, et, quid natura, docebat*, 68). The vegetarianism does, however, introduce the general principle of Pythagoras' philosophy, that change is the key to all knowledge. Pythagoras is a Lucretius (the strong echo of Lucretius in lines 145 ff. is unmistakable) providing misguided and errant humanity with the rational truth. The typical Pythagorean reason for avoiding meat (i.e. that the human soul is constantly migrating between men and animals and that, therefore, a carnivore is virtually a cannibal) is developed at line 176 into a universal principle of change. It is not merely souls that shift; the whole universe is engaged in a process of constant change (xv, 176–7):

> Et quoniam magno feror aequore plenaque ventis
> vela dedi: *nihil est toto, quod perstet, in orbe*.

And—since with sails full-spread wide seas I range—
Nothing in all the world is free from change.

This is the general principle (not vegetarianism) that is now
explained in parts *b*ii–v of the speech (table on p. 297). The principle is seen at work in the heavens and seasons (ii)—i.e. in the
broadest possible sphere of operation—before it is brought down
to specific bodies (*corpora*) at line 214 (which thus begins a new
section). Here the changes of human growth and decay (214–36)
are assimilated to the changes of all the *elements* (237–51). This
leads to a section (iv) on *change of species* (*nec species sua cuique manet*,
etc.) or, perhaps better, the instability of all forms. Nothing
perishes, but nothing remains the same. We see this in the conversion of earth into water and water into earth (262–72), and in
the alternation of salt and fresh waters, of plain and mountain (296–
306), of water and ice, of hot and cold waters, of active and
dormant volcanoes. We then come to changes of animal forms
(361–417): this is obviously the pivotal section that both leads up
to the historical-Roman conclusion of the speech and explains all
animal metamorphoses. Bodies when they decay turn into 'small
animals' just as bees arise from rotting carcasses of bulls (the
bugonia), hornets from dead horses, scorpions from buried crabs and
butterflies from worms! Mud itself has *semina* which generate
frogs. Indeed, many animals are born unfinished and only later
take on their adult shape, like birds that come out of eggs. If we
did not *know* this, we could scarcely *believe* it (xv, 388):

Ni sciret fieri, quis nasci posse putaret?

Who would believe it, if he did not know?

There are even some who believe that snakes come out of the
innermost parts (*medullae*) of dead human beings. The fact is that
nature is altogether full of marvellous metamorphoses. The one
thing that the natural scientist must avoid is incredulity. Any
change can take place!

This leads Ovid to the greater marvel of the Phoenix which

possesses the capacity to resurrect itself from its own embalmed corpse. Compared to this, there is not much novelty (*si tamen est aliquid mirae novitatis in istis*, 408) in changes of sex, colour, or consistency!

We are now ready for another application of metamorphosis (v). Ovid cannot cover all kinds of changes in nature (time itself would run out in the process); thus with the scantiest of transitions, he turns to history: *sic tempora verti cernimus* (420–1). So many great cities of the past are now but names (xv, 430):

Quid Pandioniae restant, nisi nomen, Athenae?

But the reverse is also true. Even *now* (the time is obviously that of Pythagoras, some time preceding that of Numa) Rome is laying the foundations of a mighty future. The seers are predicting her leadership of the world. Here, therefore, Ovid finds room for his own version of Helenus' prophecy to Aeneas: Troy has not wholly fallen; Aeneas will claim another land where his successors will create a powerful realm which at long last one of his own descendants (*de sanguine natus Iuli*) will make mistress of all things (*dominam rerum*), while that descendant himself is destined to reach the heavens as a new god (xv, 446–9):

Hanc alii proceres per saecula longa potentem,
sed dominam rerum de sanguine natus Iuli
efficiet; quo cum tellus erit usa, fruentur
aetheriae sedes, caelumque erit exitus illi.

When through ages long
Her noble lords have made her great and strong,
One of Iülus' blood, with whom it lies
To make her mistress of the world, shall rise,
In whom, when earth's employments let him rest,
Shall heaven's abodes, his final home, be blest.

The Augustan orientation of the whole speech is thus quite obvious. It finally ends in a renewed plea for vegetarianism, but this, as we have seen, is only part of the speech's framework or narrative context. In fact, the essential message of Pythagoras ends with the Helenus prophecy that is the real culmination of the history section (v) which is itself the culmination of the long 'Change of Species' section (iv) that contains the heart of the doctrine. We have now been, as it were, alerted for the actual fulfilment of the prophecy at the absolute conclusion of the poem. We are prepared to see in Julius and Augustus the culmination of the process of change to which the whole *carmen perpetuum* has been devoted. There can be no doubt at all that this is what Ovid both implies and says. The question, however, that remains is how far we can take this philosophy of change as an interpretative key to the whole poem or to all the preceding metamorphoses.

We are not helped very much at this point by speculations on sources.[1] The 'vegetarian' sections are so patently separated from the main body of the speech—consider especially the return to the vegetarian theme after the climax of the Helenus prophecy—and so obviously adduced by way of introduction and conclusion, that we can hardly take the whole speech as Ovid's version of a treatise of some Pythagorean–vegetarian philosopher such as Sotion, or one of the Sotions. It has long been argued, and on fairly good evidence, that Ovid might have gone back to one of Posidonius' natural-historical treatises, probably through an intermediary such as the elder Varro. It is clear, of course, that Ovid got a good deal of his philosophic style from Lucretius. The content, however, is less Epicurean than Stoic, though it is most eclectically Stoic (hence the Aristotelian tags): the same point of view and style that we noted at the very beginning (the origin from Chaos) are also to be found here. But there is surely no attempt to elaborate a very exact metaphysic or natural science. Granting that Ovid wanted to set forth the idea of 'universal change', it would not have been difficult for him to find lists of strange natural phenomena. The idea is after all very simple and Ovid's exposition is along obvious lines.

But the parallelism and verbal similarity of the Pythagoras speech to the 'introduction' of the first book (5–75) suggest

[1] See Appendix, p. 423

that Ovid at least considered the possibility of a philosophic explanation for his myths. We probably should not make too much of
his statement in I, 2 that the *gods* (*di*) who inspired his incipient
epic were also the authors of all changes of shape. For these *di* are
vague: they may be the philosophical deities of I, 5–75 or they may
be simply the usual gods of mythology. In any event, the *natura*
who presides over creation in I, 21 seems identical with the *natura*
of metamorphosis in xv, 253. Philosophy thus encloses the epic:
Ovid reverts at the end to the mood of the beginning. But what,
after all, is he saying? Scarcely more than that the chain of mythological metamorphoses—the constant process of transition that
runs through his *carmen perpetuum*—can also be described in the
language of science and philosophy. At bottom, moreover,
mythology is not more incredible than science: we should hardly
believe that birds could come from eggs if we had not seen with
our own eyes. What is important is the reality of change itself, of
the constant shifting of all the forces and elements that compose the
universe in both space and time.

But what we *cannot* do—what is in fact the cardinal sin so far at
least as the morality of literary criticism goes—is to force a coherent symbolism on the whole poem solely on the basis of these
two philosophical digressions. Ovid's attitude toward myth is to
be discovered in his treatment of myth, not elsewhere. No preliminary or final statements of intention can blot out the statement
of the stories themselves or the actual continuity and plan that they
together comprise.

It is here that we encounter the particular problem of the
Augustan ending. In what sense does this ending come out of the
body of the poem? What sort of a conclusion does it really
represent? The main Pythagoras speech (without the vegetarian
introduction and conclusion) is, as we have seen, planned as a
crescendo that rises from the most generalized 'science' to Roman
history and its climax, the Helenus prophecy of Rome's headship
of the world under Caesar and Augustus. Whatever else the
speech may mean and whatever other function it may perform, it

is certainly a rather effective device for raising the tone of the poem and introducing the Augustan theme. Its role is here quite comparable to that of the philosophical speech of Anchises in *Aeneid* VI.

The way was thus opened by prophecy for the event. Here, by an extremely clever transition, Ovid passes from Aesculapius to Caesar (xv, 745–6):

> *Hic* tamen accessit delubris *advena* nostris:
> Caesar *in Urbe sua* deus est

> *Yet he, when all is said, came over seas*
> *To join the ranks of Roman deities;*
> *Caesar is god at home,*

and forthwith attributes his deification less to his own deeds in war and peace than to his offspring! Augustus had to have a divine father (760). The burden, in fact, of the ending is not Caesar and his metamorphosis into a star, but the greater glory of his heir (xv, 850–1):

> Stella micat; natique videns bene facta fatetur
> esse suis maiora et vinci gaudet ab illo.

> *And now a radiant star,*
> *He sees his son's great exploits from afar,*
> *And grants them greater than his own to be,*
> *Rejoicing in his son's supremacy.*

The very last lines (before the epilogue) look ahead to Augustus' apotheosis according to the Horatian formula of *serus in caelum redeas* (xv, 868–70):

> Tarda sit illa dies et nostro serior aevo,
> qua caput Augustum, quem temperat, orbe relicto
> accedat caelo faveatque precantibus absens!

> *Far be the time, deferred beyond our days,*
> *When great Augustus leaves the earth he sways,*
> *And joins the gods, yet still with loving care*
> *From distant heaven shows favour to our prayer.*

The burden of Jupiter's prophetic speech to Venus (807–42) is the glorious career of Julius' avenger! Here also Augustus' prospective apotheosis is anticipated (*aetherias sedes cognataque sidera tanget*) and it is only at the end that Jupiter, as by an afterthought, reverts to Julius: *hanc animam* interea *caeso de corpore raptam fac iubar*, etc.

The flattery here seems crude and excessive. The Virgilian apparatus of gods (colloquy of Venus and Jupiter, prophecy of Jupiter—just as in *Aeneid* 1) is lugged in at the end to satisfy convention and give *éclat* to a rather routine eulogy. What does it all have to do with the natural science and philosophy of Pythagoras or with the gods of the major portion of the epic? Again we can say that the beginning of the poem—the *concilium deorum* of the first book, especially the comparison of the dismayed gods to the human race appalled at the assassination of Caesar, 1, 199 ff.—is recalled at the end, but we can hardly overlook the irrelevance of all that lies between!

The fact is that despite the evident Augustanism of the concluding section (Books xii–xv)—the movement from Troy to Rome, the successive apotheoses, the preparatory philosophy, the Helenus prophecy and the finale—its plan is really a quite external one which develops a motif that was peripheral rather than central to the preceding sections. This portion of the work has great merits: some individual episodes (such as the story of Vertumnus, the song of Polyphemus, the debate on the arms, part at least of the Pythagoras speech) are admirable specimens of Ovid's art. But the movement of the poem (up to and including the *Ceyx and Alcyone*) is effectively stopped. The apotheosis motif has little or no organic connection with metamorphosis as otherwise conceived; the history is not really assimilated to the myth. Augustus is no logical conclusion to either the mythology or the philosophy of the *carmen perpetuum*. And no one, surely, can miss the conventionality of the panegyric at the end.

But it is very difficult to believe that Ovid was wholly unaware of what he was doing. We have commented on his strange parody of Virgil, the barely disguised perfunctoriness of much of his historical liaison, the way in which his collocation of the material (e.g. the insertion of the amusing debate between the epic and tragedy of the Trojan section) deflates its sobriety, his clever use of the *Aeneid* as a frame for light love stories. It is very hard to see all this as a serious preparation for an epic–patriotic conclusion. Ovid doubtless intended the Emperor to be pleased or at least mollified. But he did not expect all his readers to take him so literally. Whatever he was, he was not naive.

CHAPTER IX

CONCLUSION

This chapter is meant to be more than an ordinary conclusion. Since the first edition of this book appeared in
1966 and particularly since the MS of it was completed in
1964, a number of books and monographs on the *Metamorphoses*
have appeared. These, along with reviews of this book (some
quite lengthy), have made me rethink a great many points in its
argument.[1] But much more important than any of these (interesting and important as some of them are) has been the experience
of facing myself in the cold objectivity of print. I will freely admit
that could I (*per impossibile*) have had this experience before
writing the book, I would in fact have written it very differently.
Macaulay once said that nobody had written as stringent a review
of his *History* as he himself could have done. I now feel much
the same though I am not thereby comparing myself with him.

As to the reviews, I shall not attempt to 'answer' them except
by an occasional and anonymous reference to certain specific

[1] The following books on the *Metamorphoses* have appeared since my typescript
of the first edition of this book was completed: Walther Ludwig, *Struktur und
Einheit der Metamorphosen Ovids* (1965); Antonio Menzione, *Ovidio: Le Metamorfosi* (1964); M. von Albrecht, *Die Parenthese in Ovids Metamorphosen und ihre
dichterische Funktion* (Spudasmata VII, 1964); Hans-Bodo Guthmüller, *Beobachtungen zum Aufbau der Metamorphosen Ovids* (Diss. Marburg, 1964); Kurt Gieseking,
Die Rahmenerzahlung in Ovids Metamorphosen (Diss. Tübingen, 1964); Ernst
Jürgen Bernbeck, *Beobachtungen zur Darstellungsart in Ovids Metamorphosen*
(Zetemata 43, 1967); Simone Viarre, *L'image et la pensée dans les 'Métamorphoses'
d'Ovide* (Faculté...Lettres et Sciences Humaines de Paris, Sér. Recherches xxii,
1964). Reviews of the first edition of this book have appeared in *AJP* 89 (1968);
CP 61 (1966); *CR* (March 1967); *REL*, 43 (1966); *Revue de Philologie*, 41 (1967);
Oxford Review (1967); *Latomus*, 25 (1966); *Mnemosyne* 24 (1967); *Classical Bulletin*
(1966); *Deutsche Literaturzeitung* (1967); *Revue Belge*, 45 (1967); *Classical Folia* 20
(1966); *Times Literary Supplement* (1966); *Durham University Journal* (1967).
Doubtless some reviews have escaped my notice.

points. The reviewer has a right to his temporary infallibility—or so at least prevailing custom decrees. The reviews have been most helpful to me by indicating the extent to which I could be misunderstood or, more exactly, the extent to which my own judgements as to what was important and unimportant in the book could be transposed and inverted. For this, as I now clearly see, there was a good deal of justification. Any book that tries to say some new things is in large part a struggle for clarity: what seems obvious to the author is dismissed by him in a few words or silently taken for granted; what seems new or unusual is explained at some length and with emphasis. Yet the obvious to him may not be obvious to anyone else, and may also be much more important than what he deems to be obscure and in need of particular elucidation.

But, be that as it may, I am more concerned now with stating the truth as I now see it. An author ought never to stand on his former opinions: if there is one rule he should not observe it is that of *stare decisis*. This is especially true in the case of books on Ovid. After a long period of relative neglect and immobility, there are signs of both interest and change within the somewhat esoteric circle of classical scholars concerned with him, and perhaps also within the wider circle of those who still read him either in translation or in the original Latin. Few critics today, I think, would deny that one of his most pre-eminent qualities is his humour or wit; yet most of the Ovidian literature of the last hundred years pays the scantest attention to it. Furthermore, most of this literature until very recently has operated by the canons of a supposedly 'objective' scholarship: the aim was not really to find Ovid himself and his actual poetry but to determine his 'models' (mostly Greek), to define the literary genres or types in which he worked, to distinguish his styles (e.g. 'elegiac' *v.* 'epic') or to analyse his verse from a quite technical perspective. I myself have become increasingly aware, especially since I have been able to see myself in the mirror of print, of how much I too was a creature of such scholarship. The last thing I wish to do is to condemn it, to ignore all that it has taught us which is a very great deal; but it is, I am now convinced, a quite Procrustean bed for the accommodation of a lively poet.

Essentially I have no great retractions to make in this second edition:[1] in any event, the chapters of this new edition that are reprinted from the old (I–VIII) represent a stage in my thinking, and perhaps in the history of Ovidian research, that I have no wish to alter; let the reader, here in this conclusion, review and criticize them together with me. The revelation of a difference of perspectives, the difference between my opinions of 1964 and my opinions of 1968 will, I think, be more helpful and interesting than any attempt to rewrite the whole. I shall doubtless change some of my views once again, yet I must also record my conviction that what I now think about Ovid is perceptibly nearer the truth.

Two aspects of the book have been especially criticized or remarked by reviewers: the schema or plan of the *Metamorphoses* (outlined on pp. 84–5, 93, 129, 168, 278) and my use of the label 'epic'. It was perhaps natural that they should invite most misunderstanding of my general intentions. And I can now see that there is real ambiguity or lack of clarity in my treatment of these matters. But essentially the trouble, as I see it, lies in the very concept of 'plan', in the very idea of 'epic'. I was quite unaware of how unobvious, how little taken for granted were the things I had fondly thought to be too obvious for explicit statement. The trouble, furthermore, has been compounded by many recent essays in the reduction of Latin authors to various mathematical or other schemes that are remote indeed from anything I had in mind.

I gather that some have thought that I had in mind an intricate, mathematically elaborated schema of symmetries (precisely matching numbers of lines, exact equivalences of themes, etc.) that, for some obscure reason, Ovid had deliberately worked out

[1] My major change of opinion concerns my appraisal of the heroic-Augustan side or 'plan' of the poem. See pp. 351 f, 368 below.

from the start or before the start of his poem. Doubtless the intri-
cate-looking chart on p. 168 would, at a superficial glance,
encourage such a judgement, though I at least tried to warn the
reader against it in my preface (to the first edition, p. xiii). But any
'plan'—let alone a 'symmetrical' one—raises a problem that I
should, I now see, have considered more carefully. What is the
point of an all-embracing 'plan' for a very long fifteen-book poem
(of some 11,793 lines) obviously meant to be read rapidly and
constructed to conceal rather than to obtrude the transitions that
its variegated content necessitated? Ovid smooths the passages
from one book to another, one episode to the next, one motif to
its successor. The very last thing seemingly that the casual reader
could feel is the sense of an architectonic whole: in this respect
the *Metamorphoses* is almost the opposite of the *Aeneid* or of any
narrative with a single plot, a single cast of characters and a single
ethos and style.

I assumed (wrongly I now see) that this obvious point needed
no special emphasis. There are in fact two meanings of 'plan'
here which need to be distinguished. 'Plan' can mean a general
architecture or 'static' structure: another meaning of 'plan' (and
much the more important for the *Metamorphoses*) is a transitional
or evolutive design that pulls the reader along as it were from
one main point to another and through many subsidiary points
as well. Actually, I think the *Metamorphoses* has both, though the
first—the 'static' or architectural plan—is of secondary importance
and is not meant to impress the reader except in retrospect and
probably only after a number of re-readings. It is, in this respect,
like any architectural plan applied to material that has only linear
or temporal extension, such as music, drama, or prose narrative.
But because of the inherently episodic and varied character of the
Metamorphoses, the architecture is necessarily more concealed and
obscure.

The best comparison here, I think, is to an elaborately
designed mural or fresco such as those of Pompeii or, perhaps
even more exactly, to a large mosaic arranged in counterposed or

symmetrical 'panels' or vignettes. In the *Metamorphoses* certainly
the succession of long and short episodes, the alternation of
elliptical or sketchy and full length or detailed narratives, of
heroic and amatory, epic and un-epic passages, the intricate
variation of contents and styles, suggest the mosaic or tapestry:
indeed the tapestries of Minerva and Arachne in Book v seem to
show that Ovid himself thought in such terms. In the first two
books, the elaborate, lengthy Creation–Flood and Phaethon
episodes do indeed look like dominant 'panels' set off by the
surrounding shorter and differently styled episodes of divine love.
So too in Books iii–vi, with the long epical Perseus 'panel' of
Books iv–v interset between the carefully framed love stories of
the Minyades and Muses, the interspersed narratives of divine
vengeance. The long and pathetic amours of Books vi–xi
(Philomela–Tereus, Scylla, Byblis, Myrrha, Alcyone) correspond
to the large vignettes of several more or less contemporary murals
and, like them, are set off by a different background—in this case
a background of moral, heroic or miracle stories. In the last four
books the massive rhetorical and philosophic sections devoted to
the debate on the arms and Pythagoras' lecture on the 'nature of
things' are again set off by the surrounding epic, tragic, amatory
and religio-patriotic narratives.

But this architectonic or 'static' aspect of the *Metamorphoses* is,
as I have said, of secondary importance for the reader—certainly
for the contemporary reader for whom Ovid wrote. The question
here is whether the poem is indeed, as has often been thought or
tacitly assumed, a planless miscellany or, what is only a rather
slight modification of this view, a miscellany strung on a loose
and highly ambiguous chronology. The basic thesis of this book,
on the contrary, is that the *Metamorphoses* is in effect a network of
related motifs moving in a definite direction. The real problem of
its unity, on this conception, is the 'gap' between the last four
books (the Augustan portion) and the preceding eleven books
or, in other words, the discrepancy between the amatory plan
(that moves toward the massive Ceyx–Alcyone espisode) and the

CONCLUSION

Augustan or heroic-epic plan that culminates in the deification of Julius and the anticipated deification of his 'son' Augustus.

Here, of course, there is much room for legitimate dispute as to detail. As will be seen and has already in part been seen in the earlier chapters, there are in fact a number of intersecting patterns or plans, a constant striving for variation and alternation of motifs, a constant shifting of narrative units or frameworks that cannot be done justice to in any one (particularly any simple) plan. It is quite false to single out one element from this complexity as if this were in any sense the 'whole story'. Nevertheless, it would, I think, be obfuscating indeed to deny the poem a general plan or intelligibility on the ground that there are many sub-plans, much designed variety, a great deal of ingenious counterpoint and cross-harmony.

We can certainly see a number of sources for parts of *the plan* (to assume for the moment that this term is justified). Thus, as Walther Ludwig[1] points out, the combination of a Creation from Chaos with a series of amours between gods and mortal women is indubitably Hesiodic (the catalogue of women was for long supposed to follow the *Theogony* without a break)[2] and was indeed a sequence that was thoroughly familiar to Augustans as we know, for example, from the 'Song of Clymene' in the *Fourth Georgic*. The addition also of neoteric amatory *epyllia* to a philosophic *Creation* is directly attested by Virgil's *Sixth Eclogue*. The idea of a series of heroic myths, or more exactly myth-cycles (e.g. the sagas of Thebes, Calydon, Athens, Hercules), with chronological linkage goes back to such prose narratives as that of Pherecydes and was set forth also in didactic verse as well as in later prose 'handbooks'. The idea of a linkage of Troy and Rome through the figure of Aeneas was of course given prominence by the *Aeneid*. Finally the use of *metamorphosis* as a unifying device was prefigured by several didactic poems such as, perhaps most notably, the *Heteroioumena* of Nicander.

[1] See footnote on p. 306. I have profited greatly from an 'Ovid' seminar conducted jointly by Ludwig and myself.
[2] See M. L. West, *Hesiod, Theogony*, pp. 48–9 and 31 f.

But there seems little doubt that only Ovid combined all these ideas in one continuous poem. So we can account for part of his plan in Hesiodic, genealogical-mythical, neoteric-amatory and Virgilian terms; we can descry a vague but obviously operative chronology; we can certainly see a principle of selection based (though very partially based) on metamorphosis. But these things do not add up to much unity: no one of these factors provided an efficient principle of combination. Put somewhat differently, each of these elements provided Ovid with certain motifs: the divine amour, the offended *numen* of a god, the pious placation of a *numen*, the battle and other *aristeiai* of heroes, the tragic destruction of children by their mothers, the tragic grief of mothers and fathers at the loss of their children, pathological eroticism (including incest), the tragic separation of lovers, the various types of metamorphosis (as motivated by divine vengeance or spite or pity, sheer inability to preserve the human condition, heroic achievement deserving and achieving apotheosis). His problem therefore was, basically, to combine these motifs in some intelligible way if indeed he did recognize and deal with such a problem.

Here the chief obstacle to understanding lies, in my view, in Ovid's deliberate obscuration of real by specious or subsidiary connections. The different episodes were not (in very many cases) intrinsically related or connected: furthermore, Ovid for good reason was bound to disregard many of the connections that he found in the available mythology or the handbooks which recorded it. The links between episodes are very often superficial, sometimes quite deliberately so. Even when Ovid is dealing with a well-known myth-cycle, he never follows the usual genealogy, always interrupts it by quite alien episodes, and in fact selects (by omission, re-arrangement and careful management of transitions) exactly the motifs that he, for quite other reasons than the simple re-telling of the cycle, wants to use. In short, the ostensible linkage of episodes is more often than not deceptive. In this sense his *carmen perpetuum* is quite superficial.

It is precisely this 'deceptiveness', this obvious lack of a clearly stated or evident unity and the apparent substitution for it of superficial or *ad hoc* 'joins' between the disunited pieces, that has so stubbornly defied attempts to produce a convincing general pattern or plan. One can of course always posit what I have called the 'static' or architectonic plan, but this by its very nature excludes true narrative or linear unity: the unity is only that of a mosaic or Pompeian mural which is based on symmetry and on framing devices that are quite extrinsic to the framed pictures. But a study of the *ad hoc* links, the very notion of *carmen perpetuum*, or of an unbroken superficial narrative, shows at least that Ovid was highly concerned with the narrative or 'linear' connection. By his insistence on the *leitmotif* of *metamorphosis* (many episodes are in fact *not* metamorphoses but Ovid nevertheless tries very hard to link them in some way with metamorphosis), on genealogy and locality (the sections on Thebes and Athens, for example), by attributing many of the episodes to a narrator or narrators (Muses, Minyades, Achelous, Orpheus), he is obviously trying to maintain his continuous narrative. It is to these devices indeed that most analysts of the poem have looked for such 'plan' as they have been able to see. Yet it seems clear that study of what I have called the 'superficial' or *ad hoc* links can never carry us very far.

Walther Ludwig (whose monograph came out when this book was first printing) made a great advance by positing a 'plan' that took into account both the genealogy and narrative 'frames' as well as the dominant themes or 'motifs' of the poem. He identifies some twelve sections of varying lengths: first (1) Creation (the *Urzeit*); then eight sections of myth (*Mythische Zeit*), one (2) on the *amor deorum*, one (3) on the Theban cycle (i.e genealogical), one short section (4) on Perseus (who had a quite different genealogy—from Belus, not Agenor), a non-genealogical section (5) that combines the *ira deorum* theme with *amores*, a long genealogical section (6) on Athens (Theseus in particular), a short section (7) on Hercules, a long section (8) unified by the 'framing' or narrating Orpheus, another short one (9) on pre-Trojan material

(Peleus, etc.); then three sections (10–12) on *history* appropriately divided into Trojan, Aenean, and Roman subject-matter.

But the problem presented by this interesting 'plan' is what in fact it really means besides the obvious transition from Creation to 'mythical' and historical times. Ludwig thinks that it shows a correspondence or matching of certain sections in a more or less coherent scheme: thus sections 2 and 5 both deal with divine love and vengeance; 3 and 4 are clearly connected genealogical sections (descendants of Agenor and Belus); section 8 is again very similar to 2 and 5, while 6 and 7 (again genealogical) are, like 3 and 4, closely connected. This looks to me like a 'combination' of static-architectural and narrative plans that does not seem to have any clear *raison d'être*. I do not think that genealogy and motif or theme can be separated in this way: both in fact overlap and, aside perhaps from the more or less closely articulated Theban section (Ludwig's 3), the genealogical sections (especially the very heterogeneous Athens section, 6) are exceedingly loose 'units' to say the very most for them. Again the 'framing' of Book x by the figure of Orpheus (Ludwig's section 8) certainly puts together a most disparate series of episodes. Is Ludwig really warranted in shifting the unifying principle of his 'units' or sections from genealogy to motif to 'frame' in this rather bewildering way? If one operates simply on genealogical and 'frame' patterns, one can come up with quite a different scheme (e.g. that of Proosdij who posits some twenty-nine sections: he includes, like Ludwig, Theban and Athenian and Orpheus 'cycles', but breaks down the *Creation* into no less than six sections!).

It is, I think, only by paying close regard to motifs that we can reach anything like firm ground. Here, it is apparent, the *raison d'être* of the scheme set forth in this book has been misunderstood by several of my critics and that my own presentation of it has provided them with some excuse for their misunderstanding. Let me then try to retrace my schema in such a way as to show its narrative or linear (in distinction from its pictorial or static-architectural) function.

314

I may remark first of all that certain major 'divisions' or breaks in the poem are of particular importance even though Ovid was much concerned to minimize all the breaks in his *carmen perpetuum*. Though there is, I think, a break at the end of Book II (the transition from divine *amor* to divine *ira* and from vague localization to a definitely Theban setting), this is of quite minor importance beside the break in Book VI (with the transition from the final episodes of divine *ira* to the strictly human *Tereus–Philomela* episode that comes between lines 412 and 424). The distinction between this and the preceding vengeance stories (Pieriae, Arachne, Niobe, Lycian Peasants, Marsyas) is that there is, in it, no divine wrath at all, no explanation of the final metamorphoses as divine *poena* or retribution. There *is* vengeance in the *Tereus–Philomela* but it is a thoroughly human vengeance. Furthermore the *Tereus–Philomela* episode represents a new genre, the full length neoteric *epyllion* based on an essentially Euripidean theme. The important point is that with it a complete transition from gods to men, from divine to human love, vengeance and tragedy is effected. On the other hand, the very logic of Ovid's continuous narrative requires preparation or anticipation of a new theme: in this sense, therefore, the *Tereus–Philomela* is anticipated by the general vengeance atmosphere of Books III–VI, by a perceptible focusing on the human aspects of divine vengeance, and by short tales of *human* life and passion deliberately inserted within the 'divine vengeance' section. On the other hand, the gods by no means disappear from the scene after the *Tereus–Philomela*. They are for example quite conspicuous in Book X and play a definite role in Book XI but no one can mistake their relative de-emphasis as compared with their relative prominence before. So the *Tereus–Philomela* implies a major transition: in other words at this point the *main* narrative or the chief episodes effectively shift from a divine to a human motivation.

The second major 'break' or transition occurs at the beginning of Book XII with the introduction of the Trojan war and the whole historical or Virgilian sequence of Troy–Aeneas–Rome. Here again Troy had been prepared for in Book XI by brief mention of Laomedon, Peleus (Achilles' father), Aesacus (Priam's son), etc., but the actual Peleus–Thetis and Aesacus episodes and, most of all, the Ceyx–Alcyone episode they enclose, are thoroughly amatory in content and clearly belong in the general human-amatory context established by the *Tereus–Philomela*, *Medea*, *Procris–Cephalus* etc. The love theme of course re-emerges in the 'historical' books (XII–XV) but again the important point is that it ceases to be dominant or determinative of the narrative flow.

Gods, men and history (or men in history) thus have each their own major sections or thirds of the poem. But what does this mean aside from the obvious transition from Creation to saga-time to history and the specious linking of Creation with Ovid's own time (*mea tempora*)? Here we must look more particularly at the detailed development.

The initial 'Creation Epic' (as I have somewhat unwisely called it) is—on this there is some agreement, certainly between Ludwig and myself—a clear unit of narrative. The original creation, the four ages, the *concilium deorum*, the flood and the re-creation after it, form a quite intelligible whole. Nor can one, I think, mistake the central or pivotal position of the *Concilium*. In this it is notice-able that Jupiter's principal motivation is not merely the genera-lized wickedness of the iron-age but the specific wickedness of Lycaon. His is the first metamorphosis of the poem and it intro-duces a dominant motif: the offended *numen* of a god and the degrading metamorphosis by which the god punishes the offence. It seems highly probable that Ovid himself inserted this into the usual Creation–Flood saga. This is furthermore coupled with its opposite, the Deucalion–Pyrrha episode that likewise introduces a less dominant but also important motif: the reward of human piety by the pleased *numen* of a god.

But, as we have seen, this incipient theodicy (this reciprocity of human wickedness and piety, of divine punishment and reward) is followed by divine *amores* (Daphne, Io) that constitute a sort of 'divine comedy'. The metamorphoses here are not at all punitive. But the divine *amores* are brief. The massive *Phaethon* episode at the beginning of Book II introduces a new set of motifs though it continues the general theme of divine *maiestas* worsted by very human emotion: here the agony of a devoted father at the loss of a child, and, most of all, the premature attempt of a mortal to acquire divine status and privilege are primarily emphasized, not at all the divine amour. Phaethon tries to be a hero and to act like a god: he fails but his attempt prefigures the true hero and his true apotheosis later on in the poem. We then revert to divine *amores* (the symmetry of Apollo/Jupiter/Jupiter/Apollo in the Daphne, Io, Callisto and Coronis stories seems clearly intentional and the stories are close enough together for it to be noticed by a rapid reader) but with a change. Callisto and the jealous Juno who effects her metamorphosis are more pathetic or less comic than were Io or the Juno of that story. In the *Coronis* the love-story of Apollo is drastically curtailed: the main emphasis is now on the god's vengeance; Coronis has terribly offended his *numen*. This is even more true of the amour of Mercury and Herse: the story really centres on the jealousy of Aglauros and Mercury's vengeance upon her. The Europa story that closes Book II is a brief reversion to the mood of the earlier divine amours but it is obviously a closing episode as well as a transition.

Here we must note not only the obvious transition from divine love to divine vengeance but the 'symmetrical' character of it. What I have called, perhaps misguidedly, the 'law of symmetrical progression' (p. 86) is simply Ovid's peculiar combination of old and new motifs by elliptically repeating the old while really emphasizing the new. This is, I think, greatly facilitated by the intervening non-amatory *Phaethon*: it is not long enough to dim the repetition effect but it is quite long enough to mark a change, a new stage in the narrative. One must not of course interpret 'symmetry' here in a mechanical or mathematical way: had Ovid made his two sets of *amores* (i.e. those before and after the *Phaethon*) equally long or equally amatory, he would of course have spoiled his transition altogether and bored his reader by unnecessary emphasis of an already elaborated motif.

With Book III and up to and including the Ino incident of Book IV (through IV, 603 in fact), we have not only entered a Theban cycle (the first of a number of mythical cycles) but, much more significantly a series of divine *irae* or vengeances which effectively dominate the main narrative until the decisive 'turning point' in Book VI (the Tereus–Philomela). Now, of course, the amatory theme is dropped: this in effect marks the transition to the fully developed *ira* (or the divine *ira* without the divine *amor*). But we do not at once revert to the sort of theodicy prefigured by the Lycaon episode. The Theban cycle is, as I have shown, arranged in a series of divine *irae* based primarily on the two gods, Juno and Bacchus. The *aristeiai* and the final metamorphosis of Cadmus form an obvious frame for their *irae*. The initial *Actaeon* with its clear-cut echoes of *Callisto* is a tale not of human sin but of human error. The wrath of Diana then becomes the model and incitement of the much more spiteful wrath of Juno. The result of this—the destruction of Semele—introduces, of course, her son Bacchus, and it is through Bacchus that we finally recover a true theodicy (his rightful vengeance on Pentheus and Minyades). But the terrible Pentheus episode and the pendant Minyades episode once more excite Juno: the *Ino* then comes as the fitting conclusion to this set of *irae*. Juno has completed her vengeance on the house of Cadmus.

Thus we can hardly mistake the 'unity' of the poem so far (up to IV, 603). Ovid's 'Hesiodic' introduction of divine *amores* after the 'Creation' had not really stopped the 'theodicy' theme of the *Lycaon* but, as it were, deferred its full elaboration. The essential transition is from amatory to punitive gods: Juno is the figure who transforms the essentially comic (Jovian) amour (Io) into what is finally a vengeance or spite-episode (*Semele*—Callisto marks the transition to it): with the *Ino*, the amorous element in Juno's motivation is dropped, or extended to an 'objective' spite against the whole Cadmean household. Pentheus and the Minyades, on

318

the other hand, are not objects of divine spite but of divine punishment in the proper sense: they are not innocent victims (like Io, Callisto, Actaeon, Semele) but guilty profaners of the *numen* of Bacchus. The transition from Juno's erotic jealousy to Bacchus' theodicy is beautifully managed. Above all the recurrence of Juno in the *Ino* espisode is especially effective: the *Ino* completes both the Juno and the Theban motifs but does not erase the theodicy motif which is to emerge definitively after the long Perseus 'panel'.

The Perseus panel (IV, 609–V, 249) is of course a separate or distinct episode. Ludwig, Proosdij and many others have recognized this mainly because of its *genealogical* difference from the preceding Cadmean–Theban or Agenorid episodes. But Perseus' ancestry is only one (and I think the least significant) aspect of his distinctiveness. The *Perseus* episode is *also* distinctive because it is not (like the main narrative of e.g. III, 1–IV, 603) a narrative of divine vengeance, cleverly as it is assimilated to or made to look like one. Perseus takes vengeance on a clearly wicked or impious opponent; he is assisted throughout by Minerva; he kills the dragon and beheads the terrible Medusa. Yet he is the human hero of an epic (of the 'epical' style of the episode we shall presently speak) even though he is the son of Jupiter. This fact indeed provides Ovid with his transition from as well as parallel to Bacchus. Both Bacchus and Perseus are sons of Jove (their mothers, Semele and Danae) but the Argive king Acrisius (grandfather of Perseus) recognizes neither the divinity of the former nor the divine paternity of the latter (IV, 604–14). Ludwig, like Proosdij, sees in Bacchus the prototype of Hercules and of the later Romans, Aeneas, Romulus, Julius and Augustus—the deified hero, the man who deserves and attains apotheosis. But it does not seem to me that Ovid emphasizes this connection (the apotheosis of Bacchus is only elliptically indicated: he is never treated as a hero who becomes a god, but rather as a god from the very start) so much as that of Perseus with his more august successors. Just as Phaethon failed to attain or maintain a divine status, so Perseus succeeded in establishing a truly heroic one. He is in a sense (as we have seen above and shall see also below) a prototype of Aeneas and his story is heavily inlaid with Virgilian reminiscences. Furthermore, the decided difference or deliberate 'isolation' of the Perseus episode (in respect to narrative connection, genealogy, motif and style) singles it out for comparison with the similarly isolated and styled episodes of Phaethon, Meleager and Hercules. These episodes are those of heroic *aristeiai* (especially epic battles) and carry the burden of the poem's 'heroic' message. In a more positive sense, these episodes associate men with gods and clearly lead to their final metamorphosis into gods. The *Perseus* is here the link between Phaethon and Hercules.

After the *Perseus* (v, 250–VI, 420), we revert to another series of divine *irae* (here indeed Ludwig acknowledges a unity or principle of connection based on *motif* rather than genealogy). But this time the theodicy motif (divine *ira* as righteously punishing offenders against a god's *numen*) is absolutely dominant: the Pieriae, Arachne, Niobe, the Lycian Peasants, Marsyas are all guilty of sacrilegious *hybris*. In the case of the Pieriae and Arachne there is an actual contest with the gods: the mortal women singing of or depicting (in tapestry) the cowardice and amatory folly of the gods: the divinities (Muses, Minerva) depicting their own beneficence as well as righteous vengeance. Here as before with the 'symmetrically progressive' amatory episodes following the *Phaethon*, the *irae* are curtailed (some 840 as opposed to 1337 lines) in relation to those before the *Perseus* (or in III, 1–IV, 603). The massive *Niobe* (with its appended, indirectly narrated short episodes of the Peasants and Marsyas) ends the section with considerable aplomb. It is worth remark that the 'correspondences' of the two *irae* sections (before and after the *Perseus*) are carefully underlined. Not only the main motif but the two framed amatory series (Minyades, Muses–Pieriae) provide an obvious balance or 'symmetry' on each side of the *Perseus*. This is even underlined by one apparently 'unsymmetrical' feature, the insertion of the *Ino* between the *Minyades* and the *Perseus*, with the resulting order: Minyades, Ino, Perseus, Muses–Pieriae, Arachne. But the reason for this is Ovid's desire to repeat the motif of the first *ira* section: the motivation of one goddess's wrath (Juno, Minerva) by the spectacle of another's successful vengeance (Bacchus' on the Minyades, the Muses' on the Pieriae). Minerva's punishment of Arachne is suggested by the Muses' punishment of the Pieriae just as Juno's punishments of Semele and Ino are suggested by Diana's of Actaeon and, most pertinently, Bacchus' of the Minyades. But this 'symmetry' is narrative as well as architectonic: the reader is meant to recall the prior motifs and thus also mark the shift or new development of them.

But what of the episodes that are not controlled by the *ira* motif—i.e. the love stories of the Minyades and Muses, the differently toned and basically amatory story of Narcissus and Echo? The basic reasons for their insertion are surely Ovid's evident desire for variety (he had to break in some way the monotony of the *ira* theme) and his equally evident desire to keep the amatory motif (of the first two books) fully alive. *Proserpina* is obviously a 'recall' of the divine *amor* theme (re-emphasized indeed by the inset *Arethusa* that particularly recalls the *Daphne*) but the three tales of the Minyades for the first time introduce the motif of essentially *human* love (without divine vengeance) and point ahead to, or 'anticipate', the next large section (VI, 420–XI, 795). Ovid however (here also true to his principle of 'progressive' symmetry) varies the 'frame' of the inset episodes: in the first set (Minyades) they are separate unrelated songs: in the second set the sub-tales (Stellio, Arethusa, Ascalaphus, Triptolemus) are included within the main Proserpina narrative. But in each case Ovid preserves the unity of the main narrative and theme (the *ira* of the gods) by subordinating the sub-narratives to it. The 'frame' device is a sort of parenthesis that indicates clearly the eccentric or digressive character of what is framed. The narrators in each case (Minyades, Muses) are themselves participants in the main story, each victims or agents of divine vengeance. Thus Ovid is careful to underline the unity of each section even while he is intent on achieving variety.

The Narcissus–Echo story is from this standpoint very interesting: not being an 'inset' or framed episode, it formally adheres to the *ira* motif—Juno takes vengeance on Echo, one of Narcissus' rejected lovers prays for vengeance on him. But in reality it is a clever *divertimento* and basically amatory in conception. I cannot but feel it is really a disguised bit of self-criticism. Ovid was well aware that he was criticized for his repetitions, his deliberate indulgence of his own genius or in this sense his excessive fondness for himself. But, be this as it may, the *Narcissus* is a refreshing variant on the main motif which yet does not distract the reader's attention from it.

So far the main narrative or motif-development has been relatively easy to follow. (The full meaning of the essentially independent or 'different' Phaethon and Perseus episodes has of course not yet come out but their very magnitude makes them easy to remember, for the reader to recall them later in the story.) But with the *Tereus–Philomela* (VI, 424 f.) we reach, as we have seen, a major divide or turning point. It, of course (Ovid always 'anticipated' his transitions), makes use of former motifs: vengeance or *ira* (though not divine), sexual *libido*, child-murder (Agave, Niobe, Ino), the horrible use or 'parody' of Bacchic enthusiasm (Ino), metamorphosis as the only available solution of an agony or passion beyond human endurance or expression (Niobe, especially)—above all, emphasis of the human (as distinct from the divine) aspect of tragedy (here again the conclusion of *Niobe* especially pre-figures the plight of Philomela or Procne—that of a woman driven out of her normal character and feelings by a massive tragedy). But there is also an essential novelty in the episode, a clearcut difference from the divine *ira* motif that has so far predominated.

The episode commences in a manner very similar to (probably in fact recalling) the beginnings of the *Ino* and the *Niobe*. Ino's *happiness* is the thing that initially excites Juno: *adspicit hanc* [i.e. Ino]/*natis thalamoque Athamantis habentem/sublimes animos.* Niobe's happiness is more directly built on her pride: *et felicissima/ matrum dicta foret Niobe, si non sibi visa fuisset.* The happiness of Procne and Tereus is seen from the start as a pernicious deception: *usque adeo latet utilitas.* But what reverses the appearances is no angered *numen* but the actual *libido* of Tereus: *hunc . . . innata libido/exstimulat, flagrat vitio gentisque suoque.* It is this that makes tragedy out of the apparently happy marriage, its fruitful outcome (the child Itys), the sisterly devotion of Procne and Philomela, the father's (Pandion's) affection for his child (Philomela). And it is this that wipes all other emotions from Procne and Philomela save the desire for revenge. The murder of the little Itys and the cannibal feast signify the degradation that the metamorphosis, as it were, ratifies: the trio are already less than human. The *libido* in other words takes the place of the god's *ira* as a motivating force of tragedy: the parallel between Niobe and Procne is clear to see.

This theme recurs throughout the whole section (through the Myrrha episode of Book x: it is slightly re-echoed in the Aesacus episode that closes Book xi). The *libido* of Medea in Book vii (*video meliora proboque:/deteriora sequor!*) causes her to betray her family, and eventually kill her own children. The female *libido* is indeed worse than the male: with Scylla (Book viii) it leads to patricide; with Byblis (Book ix) to the lust for incest; with Myrrha to incest itself.

But the perverted, pathological and destructive *libido* is contrasted with a quite different, essentially good kind of *amor*. In the seventh book, the *libido* of Tereus, the revenge of Procne are re-echoed by Medea (even though the parts of her tragedy that would repeat the Tereus–Procne motifs are barely mentioned) but the concluding *Procris and Cephalus* strikes another note that clearly recalls the *Pyramus–Thisbe* of Book iv and anticipates the *Orpheus–Eurydice* of Books x and xi, the grandiose *Ceyx–Alcyone* of Book xi. These are all tragedies—the lovers are catastrophically separated—but the endings in some sense validate the strength of the mutual affection: Procris dies in final knowledge of Cephalus' faithfulness; Orpheus and Eurydice are re-united in the under-world; Ceyx and Alcyone resume their conjugal happiness in an animal form.

Furthermore the contrast is heightened by the tales of the successful love that comes as a reward to the piety of Iphis and Pygmalion. Iphis is the obvious foil for Byblis: Pygmalion for Myrrha. Even the *amor* of the gods is softened and sentimentalized: it is no longer the near-rape of the Daphne, Io and Arethusa episodes. Apollo mourns for Cyparissus and Hyacinthus, Venus for Adonis in much the manner of Orpheus for Eurydice. We can hardly make too much of the tragedy of these brief tales: they reveal, rather, an elegiac mood, the conversion of the great gods to a tender and all-too-human amorousness.

But love is not the sole, even if the dominant, theme of this section (VI, 424–XI, 795). It is shared by two other motifs: theodicy and the hero. In Book VII Medea enacts a weird sort of resurrection or rejuvenation (Aeson) that has its painful counterpart in the pretended rejuvenation and actual murder of Pelias. Medea finally signifies nothing but evil. Yet Juno's destruction of the people of Aegina through dire pestilence is recompensed by a Jovian miracle which is really a reward for the trust and piety of Aeacus. Then at the very centre of the poem (the middle of Book VIII) the story of Philemon and Baucis spells out the theodicy theme in a definitive way. It comes furthermore as the answer to the doubts of a sceptic. Its moral is supplemented by the story of the punishment of the sacrilegious Erysichthon. The reference back to the similarly paired *Deucalion–Pyrrha* and *Lycaon* of the initial Creation episode seems unmistakeable. Finally, in Books IX, X and XI the stories of Iphis, Pygmalion, Atalanta and Midas contrast the punishment of the ungrateful or insensitive with the reward of the pious and tender. Even Venus is at last a goddess of justice and mercy.

The third major motif of this large section is the heroic: this is prefigured by the brief mentions of Theseus in Books VII and

VIII, by the heroic characters of Cephalus, Aeacus and Minos (whose heroism however is confined to brief allusions): but the only heroes who appear at any narrative length are Meleager and above all Hercules. They form an obvious contrast. The terrible boar that upsets Calydon is Diana's vengeance for the slight to her *numen*. Meleager's attachment to Atalanta is disavowed by Cupid. His impulsive murder of his own uncles receives its punishment at the hands of his own mother. He burns to death with the brand that holds his fate and there is nothing but the bitterest grief for his fate. Hercules, on the contrary, is the innocent victim of terrible jealousy and error: his great deeds guarantee his apotheosis, as Jove explains in an opportunely assembled *concilium deorum*. Even Juno cannot oppose it. We have thus reached the *dénouement* of heroism: Hercules, unlike Meleager and such other gods' sons as the immature Phaethon and the merely heroic Perseus, fully deserved his divine destiny. The whole central section of the poem (latter half of Book VIII and first half of Book IX) thus combines theodicy and apotheosis in an obviously climactic ensemble.

The combination of these three major motifs is a work of considerable art. Various 'frames' or framing devices (Athenian genealogy from Pandion to Theseus; Medea; the conversations of Cephalus and Aeacus; Minos; the journey of Theseus from Calydon to the cave of Achelous; the conversation at the cave; Hercules himself; Orpheus; Laomedon, Troy and Peleus) form the links but most of these are quite superficial. What counts is the succession of motifs at short intervals and with due allowance for variety. Procne, Medea, Scylla, Althaea, Deanira, Byblis and Myrrha all enact the fatal woman who ruins her husband, child, father or herself in a fury of erotic or consanguineal emotion. The *libidines* of Scylla, Byblis and Myrrha are remarkably similar but also ingeniously varied. The offsetting episodes of mutual love or of love rewarded are ingeniously contrasted: Procris follows Medea; Iphis follows Byblis: Pygmalion just precedes Myrrha. Though the gods are absent or inconspicuous in most of the amatory episodes, they dominate the series of theodicies which form a major contrasting element: as in the seventh book with the *Plague* and the *Myrmidons* (men from ants); in the eighth with the central *Philemon–Baucis* and *Erysichthon*; in the ninth with *Iphis*; in the tenth with *Pygmalion* and *Atalanta* (gratitude rewarded, ingratitude punished by Venus) and in the eleventh with *Midas*.

But we must not look for any mechanical or obtrusive 'symmetry' in this section. In the first place the material preceding the massive epics and theodicies of Books VIII–IX (what I have called the section's 'central core') is out of proportion to the relatively voluminous material after it: the first takes some 1421, the second some 2059 lines or about 600 lines (almost a book) more. More important is the fact that the correspondences of motif elements are a good deal less symmetrical than those before and after either the *Phaethon* or the *Perseus*. The seventh and tenth books have a quite different structure: the doublets of Book VII (Aeson/Pelias and Plague/Myrmidons) are quite unlike the doublets of Books IX and X (Byblis/Iphis *v.* Pygmalion/ Myrrha or, alternatively, Iphis/Pygmalion *v.* Atalanta/Midas). The divine amores of Book X are quite different from anything preceding. Even though there is a certain similarity between the non-amatory Daedalus–Icarus and Dryope episodes they are much more different than alike. Their main function is to provide an effective interlude or 'cushion' between major heroic and amatory episodes (*Scylla* and *Meleager; Hercules* and *Byblis*). In short the structure of this section (VI, 424–XI, 795) is relatively 'loose' in comparison with the sections preceding or following.

Yet the reason for this is obvious enough. The reader simply could not take in such extensive material with sufficient precision of memory to justify the closer kind of correspondence we find, for example, in Books I and II or III–VI, 411. Ovid would never have sacrificed a narrative to a purely 'architectonic' end. The important point is that the major motifs are present in each 'half,' i.e. that before and that following the massive *Meleager–Philemon–*

Baucis–Erysichthon–Hercules 'core'. *Tereus–Philomela, Medea, Procris–Cephalus* and *Scylla* establish the amatory and libidinous motifs: the *Aeacus* narratives (*Plague, Myrmidons*) establish the theodicy motif. *Theseus, Cephalus, Minos,* etc. pre-figure the 'heroic' core. Though all these elements are greatly developed and changed in the second half, there is more than enough parallelism or identity of motif to mark the essential correspondence of the two halves.

The main problem of the section is not its arrangement but the apparent clash or contradiction of the major motifs as well indeed as the clash between the motifs of this and those of the preceding section or sections (the decisive 'sectional' break, as we have seen, is at VI, 420).

No one can doubt that the destructive *libido* is a major if not dominant theme of the section. The important features of this *libido* (as seen in Tereus, Medea, Scylla, Byblis, Myrrha) are its *instantaneousness* (or complete lack of development or growth), its essential *immorality* (disregard of all competing obligations) and its *destructive* outcome. There seems to be no possibility of effective resistance to its fatal course: once Tereus sees Philomela, once Medea actually holds her *tête-à-tête* with Jason, once Scylla catches sight of Minos from the tower, once Byblis and Myrrha persuade themselves that they can attain their objects, there is no stopping short of the terrible *dénouement*. Nor is the *libido* less destructive of those who resist it than of those who actually harbour it: Procne and Althaea kill their children out of hate and the desire to avenge a sister or brother, but their emotions are no less fatal or terrible than the purely erotic jealousy of Medea or Deanira. Here of course Ovid employs a quite thoroughly established and highly popular motif, first developed and made influential by Euripides, then given wide currency by the Alexandrians and neoterics. Indeed Cinna's *Smyrna* was the acknowledged *chef-d'œuvre* of neoteric literature: Parthenius' *Erotica Pathemata* the quasi-authoritative handbook of plots for neoteric writers such as Gallus. Virgil, for good reason, had made the Silenus song of *Eclogues* VI culminate in the *libidines* of Sadiphae, Scylla and Tereus. But we need go no further back than the *Heroides* of Ovid himself.

The important thing, therefore, is not Ovid's adoption and use of this motif. As a neoterically educated writer with a 'Hesiodic' orientation, he could hardly have avoided it. What is of much greater interest for the understanding of his general poetic purpose in the *Metamorphoses* is the way in which he relates it to his other motifs and the total effect he thereby produces. Here two things are evident. The episodes that depict a *libido* (in the sense just set forth) are contrasted with other episodes of what we may call *mutual love*. The *libido* by its very nature is isolating, quite unreciprocated and productive only of repulsion and hatred. Tereus, Scylla, Byblis, Myrrha, Medea, are or become only monsters to the objects of their desire. Procris and Cephalus, Orpheus and Eurydice, Ceyx and Alcyone, like the prefiguring Pyramus and Thisbe, are all too human, sympathetic, pitiable and pitied. Nor, as I have tried to show in chapter VII, was Ovid here simply repeating Greek or neoteric originals. The *Orpheus–Eurydice*, of course, is heavily indebted to Virgil and treated with a lighter touch that verges on parody: Ovid was obviously determined to avoid direct or serious imitation of Virgil's masterpiece. But the *Cephalus–Procris* and *Ceyx–Alcyone* (each, it must be noted, pivotally placed in the first and second 'halves' of this section: *Procris* closing the book that begins with *Medea* and immediately preceding *Scylla* at the beginning of Book VIII; *Alcyone* concluding the whole section and described with the obvious amplitude and resonance that befits a finale) are, as I have tried to show, very drastic alterations of their Greek originals, in no sense (so far as we can tell) prefigured by neoteric predecessors.

The second important thing about Ovid's treatment of the *libido* theme is the way he relates it to metamorphosis. The *Cephalus–Procris*, of course, is not a metamorphosis (the interset metamorphoses of the dog and wolf are obviously superficial and unrelated to the main episode): the reason he nonetheless tells it is not only that he needs it in its particular context (i.e. between Medea and Scylla) but that he is not yet ready to propose a solution to the problem it presents. Or put differently: there is something quite inevitable and natural about the metamorphoses of Tereus, Philomela, Procne or Scylla (they have already cut, as it were, their links with humanity); the situation of Procris and Cephalus is not at all the same. But when we finally reach Byblis and Iphis in the ninth book, we have already been prepared for a quite different type of metamorphosis, a quite different relation of gods to men than had been formerly the case: the 'theodicies' of the eighth book have pointed the way. Iphis, unlike Byblis, desires in her piety and humanity, only a normal and mutual love: the goddess Isis rewards her with a miraculous metamorphosis. So too with the contrasted Myrrha and Pygmalion. But so also with Atalanta (rightfully penalized out of her human shape). The 'pity' of the gods in the *Ceyx–Alcyone* is, as we have seen, but a dim reflection of the pity of nature itself: nevertheless a counterforce to destructive libido and degenerative metamorphosis has at last been built up and brought to decisive action. (This is not, I think, materially diminished by the successive catastrophes of the gods' darlings in Book x. They are really nothing but pathetic objects of Apollo's or Venus' devotion and can quite appropriately become perpetual emblems of grief as cypress, hyacinth or anemone).

But how are we to reconcile this treatment of the amatory theme with the heroic deeds of Meleager and Hercules and above all with the divine love and wrath of Books I–VI, 424? Is Ovid really taking theodicy so seriously? Can we revert as it were to the 'piety' of Deucalion and Pyrrha (i.e. with their alter egos, Philemon and Baucis) despite the intervention of some seven books of divine love-making and rage? The apotheosis of Hercules is in one sense the culmination of human heroism—he achieves the divinity that Phaethon missed, that other heroes such as Perseus and Theseus had not yet attained—but it comes as an oddly perfunctory conclusion to his amatory tragedy. The stories of the Pieriae, Arachne and Niobe (even the brief episodes of the Lycian Peasants and Marsyas) are in a sense theodicies—mortal presumption and sacrilege rightly punished—but we are finally left with more of a feeling of pity for human suffering (poor Niobe and her undeservingly annihilated family) than of respect for divine justice. After this the *libido* of Tereus comes as an abrupt change of direction even though we can feel also a certain continuity of motif and tone. We have in one sense been prepared for human suffering and the metamorphosis that comes from it (not the punishing gods) but how can the gods who caused the suffering now assume an attitude of justice and mercy—no longer amorous and spiteful or rightfully, if mercilessly, avenging, but actually benevolent? There is an evident shift of point of view, an evident loss of consistency that comes with this section and the Tereus story which opens it.

There is an equally disconcerting difference of tone or loss of continuity between the amatory and the heroic episodes. The *aristeiai* of Perseus conform in a way to the vengeance theme: he as the conqueror and petrifier of Pheneus is obviously indulging in a righteous vengeance with divine aid. But the elaborate boar-hunt of Meleager, the contest of Hercules and Achelous, the apotheosis of Hercules—what have these really in common with the *libidines* and *amores* that surround them? Or, for that matter, with the theodicy theme, save in any but the most perfunctory way?

But we are vastly more disconcerted by the third and final section that follows (Books XII–XV). Here the essential divisions and 'symmetry' are fairly evident: Ludwig's scheme is to all intents and purposes the same as my own and clearly seems based on Ovid's own design. There is a big Trojan section with a large-scale battle and *aristeiai* (Lapiths and Centaurs), a rhetorical debate (Ulysses and Ajax) and a tragedy (Hecuba); then the voyage of Aeneas to Latium (though it is mainly a frame for various love-tales and parodies of Virgil and Homer) and, finally, the Roman finale (immigrant and native gods of the city framing the massive 'lecture' of Pythagoras and leading into the Julio-Augustan ending). We easily see (indeed Ovid underlines the connections) that the apotheoses of Aeneas, Romulus and Julius Caesar are meant to complete and fulfil the 'heroic' sequence that had reached a previous culmination in the apotheosis of Hercules. But the lack of continuity with the preceding section is not any the less shocking. Though there are amatory episodes interwoven with Aeneas' voyage to Latium, they come too late (after the huge, non-amatory Trojan section) and are too diffuse in tone and conception to establish any connection with the intensely amatory section that culminates in the *Ceyx–Alcyone*. Furthermore, the absurd reduction of the *Aeneid* to a loose frame for these love tales is hard—in fact impossible—to reconcile with a serious Augustan and Roman-patriotic intent.

We cannot, in fact, proceed further by consideration of motifs alone or of the 'plan' by which they are linked. It is clear that Ovid's 'design' or plan (if such there really is) was the result of a poetical intention that cannot be discovered by taking his 'motifs' or the bare plots of his stories at their face value. The *Metamorphoses* is neither serious nor obvious in the sense that the *Aeneid* or the usual epic is. There is no clear plot, no uniformity of *ethos*, no congruence between the ostensible and the actual purpose of the writer. We come to the second major problem posed on p. 308: the problem of what the *Metamorphoses* is or what sort of an 'epic' it can properly be said to be.

My use of 'epic' as label for the poem has raised some critical eyebrows. A good deal of this has been my own fault: I have failed to distinguish clearly between what I may call the superficial and the 'deeper' or less obvious meaning of the term. In any event the term can be misleading, particularly if it makes us impose merely extraneous or alien conceptions on the poem's reality. The superficial sense in which the *Metamorphoses* is an 'epic' is that suggested in Heinze's famous monograph (discussed on pp. 49 f.) even though a number of modifications must be made in his formulation of the problem. There are, at the very

331

least, many episodes in the poem that certainly show a superficial observance of epic convention: gods, heroes, long 'epical' speeches, epic descriptions or *ekphraseis*, similes and epithets, above all a 'continuity' of narrative and an objectivity of viewpoint that are quite unlike the jerky, syncopated, subjective narrative of elegy.

Yet there is in fact much variation of style and content: the huge fifteen-book poem shows a 'kaleidoscopic' (an epithet often and deservedly applied to it) diversity of episodes, characters and points of view. No deduction of a general, overall style from any one episode or passage, or even from a number of such, can do it justice. Nevertheless, there are some fundamental traits that belong to the whole poem and distinguish it from elegiac and Alexandrian hexameter verse as well as from Homeric and Virgilian epic.

The most important of these perhaps is the *continuity* of the narrative. Though episodic in the sense that it contains many episodes often quite loosely or superficially joined, the *Metamorphoses* is not episodic in the manner of the *Fasti* or other narrative elegy (such as Callimachus' *Aitia*) or in the manner of the Alexandrian and neoteric *epyllion* (or, perhaps better put, the 200–600 line hexameter poem on the order of Callimachus' *Hecale*, Theocritus' *Dioscuri*, Catullus' *Peleus and Thetis*). As Heinze pointed out, such poetry is marked by an asymmetrical structure, by which is meant a concern with the 'high-lights' or specific moments or scenes in a story rather than with the story itself. Such poetry is therefore by its very nature *discontinuous*: the main events (in a narrative sense) are hurried over, even omitted or taken for granted, so that certain piquant scenes (those that the poet is interested in) can be emphasized. In the *Peleus and Thetis*, for example, the marriage of Thetis is really a background or 'frame' for the Ariadne story and that in turn is really reduced to her formal lament on the desolate beach. The 'digression' in fact that seems to play a major role in such poetry is a clear sign of its non-narrative interest and intent. The loss of most of the so-called *epyllia* prevents us, however, from drawing too many generalizations. Yet even where there are no 'digressions' in a formal sense, the essentially non-narrative character of the poetry is evident, as we can see in comparing Theocritus with Apollonius in such episodes as those of Hylas and the Dioscuri. Ovid composed several long elegiac narratives (e.g. the Proserpina and the Lucretia episodes of the *Fasti*) but their narrative discontinuity, the neglect of substance for detail, the evident drag of their closed couplets on the progression of the story, is very plain.

Yet we must not misunderstand what 'continuity' or 'symmetrical' narrative structure here means. Clearly Ovid in the *Metamorphoses* does often summarize, truncate or lightly sketch episodes that he does not want to tell at length or episodes that would involve the wearisome repetition of motifs already utilized. Nor does the mere adoption of hexameter (as opposed to elegiac) verse entail the total abandonment of all elegiac traits: here indeed Heinze greatly overstated the distinction of styles by metre. The important and decisive point is the concern with an ongoing narrative—the concern to *tell a story* and to give at least the impression of telling a continuous story and not a string of episodes. The divers episodes of Callimachus' *Aitia* were linked by devices such as having the Muses answer a succession of discrete questions: the tales of the *Fasti* were of course linked by the calendar. Such 'links' were themselves a sign of discontinuity: the *Metamorphoses* avoided them and tried, with whatever stoppages and periphrases, to give an impression of constant forward narrative movement. Both the bulk of the narratives and the narrative *liaison* preserve the sense of story, of on-going action.

But this 'continuity' is also something very different from that of the true epic—whether Homer, Apollonius or Virgil. For the *Metamorphoses* is not only a *continuous* narrative but a *Hesiodic* or *discontinuous* medley of narratives. In other words, the *Metamorphoses*, by its very nature and certainly by the poet's intention, is not designed to preserve a single tone or *ethos*, a pervading 'high style' of the sort that Horace recommended to the would-be

Roman writer of epic. Ovid can be serious (as we shall see) but he is never serious when he echoes or recalls Virgil: his concern to distinguish his poem from the *Aeneid*, to mark the deliberate difference of tones is quite obvious and seemingly quite intentional. The plan of the *Metamorphoses* gave him scope, the possibility of variety, of an elaborate polytonality that utterly flouts the stylized uniformity, the deliberate *hypsos* or elevation of epic. His narrative continuity is coupled with great discontinuity of style and content. But here again the difference from Callimachean or neoteric poetry is evident: the continuous hexameter narrative at least made the 'high' or epic style a definite possibility of which Ovid frequently made use (as Heinze saw). Even this, as we shall see, was quite un-Virgilian and un-Homeric but it was certainly also un-Callimachean and un-neoteric. What has so often baffled the critics is the very fact that Ovid can both sink and rise, sink to a low or elegiac and rise to a high or epic style.

What has often been quite misunderstood (witness some of my critics) is the so-called 'symmetry' that goes with the 'continuity' of the style. By this I mean the fact that the story or plot (*mythos* in the Aristotelian sense) is not sacrificed to details or to what I have called elsewhere the piquant or sentimental moment, the special scene, tableau or impression. It is this, for example, that distinguishes Ovid's *Scylla* from the pseudo-Virgilian *Ciris* (cf. pp. 62–5 above) even though the *Scylla* itself is elliptical or asymmetrical by comparison with other Ovidian narratives and certainly by comparison with any narrative of the *Aeneid*.

The point is that there are no absolute breaks in the narrative, no omissions of essential *liaison*, no stoppage of the action even by the long soliloquy. This does not mean that there cannot be (as there often is) far more ellipsis and asymmetry than in a truly epic style such as Homer or Virgil. Ovid can be asymmetrical just as he can be epic in the *Metamorphoses*. But he is never (in the *Metamorphoses*) asymmetrical or elliptical in the manner of elegy or most known *epyllia*: his narrative never stops, or never stops long enough to sacrifice the plot or the action.

334

There are, of course, certain pervasive characteristics of this continuously narrative but discontinuously styled poem. One is the metre that we have briefly discussed on pp. 74–7. The principal thing, perhaps, to be said about it is that it virtually precluded the *ethos* or narrative style of Virgil in the *Aeneid*. Ovid's sense-units or 'cola' are usually brief and heavily marked by the line ends and the main pauses (especially the third foot caesura). The gradual build-up of verse-groups toward a clinching or climactic line, the long emotional sweeps of the *Aeneid*, are quite un-Ovidian. Yet this did not so much forbid the expression of solemnity or grandeur (when he wanted it) as facilitate a rapid shifting of tone and mood. In general the effect of the metre is one of lightness and rapidity. Its more important contribution, however, is its enhancement of fluidity, the impression it gives of a narrative effortlessly carrying a series of multiplex impressions and constantly changing its direction even while never giving up the sense of steadily moving toward a goal.

A second major characteristic of the *Metamorphoses* is the subjectivity of the point of view, the covert (sometimes overt) presence of the narrator as he either opens the *psyches* of his characters to the penetration of the reader or himself comments upon them and upon the action or, as is very often the case, does both things at once. Here Ovid is at once like and very unlike Virgil, and quite dissimilar to Homer and Apollonius or such Alexandrian opponents of long epic as Callimachus and Theocritus. Michael von Albrecht[1] has pointed out the striking character of Ovid's 'parentheses'—the interjections that rapidly cover an exclamation, comment or casual remark—and their largely subjective effect. We find also subjective parentheses in Virgil but Ovid's are not only more frequent but quite different in effect. It is as if he were insisting that the reader see the 'point' (often a witty or incongruous point) of the narrative. When he describes the 'virginal' Scylla (XIII, 733–4):

[1] See footnote on p. 306.

335

Virginis ora gerens et, *si non omnia vates,*
ficta reliquerunt, aliquo quoque tempore virgo

Virgin was her face, and if poets don't always lie, a virgin
once she really was.

he is obviously 'stepping outside' the story to convey his own
amusement. In this he certainly resembles Callimachus to at least
some degree, but the difference is that the subjectivity (the 'mind-
reading' and the appealing to both character and reader) is far
more pervasive and far more deeply embedded in the narrative
texture. It is not merely in parenthesis or overt appeal to characters but in the very cast of the sentence-structure (grammar and
colometry) that his personality comes out. Here again he is like
Virgil but whereas Virgil preserves at least the formal pretence of
epic objectivity (his use of the auctorial *ego* is as rare as Homer's)
Ovid emphatically does not. It is as if he were insisting on his
rights as narrator and utterly abandoning the claim to objectivity,
as when for example he describes the plight of Apollo after his
vengeance on Coronis (II, 612-13):

Paenitet, heu! sero poenae crudelis amantem,
seque quod audierit, quod sic exaserit, odit

He regrets—alas! too late—his cruel penalty and hates himself
for listening to the tale-bearer, for letting his anger flame up
in such a way.

or the worsted decorum of Jove courting Europa (II, 846-9):

non bene conveniunt nec in una sede morantur
maiestas et amor: sceptri gravitate relicta
ille pater rectorque deum—
induitur faciem tauri

There can be no harmony or lasting link between love and
royal majesty: the very father and ruler of the gods abandons
his royal sceptre and takes on the likeness of a bull.

or the crack in the wall that enables Pyramus and Thisbe to
converse (IV, 67-9):

id vitium nulli per saecula longa notatum—
quid non sentit amor?—primi *vidistis* amantes
et vocis *fecistis* iter

*No one had noticed the crack for many generations but—what
does love not notice?—you lovers saw it and made it a
passage to convey your voices.*

where not only the parenthetic question but the direct address to
the lovers convey the sympathetic Ovidian presence. We could
multiply such examples almost without limit for they represent
a primary and pervasive feature of Ovid's style. Yet it is important
to note that the auctorial viewpoint is more often indirectly than
directly expressed. In the lines about Actaeon transformed into
a stag and hunted down by his own dogs and comrades (III,
242–52):

at comites rapidum solitis hortatibus agmen
ignari instigant oculisque Actaeona quaerunt
et velut absentem certatim Actaeona clamant
(ad nomen caput ille refert) et abesse queruntur
nec capere oblatae segnem spectacula praedae.
vellet abesse quidem, sed adest; velletque videre,
non etiam sentire canum fera facta suorum.
undique circumstant mersisque in corpore rostris
dilacerant falsi dominum sub imagine cervi,
nec nisi finita per plurima vulnera vita
ira pharetratae fertur satiata Dianae.

*But his friends in their ignorance urge on the tearing pack
with their usual halloos, and keep looking around for Actaeon,
and vie with each other in calling for him as if he were really
absent (but he turned his head at the sound of his name). They
complained of his 'absence' and called him lazy for not seeing
the booty chance had offered them. He would indeed have liked
to be absent but he is present: he would have wished to see,
not also feel, the cruel prowess of his hounds. They hem him
in on every side, sink their teeth in his body and tear in
pieces their own master hidden under the likeness of a
deceptive stag. Nor was the wrath of Diana said to be satisfied
until his life was ended by innumerable wounds.*

we are drawn by the historical presents (*quaerunt, clamant, refert,* etc.) into the immediate action: we hear the shouts of his comrades; see the pathetic responsive motion of Actaeon's head; read his thoughts (*vellet abesse quidem*); our attention is drawn (by the author of course) to the paradox of Actaeon's unwilling presence and his ignored identity; and we finally receive an implicit comment on the *ira* of a goddess whom only the complete laceration of her victim could satisfy. Ovid insists that we experience the paradoxical pathos of Actaeon's situation and so also the full cruelty of the divine *ira*: the short metrical and grammatical cola admirably underline the points insisted upon (247–8):

> vellet abesse quidem sed adest! velletque videre
> non etiam sentire canum fera facta suorum.

He would indeed have liked to be absent but he is present: he would have wished to see, not also feel, the cruel prowess of his hounds.

The salience of the short colon *sed adest* and of *sentire* (with ictus and accent on the long penult) is enhanced by the strong breaks in the first line and the deliberate omission of the third foot caesura in the second. The parallelism of the two *vellets* and the two infinitives that complement them in I, 247 is deliberately broken by the parenthetic *sed adest* (the change of mood indicates the change from character's to narrator's view-point); then the contrast and placing of *videre* and *non etiam sentire* give a final twist, as it were, to the paradox. It is all very rapid—the dogs are now upon Actaeon—but the action is not interrupted by, rather narrated through, the incongruities of which it consists.

But, again, this subjectivity is never elegiac—that is to say it never sacrifices the sense of real event, of objective event, to the author's whim or fancy. We can say perhaps it is more elegiac than Virgilian or Homeric: nonetheless it is always subordinated to the narrative, never in radical opposition to it, never arbitrarily deflecting the narrative sequence, wantonly or avowedly

interrupting it, stopping it or ignoring it in the manner of Callimachus in the *Aitia* and Ovid himself in his *Fasti*.

The third and final characteristic of Ovid's *general* style on
which I would here insist is its precision and lucidity. The grammar is simple; the cola short; the climactic structure of Virgil or
the rhetorical structure of Lucan are alike avoided. In Ovid repetition, antithesis, simile, etc. clarify rather than complicate the
thought. Such lines as these on Narcissus (III, 353–5):

> multi illum iuvenes, multae cupiere puellae,
> sed—fuit in tenera tam dura superbia forma—
> nulli illum iuvenes, nullae tetigere puellae

*Many the youth, and many the girl who desired him, but so
harsh was the pride within his tender body that no youth, no
girl ever touched him.*

are characteristically Ovidian though the anaphora is not usually
carried to the length of whole lines. In the verses describing Echo
excited by Narcissus (III, 370–1):

> vidit et incaluit, sequitur vestigia furtim
> quoque magis sequitur, flamma propiore calescit

*She saw him and grew hot and furtively follows his footsteps:
the more she follows, the closer the heat with which she glows.*

the repetition of the *sequitur* and the use of it in a clause designed
to reintroduce the idea of *incaluit* (though with much greater
emphasis and immediacy; note the shift of tense from *incaluit* to
the inchoative *calescit*) lead up to and are given precision by the
ensuing simile (373–4):

> non aliter quam cum summis circumlita taedis
> admotas rapiunt vivacia sulphura flammas.

*Just as live sulphur smeared on the ends of torches snatches
the flame brought close to it.*

The combustion of the torch by the flame exactly describes the
effect of pursuit on Echo's feelings: the simile gives precision and
pictorial quality to the relatively simple idea of the original

incaluit. Echo is already, so to speak, inflammable sulphur; only the proximity of Narcissus is needed to set it off. What these lines illustrate particularly is Ovid's assimilation of various devices (here anaphora, simile) to a single end that we might call pictorial accuracy. Neither the rhetorical devices nor the epic conventions (especially the simile) are used in a traditional epic way, e.g. as a means of inflating the content to a certain dignity or stylistic amplitude.

The result is often a definite modernization of both language and content. Ovid for example knew that similes were *de rigeur* in epic: this is why they are vastly more frequent in the *Metamorphoses* than in the *Fasti*.[1] But his similes, like the sulphur torch just mentioned, are often oddly modern or 'unepic'. Pyramus' blood, for example, spurts up like a stream of water from the break in a *lead* pipe. The Hermaphrodite's body gleams in the clear water like ivory or lilies *under glass*. Perseus' dragon is as far away as the distance covered by a lead bullet shot from a Balearic sling, etc. Even when the similes are traditional, they are given an odd precision as in Ovid's remarkable development of the Homeric storm/siege simile in the Ceyx–Alcyone episode. But the precision is characteristic of the whole style, not just of the similes. The deliberate archaisms and Homericisms of Virgil are largely abandoned. Epithets and patronymics are used in a context that mocks or parodies their traditional meaning. Furthermore Ovid often abandons the use of either epithet or simile for long stretches of the narrative. But his style is always clear, precise, fluid and personal.

But his style is not uniform. There are some obviously epic episodes; others—the *Pyramus and Thisbe* is a good example— are not epic at all. The general features of the style that we have so far considered are wholly compatible with a number of types of narrative. Though it certainly differs from the elegiac in both plot and verse structure as well as in grammar and diction (it is

[1] See the discussion of similes in the *Metamorphoses* by Theodore F. Brunner, *Classical Journal*, 61 (1966), pp. 354–63.

not interrupted by closed distichs and alternating pentameters), it can in fact come very close to the elegiac mood or tone as well as to other unepical moods and tones. The fact that the style is continuous, rapid, personal (or subjective), clear and precise may exclude the Virgilian *ethos* or the elegiac jumpiness and ellipsis but is nevertheless quite compatible with either an epic or an elegiac effect. Above all, it is neither comic nor serious *per se*. This fact is, as we shall see, of the very greatest significance.

By and large his style is more or less consciously epic when he is dealing with the gods and with heroes. Here style and subject matter conform even if the conformity is in large degree superficial. But here again there are all manner of degrees and variations in both style and subject matter. There is no more uniformity to the epic than to the unepical Ovid. Thus, the critical Creation–Flood episode is centred around an obviously epic *concilium deorum* presided over by Jupiter. The setting, diction, formal speech (of Jupiter) have a quasi-Virgilian ring. Yet the whole Creation episode does not quite preserve this level of dignity though it does not fall very far beneath it. The ensuing Daphne and Io episodes, however, are quite different: they are first of all much shorter, much more elliptical, much less ample or stately. The speeches are more hurried, more emotional; the subjectivity of the author more pronounced; the tension and *ethos* very much relaxed. The Phaethon episode reverts to a more obviously epic style: its size, its epic descriptions, speeches, epithets, diction are obviously meant to make an epical impression. But again the Callisto and even more the Coronis and Battus episodes fall much below this epical height. The *Herse–Aglauros* is a little more epic—there is at least the epic hypostasization of *Invidia*—but it is also very elliptical. The *Europa* is not epic at all: Jupiter has now given up all his dignity.

There can be little doubt what has happened. I have already described it in chapter IV. The struggle between divine *maiestas* and divine *amor* is also a struggle between incompatible styles of life and of poetry. Apollo, Jupiter, even Hermes try to maintain

341

an epic dignity but under the emotional disturbance of love they find they cannot succeed. I should like to add however to what I have said a shrewd observation from an unpublished Stanford dissertation of my student Daniel Arnaud: the amatory gods are ridiculous not simply because they strive vainly to act in a Virgilian manner but because their elegiac behaviour belies their epic pretensions. The role of the elegiac lover who avows himself the humble slave of a haughty mistress—an intrinsically unepic stance—is now played by the gods themselves. Apollo's incongruous courtship of Daphne, Jupiter's elaborate self-introduction to Io, the deliberate humility and coy behaviour of Jupiter in the disguise of a pretty white bull (here even Moschus is reduced to Roman elegiac terms), Hermes 'slicking himself up' for Herse, are all incipiently elegiac. We see this even more strikingly in the later (Book v) Proserpina episode (clearly a 'recall' of the divine *amores* of Book i): Dis, of course, merely grabs Europa and has no time for elegiac courtesies; yet his *properatus amor* is reprehended by the shocked Cyane as in very poor taste. She herself had succumbed to a lover but only after a proper courtship—*exorata tamen, nec ut haec* [i.e. Proserpina] *exterrita nupsi*!

Yet the scene and to some extent the style change when the gods shift their behavior from love to vengeance. Here the epic touches are still essential means of bringing out the incongruity between divine power and very human emotion, but the comic now makes room for the grotesque, for the fundamentally macabre. Diana's dignity in the Actaeon episode is that of a wealthy and punctilious Roman lady: its result is the grotesque paradox of Actaeon's death. Here the epic dog-names, the paraphernalia of an epic hunting scene are patently absurd: yet everything accentuates the sense of Actaeon's lost identity, his tragic inability to communicate. The *Pentheus* is really a heightened version of the same thing: like Actaeon, he lacks the human arms (they have already been torn away by his Bacchically maddened mother and aunts) with which to plead: his identity also is incommunicable. The *Ino* is a particularly good example of how Ovid can reduce the epic to the grotesque: the comic, pseudo-Virgilian Juno, her incongruous visit to the Furies (the atmosphere of a social call, even of feminine primping, is imposed as it were on the inner circles of Hades!), the hasty toilet of Tisiphone—all prelude another tragic loss of identity: Ino and Athamas, however, are now the hunters, not the hunted, though their unconscious infanticide is just as destructive of their real selves. The apotheosis of Ino is an exceedingly poor compensation for her tragedy.

The 'epic' of the gods, in other words, is in fact a travesty, an obvious essay in the mock-heroic and anti-epic. Yet here again Ovid is not to be ticketed on the basis of any one part of his poem. His own identity is as elusive as that of his characters. The later episodes of divine vengeance (those after the central Perseus 'panel') are obvious theodicies: the Pieriae, Arachne, Niobe are all guilty of presumptuous *hybris*. Yet the *Niobe* is much more than grotesque: the incongruity of divine-epic and human-maternal elements is really taken seriously. The death-scene of the sons is a sort of architectural epic: Ovid obviously relished the ingenuity of his variations on the way a man can be shot dead by an arrow. We feel no emotion at all. But the final scene of the killing of the daughters and the petrifaction of Niobe is full of real pity. We are meant to be shocked at the excess of the vengeance and are given a hint at least of another and better power—the power that relieves Niobe of her exhausted sensibility. The style of the last part of the *Niobe* is wholly different from that of the beginning.

After this (the *Niobe*), of course, the gods make occasional if much rarer appearances. There is the Plague that Juno sends, the miracle of the Myrmidons in Book VII, the central pair of theodicies (Philemon–Baucis, Erysichthon) in Book VIII, the *concilium deorum* that decrees the apotheosis of Hercules in Book IX, the quite differently styled theodicies of Books IX, X and XI (Iphis, Pygmalion, Atalanta, Midas), the Cyparissus, Hyacinthus, and Adonis episodes (the gods as doting lovers tragically cheated of their darlings) of Book x, the amores of Circe, Glaucus and Vertumnus in Books XIII and XIV, the apotheoses of Aeneas and Romulus, the new gods of Rome (especially Aesculapius), the final Virgilian conversation of Venus and Jupiter at the very end. It is difficult to draw any clear conclusion from these incidents. The pretty tales of loving gods in Book x (Orpheus tells two of them, *Hyacinthus* and *Adonis*) are obviously quite un-epic: here Apollo and Venus have wholly succumbed to a sentimental *eros* succeeded by an equally sentimental (and quite untragic) *pathos*. The style is markedly elegiac. But these are the exceptions. The later stories of Galatea, Glaucus, Circe, Vertumnus and Pomona are light, colourful offsets to the heavier epic and philosophical, Roman and patriotic themes. The important new development on the divine scene is obviously the theodicy-apotheosis of Books VIII–IX and its Roman sequel in the last two books. (The four related 'theodicies' of Iphis, Pygmalion, Atalanta and Midas belong as we shall see to quite another ensemble.)

The *Philemon–Baucis* comes at the exact centre (line-wise) of the whole epic. It is introduced as a solemn proof that the sceptics are wrong, that the gods do really have power and that metamorphoses do really occur. There can thus be no doubt of Ovid's emphasis: the episode is meant to stand out, to offer a central 'message'. Nor is there anything in its content—it is definitely not an epic, but an idyll, a homely moral tale—that contradicts this impression. Yet its obvious counterpart or continuation, the *Erysichthon*, is definitely mock-epic. Ovid wrings the last drop of paradox and grotesquerie from his bleeding oak tree and elaborate divine machinery. Also Erysichthon has a daughter who supports him by indulging in a series of comic metamorphoses. It is exceedingly difficult to reconcile the tone or mood of the two 'theodicies' but as I have pointed out in Chapter VI, there is much reason to believe that the difference is deliberate, that Ovid was quite consciously 're-doing' two Callimachean pieces in deliberately contrasted styles.

The problem deepens when we take into account the setting of

the two episodes: they are preludes, so to speak, to the Hercules
story, the central instance of divine reward for heroic behaviour
and the key example of the successful, upward metamorphosis.
Up to VI, 420 the major amatory and wrath themes are broken or
interrupted by the Creation, Phaethon, and Perseus episodes—
episodes that obviously 'stand out' from the main narrative in
respect to both content and style. Similarly between VI, 424 and
the end of Book XI, the Meleager–Theodicies–Hercules complex
displays an equal divergence in style and content from the prevailing amatory mood of the whole section (the only other non-
amatory parts are the very brief 'miracles' of Book VII, the short
Icarus and Galanthis–Dryope tales, and a certain amount of
obvious *liaison* such as the passages concerning Theseus and
Achelous).

Broadly speaking, all these large 'eccentric' portions of the
poem are heroic in content, epic in style. They are also on a
larger scale than other episodes (400–500 or more lines) and can
thus easily be kept in mind and associated together as a more
or less related or continuous line of development. Jupiter's
concilium deorum (with the Lycaon–Deucalion–Pyrrha theodicies)
asserts the overruling control of the gods. Phaethon makes a
premature, misguided attempt to attain divine status, to act like
a god. Perseus is a true 'Virgilian' hero; Meleager is a hero thwarted by his own passion and the resentment of his mother. But the
gods are just (as the two interspersed theodicies assert) and true
desert (as with Philemon and Baucis) can win its reward in
quasi-divinity: *cura deum di sint et qui coluere colantur*. Hercules is a
hero who triumphs over the jealous folly of the passionate
Deanira precisely in virtue of his superior achievements. With
him, therefore, the hero finally achieves a true apotheosis and,
in another *concilium deorum*, Jupiter compels the gods' assent to it.
It is clear that the precedent has at last been laid for the great
Roman apotheoses that will conclude the whole poem.

But when we actually look at the style and the full content
of these episodes their mock-heroic character clearly emerges.

The *Phaethon* we have already discussed (chapter IV) in sufficient detail. The *Perseus* however needs further consideration: in one sense it is, as we have seen, bathos; in another, as I am now fully convinced, it is deliberate bathos, a true parody of epic.

Perseus is introduced in a cleverly elliptical way: Acrisius of Argos, we are told, was to repent equally of his behaviour towards the two sons of Jupiter, Bacchus and his own grandchild, Perseus. The former was raised to heaven: the latter (IV, 615–16):

> viperei referens spolium memorabile monstri
> aera *carpebat* tenerum stridentibus alis.

> *Bearing back the memorable spoil of the snaky monster, was*
> *sweeping through the thin air on whistling wings.*

We are thus at once in the air with the new hero already equipped with the Medusa head. The transition strikes us by what I might call its un-epic and elliptical ingenuity. So too with the sequence: Perseus tries his new winged sandals on broad sweeps in all directions but prudently refrains from a night flight, *cadente die veritus se credere nocti.* He asks for hospitality from no less a person than Atlas. But Atlas churlishly dismisses him and adds a threat of violence. Obviously Atlas is unbeatable—*quis enim par esset/ Atlantis viribus?* (an eminently Ovidian parenthesis)—so Perseus repays the slight to his reputation (Atlas had refused to believe in his predicted *gloria*) by a quite different sort of *gift*, a view of the Medusa head. The Ovidian phrasing of his retort to Atlas is neat (654–5):

> at quoniam parvi tibi gratia nostra est
> accipe munus!

> *But since you care so little for my esteem, take then my gift!*

But even when turned into a mountain, Atlas can still sustain the heavens. The only difference is that his beard and hair are now trees; his head the mountain-top; his bones stones.

But Perseus proceeds and 'sights' Andromeda, a beautiful picture indeed. But for the motion of her hair and the trickle of her tears, he would have taken her for a marble statue (*marmoreum ratus esse opus*). He speaks to her and finds her modest enough. She would certainly have covered her face had her hands not already been chained! But she can hardly falter out the most essential information (*nomen terraeque suaeque*, etc.) before the water resounds with the noise of the approaching dragon. Soon he is only a sling-shot's distance off. There is a general lamentation but Perseus cleverly seizes the opportunity to put through a formal contract of marriage. His speech (nine lines) pays some deference to epic oratory (epithets, elaborate relative and conditional clauses, resounding cola) but also manifests a definite desire to get to the point. After all he is exacting a promise from people already *in extremis* and only too ready to comply. There will, as he reminds them, be plenty of time to weep: first aid is the present necessity (*ad opem brevis hora ferendum est*).

The fight with the dragon again shows Perseus' great presence of mind. He adroitly attacks him by clever use of his winged sandals (he goes for vulnerable places such as the tail and then gets away before the clumsy dragon can respond) until the sandals get soggy from the monster's effusions of bloody water. At that, Perseus prudently perches on a rock just above sea level and from there manages to finish the beast off.

After this there is of course a victory as well as hymeneal banquet at which Perseus becomes *raconteur* and recounts his acquisition of the Medusa head and the *raison d'être* of Medusa's peculiar coiffure. With this the first phase (in Book IV) of the story comes to an end.

The next (beginning of Book V) is far more epic and pseudo-Virgilian: the parallel of Aeneas/Turnus/Lavinia/Latinus with Perseus/Phineus/Andromeda/Cepheus is fully drawn; the martial *aristeiai* of the hero are now set forth at some semblance of Homeric–Virgilian length (235 lines). We need not follow the fight in detail. It is a peculiarly Ovidian mixture of parody and the grotesque. There is for example a clear reminiscence of Virgil's Nisus/Euryalus in the episode of Athis and Lycabas.

They are evident homosexuals and Ovid spares no pains to make this plain. Athis, a 16-year-old of East Indian extraction, is clad in a Tyrian cloak with a gold band: his neck is loaded with bracelets; his hair scented and topped with a comb. Perseus kills him with a big log snatched from the fire, at which his lover Lycabas, in true Nisus fashion, tries to retaliate (with an arrow) only to receive a blow from Perseus' Medusa-proof hatchet. He dies, Nisus-like, with his eyes on his beloved (72–4):

> iam moriens, oculis sub nocte natantibus atra,
> circumspexit Athin seque adclinavit ad illum
> et tulit ad Manes iunctae solacia mortis.

> *Now dying, his eyes swimming in the approaching darkness*
> *he looked round for Athis, bent himself toward him and bore*
> *to the shades the solace of their united death.*

The other victims of Perseus are described with truly epic but obviously meaningless nomenclature (85–8):

> inde Semiramo Polydegmona sanguine cretum
> Caucasiumque Abarim Sperchionidenque Lycetum
> intonsumque comas Helicem Phlegyamque Clytumque
> sternit et *extructos morientum calcat acervos.*

> *Then he strikes down Polydegmon, sprung from the blood of*
> *Semiramis, and Caucasian Abaris, Sperchian Lycetus, Helice*
> *of unshorn locks, Phlegyas and Clytus—strikes them down*
> *and tramples on the heaped-up piles of the dying.*

The last line is a fitting finale to the gory paragraph. The longer death scenes have each their bit of ingenious parody as, for example, when Pedasus kills the singer Lampetides with the injunction to 'finish the song in Hades' (*Stygiis cane cetera . . . manibus*). But the petrifactions (Perseus is so outnumbered that he has to resort to Medusa) are more amusing, especially the unfortunate fate of the Persean partisan, Aconteus and of his opponent Astyages: the latter, still thinking the new life-like statue to be a live man, strikes it only to get the *tinnitus* of metal against stone. He is of course astonished and thus petrifies with his mouth open.

On the amusing and final petrifaction of Phineus we have commented sufficiently in chapter v. The whole scene is a brilliant parody. I trust the reader will accept my recantation of my former misconception and misestimation of its significance. I had simply not read it carefully enough.

It is unnecessary to analyse the Boar Hunt of Meleager or the Hercules–Achelous combat in similar detail. They are not, I think, equally amusing but in purpose and character they are very similar to the Perseus episode. The incongruity between the reputation and the feeble prowess of the heroes at the Hunt is very much in the mock-heroic vein. The 'tragic' portions of the Meleager/Hercules stories (Althaea, Deanira) are not comic but they are certainly more ingenious than tragic. The soliloquy of Althaea is a heightened, exaggerated, and rhetorical version of the so-called 'monologue of conflicting impulses' that goes back, of course, to the famous 'to kill or not to kill my children' speech of Euripides' *Medea* and is also a clever variant on Ovid's own version of Euripides in *Metamorphoses* VII. Deanira's corresponding speech of 'indecision–decision' is much shorter: here it is the agony of Hercules, not Deanira's *femineus dolor*, that Ovid wants to emphasize. The striking feature of the Hercules episode, however, is not the agony but the quite jovial indifference to the agony which Jupiter displays. To the gods perturbed and uneasy over the terrible suffering of Hercules, Jupiter nonchalantly declares that he finds their concern a real pleasure (*nostra est timor iste voluptas*). Hercules, in virtue of his divine 'half' or inheritance from his father, is to be saved and made a god. But there is little interest in his mortal tragedy. The deliberate discrepancy of tones and attitudes (the exaggerated agony; the flippant apotheosis) is quite unmistakeable. Ovid, like Jupiter, is very much at his ease with heroic material.

All this explains the extraordinary character of the last four books. The *Lapiths–Centaurs*, the debate on the Arms, even the rhetorical rehash of Euripides' *Hecuba* mark an absolute break with the amatory emphasis of the preceding books: we have certainly reverted to the mood of mock-epic. This is evident enough in the *Lapiths-Centaurs* itself, but the cleverness of Ulysses in the debate (the conquest of arms by words and wit) and the exaggerated agony of Hecuba, serve also to deflate the epic and heroic mood. As for Aeneas, his role in fact is to provide *liaison* to rather light love stories and to such overt parodies as the story of Polyphemus' cannibalism (Achaemenides) or courtship of Galatea. The apotheoses of Aeneas and Romulus are in the main perfunctory repetitions of that of Hercules. After all it was enough for Aeneas to see the Styx once! Finally the great end pieces—the Pythagoras lecture and the Venus–Jupiter colloquy which prelude the Julio–Augustan conclusion—are hardly calculated to produce a serious final impression. The Helenus prophecy of Augustan greatness emerges from the deliberately un-epical or 'philosophical' Pythagoras episode. It is a perfunctory, incongruous sequel to the catalogue of changing natural phenomena—a *tour de force* that scrambles myth and philosophy, Pythagoras and Virgil in a patently artificial way. The concluding Virgilian dialogue of Venus and Jupiter has as its main purpose the explanation of the Julian apotheosis as a necessary prelude to the future and greater apotheosis of Augustus: Octavian had to have a divine father just like Hercules, Aeneas and Romulus before him! In short, the whole 'historical' or 'Roman' section simply belies—as it seems to me—any serious or seriously Augustan interpretation.

But what conclusion can we draw from all of this? Certainly the divine, heroic and historical episodes (a good half, at least, of the whole poem) can be fairly described as a sort of 'anti-epic' or as a facetious inversion of normal epic and particularly of Virgilian epic. There is, however, nothing like consistency of tone and style: Ovid in fact seems to take an almost 'impish' delight in being inconsistent. The *Phaethon, Perseus, Meleager, Lapiths and Centaurs* are big, emphatically epic pieces: they show the epithets, similes, formal speeches, *ekphraseis*, battle *aristeiai*, diction and amplitude of Homer or especially Virgil. Yet all these things are 'undercut' by an Ovidian ingenuity and humour, either a bit of quite un-epic ellipsis, a shockingly 'modern' simile, a snatch of parody, or a prosaic detail—in sum, an adroit deflation of both the seriousness and the reality of the heroic saga. The sections on the gods—whether of their love or their wrath—are also deflationary or a reduction of the material to the comic or the grotesque. The very collocation of episodes, further-more, especially in the last four books, indicates their incongruity: the setting for example of the epic and comic *Erysichthon* against the idyllic *Philemon and Baucis*, of the jaunty apotheosis against the intensified pathos of Hercules, of the exaggeratedly epic *Lapiths and Centaurs* against the clever debate on the arms, etc.

It seems, on the face of it, unlikely that Ovid would have consciously written an anti-Augustan poem, a mock-epic with a mock-Augustan ending. But I quite fail to see how we can other-wise interpret a large part of the *Metamorphoses*. Ovid was not naive: he knew what he was doing. There is certainly an occasional pretence of seriousness, an avoidance of overt *lèse majesté*. But the heroic and the Augustan elements are nonetheless 'undercut'. Virgil is turned inside out and this is true whether we consider the indirect parody of the *Perseus*, the direct parody of the *Orpheus* and *Achaemenides* or the truly comic ellipses of the later 'summaries' of the *Aeneid*. The apotheoses—including that of Julius and pros-pectively that of Augustus—are all assimilated to the realm of amusing fantasy.

From a literary point of view, however, what matters is not Ovid's 'anti-Augustanism' but his attitude toward epic and its traditional content. Ovid knew well enough that though one may archaize the modern (as in 'epics' of Roman wars), one can-not modernize the archaic without making it ridiculous. When Perseus takes note of his 'bibulous' sandals or remarks that the petrified Phineus will be a nice addition to the decor of his wife's mansion, when Diana's chief attendant is a hairdresser and the fiend Tisiphone ties up her *palla* with a snake, the result has to be comic: Hamlet 'in modern dress' may be serious; a modern Perseus, Diana or Tisiphone is not.

In one sense therefore we can rightly point to the 'epic' or 'anti-epic' character of the *Metamorphoses*. But we cannot describe all of the poem as we can the episodes (gods, heroes, Romans in effect) so far considered. As we have seen, the concluding portion of the *Niobe* is serious *pathos*, a quite sincere narrative of human suffering. With the following *Tereus–Philomela* and the subsequent narratives of female *libido* and heterosexual *amor* (until indeed we conclude the culminating *Ceyx–Alcyone*), we enter a quite different world, an essentially but not exclusively amatory world, displayed in episodes that are markedly un-epic in style and basically serious in mood.

For this indeed we have been prepared by the love-tales of the Minyades in Book IV: with their first tale, *Pyramus and Thisbe*, we find ourselves at once in a startlingly different milieu from that of the immediately preceding *Pentheus* or from the *Ino* and *Perseus–Andromeda* that close the same book. No one can miss the subjectivity (the indirect method of narration helps: it is ostensibly not Ovid but one of the Minyades who tells the story), the elegiac ellipsis and emotion, the quite un-epic style of the narrative. But one swallow does not make an Ovidian summer. The major amatory stories and other 'un-epic' episodes after VI, 424 are in a number of styles: the *Tereus–Philomela* is 'tragic', the *Ceyx–Alcyone* 'epic', the *Scylla*, *Byblis* and *Myrrha* 'neoteric' or 'epylliac'; the smaller *Iphis*, *Pygmalion*, *Atalanta*, *Cyparissus*, *Hyacinthus*, *Adonis* are again elegiac or 'quasi-elegiac'. None however is epic or anti-epic in the sense that the *Perseus* or *Lapiths–Centaurs* are or even in the sense that the *Proserpina*, *Ino* or *Pentheus* are. There is of course no cessation of the Ovidian wit, exaggeration, paradox and ingenuity but there is no inherent contradiction between the mythical and the real, no comic modernization, no elaborate deflation of an elevated style by a lowly content. The reason is quite simply that, aside from the actual metamorphoses themselves, the contents (*libido* or *amor*, occasionally jealousy, rage or piety) are all human, all quite contemporary or universal in substance, all concerned with credible reality rather than incredible myth. Even the 'miracles' (e.g. Atalanta, Midas, Iphis, Pygmalion) are deliberately such—that is to say they are extraordinary events that happen to ordinary or quite human people and the discrepancy is emphasized: we are not in a purely fantasy world where gods become amorous bulls and Furies erupt on the stage.

There always remains, of course, the *metamorphosis* but this is itself now given a 'natural' or realistic colour: it is the only 'way out' of an *impasse*; the symbolic expression of an already dehumanized condition, or alternatively, the 'miracle' that rewards true piety or punishes ingratitude and stupidity. We shall revert to the meaning of this type of metamorphosis later on: here it is only the 'difference', the new character of metamorphosis in this amatory section that I want to emphasize.

I need not here repeat my account (chapters VI, VII) of the development of the love theme in this section of the poem (i.e. through Book XI). Ovid's narratives here are clearly 'stylized' to fit this 'development'. The *Tereus–Philomela* is tragedy (basically Euripidean) though reset in a narrative mould. Here there is, I think, a quite limited 'sympathy' with the rather horrendous characters: the tragedy is intense but we are hardly moved to much 'pity and fear'. So too with Scylla: she is too obviously wicked to excite much emotional response. The immediately following *Daedalus–Icarus* contrasts two fathers, the sincerely mournful Daedalus with the vengeful Nisus: but their children are extreme opposites, Icarus an endearing, if foolish, boy; Scylla, a parricidal perversion of the filial relationship. With the *Byblis*, however, we have a truly sympathetic portrait of a perversion, of a *libido* destroying a weak but nonetheless comprehensible and pitiable girl. The elegiac soliloquies and letter (the kinship to Ovid's *Heroides* is pronounced) and the narrative itself are all movingly subjective. Ovid's sympathy with Iphis and Pygmalion is pronounced: the *Myrrha* is more melodramatic (the 'horror' is stagey) than real.

In the *Ceyx–Alcyone* the epic–mythical and amatory–real are truly and fully contrasted: the 'epic' parts of the story (the storm and the sleep episode) are implicit contradictions of the usual theodicy. The traditionally epic storm and the traditionally epic wave-siege simile are each 'exaggerated' to the point of parody but the exaggeration also reveals and explains a quite new relation of man to nature: waves and winds are made actors in a true drama of destructive violence and eventual reconciliation. The traditional gods, *per contra*, are only concerned to preserve the proprieties: Alcyone's grief is 'technically' sacrilegious. The metamorphosis is 'natural' in the sense that it completes a quite human or 'natural' episode. Thus the 'incongruity' of the epic–mythical and human–natural elements is not comic (though there are of course comic details) but deliberate and serious. It is almost as if Ovid wished to underline the difference between the two moods and styles of his poem: between the mythical, epic and unreal, on the one hand; and on the other hand, the human, amatory, natural and what is in the deepest sense real.

The great contradiction of the poem is thus, I hope, beginning to emerge. Against the 'anti-epic', the comic, the *anti-Augustan Metamorphoses* must be set the serious, un-epic and amatory *Metamorphoses*. There is here an essential opposition of style, content and purpose. How are we to explain it? How does it fit the 'plan' of the whole poem? For it is clear that a plan, in some sense, there is. The divine *amores*, divine *irae*, heroic episodes, apotheoses and Trojan–Roman conclusion all belong together in a great 'epic' that ostensibly reveals a divine order, a human association with it and eventual assimilation to it, and a historical culmination of both in Rome and Augustus, yet which in fact undercuts this order by reducing it to an absurd and grotesque fantasy. On the other hand, there is a quite different movement of motifs and styles which belongs to an amatory theme that in some sense reaches back to the divine *amores*, then clearly emerges in the very midst of the narrative of divine *irae*, culminates in the great love 'epic' of the eleventh book and is at least faintly re-echoed thereafter. The two 'plans' are thus intertwined: they reach through the whole poem; they cannot arbitrarily be separated into distinct, detachable sections or parts. The associated motifs, for example, are quite intricately related and constantly react on each other: there is a designed ambivalence between the divine and human aspects of *amor*; of *ira*, of maternal and paternal affection; a close association of epic and amatory themes; a designed recurrence of earlier themes as well as a designed anticipation of later ones. Before we can reach a judgement as to the meaning of this odd structure of competing 'plans' we must go beyond the mere arrangement of motifs and the distinction of styles to the actual or 'living' movement of the poem.

This movement can be understood only as a blend of many separate antithetical movements: a unity made out of change; a ceaseless weaving of separate motifs into a finally recognizable design. From one standpoint the pivot of the poem—the key to the design—comes at the exact centre of the fifteen books and 11,793 lines, that is to say in the latter half of the eighth book, at the *Philemon–Baucis* episode to be exact, though this itself as we have seen belongs to a broader context, the great epic-theodicy of the Meleager–Cave-of-Achelous–Hercules episodes that overruns the latter half of Book VIII and the first half of Book IX. From another standpoint the poem breaks into two unequal segments: the divine–mythical portion that embraces the first eleven books; the historical portion comprised in the last four. The first of these or the long eleven-book segment has also its mid-point at the break in the sixth book where the episodes of divine love and wrath conclude and the episodes of human love and wrath begin. Each of these general themes (the human and the divine) takes almost exactly five and a half books. There is of course no peculiar magic in the evenness of these divisions: they are nonetheless a valuable clue to the whole design.

The two points of division (in Books VI and VIII) in fact stand for the two 'plans' of the poem: that embracing the whole fifteen books, to some degree at least, and linking the big 'panels' or 'sub-epics' that always come at crucial breaks in the narrative (the initial *Creation, Phaethon* that separates the two sets of divine *amores, Perseus* that separates the two sets of divine *irae, Meleager–*

Hercules that separates the two sets of human *amores*) with the Trojan–Roman material of the last four books; and that embracing the two themes of divine *amores* and *irae* (first five and one-half books) on the one hand; the human *amores* and *irae* (though more *amores* than *irae*) on the other. There is of course continuity as well as diversity here: the gods are throughout concerned with mortals, as a parent in the *Phaethon*, or as aids or superintending presences in the *Perseus* and *Meleager*; or as, finally, co-equals in the *Hercules* and Roman apotheoses. The gods also play a slight amatory role in the 'human' sector (Books VI–XI, especially in X) as do most of the heroes (divinely descended men) also.

But the basic distinction is nonetheless clear: the gods dominate Books I–VI, 400; ordinary men and human passions dominate Books VI, 420–XI; heroes (men descended from gods and, so to speak, on their way to divinity) dominate the great 'mythical' panels and the last four books. In short there is a clear difference between the divine, human and 'heroic' sectors despite their overlapping and crosscutting. Broadly speaking each sector has special points of similarity and dissimilarity with the other: thus the gods love and show anger in a quite human way; the heroes act like the divine children they are and some of them eventually become gods; the men (and women!) are subjected to divine justice and in most cases undergo that peculiar manifestation of 'divine' will that is metamorphosis. Yet all these similarities or relationships only point up the divergencies: the gods are *not* human; the heroes are *not* gods (save for the exceptional apotheosis) and cannot behave like them (for profit or pleasure); and the mere mortals are neither divine nor heroic but live in a radically different world.

The great difference here is really that between mortals and heroes–gods or between ordinary and mythical existence. In stylistic terms this is equivalent to the difference between epic (subject matter: gods and heroes) and all that is not epic (subject matter: mere humanity). It is when dealing with gods (especially

Books I–VI) and with heroes (especially the *Perseus*, *Meleager*, *Hercules* and the last four books) that Ovid's 'epic' style is most in evidence and therewith, as we have seen, his essentially anti-epic or comic-grotesque intention. Here too there is a difference: the *amores* and *irae* of the gods in Books I–VI are less obviously epic, less ample in extent and grandiose in diction than the great 'heroic' panels of Phaethon, Perseus, Meleager etc.

The means by which the ostensibly epic is deflated or converted into anti-epic have already been indicated and need only to be briefly recalled: Ovid *humanizes* his gods, *modernizes* his narrative and diction (through realistic detail), and accents the *incongruity* of the myths by their position and collocation in the 'continuous' narrative. But he does more than this: he actually refutes his myths or subjects them to the test of science or philosophy.

Let us consider in this connection the beginning and the conclusion of the whole poem. We start in Book I with a philosophical, didactic introduction: the emergence of the cosmos from chaos, the creation in this 'scientific' sense, not in that of the Hebrew *creatio ex nihilo* by a single omnipotent, personal Creator. The Creator is anonymous, a *deus et melior natura*: the phrase reminds us indeed of the Spinozan *deus sive natura*. It is not until we reach the silver age (of the Hesiodic degenerative *saecula*) that the reign of Jupiter begins (I, 113: *sub Iove mundus erat*). We move thereafter in the traditionally mythical world, a world governed not by *natura* but by thoroughly anthropomorphic gods. These are at once reduced to a modernity, a bourgeois-Roman aspect which is quite imcompatible with serious religion, theodicy or poetry: the mock—or counter—epic begins. Jupiter holds his *concilium* on a celestial Palatine; the plebeian gods live in their own inferior quarter. Yet Jupiter, like a thoroughly conscientious administrator, feels his responsibility for them (I, 192–5):

> sunt mihi semidei, sunt rustica numina, nymphae
> faunique satyrique et monticolae silvani:
> quos, quoniam caeli nomdum dignamur honore,
> quas dedimus certe terras habitare sinamus.

And I have in my domain demigods, rustic divinities, nymphs,
fauns, satyrs and silvan deities of the hills whom we may deem
as yet unworthy of a celestial habitation but should at least
grant the right to dwell in the lands we have given them.

He is careful in choosing the right punishment for the wicked
iron-age people, to calculate the damage in advance: flood is a
better risk than fire! The gap between such sober behaviour and
the philandering of the Daphne and Io episodes, which follow
the *Creation* and *Flood*, is in one sense considerable; in another
very slight. Jupiter and Apollo are simply 'off duty' and free to
relax. But Apollo when he chases Daphne is quite conscious of his
compromised dignity as is Jupiter during his ridiculous courtship
of Io. The eminently bourgeois problem of Clymene—a former
flame of Phoebus, now respectable married—her attempt to
explain and prove the paternity of the young Phaethon, provides
the *raison d'être* of the next universal catastrophe, the fire that
really turned out to be the excessive risk that Jupiter had once so
prudently avoided. That Jupiter should then become an enticing
bull—the very symbol of masculine violence now behaving in a
coyly elegiac way—marks as it were the first climax of the comedy
that is an anti-epic.

We note here the evident humanization of the gods, the
modernization of locale and of manners, the incongruous collocation of *concilium deorum*, flood, *amores* etc., but above all the
tacit refutation of the myth by the philosophy–science of the
exordium. The sequence (creation from chaos, to gods, to *amores*
of the gods) is of course Hesiodic but the *melior natura* is not:
whether the expression is Stoic or Peripatetic or of some other
philosophical origin it represents a quite non-hesiodic and 'demythologized' point of view.

The same sort of thing marks also the conclusion of the poem.
Book XII opens with an elaborate Trojan section that, by a trick
of *liaison*, leads into the lengthy 'epic' of the battle of Lapiths and
Centaurs. This resembles the mood and style of the Perseus–
Phineus conflict. The gouging of Gryneus' eyes by the two prongs

of an antler-trophy; the bubbling of Charaxus' blood; the impaling of Dictys on the splintered trunk of a tree that he himself has snapped in two; the brief digression on the endearments of the Centaur couple, Cyllarus and Hylonome (she bathes twice a day, is very careful about her hair and dress—quite as careful as a lady Centaur could be—*cultus quoque quantus in illis/esse potest membris*); and very much else—indicate clearly enough the character of the 'epic'. We then revert to the death of Achilles and the Trojan war: the debate on who (Ulysses or Ajax) should possess his arms follows in the next book (XIII).

Here again Ovid's deflationary technique is evident. Ajax ends his plea by averring that Ulysses' shield is quite intact (so rarely has it been exposed in battle) while his own is full of holes and badly needs a replacement! This clever turning of the hero's pride in his martial *aristeiai* into a utilitarian argument from need (almost as if he were asking for a new pair of shoes) is quite typically Ovidian. The reply of Ulysses is in essence a defence of art and *ingenium*, even of aesthetic sensitivity (Ulysses knows a work of art when he sees it). By the time he is finished, the heroics of war have been cleverly 'debunked'. Ulysses excuses his attempt to escape the war 'draft' by citing the example of Achilles himself. Yet his cleverness caught Achilles as Ajax certainly could not have caught him: *deprensus Ulixis ingenio tamen ille, at non Aiacis Ulixes*!

After this we have, of all things, the tragedy of Hecuba! This is no parody: but it can hardly be taken as a 'serious' counterweight to the epic and oratory that have preceded it or to the love tales and parodies that follow it. Here again their collocation with the barest possible summary of the *Aeneid* is unmistakeable evidence of Ovid's intention. The apotheosis of Aeneas is very perfunctory and altogether tongue-in-cheek. It is preluded by a little *concilium deorum* in which Venus *campaigns* among the gods (*ambieratque Venus superos*) and finally exercises her charms upon Jupiter with the amusing words (XIV, 586-91):

> 'numquam mihi' dixerat 'ullo
> tempore dure pater, nunc sis mitissimus, opto,

Aeneaeque meo, qui te de sanguine nostro
fecit avum, quamvis parvum des, optime, numen,
dummodo des aliquod: satis est inamabile regnum
adspexisse semel, Stygios semel isse per amnes.'

*'Though you never at any time,' she had said, 'have been a
harsh father to me, now I implore you to be as mild as possible
and allow my Aeneas, who has made you a grandfather
through his descent from me, to become a god—a little one if
you like, but some sort of god at any rate. One visit to the
disagreeable Styx, one passage of its waters, is enough!'*

We then enter the strictly Roman section of the *Metamorphoses* (XIV, 609 to the end of the poem). Here the big Pythagoras lecture is surrounded by evidently lighter episodes: ostensibly episodes of the native and immigrant gods of Rome, actually amusing tales such as the cleverly varied amour of Pomona and Vertumnus (with its piquantly inset *paraclausithyron*) and the 'epic' progress of the Aesculapian serpent. The lecture itself, however, is a definite piece of philosophy–science and a clear reversion to the *natura* of the original Creation. We are once more 'out' of a mythical milieu. We cannot therefore (as I see it) escape the shock of the supposedly climactic Helenus prophecy (at least the lecture's arrangement indicates that Ovid planned it as a climax: see pp. 298–301 above): after the long account of physical and biological mutations Ovid suddenly cuts himself short (time would run out, he says, before he could get through all the changes) and leaps from nature to history. But even history is given very short shrift (some seven lines for everything before Rome: some five lines on Rome) and is introduced only as a means of bringing in Augustus: to show that his apotheosis had already been predicted by Helenus to Aeneas.

The disjunction of styles, ideas, thought-worlds is barely disguised. In the philosophic–scientific thought-world of the Pythagoras lecture, the rise of civilizations is explicitly bound up with their fall: as with Sparta, Mycenae, Thebes, Athens so also with Rome. The moral is clear: Rome too is part of a natural process of growth and decay. But this obvious logic is suddenly brushed aside by the startling introduction of the *Aeneid* which marks of course a reversion to the world of epic and of myth, of anthropomorphic gods and the old sagas. It is by means of the Helenus prophecy that the final conversation of Venus and Jupiter (the explanation of Julius' deification as a necessary prelude to that of Augustus) is prepared or anticipated, though it had already been anticipated by their conversation (just alluded to) before the apotheosis of Aeneas. We get in short almost exactly the same kind of incongruity—the abrupt conjunction of science and myth—that we have already seen in the account of creation. The two of course are meant to correspond: both the philosophy and the references to Caesar and Augustus (cf. I, 199–206) are deliberately brought in at the beginning and end of the poem.

Thus I need hardly point out the identity of the 'deflating' techniques at both the beginning and end of the *Metamorphoses*. The humanization of the gods (Pomona, Vertumnus, especially Jupiter and Venus), the modernization (e.g. the lawyer-like *suasoria* of Ulysses), the incongruous collocations are evident enough. But more significant is the implicit 'refutation' of the myth by the science, here accentuated by the perfunctoriness and frivolity of the Helenus passage and the final conversation between Jupiter and Venus. The echo of Virgil is of course a clue to Ovid's intention: the *Aeneid* is parodied (Achaeminides), absurdly truncated, incongruously juxtaposed to a series of *amores*, finally made the tag end of a scientific disquisition and, then, at the last possible moment, turned into an obsequious compliment (Julius as the necessary 'divine father' of Augustus).

We need not retrace the relation of this beginning and this end to the rest of the mythical material—the gods and the heroes. If the *Metamorphoses* were limited to this material alone it could be rightly called an anti-epical as well as an anti-Augustan poem. In one sense what Ovid did here was obvious and natural enough. What he was writing about was myth or fantasy: few educated men of his time, or indeed few educated men since the days of the Sophists and for long before that, believed in its reality or truth. No educated Augustan for that matter believed in the *de facto* apotheosis of Julius or in the spurious association of the Julians with the divine son of Venus or justified the dressing-up of modern events in the garments of ancient myth for any but political or propaganda reasons. Nor was there any lack of precedents for the poetical and literary expression of incredulity or practical atheism. The game of 'modernizing' or 'humanizing' the gods was an old one that the Alexandrians had played very skilfully and to occasional comic effect. Only a few years later Seneca was to write a skit on the 'pumpkinification' of Claudius.

But despite all this and much else, Ovid did something that was quite new and original. No such sustained, continuous 'modernization' of a large body of mythical material, no such extensive parody of epic (and Virgilian epic at that), no such audacious treatment of Augustus, no such grandiose experiment in deflation had ever before been attempted. Here the 'continuity' of the *Metamorphoses* is of special significance: the myth is pursued from Creation to Augustus with relentless insistence; it is not merely a detail, an off-beat episode that is treated (as in Alexandrian and elegiac poetry) but the whole mythological fabric itself (such at least is the impression, even if in fact a very great deal is omitted).

It is not necessary to exaggerate here the sheerly comic side of this, the mere parody, the intent to 'debunk'. There is enough pretence of seriousness to deceive (as it has deceived) the unwary reader. There is also a considerable amount of neutral narrative, of filling, of probably unintentional bathos. But the grandeur and audacity of the anti-epic cannot, I think, be denied or analysed away. It is there.

But there is also quite another Ovid at work in the *Metamorphoses*. Most of the long section (VI, 424 to the end of Book XI) on human as distinct from divine and heroic themes is not fantasy or myth, is not (for the most part) epic in style, and is not therefore to be taken as parody or comedy or anti-epic. The tragedy of Tereus, Procne and Philomela is (aside from the final metamorphoses) a quite human thing: the lust, the rape, the revenge, even the cannibalism are quite humanly motivated. So too with the love-story of Cephalus and Procris, the love (aside from the sorcery) of Medea, the incestuous desires of Byblis and Myrrha, the marital tragedy of Ceyx and Alcyone, the dilemma of poor Iphis, the idealism of Pygmalion. These as before them Pyramus and Thisbe, Salmacis or Leucothoe are engaged in no fantasy or myth but a quite intelligible and real experience. Or, put somewhat differently, they have no divine or heroic dignity to keep, no superior powers to use or abuse, no ridicule to fear when they are put in a modern or human context for they are in such a context already. Their stories lack the intrinsic incredibility of myth, of anthropomorphic gods and the supernatural, of amatory and punitive metamorphoses willed by Olympian caprice.

The great problem, however, is the combination of such humanity with what seems to be a mythical outcome, the final metamorphosis in which, for example, the *Tereus–Philomela*, *Byblis*, *Myrrha*, *Iphis*, *Pygmalion* and *Ceyx–Alcyone* end. But these metamorphoses are in fact very different from those of the 'divine' or 'heroic' sections of the poem. There are no human stags or bears like Actaeon or Callisto, no comic dolphins, no sudden laurel-bushes, no petrifactions by a Medusa head. Indeed (save for the quite distinct Iphis, Pygmalion and Atalanta episodes) the Olympian or known gods do not seem to cause the metamorphoses at all. Procne and Philomela are suddenly birds (VI, 666–8):

> munc sequitur [i.e. Tereus] nudo genitas Pandione ferro.
> corpora Cecropidum pennis *pendere putares:*
> *pendebant* pennis.
>
> *Now Tereus pursues Pandion's daughters with drawn sword.*
> *You'd think their bodies were hanging on wings, and on wings*
> *indeed they were hanging.*

The difference between the *pendere putares* and the *pendebant* tells the story. There is no apparent transition, no divine intervention.

So too with Byblis when she weeps herself into water; with Scylla unable to keep her hold on Minos' ship. Myrrha prays to whatever deities are accessible to confessed sinners (*O si qua patetis numina confessis*) for a change of shape that will remove her from both the living and the dead: it is the only possibility left her. The gods comply, but their identity is hidden: *ultima certe vota suos habuere deos.* The change in Ceyx and Alcyone is almost automatic: one moment they seem human; the next they are birds. Only at the end are we told of divine pity in a brief anonymous reference to the gods—*superis miserantibus.*

The best way to describe these metamorphoses is by the adjectives *natural* or *symbolic.* In them mortals are no longer playthings of the gods—subject to the whims of divine love or jealousy, wrath or vengeance, even gratitude or benevolence— but victims of a passion or a condition that makes human existence unendurable and seems almost naturally to leap the barrier between species. On the one hand, they exhibit a natural law, the law that everything changes and nothing perishes: *ex aliis alias reddit natura figuras nec perit in toto, quicquam, mihi credite, mundo.* On the other hand, they indicate a control, a principle of natural order and beneficence for which the gods, the collective or anonymous deities that are virtually coterminous with nature, are only one of several possible labels. *Melior natura* is another. Of course the metamorphosis *per se* is incredible: the point is that it comes at the climax of a human drama and is invested with natural inevitability; it is not the interference of gods but the human situation itself that seems to demand the change. Ultimately the distinction of man and animal disappears: the naturalism of humanity becomes identified with the humanity of nature.

The shorter Iphis, Pygmalion, Atalanta and Midas episodes, however, are different from the longer episodes (Tereus–Philomela, Byblis, Myrrha, Ceyx–Alcyone) just considered. Here the personal deities do directly intervene and effect the metamorphosis: Isis that of Iphis; Venus those of Pygmalion and Atalanta; Apollo that of Midas. Furthermore they are, formally considered, theodicies—rewards or punishments for piety or impiety. But they are, for this very reason, important indices of Ovid's poetical intention. Iphis is a cardinal instance of a *libido* controlled: she desires Ianthe but she recognizes and abhors the abnormality of the desire. She is a victim of a social situation (the cruel custom of infanticide and of the poverty that justified it) and of the piety (a mother's obedience to Isis) which has not resolved, only deferred, its eventual impact upon her. The metamorphosis therefore comes as a validation of both social and natural right. In this sense true or natural piety is justified.

So too with Pygmalion. In his abhorrence of depraved femininity—prostitutes such as the Cerastae—he constructs an ideal but artificial image of the true woman. But the image is not, as it was in Ovid's source, a mere instrument of his *libido*. It is after all reality, the realization of the ideal, the coming to life of his image, that he craves. In this sense he is pious or faithful to Venus. This is why his art is finally acknowledged as the true prototype of nature and thus worthy of identification with it. The metamorphosis is in effect the true artist's recognition by nature and by love.

In the stories of Atalanta and Midas the same situation is reversed. Atalanta is not, I think, an episode that contains a 'profound' or symbolic meaning though it forms an obvious contrast to the 'piety' of Pygmalion. But Midas is the philistine, the boor who can see no value but gold, who can make no distinction between the music of Apollo and the music of Pan. He deserves the ass's ears that he receives. Here a misconception of art goes hand in hand with a misconception of beauty and of the natural goodness man would foolishly turn into gold.

The difference between the behaviour of Isis, Venus or Apollo in these cases and that of these and the other gods and goddesses in their other amours and vengeances, is quite apparent. Ovid is saying that there is after all such a thing as natural justice, beauty and goodness and that human recognition of what is normal and beautiful in nature will be recognized by nature in its turn. The metamorphosis of *libido* is a necessary but tragic confirmation of a destructive loss of humanity. The metamorphosis of true *amor* and true art, is on the contrary a validation of the true and an expression of the normal humanity.

Of the tragedies of mutual love—the *Pyramus–Thisbe*, *Orpheus–Eurydice* and *Cephalus–Procris* are not metamorphoses (save for incidental details)—the *Ceyx–Alcyone* is of quite crucial significance. There is no need to repeat my long discussion of it in chapter VII. Here I would only call attention to the fact that the epic parts of the long narrative (the storm, the sleep section) are quite deliberate reversals of their epic models and in all probability of Ovid's model here, a hellenistic or neoteric (possibly even Ciceronian) *epyllion*. As one of my reviewers has pointed out, I did not (in my analysis) make explicit (though I think I implied as much) the literal fulfilment of Alcyone's initial wish that she and her husband might be borne together over the waves (*quidquid erit, pariter super aequora lata feremur*). What counts is the fact that the winds and waves, who so outvie the best efforts of Virgil and Homer (here the parody is much more than merely humorous), do in fact fulfil both Alcyone's and Ceyx's desire while the gods do nothing. That Ovid deliberately omitted the impiety of the devoted couple and the divine (vengeance) motivation of the storm, both of which he found in his source or sources, seems to me all but certain. On the other hand it seems to me equally certain that he transferred the action of Juno from the storm (as it was in his source) to the sleep episode, thereby of course effecting a most poignant contrast between the religious *punctilio* but real indifference of the epic gods and the passion but essential mercy of the purely natural forces, the winds and the waves. The metamorphosis is therefore a true expression or symbol of what we might call the natural victory of love, or, perhaps better put, the beneficent identity of man and nature. The epical elements are set against their human and natural opposites. The epic parody is used to accent and relieve an un-epic but serious reality.

There are then two major elements, subject-matters or 'plans' contained in the poem: the fantasy, the myth, the gods and the heroes, the apotheoses and the Augustan finale on the one hand; the human beings, the human *love* and *libido*, what we might call the theodicy of nature, on the other. One is essentially anti- or mock-epic: the fantasy is reduced to a modernized and deflated make-believe. The other is essentially serious and un-epic: a scheme of positive values, a vague but nevertheless real and serious theodicy of nature is implicitly postulated. To call this latter or 'human' *Metamorphoses* an 'epic' is of course to use the word 'epic' in a quite symbolic and non-technical way: in doing so I opened myself to much pointless misunderstanding. It is, I now think, better to avoid such a confusing usage of the term. The important question is not about labels but about what Ovid meant by thus juxtaposing the 'anti-epical' and 'un-epical', the mythical and the human elements or plans of his poem. The only conclusion, I think, to which we can come is that he did it deliberately; in fact it is precisely in this 'tension' of opposites that the fundamental meaning or sense of the *Metamorphoses* is to be found.

It is important, first of all, to understand that the two 'elements' or 'plans' are not crudely or obviously separated but in fact interweave in a quite subtle way even though it is not usually too difficult to distinguish their major lines or demarcation points as we have already seen. There are of course the big panels that are meant to stand out and be distinct, the marked difference or disjunction of the last four books, the pivotal divide of the divine and human episodes in the middle of Book VI. But the human or non-mythical element emerges clearly in Book IV with the *Minyades*, and the human beings of the divine wrath and love episodes are often important in their own right, or often 'human' in a manner that does not differ greatly from that of the characters in the strictly human episodes. The heroes of saga are not only to be found in the great epic panels: Theseus, Minos, Peleus etc. are important 'links' between the human or amatory episodes; Cephalus is the narrator of one of the most moving of such episodes; Medea is closely related to the Argonauts, Jason and Theseus himself; Peleus to Ceyx and Alcyone. Aeneas of course forms the *liaison* of the final series of amours. On the other hand all of the epic panels contain an amatory element: Andromeda in the *Perseus*, Atalanta in the *Meleager*, Deanira in the *Hercules*.

Yet the basic distinction remains. Many years ago I tried to account for it in terms of Ovid's desire to reach an Augustan conclusion or give an Augustan orientation to his poem. Even in some of the chapters of this book (though not certainly in all: here I must acknowledge a decided ambivalence or even contradiction of views) I state or imply the thesis that Ovid's desire to write an 'amatory epic' was warped so to speak by the necessity of writing an Augustan one. Pushed to an extreme, this would appear to mean that what I now call the 'mythical' or 'anti-epical' *Metamorphoses* was imposed on Ovid by Augustan or political considerations. It can be seen from the argument of this chapter that I now wholly repudiate any such conception. It is indeed quite indefensible. Ovid did not intend to write an 'amatory' or human 'epic' that was, as it were, deformed and cut short by a competing heroic–mythical–Augustan 'plan'. I still think that the last four books represent a decided break with the previous eleven but their foundation, nevertheless, was firmly laid from the very beginning.

On the other hand, the attempt of some to force the plans together, to treat the whole poem as a single or homogeneous 'anti-epic' or parody of epic, is in my opinion equally if not more misguided. A measure which fits the divine *amores*, the *Phaethon*, *Actaeon*, *Ino*, *Perseus*, *Meleager*, *Hercules* and the Trojan–Roman material will not at all fit the *Pyramus–Thisbe*, *Cephalus–Procris*, *Byblis*, *Pygmalion*, or *Ceyx–Alcyone*. Even a criterion which does justice to the divine amours of the first two books will not suffice for the divine amours of Book x, where the gods themselves have become as sentimental as the human beings. We cannot, except at our peril, ignore the essential opposition of the two major elements of the poem.

What then does this opposition mean? We can, I think, at least partially answer the question by considering certain passages of the poem wherein Ovid does seem to express something like a poetical purpose. In Book VI Minerva enters a weaving contest with Arachne: each constructs a wondrous tapestry crowded with divers episodes. Minerva's has a centre-piece depicting her contest with Neptune for the greater benefit of Athens (she endows Athens with the olive: he with a stream of salt water) but the four corners contain vignettes of four impious mortals each of whom defied the gods and each of whom was accordingly punished by metamorphosis into an animal or object (mountain, crane, stork, temple-steps). Arachne wove a very different composition and, seemingly, a far more attractive one: her tapestry depicted the animal-forms under which the Olympians (Jupiter, Neptune, Phoebus, Bacchus, Saturn) effected their seductions of mortal women. The motif is a slight variation of that of the preceding Muses–Pieriae contest but there the episodes are sung: the divine amours by the righteous Muses; the cowardly behaviour (the use of animal disguises) of the gods by the impious Pieriae. Here we see clearly enough not only Ovid's concern with a contrast of motifs but with what we may call a contrast of two motif-series. We see much the same thing also in the Minyades episode: here the quite human love-stories are set inside a story of divine wrath which is itself one of a series of wrath stories. The striving for deliberate contrast is quite evident.

Other contrasts in the *Metamorphoses* are even more significant. We have referred above to the use of the *suasoria* of Ulysses, the 'scientific' lecture of Pythagoras, as means of 'deflating' the *aristeiai* of epic or the divine machinery of Virgil. Ovid is, among other things, deliberately exposing his myth or 'epic': it is part of his 'anti-epic' technique. But the deflation of myth has another side: the assertion of reality. Here the 'frames' of the eighth book theodicies or of the *amores* of the tenth book are in my opinion quite enlightening.

The cave of Achelous is strangely unreal, deliberately fantastic. The piety of Lelex, the narrator of the *Philemon–Baucis*, the decor of the scene (including the barefoot water-nymphs who wait on table), the odd collocation of the two theodicies and the curious contest of Achelous and Hercules—all add to the impression of incongruity and paradox. The ostensible moral of the whole scene is one of belief in and obedience to the gods: the actual effect is one of incredulity or, better put, of deliberate indulgence in farfetched fantasy. The unreality of the epic setting is, as it were, insisted upon.

In contrast the Orphic 'frame' of the tenth book leaves a quite opposite impression. The book commences with a partial re-echo and parody of Virgil's *Orpheus–Eurydice*. Cyparissus is introduced as one of the trees in Orpheus' audience (this is Orpheus' 'homosexual' period after the loss of Eurydice). His story is then told briefly after which we hear from Orpheus himself: he will not, he says, sing epic any more; there is need now for song in a lighter vein (x, 148–54):

> Ab Iove, Musa parens, (cedunt Iovis omnia regno!)
> carmina nostra move! Iovis est mihi saepe potestas
> dicta prius: cecini plectro graviore Gigantas
> sparsaque Phlegraeis victricia fulmina campis.
> nunc opus est leviore lyra, puerosque canamus
> dilectos superis inconcessisque puellas
> ignibus attonitas meruisse libidine poenam.

> *Begin my song with Jove, O Muse, my mother (all things
> yield to Jove's dominion). Often before I told of Jove's power:
> I have sung in solemn strain of the giants and of Jove's
> victorious thunderbolts scattered over the Phlegraean fields.
> But now I want a lighter note and wish to sing of boys beloved
> by gods, and of girls who were overcome by forbidden passions
> and paid the penalty for their lust.*

His long 'song' which embraces the entire remainder of the book (or 592 lines) is thus ticketed as 'un-epic' or Callimachean-elegiac (*leviore lyra*) and its subject corresponds to its style: boys loved by gods; girls deserving the penalty that comes from the indulgence of illegitimate or unnatural desire.

It is clear, however, that the subject-matter of the song is in fact quite independent of Orpheus and his elegiac mood: the love of gods and boys had already been introduced just before the song began (Cyparissus); the incestuous *libido* of Myrrha had already been paralleled by the very similar *libido* of Byblis in the preceding (ninth) book; even the contrasted theodicy of Pygmalion had been anticipated by that of Iphis. Orpheus, in fact, defines the subject-matter and style of the whole second part of the amatory or human–amatory section (i.e. all the material between the end of the *Hercules* and the beginning of the *Ceyx–Alcyone*). He thus inaugurates a new approach to new material, in a sense a new beginning: this part of the poem starts not from chaos but from Jove, is not epic but elegiac or Alexandrian. But here also we proceed from gods to mortals.

Yet the divine amours here are very different from those of Books I and II. It is not merely that the amours of Apollo and Jupiter with Cyparissus, Ganymede and Hyacinthus are homosexual (they are in fact quite parallel with the heterosexual amour of Venus and Adonis) but that the amours are frustrated; the gods lose their loves and can only convert them into emblems of grief —the cypress, hyacinth, or anemone. Apollo and Venus are in all but name the lovers of elegy: their attitude is tender or sentimental; the pretty boys are really quite indifferent to them or else concerned with quite non-amatory interests such as Cyparissus' tame stag, Hyacinthus' athletics, Adonis' hunting. In short the tone of these episodes is anything but divine: the loving gods are 'human' in a very different way from that of the first two books. There is thus no great gap of feeling or style between these episodes and the central *Pygmalion* and *Myrrha* that they enclose or 'frame' (The order of episodes in the book is: Orpheus–Eurydice, Cyparissus, Ganymede, Hyacinthus, Cerastae, *Pygmalion*, *Myrrha*, Venus–Adonis (with inset Atalanta).) Nevertheless it is equally clear that the two subjects (divine and human) of Orpheus are meant to be different, to form a contrast. The centre, the point of emphasis, is the human love and this is very different in tone and substance (in the sense of reality and in the seriousness of the author's purpose) from the slight *amores* of Apollo and Venus. We see this furthermore in the very fact that the centre of Orpheus' song—the *Pygmalion* and *Myrrha*—is obviously an intentional echo and development (according to our 'law of progressive symmetry') of the *Byblis* and *Iphis*.

The difference then in style, subject-matter and poetical intention between what happens in the cave of Achelous and what Orpheus sings and between the two themes of Orpheus' song is quite plain. We can see the same thing in the framing of the seventh book (the book that in effect 'balances' the tenth): here Medea frames a set of magical transformations; Cephalus frames another set of divine transformations. Both Medea and Cephalus are related to the heroic or epic 'element' of the poem; Medea to the Argonauts and Theseus; Cephalus to Athens, Aeacus, Minos etc. But the pivotal episodes—the real emphasis—are at the beginning and end of this very well organized and unified book: Medea's love soliloquy; the romantic attachment and tragic end of Cephalus and Procris. Again the difference between the legendary and mythical (magic, heroes, divine miracle) and the realities of human passion is very evident. The difference between Books VII and x is that in the first the two elements are simply juxtaposed; in the second atmospherically merged, for here epic style and subject-matter are deliberately kept out.

All this shows, I think, that the contrast and tension between the 'anti-epical' saga (the world of myth and fantasy) and the human (especially the amatory side of humanity) is deliberate and quite intentionally Ovidian. He is, in one sense and aspect of his poem, saying that myth is false and human passion and love are true, that the connection of Julius and Augustus, of modern Rome, with the saga-world of heroes and gods, apotheosis and miracle, is both unreal and ludicrous. The chronologically linked Creation, saga-cycles and Rome, the fusion of Hesiodic epic, mythical genealogy and history constitute in effect the 'epical' content which is deflated in the great 'anti-epic' whose extent can be approximately (but only very approximately) defined as that of the first five and a half books, the *Meleager–Hercules* complex and the last four books (or somewhat more than a good half of the entire poem). (Excluding the last four books, however, the division of 'anti-epical' and 'un-epical' (or human) material is approximately equal.)

Put somewhat differently, the poem has two climaxes: the triumph of human love of the *Ceyx–Alcyone* in Book xi and the triumph of heroic virtue, the Julian apotheosis, in Book xv. The tension of the two themes is designed, is meant to be felt. Ovid, however, keeps both themes going throughout the entire poem; his constant 'modernization' or depreciation of the myth, of the incredible fantasy, the false propaganda, goes hand in hand with his assertion of human reality and its ultimate validation by that *melior natura* which works the great amatory metamorphoses. But in the first aspect or theme he is humorous or sceptical, concerned with producing a comic or grotesque effect: in the second, he is, in the main, serious and truthful.

But the tension of the two elements represents more than a mere desire to tell the truth, to distinguish fantasy from reality. In one sense the poem is chronological, a progression from aboriginal chaos to the poet's own times (*mea tempora*), a movement from the Creation and Deluge through the great myth-cycles of Homeric epic to Roman history. But in reality all this is a shifting illusion: change is the only constant and the change is down as well as up, pejorative as well as ameliorative, a thoroughly and everlastingly cyclical phenomenon. There is no permanent progress, no reason why Rome must not endure the fate of Thebes or Athens (xv, 420–2):

> sic tempora verti
> cernimus atque illas adsumere robora gentes,
> concidere has

> *So we perceive the changing of the times, how certain peoples*
> *wax in strength and others wane.*

373

In such a phantasmagoria of impermanent things, such a condition of instability and flux, the only stable reality is that of nature itself, a better nature (*melior natura*), that is always overcoming chaos, always concerned to protect what is fundamentally good, to withstand and punish what is fundamentally bad. Here the forces of libido, hate and vengeance are continually engaged with the powers of love and pity. Here the passion between man and woman is a perennial reality, always modern because never obsolete. It is itself a major manifestation of *natura* and metamorphosis is the great agent of this *natura*: that which preserves the proper distinction of human and non-human and at the same time maintains their fundamental identity. Here we can perhaps speak of a symbolically true as opposed to a symbolically false mythology and conclude that the tension between myth and reality is not in this sense ultimate. The 'false' mythology was Ovid's inheritance from epic, from Homer, the Cyclics and Virgil: the 'true' mythology was, basically, Alexandrian and neoteric and in some degree originally Ovidian. But the juxtaposition of the two, though faintly foreshadowed in such 'Hesiodic' sequences as the Silenus song in Virgil's sixth eclogue, was mainly Ovid's own doing. Against the antique mythology of Homer and against also the modern, Augustan use of it by Virgil,—he set his own peculiar blend of iconoclasm and human sympathy. This is what makes the *Metamorphoses* so much more than a mere 'anti-epic or 'anti-Augustan' manifesto. When all is said and done, the poet's own humanity comes through.

ON THE SOURCES USED
BY OVID

THERE are two main ways of determining the 'originality' of
Ovid's *Metamorphoses*. 'One is by examination of the general
or overall style and structure. The other is by comparison of
the Ovidian text with the actual or probable or merely hypothetical
'sources' that Ovid used. The whole argument of this book is, of
course, an implicit denial of the thesis once widely held (cf. e.g.
Kienzle, Peters and other works listed in Schanz–Hosius, pp. 240–2
and Martini II, pp. 37–8) that Ovid followed, more or less faith-
fully, the plan of a mythological 'handbook' or 'compendium'. It
is obvious that Ovid used genealogies and didactic collections of
myths and metamorphoses, but it is also clear that he always fitted
such material to his own plan and supplemented it by his extensive
reading in Greek and previous Roman literature. We can see
this, for example, in his departures from the normal genealogical
or chronological order in a number of places (see pp. 130, 174).

By and large, his structure or plan was his own. So also was
his style. And this is quite evident in itself. We do not even need
to compare him with his sources in order to see that he wrote in
his own, Ovidian way. But his originality is both confirmed and,
above all, elucidated by such comparison. Yet in most cases his
sources are by no means clear: we cannot in many instances be
certain whether he actually altered a given source or whether he
chose between several alternative sources in a given myth or
episode. The important thing to note, however (and this point has
often been neglected), is that both alteration and selection had
much the same purpose: to bring out the tone, idea or style that
Ovid wanted for each successive portion of his 'perpetual song'.

A good example of this is the Proserpina episode: here opinion has long been divided as to whether Ovid himself altered his earlier elegiac version of the story (*Fasti* IV, 417–620) for the *Metamorphoses* (V, 341–661) or whether he drew (as e.g. Herter now supposes: see p. 50, n. 1 above) on a different source, but, in either case, he suited the content to the style (epic as opposed to elegiac).

The episodes that we can definitely attribute to a particular known source are quite limited. His direct use of Virgil in the Achaemenides and Orpheus episodes and his oblique use of him in the long Perseus–Phineus and Ino episodes are obvious and certain. His general use of Callimachus is indubitable, but we cannot be certain of its extent even in such 'Callimachean' episodes as the *Erysichthon*, *Actaeon* or *Baucis–Philemon* since (*a*) he was almost certainly diverging (probably deliberately) from Callimachus in these stories and (*b*) he also used other sources besides Callimachus. His use of Nicander seems overwhelmingly probable in three or four episodes (see below), but in none can we be sure that Nicander was his sole or only source. Obviously also he knew of and used various Latin and Greek short epics or so-called *epyllia*, certainly those of Cinna, Valerius Cato and Gallus in Latin and of Euphorion and Parthenius in Greek. But the loss of all his originals makes any exact determination of originality and dependence quite impossible. The same conclusion applies to his use of lost tragedies such as Sophocles' *Tereus* or Euripides' *Phaethon*. Nevertheless we can, at certain points (e.g. in the Medea, Hecuba and Hercules episodes), be certain of his specific indebtedness to Sophocles and Euripides, though this does not help us very much. Despite all this uncertainty, however, we can, with reasonable assurance, see, first, how by alteration, selection or both he achieved the effects he wanted in certain pivotal episodes such as the *Phaethon*, *Byblis*, *Pygmalion* and *Ceyx–Alcyone* and secondly, how *in general* he treated his Hellenic, Hellenistic and Latin sources. The importance of the second point has often been overlooked by many of those engaged in Ovidian *Quellenforschung*. Comparison of Ovid's and Callimachus' *Erysichthon*, for example, is not primarily valuable for the determination of Ovid's original use of *content* (it is in fact possible that Ovid deliberately followed an alternative or non-Callimachean source), but it is most valuable for the determination of the stylistic differences between the two *types* (Ovidian and Callimachean) of narrative. Again, comparison of Ovid's *Scylla* and the pseudo-Virgilian *Ciris* is valuable only because the *Ciris* gives us some idea of how Ovid's narrative diverged from that of a highly derivative but, for that very reason, rather typical *epyllion*. The *Ciris* is decidedly inferior to Catullus' *Peleus and Thetis* (64) but resembles it in just those respects in which it does *not* resemble Ovid's *Scylla*. We can thus gain some insight into Ovid's general divergence from the neoteric narrative style by making the comparison. In what follows, I give what seems to me the relevant evidence for the more generally stated conclusions of the text proper with some indication of what we must still call hypothetical or doubtful and what seems to possess a higher degree of certainty. I take the episodes in the order of the poem itself.

I. CREATION EPIC (CREATION, FOUR AGES, FLOOD, DEUCALION-PYRRHA, RE-CREATION) (I, 5-415)

As indicated in the text (pp. 93 f.), the whole episode forms a symmetrical unit in which *Creation* (lines 5-88) and *Re-creation* (313-415) as well as the Four Ages or *Fall* (89-162) and its punishment, the *Flood* (253-312), correspond: the centre is the great *Concilium Deorum* (163-252). The sources for this 'Creation Epic' are somewhat various. We find the idea of a continuous poem *a Chao* in Virgil's sixth Eclogue (31-40) and fourth *Georgic* (347). The philosophic style of lines 5-88 corresponds closely to that of Eclogue 6. 31-40. Other instances of the use of the Creation theme are to be found in Apollonius (*Arg.* 1, 476 ff., Song of Orpheus), *Aeneid* 1, 740 ff. (Song of Iopas) and, above all, in Ovid's own *Ars* (II, 467 ff.) and *Fasti* (I, 103 ff.; V, 11 ff.). On Ovid's philosophic sources see especially L. Alfonsi in *Ovidiana*, pp. 266-7 (better than E. E. Robbins in *CP*, 1913, pp. 401 f., or De Lacy in

CJ, 1947, pp. 153f.). Parallels with Aristotle's *Protrepticus* (e.g. *deus et melior natura* and ἡ φύσις ἡμᾶς ἐγέννησε καὶ ὁ θεός) are rather striking, but it seems to me that one can easily exaggerate Ovid's Aristotelianism as well as Stoicism here. He is concerned only to produce a philosophic piece at the beginning of his *carmen perpetuum* (it is the period before the gods) and one which gives dignity to the origin of man that closes the Creation proper: *sanctius his animal...divino semine fecit ille opifex rerum*, mundi melioris origo *sive* [Prometheus] *finxit* [recentem tellurem] *in effigiem moderantum cuncta deorum*. The Four Ages (89–162) carry man from this god-like state to a depraved condition devoid of all *pietas*: to such men are added the terrible men from the defeated giants' blood (160 ff.). Ovid here developed a well-worn theme that we find in Hesiod's *Erga*, Aratus (105 ff.) and elsewhere. We do not know his source for the Lycaon story (cf. the discussion of it by G. Vollgraff, *De Ovidi Mythopoeia*, 1901, pp. 1–36), but the inclusion of it within the Jupiter speech of the *Concilium deorum* was certainly his own invention. Ovid needed such a *concilium* to start his epic on the grand note, and the echo of Virgil (see pp. 96–7 above) is obvious and deliberate. The ensuing *Flood* and *Deucalion–Pyrrha* were of course traditional: cf. the phrase of Eclogue 6 (41) that directly follows the Creation theme: *hinc lapides Pyrrhae iactos*. Ovid clearly emphasizes the *piety* of the couple and the wondrousness of the miracle. He wanted not only to start the *Metamorphoses* on an exalted note but to emphasize the contrast with its counterpart to come, the *Phaethon*. The real originality of this 'Creation Epic' consists in the careful way that the Flood is introduced by means of the *Concilium Deorum* and in the deliberate and artful contrast of the wicked Lycaon with the good Deucalion (a contrast re-echoed at the dead centre of the poem, VIII, 616–878, by that of Erysichthon and Philemon. See pp. 201 f. above). Deucalion was of course to be expected in this sequence, but Lycaon seems to be Ovid's own addition to the Creation story. The general parallelism of Flood and Fire (Phaethon) is unmistakable (see pp. 91 f. above).

II. DAPHNE-APOLLO, IO (452–746), CALLISTO (II, 401–530), CORONIS (531–632)

The important point about these stories is that they are *arranged* in symmetrical sequence around the *Phaethon* (cf. p. 93 above). The two amours of Apollo and two amours of Jupiter correspond in chiastic order. Ovid clearly arranged the liaison as well as the counterpoint of motifs: he strove for similarity as well as difference within a common theme and also for a definite progression of tone and emphasis (i.e. progression from the essentially *humorous* theme of the frightened virgin to the quasi-tragic theme of jealous revenge). These were the essential considerations that determined his choice and use of sources.

It is first of all clear that the liaison is wholly Ovid's invention, i.e. the connection of the Flood, Apollo's conquest of Python and consequent contretemps with Cupid; the connection of the two stream-fathers, Peneus and Inachus (hence of the Daphne and Io stories); the connection of the Conflagration caused by Phaethon with Callisto; and the curious introduction of Coronis by means of a comparison between the crow and the peacock (Argus' eyes). He wanted these stories in just this order and he resorted to a series of *tours de force* to bring them together. But his handling of the motifs is no *tour de force*. His main sources can be listed as follows:

(1) The *Io* of Calvus.

(2) The normal or Arcadian version of the Daphne story (well described by H. Magnus, 'Ovids Metamorphosen in doppelter Fassung', *Hermes* 40 (1905), pp. 200–1). This is perhaps best seen in Tzetzes *ad Lycophr. Alex.* 6 (reproduced in Magnus). Here Daphne is the daughter of the river Ladon and Ge or Earth. When pursued by Apollo, she prays to her mother, Earth, for protection and is accordingly swallowed up by her. Apollo in compensation receives a plant of the same name as Daphne. Wolfgang Stechow (*Apollo und Daphne, Studien der Bibliothek Warburg*, XXIII (1932), pp. 64–5) points out that Magnus was wrong in attributing a

metamorphosis to this version of the story: the laurel was a *substitute* for the vanished Daphne, not Daphne in another form. But some texts (e.g. Libanius, *Progymn.* 13′, Teubner VIII, 44) do mention the metamorphosis, and we cannot assume, as Stechow does, that contamination with Ovid's version is necessary.

(3) The Laconian version (to be found in Plutarch, *Agis* 9. 2, Pausanias, VIII, 20, and above all Parthenius, *Erotica Pathemata*, XV), according to which Daphne is the daughter of Amyclas of Laconia. She reveres Artemis and becomes a virginal huntress. But Leukippos, the son of Oenomaus, sees her, falls in love with her and tries to win her under female disguise. He becomes, as such, her dearest friend, but his game is abruptly ended when his sex is inadvertently revealed in a bathing scene (obviously the original of the similar scene in Ovid's *Callisto*, II, 451–65). This gives the god Apollo, who was already jealous of Leukippos, the chance he desires. When Leukippos flees from the spears of the enraged virgins around Daphne, Apollo appears and pursues Daphne in earnest. She prays for help to Zeus and is made a laurel-tree. This version is attributed to Diodorus the Elaite (elegiacs) and also to Phylarchus. It was obviously well known to Ovid.

(4) Ovid certainly had a Hellenistic source for his *Callisto* though we cannot be sure that the Homeric scholiast's (*ad Il.* XVIII, 487) version is necessarily that of Callimachus (see Pfeiffer, I, frag. 632). Here Zeus secretly seduces Callisto (Lycaon's daughter), Hera turns her into a bear and Artemis (at Hera's instigation) innocently kills her as such. Zeus then makes her the constellation, *Ursa Major*. Apollodorus (*Bibl.* III, 100 f.) represents *Zeus* as the author of her ursine metamorphosis (so as to deceive Hera). Hera, as before, persuades Artemis (who did not know Callisto's real identity) to kill her after she had taken the shape of a wild beast (ὡς ἄγριον θηρίον). But Apollodorus also adduces other sources (εἰσὶ δὲ οἱ λέγοντες) who ascribe a quite different motive to Artemis: anger at Callisto's loss of virginity.

(5) The odd disguise (that of Diana or Artemis) assumed by Jupiter in Ovid's *Callisto* (II, 425 ff.) was an invention (apparently)

of Amphis, an early writer of New Comedy (cf. Edmonds, *The Fragments of Attic Comedy*, II (1959), p. 323).

(6) Callimachus was a general source. Certain or assured Callimachean reminiscences in these episodes are from the Hecale (the talking crow, cf. Pfeiffer, II, frag. 260, pp. 251 f.) and the fifth Hymn (on the 'undress' of Athene, cf. de Cola, p. 42).

Former treatments of Ovid's use of these sources in these episodes (e.g. Magnus and Stechow just cited; de Cola; Heinze, pp. 106–10 for Callisto; Sudhaus, 'Die Ciris und das Römische Epyllion', *Hermes* 42 (1907), pp. 469–504; W. Ehlers, 'Die Ciris und ihr Original', *Mus. Helv.* 10 (1953), pp. 65–88; Haupt–Ehwald, *ad loc.*; Castiglioni, pp. 114 f.) do not take into account Ovid's overall planning (and hence use of source material) in the four episodes. Thus source (1) above (Calvus' *Io*) appears in both Ovid's *Daphne* and *Io*; source (3) (the Laconian or Parthenian version of Daphne) in both his *Daphne* and *Callisto*; while his omissions and abbreviations (e.g. the omission of Cupid's arrows in the *Io*, abbreviation of the Syrinx sub-episode and the 'chase' in the *Io*, omission of Diana or Artemis in the *Daphne*) are obviously motivated (at least in part) by a desire to avoid wearisome repetition as well as by an intention to advance the movement of the narrative from old to new motifs. His own innovations also emerge much more clearly when the ensemble of four episodes is seen in its entirety.

The *Daphne* is obviously intended to be a straight story of a god in love. Daphne is the determined virgin who provides the proper means to his complete discomfiture. Magnus (*op. cit.*) has made much of Ovid's innovation in introducing a Thessalian (instead of Arcadian) locale and Peneus (not Ladon) as Daphne's father. But Ovid seemingly was not so much interested in bringing the scene closer to Delphi (as Magnus thought: cf. O. Gruppe, Bursian *Jahresbericht*, Supplement, 1908, pp. 449 f. on this) as in marking his definite departure from the usual Arcadian version (that accents the mother). What he wanted was two prominent river-fathers for both Io and Daphne (for the parallel had to be made clear). It is, in any event, by no means clear that Ovid himself invented the Thessalian locale, as Magnus thought (P. J. Enk, *Ovidiana*, p. 327, cites a Thessalian Daphne from a scholium to l. 198 of Nicander's *Alexipharmaka*, but Castiglioni is much fuller here, pp. 118 f. The Thessalian legend seems to have been known to Nicander himself). The important point is that Ovid omitted the appeal to Earth (here the lines of the so-called 'double recension', *Met.* 1, 547a and b in Magnus' text, seem clearly non-Ovidian or, at any rate, remnants of a prior version that Ovid had definitely rejected) and reduced the caste of characters to Daphne, her father, and the god, Apollo. But he made one other omission and one addition that are quite significant.

Sudhaus (*op. cit.*) has argued quite convincingly that certain lines of the pseudo-Virgilian *Ciris* reflect Calvus' *Io*. The *Io* line (Morel, Calvus, frag. 12, p. 86):

Frigida iam celeris †vergatar† vistinis ora

that must be corrected (following Sudhaus) into something like:

Frigida iam celeri superata est Bistonis ora

is obviously reproduced (directly or indirectly) in *Ciris* 165:

Saeva velut gelidis Edonum Bistonis oris.

Here the MSS. ARU read

Saeva velut gelidi sydonum Bistonis honores

where *honores* seems an obvious corruption of *oris*. We find a similar phrase in Ovid's *Heroides* 16. 346:

Et tuta a bello Bistonis ora fuit

and at *Heroides* 2. 90:

Fessaque Bistonia membra levabis aqua.

But there is no reason not to believe that the author of the *Ciris* did not go directly to the *Io* as he undoubtedly did to Catullus' *Peleus and Thetis* and Cinna's *Zmyrna* (see pp. 391 f. below). This is confirmed by the curious *non sequitur* in *Ciris* 156-62 (the lines that just precede the imitation of the *Io* at line 165):

Etsi quis nocuisse tibi periuria credat?
causa pia est: timuit fratri te ostendere Iuno.
At levis ille deus, cui semper ad ulciscendum

quaeritur ex omni verborum iniuria dicto,
aurea fulgenti depromens tela pharetra
(heu nimium † terret, nimium † tirintia visu)
virginis in tenera defixerat omnia mente.

As Sudhaus (pp. 499 f.) acutely points out (cf. also here Ehlers, pp. 77–8), the author of the *Ciris* seems to be inserting lines from a poem in which Juno is, to her own regret, worsted by *Amor*. *Timuit fratri te ostendere Iuno, at levis ille deus* seems clearly to mean that Juno feared (for obvious reasons) the result of Jove's acquaintance with some girl (i.e. the *te* addressed) but that Cupid (light-hearted god that he was) anticipated Juno's action to prevent or stop the acquaintance. It scarcely fits the general sense of the broader *Ciris* context (i.e. that Juno is using Cupid to punish Scylla for her quite unwitting profanation of the temple) or else is extraordinarily elliptical: why should Cupid be so prompt an avenger of *impious* words? Furthermore, the golden arrows extracted by Cupid from his quiver at l. 160 can hardly have been meant (in the original source) to lead up to such a lame and vague conclusion as l. 162: *in tenera defixerat omnia mente.* The whole thing becomes clear if we assume that ll. 155–62 are, like much of the rest of the *Ciris*, a pastiche and are drawn in part from a poem concerning Juno's jealousy of some girl for whom Jove has been 'wounded' by a direct hit from Cupid. All this is surely as appropriate to Io as it is not to Scylla.[1]

Now no extant version of the *Daphne* (apart from Ovid's and so also Nonnus', see p. 374 below) makes any mention of Cupid and his arrows. Furthermore, Ovid's lines (I, 468–72):

Eque sagittifera *prompsit* duo *tela pharetra*
diversorum operum: fugat hoc, facit illud amorem.
Quod facit, auratum est et cuspide fulget acuta.
Quod fugat, obtusum est et habet sub harundine plumbum.
Hoc deus in nympha Peneïde *fixit*

[1] As Sudhaus also points out (pp. 481 f.), l. 184 of the *Ciris* seems also a plagiarism from the *Io*. *Fertur et horribili praeceps impellitur oestro* fits Io but hardly suits Scylla !

do seem reminiscent of *Ciris*, 160, 162:

Aurea fulgenti *depromens tela pharetra*

★   ★   ★   ★   ★   ★   ★

virginis in tenera *defixerat* omnia mente.

That Ovid himself had Calvus' *Io* in mind in the immediately ensuing Io episode is certain, for he obviously refers to Calvus' *Io* (Morel, frag. 9, p. 85):

A virgo infelix, herbis pasceris amaris

in describing Io at 1, 631–3: *amara pascitur* [Io] *herba*...incubat *infelix*. Again, Ovid's account of Argus' sleepiness (713):

Succubuisse oculos, adopertaque lumina somno

obviously reflects Calvus (Morel, frag. 11):

Cum gravis ingenti conivere pupula somno.

What Ovid has done is thus clear enough. He has transposed the Cupid scene from Calvus' *Io* to his own *Daphne*. Furthermore, he has cleverly parodied it (the *Io* was assuredly a serious poem, as we shall see) by introducing the double arrow-points (gold and lead). Ovid was not a poet to copy slavishly and, in any event, he wanted to make the point that the girl was as reluctant as the god was eager: Apollo must be put in the most ridiculous possible position. He doubtless got the hint for the two arrows from Euripides' *Iphigenia at Aulis* (548: the arrows that bring luck and disaster respectively). In any event, neither he nor Calvus would have put Jupiter in the same position (cf. Ovid, line 600) as Apollo. Io, like Callisto, cannot resist Jove: *quis...puella Iovem ...superare poterat?* (II, 436–7).

On the other hand, Ovid clearly had no use for the intrigue of Parthenius (source 3 above): it was the plight of Apollo that interested him here. One hardly needs to demonstrate that the detailed account of Apollo's incongruous dignity (his courtship speech, etc.) is Ovid's own contribution to the episode. Castiglioni (pp. 117–64) has given us a good deal of detail on Hellenistic or Alexandrian treatments of Daphne and similarly placed heroines. It may well be that Daphne's relation to Diana, the relative emphasis and placing of chase *vis-à-vis* courtship, the nature of Apollo's approach to Daphne, the different ways in which Daphne is depicted (as rough huntress or beautiful lady), were all points of interest in Alexandrian circles and showed the Alexandrians' desire to 'humanize' the gods and their amours. Nevertheless, Castiglioni pays the scantest attention to Ovid's own innovations: surely the combination of courtship and chase (especially the courtship-speech delivered on the run and its amusing mixture of passion and solicitude, violence and politeness) is of the very essence of Ovid's comedy and not a mere reproduction of some Alexandrian or Hellenistic model. Cf. the various references to Daphne in Nonnus (mentioned in Braune (see p. 361 below), pp. 38–41). Castiglioni also ignores the obviously 'epic' stylization of Ovid's narrative: for this cf. my comparison of Ovid's and Callimachus' *Erysichthon*, pp. 65–70. Yet Castiglioni has quite correctly emphasized the importance of general motifs as opposed to specific detail in each legend.

We unfortunately lack enough of Calvus' *Io* to make more than a very few remarks on Ovid's adaptation of it to his own purposes in his own *Io*. Such stray lines as (Morel 9)

A virgo infelix, herbis pasceris amaris

and (Morel 10)

Mens mea dira sibi praedicens omnia, vaecors

indicate it is a serious poem (as Ovid's is certainly not). Fragment 11 (quoted above) also indicates that it included the business of Argus and his anaesthesia (probably also by Mercury). But it is all but certain that Ovid alone effected the anaesthesia by the device of the Syrinx story. The story is introduced because it is completely analogous to the *Daphne* (only Pan's girl becomes a reed, not a laurel) and is, therefore, for this very reason cut off at an early stage (just before Pan can begin his courtship address). As Quirin (p. 24) has aptly remarked: 'so gewinnt Ovid die Zeit, die notwendig ist um den Schlaf des Hundertäugigen zu motivieren'. But the humour of reintroducing the motif of the *Daphne* by way of a soporific (really a delightful piece of self-parody) and the clever method of abbreviating, or rather truncating, a tale that would be only repetitious, are charming in themselves.

Ovid had thus developed the divine amour away from the mere pursuit toward conjugal jealousy (Juno) and a much more active kind of metamorphosis (Io's change of shape, unlike Daphne's, is in itself a humorous device). But he had now (after the *Io*) exhausted the pursuit theme (it had been greatly abbreviated even in the *Io*) and he therefore turned to quite different aspects of the god–virgin encounter, namely, the *shame* of the defeated virgin and the near-tragedy of her metamorphosis. These ideas had been humorously adumbrated in the *Io*: now they were emphasized and, at the same time, taken much more seriously.

In the *Io*, the humour of Jupiter's attempt to deceive Juno by the pretty cow seems an obviously Ovidian invention. It was in fact Callisto whose shape, according to Apollodorus (see source 4 above), had been changed for the purpose of deceiving Juno: in Apollodorus (II, 1. 3), Zeus made Io a cow not so much to deceive as to appease Juno (φωραθεὶς δὲ ὑφ᾽ ῞Ηρας τῆς μὲν κόρης ἁψάμενος εἰς βοῦν μετεμόρφωσε λευκήν, ἀπωμόσατο δὲ ταύτῃ μὴ συνελθεῖν). Ovid thus seems to have used a Callisto-motif in his *Io* very much as he had used an Io-motif in his *Daphne*. He makes Callisto's metamorphosis (she becomes a bear) an act of Junonian vengeance that comes as an additional and final touch to a previous tragedy. This change (cf. all the extant accounts of Callisto) is almost certainly due to Ovid alone (cf. Heinze, pp. 105–8). That is, Ovid separates and isolates the roles of Diana–Artemis and Hera–Juno and defers the metamorphosis until after Arcas' birth: it is in fact Callisto's pregnancy and the subsequent birth of Arcas which anger Juno. Diana–Artemis has no part in the metamorphosis or in the (attempted) killing of Callisto (cf. source 4 above). Ovid, in fact, seems to have changed the ending entirely so that the son (Arctophylax in the *Catasterismi* of pseudo-Eratosthenes: I follow the Olivieri, Teubner edition = *Mythographi Graeci*, III, fasc.

1, pp. 9–11) is not threatened along with the mother (as in pseudo-Eratosthenes) but rather himself plays the role attributed by one of Apollodorus' sources to Artemis (i.e. that of the unwitting murderer: he, like Apollodorus' Artemis, does not know that the bear is really Callisto in disguise).

Thus the relations of Diana, Juno, Callisto and her son, Arcas, are given an entirely new content and emphasis. By separating the wraths of Diana and Juno, Ovid was able to introduce two new motifs that he was to develop at length in the Actaeon episode to come. These are (1) the *wrath of shocked virginity* (*severa virginitas*, cf. *Met.* III, 254–5) and (2) the essentially Callimachean motif of a *naked goddess surprised at her bath* (Hymn v of Callimachus, the *Baths of Pallas* in particular). But these two motifs are introduced only after the essentially comic courtship (401–40). Here Ovid used the humorous business of Amphis' comedy (Jove disguised as Diana, cf. source 5 above) to reproduce the tone of the *Daphne*: the similarity of the two courtships is obvious and intentional (see p. 117 above). With Callisto's pregnancy (441 ff.), however, a quite new phase of the story begins. Here Ovid combines the Callimachean bathing scene with the *pathos* of Leukippos (source 3 above). In Parthenius (xv), when the disguised Leukippos hesitates to undress at the spring, the virgins with Daphne tear off his clothes (περιέρρηξαν αὐτόν). Then when they finally discover his sex and grasp the deception, they hurl their hunting spears at him. The passage is surely reflected in Ovid's lines about the similarly reluctant Callisto (II, 460–2):

> Parrhasis [i.e. Callisto] erubuit. Cunctae velamina ponunt:
> una moras quaerit. Dubitanti vestis adempta est,
> qua posita nudo patuit cum corpore crimen.

Diana's response (*i procul hinc...nec sacros pollue fontis!*) is, of course, reminiscent of Callimachus and possibly indebted to his fifth Hymn. But, as Heinze (pp. 109–10) has seen, the introduction of these motifs (bath, exposure, etc.) into the Callisto story is wholly Ovidian. Ovid, by such means, brought out the feelings or psychology of Callisto: her shattered innocence, and the shame which it caused her, give a quite different atmosphere to the ensuing metamorphosis. The near-tragedy of death at the hands of her ignorant son is thus in full keeping with the whole episode. The catasterism saves the situation, but it is a 'near-miss', so to speak, that sets the right mood for the vengeance stories to come and most of all for the *Actaeon*.

We need not linger over the final member of the sequence, the Coronis episode, whose inspiration is primarily Callimachus' *Hecale* (see source 6 above) though Ovid got the details about Coronis from another source that we do not know. He just touches on Apollo's love for the supposedly chaste girl (*placuit tibi, Delphice, certe dum vel casta fuit vel inobservata*) since the god–virgin motif needs no further repetition (Ovid thus indicates the parallelism in the fewest possible words). He puts only slightly more emphasis on the god's jealousy (for this continues the jealousy-motif of the *Io* and *Callisto*). His primary concern is now with the tale-bearer and the tragic outcome: Coronis, unlike Daphne, Io and Callisto, actually perishes before she can give birth to the future Aesculapius. The great interest of the crow narrative lies in its expansion of Callimachus: actually Callimachus' crow refers to Coronis in a scant verse or two (frag. 260, lines 59–61), amid a farrago of antiquarian lore, whereas Ovid's raven gives a quite clear-cut account of her own metamorphosis and error and displays her superiority (to the crow) in a characteristically Ovidian piece of narrative.

The following table shows the respective sources and Ovid's use of them and additions to them in these four episodes:

SOURCE or Representative of Source	OVID Borrowings and changes
Calvus' *Io* (Source 1)	Ovid's *Daphne* (arrows); in his *Io* Ovid changes Calvus' *Io* by introduction of Syrinx episode, omission of Cupid's arrow
Arcadian Version of *Daphne* (Source 2)	Main outline of Ovid's *Daphne* minus *Earth* as Daphne's rescuer

SOURCE or Representative of Source	OVID Borrowings and changes
Laconian Version of *Daphne* (Parthenius) (Daphne's prayer to Zeus) (Source 3)	Daphne's prayer to stream-god, Peneus; part of Bathing Scene in *Callisto*
Callisto in Callimachus (Source 4), Apollodorus, and Pseudo-Eratosthenes	Separation of roles of Artemis (Diana) and Hera (Juno); Bathing Scene added; Arcas' attack on Callisto added
Amphis (Source 5) (Zeus as Artemis)	Callisto (Jupiter as Diana)
Callimachus' *Hecale* (crow) (Source 6)	Coronis (raven, crow)

We cannot be sure of Ovid's absolute originality in all cases, but his general procedure is clear: Calvus, Parthenius and Callimachus were probably his main sources though he certainly got details from elsewhere (e.g. Amphis, the Arcadian form of the *Daphne*, some Hellenistic account of Callisto). It is evident that he (1) added many features on his own initiative, (2) transferred motifs from one legend (or version of a legend) to another, (3) varied the motifs according to a careful plan, (4) invented the elaborate liaison and (5) altered the tone and psychological content of his originals to suit his own 'empathetic' style.

III. PHAETHON (I, 747-II, 339)

Here Alfred Rohde (pp. 7-29) has made the essential points (cf. the able reviews of his monograph by Hans Herter in *Gnomon* 9 (1933), pp. 28-35 and F. Lenz in *Philologische Wochenschrift*, 1932, pp. 634-41). The major discussion of the sources is still that of Georg Knaack (*Quaestiones Phaethonteae, Philologische Untersuchungen*, VII, 1886).

Ovid had two main sources: a Hellenistic poem or 'short epos' and Euripides' *Phaethon*. The former is clearly reflected in Nonnus (*Dionysiaka* XXXVIII, 105-434) and Lucian (*Dialogi Deorum* 25). Euripides gave Ovid the 'promise' of the sun-god and the business of Phaethon's disbelief in his true paternity; the other source gave him the general outline of the rest of the episode (save for the Hesiodic conclusion, the locale of the drowning, Phaethon's

catasterism and a few other details). Nonnus and Lucian certainly
seem to go back to a common source (the motive of the famous
ride is the same: not a 'promise' whose fulfilment is designed to
prove Phaethon's paternity but the giving in of Phoebus to the
reiterated entreaties of Phaethon and his mother Clymene), but
Julius Braune (*Nonnos und Ovid*, Greifswalder Beiträge zur Literatur und Stilforschung, Heft 11, 1935) has argued that Nonnus
himself drew on Ovid in this episode. There are thus two main
problems to be discussed: the relation of Ovid (*a*) to Euripides and
(*b*) to Nonnus.

(*a*) Euripides' *Phaethon* has been ably discussed by Wilamowitz
('Phaethon', *Hermes* 18 (1883), pp. 396–434) in an article written
some eighty years ago. Not much, if any, new light has been
thrown on the subject since then (cf. the remarks of G. Türk in
PW under *Phaethon*). Some fairly long fragments of the *Phaethon*
have been preserved in the Codex Claromontanus (now Parisinus
107) and are printed in Nauck's *Tragicorum Graecorum Fragmenta*.
Phaethon is introduced as the supposed son of Merops, King of the
Aethiopians, and Merops' wife Clymene, but his real father was the
sun-god, Phoebus, with whom Clymene had had an affair prior to
her marriage. Phaethon's ostensible father, Merops, has, at the
start of the play, arranged a marriage between Phaethon and some
goddess of doubtful identity (Wilamowitz, probably erroneously,
took her to be Aphrodite). Phaethon resists the marriage for
reasons that are not altogether clear but, in any event, Clymene
tries to overcome his resistance by revealing his true paternity. If
he doubts her, as she tells him, he can convince himself by going
to Phoebus and demanding the single boon that that god had
promised Clymene (for herself or her son) at the time of his conception. We have, fortunately, her exact words to Phaethon on
this point (Nauck, Euripides frag. 773 = p. 602):

> μνησθεὶς ὅ μοί ποτ' εἶφ' ὅτ' ἠυνάσθη θεός,
> αἰτοῦ τί χρήζεις ἕν· πέρα γὰρ οὐ θέμις
> λαβεῖν σε· κἂν μὲν τυγχάνῃς [ὅτου θέλεις]
> θεοῦ πέφυκας· εἰ δὲ μή, ψευδὴς ἐγώ.

This presages the promise to which Cicero refers in his *De Officiis* (III, 25. 94): *sol Phaethonti filio (ut redeamus ad* fabulas*) facturum se esse dixit quidquid optasset.* By *fabulae*, as the general context shows, Cicero means *plays of Euripides or Roman dramatists*, generally those of Euripides. Obviously, as A. Rohde has remarked, all who heard Clymene's words knew what request Phaethon would make. Ovid, however, altogether omitted the prospective marriage (his Phaethon is emphatically a boy, not a marriageable youth) and Phoebus' antecedent promise to Clymene. Ovid's Phoebus only commits himself, on the spur of the moment, when he first sees the *boy*: the whole force of the episode depends on the unpremeditated rashness of the god and the mixed motivations of Phaethon (he is prematurely and unepically suspicious, but he is nonetheless a thoughtless and irresponsible boy). Hence the comic disproportion between the cause and the extent of the disaster that ensues, as well as the peculiarly comic tension between the paternal and the divine aspects of Phoebus.

What Ovid did is thus clear enough though no one (not even Rohde) seems to have pointed it out in explicit terms. Ovid has combined the boyish Phaethon of Nonnus and Lucian with the sceptical and recalcitrant but *adult* Phaethon of Euripides. This is also evident from the rest of the episode: Euripides' Phaethon brings on no cosmic disaster; Merops does not even know of his death until his burned body has been brought in and he (Merops) finds it on investigating the smoke that has invaded his treasure house (frag. 781). The sun-god in fact rides the horses with Phaethon (frag. 779) and himself brings the chariot home, after Phaethon's fall (cf. Cicero, *De Natura Deorum*, III, 76). In other words, Ovid's general narrative is quite like that of Nonnus and unlike that of Euripides except in this one very important detail.

(*b*) Nonnus' (and Lucian's) Phaethon is emphatically a mere boy. Clymene has no second husband (Merops seems an innovation of Euripides alone). In Nonnus at least, the boy is assured of his paternity from the start and has from babyhood been consumed with a desire to drive the sun-chariot; he even amuses himself by making a toy chariot like that of his father (lines 167-83). The gift of the actual chariot is the result of no distant promise but of most active entreaty by both Phaethon and Clymene (Nonnus, 184-95; Lucian says much the same thing: κατελιπάρησε δακρύων καὶ ἡ μήτηρ Κλυμένη). To be sure, Phoebus' submission to such pressure is not fully compatible with his great responsibilities (it is this aspect that Lucian makes much of), but the general tone of both Nonnus and Lucian is not comic in Ovid's sense. The ridiculousness of the fond father and his rash oath is, instead, replaced by a quite pathetic scene (Nonnus, 212):

πάις δὲ γενήτορα νύσσων
δάκρυσι θερμοτέροισιν ἑοὺς ἐδίηνε χιτῶνας·
χερσὶ δὲ πατρῴης φλογερῆς ἔψαυσεν ὑπήνης,
ὀκλαδὸν ἐν δαπέδῳ κυκλούμενον αὐχένα κάμπτων,
λισσόμενος· καὶ παῖδα πατὴρ ἐλέαιρε δοκεύων.
καὶ κινυρὴ Κλυμένη πλέον ᾔτεεν· αὐτὰρ ὁ θυμῷ
ἔμπεδα γινώσκων ἀμετάτροπα νήματα Μοίρης
ἀσχαλόων ἐπένευσεν, ἀποσμήξας δὲ χιτῶνι
μυρομένου Φαέθοντος ἀμειδέος ὄμβρον ὀπωπῆς
χείλεα παιδὸς ἔκυσσε.

This is why the subsequent speeches and the details of the ride have such a different effect in Ovid, closely as he seems to follow the probable source of Nonnus. Rohde has admirably treated the similarities and dissimilarities here even though he fails, on the whole, to perceive how Ovid's whole treatment has been affected by his Euripidean motivation of the episode. We can briefly list the main differences as follows:

Nonnus (196-409)	Ovid (50-300)
1st Speech of Phoebus (196-211) starts with ἄλλο γέρας μάστευε and heaps up *exempla* of gods unable to manage the chariot (Ares, Hephaestus, Apollo, Hermes, Zeus) [note that it is Phoebus' first speech that is *short*; his second that is *long*].	1st Speech of Phoebus (50-102) Ovid inverts Nonnus' order (ends with *sed tu sapientius opta*), uses only one *exemplum* (Jupiter) and brings in the astronomical lore of the second Zeus-speech (in Nonnus) in order to dissuade the boy [note that Phoebus' first speech is long; his second, short].

Nonnus (196–409)	Ovid (50–300)
2nd Speech of Phoebus (222–90), a straight astronomical account of the sun's course: with full description of signs of Zodiac, seasons, etc.	2nd Speech of Phoebus (126–49), brief account of road (15 lines). The time is late and Phoebus cannot delay further: *non est mora libera nobis!*
Description of horses and chariot, 291–300, *follows* Phoebus' second speech.	Description of horses and chariots (103–21). Unlike Nonnus, Ovid makes this *precede* the final (second) speech of Phoebus.
Detailed description of disturbance of the constellations (all signs of Zodiac plus many others), 318–409. No attention paid to Phaethon (save brief allusions at 308, 323, 347) before he is struck down.	Ovid mentions only *three* constellations and puts his main emphasis on Phaethon (150–209) and his feelings.
No corresponding destruction passage in Nonnus.	General destruction of earth, ocean, etc. (210–78).
Tellus' speech omitted in Nonnus, but speech of Phosphorus (333–46) on the constellations (not in Ovid) is included earlier in the episode.	Speech of Tellus (279–300) reintroduces theme of universal destruction (from the Flood episode of the initial Creation Epic).
Catasterism.	Catasterism omitted.

It is plain that Ovid puts his emphasis on Phoebus' dissuasive purpose, Phaethon's emotional reaction to the ride, the suffering of Tellus and the embarrassment of Jupiter when compelled to use the thunderbolt. The astronomical lore of Nonnus is adapted to a very different end. Thus the first speech of Phoebus (in Ovid) is a fine exhibition of the god's discomfiture: all his dissuasive rhetoric and astronomical expertise is grotesquely unsuited to his auditor. The embarrassment of the pleading god is well brought out as is, later, that of Jupiter before Tellus and that of Phoebus himself. The mighty astronomical background is always made to serve, not conceal, the human foreground. Furthermore, Ovid, unlike Nonnus, has designed his 'little epic' to culminate in the Hesiodic cataclysm (the exact parallel of the Hesiodic 'flood', cf. above, pp. 91–2).

It is evident that Ovid was here following a Greek source (probably, as Knaack supposed, an Alexandrian or Hellenistic 'little epic'); only so can the agreement of Nonnus and Lucian be accounted for and also the essential divergence of Ovid and Nonnus. Even Braune admits that Nonnus had another source than Ovid or Euripides though his thesis is in general the dependence of Nonnus on Ovid. This thesis, of course, is not so much objectionable in itself (see pp. 372–4 below) as in its application to arrangement of plot and narrative. In other words, divergence of plot (and source) can go with a good deal of actual imitation (in this case, of Ovid *by* Nonnus).

But Braune's thesis (as concerns the basic plot) has not as yet been generally accepted (Kreydell in *Gnomon* 11 (1935), pp. 597–605, upheld it; P. Maas (*Byz. Zeitschr.* 35 (1935), pp. 385 f.) denied it and H. Herter (*Ovidiana*, p. 58 n. 1) agrees with him and upholds Knaack) and contains obvious difficulties. Quite apart from the fact that Nonnus shows no trace of the Euripidean version of the story (a version known to Ovid, as Braune himself emphasizes, from direct inspection of Euripides' *Phaethon*) and clearly agrees with the source known to Lucian, the plot-similarities between Ovid and Nonnus are all best explained on the hypothesis of the priority (to Ovid) of Nonnus' Greek source. It is much easier to believe that Ovid had before him an astronomically oriented speech (like the second Phoebus speech in Nonnus) which he then adapted to the psychological condition of the embarrassed Phoebus than that Nonnus could make a rather bald astronomical itinerary out of the clever *suasoria* of Ovid's Phoebus. Furthermore, both the beginning and ending of Nonnus' account are radically un-Ovidian: the whole emphasis of Nonnus (ll. 318–423) is on the stars or heavens; Ovid's (ll. 210–328, as opposed to ll. 150–209) is on the damage to the earth and the acute discomfiture of Tellus (the catasterism of Phaethon is omitted). If Nonnus copied or used Ovid (which as regards certain details is quite possible) he illustrates the remarkable difference between Greek and Latin narrative style (cf. pp. 318 f. above and p. 374 below). But in fact the differences are so great (even where the similarities are

most apparent) that the supposition of a common Hellenistic or
Alexandrian source (and one far more accurately reflected by
Nonnus than by Ovid) is more probable, at least for this particular
episode.

In any event, we must posit two sources for Ovid: (1) Euripides'
Phaethon; (2) a Hellenistic version which lay behind the obviously
non-Ovidian details we find in both Lucian and Nonnus. Here
Phaethon was represented as a child and Merops did not exist. This
source also was mainly astronomical in its emphasis and contained
Phaethon's catasterism (cf. Philostratus, *Imagines*, I, 11).

Ovid alone conflated the two sources and thus gave his version
the peculiarly comic or mock-epic character which makes it the
chef d'œuvre it undoubtedly is. Knaack's hypothesis is that Ovid
found the two sources *already conflated* in a mythological *syntagma*
(*necessario adducimur ut syntagma a nescio quo mythographo conditum
in Ovidii manibus fuisse statuamus*, pp. 67–8) but this view was long
ago rejected by Ehwald and Lafaye (pp. 148–50). It needs no
further refutation. The blending of the sources is so subtle and,
above all, so intimately connected with the obviously Ovidian
liaison between the *Io* and the *Phaethon* (see p. 108 above) that it
cannot possibly be ascribed to the crude hands of a mythographer.

IV. EUROPA (II, 833–75)

We need not linger over this episode. No one can *prove* that
Ovid used Moschus, but the descriptions of the bull (Moschus,
Europa 80–8 and *Met.* II, 851–8) and of Europa's approach to it
(Moschus, 89–100; Ovid, 858–61) reveal just the likeness and difference we should expect: Ovid never imitates literally. And his
emphasis, unlike that of Moschus, is on *Jupiter*, on the incongruity
of his disguise (846 ff.) and on his amorous feelings (862 ff.).
Furthermore, Ovid's beginning and ending Jupiter's *amores* (in this
section, I) with the two myths of Moschus (Io and Europa) can
hardly be accidental (cf. our discussion in the text, pp. 92 f. above).
In general, the comparison of Moschus and Ovid here is most
instructive. Sentimental and erotic as is Moschus' idyll, it quite

lacks the empathy of Ovid. Europa's and Zeus' actions (Moschus, 93–100) are primarily physical in Moschus: Ovid (897 ff., 862 ff.) gives us the feelings and thoughts of the two. Cf. Heinze (pp. 58–9 note) on the difference between the Europas of the *Metamorphoses* and the *Fasti* (v, 603–20). He sees clearly that the elegiac version is static or descriptive rather than narrative, whereas the epic 'hält vielmehr an fortschreitende Handlung in der ein Glied am andern hängt'. This distinction also holds for Moschus. As Heinze sees, Moschus composes his poem of little static pictures (*Zustand-schilderungen*): the dream, the basket, the flower-picking, the Bull, the voyage, and the three monologues of Europa. Ovid in the *Metamorphoses* gives us a compressed but *continuous* narrative: *gaudet amans et* dum veniat *sperata voluptas, oscula* dat *manibus. vix* iam *vix cetera differt, et* nunc *adludit,* …nunc *latus,* etc.… *deponit,* paulatim metu dempto *pectora* praebet, etc. The temporal succession is clearly marked. But Heinze failed to see that this sort of narrative is quite as emotional as that of the more static Moschus or the elegiac Ovid. The contrast is not one between elegiac emotion and epic frigidity or dignity but between a narrative in one tone (elegiac, light, amorous) and a narrative in two tones (epic majesty struggling with amorous feeling). Thus Heinze tended, on the whole, to miss the comedy or humour of Ovid. His analysis, so far as it goes, is basically correct but fails to penetrate through to Ovid's real intention. Cf. my discussion of the Proserpina episode above (pp. 50–9).

V. ACTAEON (III, 131–252)

Undoubtedly Ovid had two main sources: (1) Callimachus' *Baths of Pallas* (Hymn v); (2) a hexameter short epic or *epyllion* of the form attributed by Apollodorus (III, 30–2) to the majority of writers on the theme (οἱ πλείονες), i.e. that Actaeon saw Artemis in her bath, was immediately (παραχρῆμα) turned by her into a stag or deer and was then killed and eaten by his own hounds. Some of the MSS. (ES excepted) of Apollodorus add a number of verses on the names of the hounds (cf. also the lists in Hyginus 171, Rose ed. pp. 126–7). It seems clear that Ovid's source contained a list of hounds though there is a considerable difference of names in the sources (Apollodorus, Hyginus) we have. It seems most probable that Actaeon's act (in this source or category of sources) was inspired by direct or indirect lust: this is not stated (nor denied) in Apollodorus but is stated in both Nonnus and Hyginus: Hyginus 180 says: *Actaeon...Dianam lavantem speculatus est et* eam violare voluit. Nonnus (*Dionys.* v, 305 ff.) represents him as a greedy and lustful *voyeur* (θηητήρ...ἀκόρητος) observing the naked Artemis from a tall oak tree (later a poplar) until a nymph spies him and shrieks in horror.

Who first combined Callimachus with the usual Actaeon legend is uncertain. Undoubtedly Kleinknecht ('Λουτρὰ τῆς Παλλάδος', *Hermes* 74 (1939), pp. 333–9) is correct when he argues against Wilamowitz's thesis that it was Pherecydes who remodelled the Tiresias story on the analogy of Actaeon: Callimachus himself was more likely the first to represent the fate of Actaeon as a parallel or *exemplum* to be set beside the much milder treatment (by Athene) of Tiresias. Callimachus' apologetic purpose (he was trying to show the mercy or kindness of Athene despite the apparent harshness of her blinding of the innocent child or lad, Tiresias) made the comparison meaningful. It is most unlikely that Pherecydes' genealogical work would have necessitated this kind of comparison or 'remodelling'. Yet clearly Callimachus influenced later versions of *Actaeon*, as we can see from Nonnus (337 ff. where Actaeon in his death-agony expatiates on the relative blessedness of Tiresias). Nonnus or his source obviously knew Callimachus: Actaeon's lament (as given by Nonnus) could not have been derived from Ovid alone or indeed from Ovid primarily, for Ovid does not make any explicit parallel between Tiresias and Actaeon (all that Ovid's Actaeon wants to say at the fatal moment is one line: 230, '*Actaeon ego sum, dominum cognoscite vestrum*', but he is, in his capacity of stag, *unable* to say it). Nonnus, of course, may have used Callimachus directly though it is possible that his knowledge of Callimachus was only second-hand. Castiglioni

(*Studi Alessandrini*, II, in *Studi Critici off. a Carlo Pascal*, 1913) holds that Nonnus had two direct sources: Callimachus' Hymn and a Hellenistic poem, itself influenced by a post-Euripidean tragedy and possibly by Ovid himself. Braune (*op. cit.*) sees, of course, the influence of Ovid and holds that Nonnus even 'repeated' his basically Ovidian version in an intensified form (*Dionys.* v, 287–369 and 415–551). In any event, there certainly existed an *Actaeon* (probably a short *epos*) that had a very different motivation (as regards the 'viewing' of the goddess) from Ovid's and that is surely to some degree reflected by Nonnus. Ovid himself must have known such a version though line 479 of the *Ibis* (*quique verecundae speculantem labra Dianae*) is too brief and ambiguous to justify certainty.

It thus seems certain that one or more Hellenistic poems existed which contained the following features: (1) the sensual motivation of Actaeon; (2) the punishing wrath of Artemis–Diana; (3) the list of dogs; and possibly also (4) the Callimachean parallel of Actaeon and Tiresias adapted to the other three (above) features, and thus taken out of the mouth of the benevolent goddess and attributed instead to the dying Actaeon (as in Nonnus).

Ovid, however, certainly knew both Callimachus and the Hellenistic poem or poems just referred to. From the one (Callimachus) he took the innocence of the victim; from the other (the source or sources represented by Apollodorus, Hyginus and Nonnus) he took the unmitigated wrath of the goddess. This is why he represented her as a haughty Roman matron puritanically preoccupied with *severa virginitas* and surrounded by properly obsequious *famulae* at her incongruously unsylvan toilet. The bath itself, however, is obviously an Ovidian 'parody' of Callimachus. Maria de Cola is quite correct when she says (p. 47): 'La sensuale fantasia di Ovidio ha trasformato il bagno della Dea semplice e vergine, riservatamente accennato dal suo modello [i.e. Callimachus], in quello di una donna del suo tempo raffinata e compiacente. La purezza della narrazione callimachea è completamente svisata.' But she sees that Ovid, unlike Callimachus, is

emphasizing the drama of the episode, especially in the affecting
death scene (e.g. the pursuit and emotional reaction of Actaeon is,
as she recognizes, an 'assoluta creazione di Ovidio'). What she
misses, however (as also Couat, *La Poésie Alexandrine*, 1890, p.
290), is Ovid's purpose or intention in this episode. Ovid, unlike
Callimachus, is concerned not to save but to destroy the idea of a
benevolent goddess. He accents the innocence of Actaeon in order
to convert the goddess' wrath into something approaching cold
malevolence or, better, a frigid puritanism that even the gods find
questionable. The Callisto episode had already prepared us for this
sort of Diana. We cannot be sure that all his sources gave him a
merely lustful Actaeon who deserved what he got (i.e. a proper
vengeance), but it is certainly a possible, or even probable, hypothesis. In any event, Ovid deliberately reversed the emphasis of
Callimachus and, unlike the Hellenistic version or versions of the
story, made the innocence of Actaeon an essential preliminary to
his tragic end. His 'empathetic-sympathetic' treatment of the
pursuit and death (lines 198–205, 225–48) is surely his own: the
story, at his hands, becomes one of suffering innocence and undeserved vengeance with heavily Roman undertones. As has often
been remarked, his listing of the dog-names is obviously perfunctory: Ovid breaks off the list (l. 225) with the words: *quosque* [i.e.
the rest of the dogs] *referre mora est*. He does, however, show by
the list of names that the dogs are real individuals whom Actaeon
could call off, had he but the voice to do so: *clamore libebat 'Actaeon
ego sum, dominum cognoscite vestrum!' Verba animo desunt*. Here the
difference between Ovid and Nonnus is striking: Nonnus' Actaeon
utters a long soliloquy (337–65) that reveals human feelings (ὑπὸ
βροτέη...μενοινῇ line 335) but remains the inarticulate voice of a
beast (ἀντὶ δὲ φωνῆς ἀνδρομέης κελάδῃσεν ἀσημάντου θρόος ἠχοῦς,
lines 368–9). Ovid empathetically reveals Actaeon's feelings *in the
narrative itself* and carefully denies him the ability to put his
thoughts into any kind of direct discourse (even the 'translated'
discourse that Nonnus attributes to him). That Actaeon cannot
speak (even though he thinks) like a man, constitutes his *pathos*.

Ovid's empathetic style (cf. ll. 247 f. *vellet* [i.e. Actaeon] *abesse quidem, sed adest; velletque videre, non etiam sentire canum fera facta suorum*) here reveals the *pathos*, as Nonnus' clumsy soliloquy does not.

The long ghost-scene in Nonnus (415–531: the return of Actaeon's ghost and its request for a proper burial) is altogether superfluous. The mother's neglect of the animal bones, the ghost's forgiveness of his ignorant dogs, are meant to be touching but are only grotesque. But Actaeon again emphasizes his original motive (cf. 432 ff., 478 ff.) and in much stronger terms. Thus, however much Nonnus may here be indebted to Ovid (and we probably cannot exclude some indebtedness, see my discussion of the *Ino* below), the essential motivation of the story and the style of the narrative are very different.

VI. PENTHEUS (III, 511–733)

It is impossible to tell exactly what source was used by Ovid. He knew Euripides' *Bacchae* and imitates it in a few places, but the *Bacchae* was certainly not his chief model. The episode of the Tyrrhene sailors is told in the seventh Homeric Hymn, Hyginus (134), Apollodorus (III, 37), Nonnus (XLV, 96–168) and also Seneca (*Oedipus*, 445–73). But only Nonnus makes it an integral part of the Pentheus story (it is a cautionary tale told to Pentheus by the prophet Tiresias). Servius auctus (*ad Aen.* IV, 469) describes Pacuvius' *Pentheus* as containing an Acoetes brought as prisoner to Pentheus in lieu of the missing Dionysus: *misit* [Pentheus] *satellites qui eum* [Liberum] *vinctum ad se perducerent. Qui cum ipsum non invenissent, unum ex comitibus eius Acoetem captum ad Pentheum perduxerunt.* This agrees closely with Ovid (III, 562–3, 572–6). Thus it is possible that Ovid found the story of the Tyrrhene sailors attributed to Acoetes in Pacuvius (where it likewise may have constituted the substance of a long speech by Acoetes). Or, on the other hand, Nonnus may represent a Hellenistic conflation of the *Pentheus* and *Tyrrhene Sailors*. There is no apparent way of deciding the question: Pacuvius is perhaps the most likely model, if model there really is, for the *combination* of the two stories (*Pentheus* and the *Tyrrhene Sailors*). Certainly the detailed account of the metamorphosis (cf. Quirin, pp. 54–5) is Ovid's own, as is the pathetic reference of Pentheus to Actaeon. The structure of Ovid's *Pentheus* is dramatic (especially so in his reliance on dialogue and speeches) which again points toward Pacuvius. But the name *Acoetes* occurs only in Pacuvius (as recorded by Servius) and in Hyginus (who despite Rose *ad loc.* may well represent Ovid himself). Hence it is conceivable that Ovid took only the name from Pacuvius but himself attributed the legend of the sailors to the man called Acoetes. The name is presumably only an *alias* for Dionysus. As for Nonnus' possible or probable dependence on Ovid, see my discussion of the *Ino* immediately following. On the whole, the most likely hypothesis is that Ovid himself first added the metamorphosis narrative to the essentially dramatic *Pentheus* and himself attributed the narrative to Acoetes (the name does not occur in the Homeric Hymn). Nonnus is here only a belated reflection of Ovid.

VII. INO (IV, 416–542)

The basic problem of the sources here is quite simple. The Athamas–Ino legend was very well known and came down to Ovid without significant variation (cf. *Od.* v, 333; Pindar, *Ol.* 2. 30; *Pyth.* 11. 2; Euripides, *Medea*, 1284 ff. and Callimachus frag. 91 Pfeiffer). Ovid himself had told the story in the *Fasti* (VI, 485 ff.) though he there, naturally enough, gave it a Roman ending. But the great innovation of Ovid in the *Metamorphoses* version of the story was his extensive use of Virgilian motifs. The wrathful soliloquy of Juno (422–31), her use of the fury Tisiphone (481 ff.), the mock-Bacchic revel of Ino (512 ff.), obviously recall the Juno, Allecto and Amata scenes of *Aeneid* I and, particularly, VII. Ovid's variations on Virgil are also obviously his own, particularly the amusing journey of Juno to the underworld. But Castiglioni (pp. 287–99) has pointed out the striking resemblances of Ovid and Nonnus in this episode. We thus get the *furor* of Juno in

Dionys. I, 325 ff. or VIII, 34 ff. (Hera and Phthonos), the madness of Athamas himself (x, 25 ff.), and above all the journey of Hera to Hades (XXXI, 24 ff.) in order to bring up the fury Megaira, and panic the forces of her enemy, Dionysus. Castiglioni sees in such passages the remains of Hellenistic motifs that exerted an independent influence on Ovid above and beyond that of Virgil. He says (p. 297): 'Ma per quanto, ripeto, si voglia ricorrere ad influssi retorici ed epici, rimane sempre inconcusso che da questa parte del libro XXXI delle Dionisiache possiamo trarre la conclusione che non tutti gli spunti dei monologhi e dialoghi ovidiani, a proposito di Giunone, nè l'intiera descrizione del viaggio dell'irosa dea ai regni sotterranei, sono un possesso che Vergilio lasciò, come modificatore e creatore esclusivo, alla poesia latina.' He also sees in the *Culex* (that in his view reflects an Alexandrian *epyllion* however it may be related to Virgil and whether or not it is posterior to Virgil in date) the remains of a Hellenistic description of the underworld on which Ovid, like other Latin poets, has drawn.

No one can doubt the similarity of these passages in Nonnus and Ovid, or, indeed, their common origin somewhere. Nonnus in fact combines Ovidian, Homeric and other motifs in the most elaborate way (e.g. the underworld journey of Hera and the Homeric 'deception of Zeus' in *Dionys.* XXXI–XXXII). The question at issue really is whether he reflects Ovid himself or, as Castiglioni thinks, prior Hellenistic or Alexandrian models. The answer to the question is, it seems to me, contained in Castiglioni's own admission (p. 288) that one hardly needs to go beyond Virgil to explain Ovid's additions to the Ino legend. The soliloquies of Hera and the Hera–Megaira episode of Nonnus, in their turn, have a quite adequate source in Ovid and Virgil themselves. While Nonnus (as we have seen in respect of the Phaethon, Actaeon and Pentheus stories) certainly knew other sources beside Ovid (Homer and Callimachus in addition to lost Hellenistic material), his knowledge of Ovid (and perhaps Virgil) is by far the most likely explanation of the passages that Castiglioni here refers to. Braune did not treat the *Ino* in his monograph, but it provides, in my view, a far more impressive demonstration of his general thesis of Nonnus' dependence on Ovid than the episodes he does treat. Nonnus, however, imitates Ovid in the most eclectic manner, using motifs rather than whole episodes from the *Metamorphoses*. This is apparent when we put both authors side by side. I list the details in Ovid's order:

Ovid	Nonnus
4. 416–31. Juno's soliloquy	I, 325 f., VIII, 34 f. Envy's colloquy with Hera
	IX, 268 f. Semele's taunting of Hera
432 f. Juno's descent to Hades	XXXI, 24. Hera's descent to Hades
473 f. Tisiphone	X, 1–44. Madness of Athamas, Megaira and Tisiphone
	XXXI, 75 f., XXXII, 98 f. Megaira
515 f. Athamas and Learchus	X, 72 f. especially the words: παππάζων δ' ἰάχησεν ἑὸς πάις

(cf. also 6. 640, Tereus and Procne:
*et 'mater, mater' clamantem . . .
ense ferit Procne'*)

Nonnus, compared to Ovid, is complicated and difficult; he quite lacks the concreteness and dramatic force of Ovid. He is, in fact, not influenced by Ovid's narrative or plot so much as by the piquantly Ovidian motifs. His narrative style is, in other words, the very reverse of Ovid's. Where Ovid assimilates thought and emotion to the narrative proper, Nonnus uses monologue (soliloquy) and speech; where Ovid is Virgilian, Nonnus is Homeric; where Ovid is condensed, Nonnus is repetitious. Nonnus, as it were, *homerizes* or *hellenizes* his Ovidian motifs. Furthermore, Nonnus always follows a non-Ovidian source at one or more essential points of his main narrative (cf. our discussion of the Phaethon, Actaeon, Pentheus episodes). Once, however, this basic difference of approach is recognized, the numerous Ovidian motifs in Nonnus can be clearly discerned. Nor does anything in extant Alexandrian verse (Callimachus, Apollonius, Theocritus) require us to contradict this verdict.

APPENDIX

VIII. NIOBE (VI, 146–312)

The major work on Ovid's use of his sources here is, beyond question, the article of Ludwig Voit, 'Die Niobe des Ovid' (*Gymnasium* 64 (1957), pp. 135–49). A good survey of the sources, etc. is given in Lesky's article *Niobe* in PW (s.v. 'Niobe'), to which K. B. Stark's *Niobe und die Niobiden* (1863) forms a useful supplement. Ovid differed from Aeschylus and Sophocles (who both wrote *Niobes*) in the following major respects: (1) Ovid concentrates his events in one place and time (cf. Voit, p. 147); (2) he eliminates (save for one reference, line 271) the husband, Amphion, and omits all mention of Niobe's prior association with Latona (Niobe is thus represented as completely human); (3) Ovid makes the petrifaction follow the killing of the children without any pause or interruption. Not so Sophocles (and presumably Aeschylus): schol. *Il.* XXIV, 599 ff. Σοφοκλῆς δὲ τοὺς παῖδας ἐν Θήβαις ἀπολέσθαι, νοστῆσαι δὲ αὐτὴν εἰς Λυδίαν; (4) Ovid does *not* (like Sophocles and Aeschylus) represent the petrifaction as a punishment (cf. Mette, *Die Fragmente der Tragödien des Aischylos*, 273, pp. 96–7). The remains of the two *Niobes* (cf. Mette and Nauck) make this at least very probable if not certain.

Though the 'killing of the sons' is a rather cold set of variations on a single theme, it at least provides both preparation and contrast for the final blow, the killing of the daughters. Ovid's plan or design is apparent. The relative balance of the two death scenes is indicated by the two boastful speeches of Niobe (170–202 and 280–5): the first (thirty-three lines) justifies and causes the punishment; but the second (six lines) is hardly sufficient to justify an exact repetition of it. By the time the arrows have killed all but the last remaining girl, Niobe has quite lost her pride and asks only for the life of the one left: '*unam minimamque relinque! de multis minimam posco*'. Her ensuing death thus explains the mother's passage from active grief to sheer stupefaction. By this time our feeling for the punitive aspect of the narrative has quite disappeared or rather been replaced by sheer pity. But the gods are far too much involved in the vengeance to be associated with pity. The petrifaction is, as Voit points out, the 'natürlich fast psychologische Folge ihres maßlosen Schmerzes' (p. 146). Here Ovid's 'empathetic-sympathetic' narrative style has made possible a most significant variation on the Niobe theme. Though we have but few fragments of either play (especially of the Sophocles *Niobe*) it is all but certain that they did not possess the arrangement and climax just indicated.

The climactic effect of the metamorphosis is clearly brought out in the remarkable lines (VI, 298–303):

> Ultima restabat. Quam toto corpore mater,
> tota veste tegens 'unam minimamque relinque!
> De multis minimam posco' clamavit 'et unam.'
> Dumque rogat, pro qua rogat, occidit. Orba resedit
> exanimes inter natos natasque virumque,
> deriguitque malis: nullos movet aura capillos.

Here the succession of tenses (*restabat, tegens, clamavit, dum rogat, pro qua rogat, occidit, resedit, deriguitque, movet*) is remarkably effective. The imperfect *restabat* serves to prolong or 'hold' the final moment of the tragedy (the last daughter's momentary survival and death). The presents *rogat, occidit* then bring the tragedy directly under the reader's vision. Then the perfects *resedit, deriguit* represent the swift consequence which is itself a reversion to the dead past, or to the petrifaction of the present in the past. The contrast also between the impassioned oratory of lines 299–300 and the gloomy quiet of lines 302–3, between the staccato action of line 301 and the heavy 'deadness' of line 302 (the spondees, the caesurae after *exanimes, inter, natos* and the repetition of *natos, natas, -que, -que*), greatly intensifies the effect of the words *deriguitque malis*. The immediate indication of the new present in the abrupt clause *nullos movet aura capillos* is also very striking.

IX. PROCNE, PHILOMELA, TEREUS (vi, 424–674)

The chief monograph on Ovid's sources for this episode is that of Ignazio Cazzaniga: *La Saga di Itis nella Tradizione letteraria e mitografica Greco-Romana*, Part I (1950) and Part II (1951), each paged separately. The second part has the separate title: *L'episodio di Procne nel libro Sesto delle Metamorfosi di Ovidio: ricerche intorno alla tecnica poetica ovidiana*. Cazzaniga holds in brief that: (1) Ovid's essential 'model' is Sophocles' *Tereus* (which he dates *after* Euripides' *Medea* of 431 B.C.); (2) but only lines 587–674 are based on Sophocles. The earlier part of the episode (ll. 424–586) shows a different style, that of the 'novella' or Hellenistic *epyllion*, though there was no direct Hellenistic model. Cazzaniga points to various features of 'novellistic' technique in lines 424–586: the premonitions of lines 424–38 (here he compares Musaeus' *Hero and Leander* 274–80); the stress on the unexpected (*aprosdoketon*) and the contrast of happy beginning with tragic ending, 434 ff.; the suddenness of Tereus' passion; the emphasis on contrast and *ekplexis* and the marvellous (e.g. Philomela's moving tongue after the *glossotomia*, 557 ff.).

He sees a marked difference after 587. Procne is now the typical *paidophonos* of tragedy (like, for example, Medea and Althaea); Tereus the typical exponent of *hybris* reduced to misery. The speeches of Philomela had already revealed (a fact that would seem inconsistent with Cazzaniga's sharp division of ll. 424–586 from ll. 587–674) a true tragic *ethopoeia* (496–502, 533–48), and the omission of sensuous detail (as at ll. 524 ff.) shows the tragic intent (in contrast, for example, to the Salmacis episode).

I need not repeat my reasons (given in the text) for rejecting Cazzaniga's thesis. There is no reason to doubt Ovid's familiarity with Sophocles' *Tereus* or, much more significantly, with Accius' tragedy of the same name. As we know from Cicero, Accius' *Tereus* was a stage favourite of the late republic and there is every reason to suppose that Ovid himself had seen it as well as read it (cf. Cicero *ad Att.* XVI, 2. 3 and 5. 1). Accius' lines (Nonius 270. 24):

Tereus indomito more atque animo barbaro
conspexit in eam; amore vecors flammeo
depositus, facinus pessimum ex dementia
confingit

are suggestively close to Ovid's (VI, 455 ff.):

Non secus exarsit *conspecta virgine* Tereus,
quam si quis canis ignem supponat aristis, etc.

★ ★ ★ ★ ★ ★ ★ ★

                hunc innata libido
exstimulat, *pronumque genus regionibus illis
in Venerem* est: flagrat vitio gentisque suoque.

★ ★ ★ ★ ★ ★ ★ ★

Et nihil est, quod non *effreno captus amore*
ausit; nec capiunt inclusas pectora *flammas*.

But the subject was also exactly suited to the amatory *epyllion* of
Parthenius and his disciples, Cinna and Gallus. Its plot has much
in common with the *Ciris* or Cinna's *Zmyrna*. Virgil mentions it at
the end of a list of neoteric subjects (*Ecl.* 6. 74–81):

Quid loquar aut *Scyllam Nisi* quam fama secuta est
candida succinctam latrantibus inguina monstris
Dulichias vexasse rates et gurgite in alto
a, timidos nautas canibus lacerasse marinis,
*aut ut mutatos Terei narraverit artus,
quas illi Philomela dapes, quae dona pararit,
quo cursu deserta petiverit et quibus ante
infelix sua tecta supervolitaverit alis.*

It is obvious that a writer of narrative verse was not bound by the
restrictions of drama. Thus the lines of Accius just quoted are
obviously taken from the Euripidean prologue of his play (the
action of his play began, as I see it, with Philomela's arrival at
Tereus' palace = Ovid, 601 ff.) but they correspond to an integral
part of Ovid's narrative. We do not know whether the Tereus
theme was ever made into a neoteric *epyllion* (there is no record of
it) but Virgil's eclogue certainly shows that it was a quite accept-

able subject for one and that there was nothing in the least unusual about putting a tragic plot into 'epylliac' form (cf. Virgil's
account of *Pasiphae* in the same eclogue).

Obviously Ovid, like the tragedians, prepared his climax with
some care, but there is no 'gap' or sudden shift of narrative technique such as Cazzaniga supposes. This can be easily seen in a
schematic analysis of the narrative:

(1) The episode starts with the marriage of Tereus and Procne
but this is emphasized (428–32) only to stress its causative importance for the whole narrative: it is the mating of opposites that
carries the seeds of all the trouble to come.

(2) lines 433–8 constitute a rapid *praeteritio* that takes us from
the wedding to the birth of Itys (the ominous *parentes*) and then to
the birthday of Itys (five years later) at which the continuous or
true narrative begins (438). The abrupt transition between the
gnomic *usque adeo latet utilitas* and *iam tempora Titan quinque per
autumnos...duxerat* indicates the dividing point between the preliminary period of apparent happiness (so deceptive) and the
actual tragedy that now begins.

(3) lines 438–46 describe both the voyage of Tereus (to Athens)
and its motive (Procne's affection for Philomela). The quick
obedience of Tereus (he does not even reply to Procne but at once
orders out his ships, l. 444) is again a dramatic indication of the gap
between appearance (Tereus' conjugal eagerness to comply with
Procne's wish) and the reality so soon to be manifested. The main
point of these lines is of course to introduce Procne at the start and
thus prepare the reader for her definitive re-emergence at the close
of the episode.

(4) lines 447–82. Here the true nature of Tereus is revealed as
soon as he sees Philomela, but this is only to the reader (as the
author empathetically penetrates Tereus' mind): to Pandion,
Philomela and the Athenians in general he puts on an impressive
show of *pietas* as if it were only the *mandata Procnes* that motivated
him.

(5) lines 483–510. Here the difference between the pious Philomela (so devoted to both father and sister) and the lustful Tereus is carefully brought out. The scene marks the narrative interval between the actual success of Tereus' plan (to get possession of Philomela) and its overt realization. Thus dramatic suspense is intensified.

(6) lines 511–30. With *ut semel* (l. 511) the mask is thrown off: Philomela learns and experiences the true nature of Tereus. The rape itself is passed over in a single phrase (*vi superat*, 525). Suspense, however, is maintained by our knowledge of Procne's ignorance. Though 'off the stage', she determines the action as both Tereus' secrecy and Philomela's isolation clearly show.

(7) lines 531–62. These contain the protest of Philomela and the *glossotomia*. Tereus has failed in his effort to exact Philomela's consent or silence. He commits another crime in order to preserve even now his false relationship with Procne. Thus the 'web' episode is motivated.

(8) lines 563–86. Now, however (it is a year later, 571, and Philomela seems isolated and unable to communicate with Procne), the device of the web reverses the previous situation: it is now Tereus, not Procne, who is kept in ignorance. The pivotal lines (582–3):

> Germanaeque suae carmen miserabile legit
> et (mirum potuisse) *silet*. Dolor ora repressit

mark the transition from one silence to another. Procne's repression of emotion and secrecy is the starting-point and condition of her revenge. The dramatic suspense rises markedly.

(9) lines 587–646. Here the vengeance is prepared (even to the murder of Itys). Without the previous narrative (the false piety and lust of Tereus, the rape, the *glossotomia*) the child-murder would be merely grotesque. Here it is amply motivated. Yet the scene, dramatic as it is, does not interrupt the suspense but actually heightens it: all this is but preparation for the dénouement to come.

(10) lines 647–74. With the cannibal feast, the narrative of course comes to its end. The metamorphosis is briefly related as an

all but inevitable result of the sheer animality to which each of the three has already been reduced.

The whole episode is admirably unified. There are of course two parts to it (one in which Tereus tries to keep Procne in ignorance; the other in which Procne tries to keep Tereus in ignorance), but Philomela is the dramatic link between them. Procne's brief emergence at the beginning is absolutely essential to her dominance at the end; the relative eclipse of each spouse (Procne from ll. 447–562 and Tereus from ll. 566–646) is in fact the very basis of the dramatic suspense: it is the one's ignorance of the other's actions that makes possible the final dénouement. But while the episode is dramatic, it is also dramatic narrative. The effects just indicated could not have been achieved in a drama of Sophocles, Euripides or one of their Latin imitators. Ovid's narrative embraces a number of places (Thrace, Athens) and a difference of times (the year between Philomela's departure from Athens and communication with Procne) that the Greek dramatic form could not compass. But a prologue (like that of Accius' *Tereus*) could have been substituted for the first part of the Ovidian narrative. On the other hand, though Ovid may have used a lost *epyllion* such as Virgil referred to, the masterly dramatic narrative seems to be entirely his own: the style is quite unlike any known neoteric *epyllion* (cf. my analysis of the *Ciris*, pp. 62–5 above and remarks on the *Myrrha* below, pp. 391–2). There is no apparent similarity between Euphorion and this episode: cf. the fragments of Euphorion's *Thrax* (D. L. Page, *Greek Literary Papyri*, 1 (1942), pp. 494 f.) and K. Latte's discussion of it ('Der Thrax des Euphorion', *Philologus* 90 (1935), pp. 152–3).

X. PROCRIS-CEPHALUS (VII, 694–868)

The two principal treatments of the sources here are those by Rohde, pp. 30–51, and Viktor Pöschl, 'Kephalos und Prokris in Ovids Metamorphosen' (*Hermes* 87 (1959), pp. 328–43). The story (so far as Procris' 'error' and death are concerned) was also told by Ovid in *Ars Amatoria* III, 687–746. Ovid was probably most indebted to Nicander represented by Antoninus Liberalis, *Met. Syn.* 41 ('Αλώπηξ, Cazzaniga ed. pp. 75–7; Martini ed. pp. 123–7). But the versions of Hyginus (189 = Rose ed. pp. 133–4), Apollodorus (III, 197–8 and II, 57–9) and the scholium to *Odyssey* XI, 321 (this reflects Pherecydes as it says: ἱστορία παρὰ Φερεκύδῃ ἐν τῇ ἑβδόμῃ) add interesting details. The principal variations can best be indicated in parallel (cf. p. 177):

Hyginus, 189	Pherecydes (*Od.* scholium)	Nicander	Apollodorus
Cephalus rejects Aurora's advances, who then changes his shape. Thus disguised, he 'seduces' Procris. At the discovery of C.'s identity, she flees, lives with Diana and is given the magic spear and dog. Then, disguised as a young man, she rejoins Cephalus. In order to secure dog and spear, he consents to her apparently homosexual solicitation. P. then discovers her true self. They are reconciled. Finally she is accidentally killed by his spear as, still jealous of Aurora, she secretly observes him from an ambush in the bushes.	Cephalus tries to 'prove' Procris' virtue by an 8 years' absence and return in a disguised form. He then tries to seduce her; she yields. He reveals his true identity but is reconciled to her. Later Procris becomes jealous of the 'cloud' (νεφέλη) to which or whom Cephalus has been heard to speak. She is, as in Hyginus, accidentally killed.	Eos (Aurora) seduces Cephalus. Then C. tries Procris by pretending absence and sending messenger with offers of money, as if from a stranger who wanted to seduce her. She finally consents; C. reveals the truth; she flees and stays with Minos but returns to C. (disguised as young man) with the dog and spear. She makes same offer as in Hyginus, then reveals herself. Nothing about her final jealousy and death.	Procris, the wife of Cephalus, sleeps with Pteleon for the price of a golden crown. Cephalus discovers her deed. She flees to Minos in Crete. Minos falls in love with her and she gives in to him after overcoming Pasiphae's witchery. But fearing Pasiphae, she flees, returns to Athens and is reconciled to Cephalus. Finally Cephalus kills her (with spear) by mistake while hunting.

Here the essential differences between Ovid and his sources (certainly one of them was Nicander) have been sufficiently discussed in the text (pp. 177–81 and 268). In general, I fully subscribe to Pöschl's excellent analysis. Ovid transformed the neatly balanced tale of double seduction (the 'novella' of masks) into a melodrama of fully mutual passion. As Pöschl truly says (p. 340): 'Bei Ovid ...ist nicht die Gleichheit, sondern der Gegensatz der beiden hervorgehoben, und das ist nicht ein Gegensatz zwischen Treue und Untreue, Liebe und Nichtliebe, sondern der Kontrast zweier Naturen, die beide von tiefer Liebe erfüllt sind.' But Pöschl fails to see the extent to which Ovid has here seen the episode through Cephalus' own eyes. The references to Procris' homosexual advances in ll. 751 and 687–8 cannot possibly be accounted for as interpolations (a notion that Pöschl will not exclude: 'was ich nicht für völlig ausgeschlossen halte'); nor is Ovid concerned simply with indicating that he knew the story as it stood in Nicander or some similar source. The double seduction was real enough, but Cephalus' love was sufficient to ignore (or almost ignore) it: despite all their jealousy and cupidity and the ignoble means to which they both resorted, Procris remained his true love as he had, till her death, remained hers (vii, 859–61):

> me spectat, et in me
> infelicem animam nostroque exhalat in ore,
> sed vultu meliore mori secura videtur.

Few episodes are more instructive for the student of Ovid. The element here added to the sources is something unknown to Hellenistic literature but characteristically and crucially Ovidian. Cf. the discussion on pp. 268–73.

Wilamowitz, therefore, was right when he said (*Hermes* 18 (1883), p. 425 n. 2): 'das ärgste muß Ovid verschweigen weil bei ihm Kephalos selbst erzählt', and Rohde (p. 41) wrong in attributing Ovid's 'silence', or toning down of the *lasciviora* in the sources, to the decorum of epic. There is plenty of lasciviousness elsewhere in the poem! On the other hand, Rohde makes a very apt observation when he attributes Ovid's description of the hesitant

Cephalus of ll. 714–29 to the poet himself. He is good also on the aesthetic reasons for Ovid's placing of the wolf-metamorphosis (p. 45). But Rohde, despite the acuteness of his analysis, tended to treat Ovid's manipulation of sources as a mainly stylistic or artistic phenomenon. What is important, however, is the new conception of love that underlies the whole episode and is illustrated also in the following *Iphis*, *Pygmalion* and *Ceyx–Alcyone* (see pp. 268–73 above).

XI. *PHILEMON-BAUCIS* AND *ERYSICHTHON*
(VIII, 616–878)

These episodes have often been discussed since they, more than any others, provide an opportunity for the direct comparison of Ovid and Callimachus (particularly of Ovid's *Erysichthon* with Callimachus' (Sixth) *Hymn to Artemis*). Of the many treatments of the *Erysichthon*, the most significant are probably: Wilamowitz, *Hellenistische Dichtung* (1924), II, pp. 43–4; Lafaye, pp. 132–40; de Cola, pp. 67–71; Diller, pp. 25–9.

All the critics (cf. Lafaye) have noticed the extent to which the 'epic' and allegorical style of Ovid's *Erysichthon* all but excludes the familiarity and charm of Callimachus. Heinze (p. 12 n. 2) of course pointed out that Lafaye missed the decisive point (*das Entscheidende*), which was that Ovid was translating the 'fairy-tale' tone of Callimachus into epic. But this is hardly a sufficient explanation of what all must feel to be the exaggeratedly 'epic' manner of this episode. Other episodes (e.g. *Salmacis*, *Pyramus and Thisbe*, most especially the preceding *Baucis and Philemon*) are not nearly so 'epic'. Here Diller made a real contribution when he pointed to the wit, paradox and verbal posturing of Ovid, but again he over-extended the comparison by deducing from it the principles of Ovid's general style in the whole *Metamorphoses*. The fact is that quite insufficient attention has been paid to the *position* of both *Baucis–Philemon* and *Erysichthon* in the schema of the poem. They stand *within* the grand double panel of Section III (see above, pp. 194–205) and are designed to be theodicies, setting forth the justice and power of the gods. Furthermore, there is an obvious striving for contrast: the *Erysichthon*'s epic is meant to balance the more idyllic and homely style of the *Baucis–Philemon*. (This is true even of the grammar and metric; compare ll. 664 ff. with 819 ff.) It hardly seems an accident that these two tales of reward and punishment (for piety and impiety respectively) stand in the very centre of the poem, while two quite similar reward and punishment tales (*Lycaon, Deucalion–Pyrrha*) stand at its beginning (Creation-Epic).

Again, it seems evident that Ovid did not want to reproduce a Callimachean effect when dealing with themes that Callimachus had made famous for all educated men of the time. He wanted, in other words, to show how differently he could treat the themes of the Artemis Hymn and the *Hecale*.

Most critics, however, have felt (and in my view rightly felt) that Ovid, for all that, had his eye on Callimachus and was using Callimachus as at least his partial 'model'. The innovations (that is, differences from Callimachus) have been thought, for the most part, to be Ovidian. It is clear, of course, that Ovid got Erysichthon's daughter (Maestra or Mestra, though he does not use the name) from a non-Callimachean source and that this of itself differentiated his story from that of Callimachus: as Maria de Cola points out, the very fact that Ovid's Erysichthon is a mature man with a marriageable daughter excludes the characterization of Erysichthon in Callimachus (the mere lad living at home with parents and family). But it has not usually been thought necessary to ascribe all Ovid's non-Callimachean touches (the bleeding tree, the elaborate divine machinery, the personified Fames, etc.) to a separate version of the story that he used. It seems clear that he was in fact 'Virgilianizing' Callimachus. Erysichthon is, like Mezentius, a *divum contemptor* (cf. ll. 739–40 *qui numina divum sperneret*); the tree bleeds like Polydorus (Wilamowitz also calls attention to the reminiscence of Apollonius' Paraebius, *Arg.* ii, 476 ff.); Fames is certainly more than reminiscent of Fama and Allecto. Callimachus' poplar is in Ovid a mighty oak and the Virgilian echo is obvious:

414 BOO

velut *annoso* validam...*robore quercum*
$$(Aen. \text{ IV}, 441)$$
Stabat in his ingens *annoso robore quercus*
$$(Met. \text{ VIII}, 734)$$
So, too, with the bleeding tree:
Ater et alterius sequitur *de cortice sanguis*
$$(Aen. \text{ III}, 33)$$
Haud aliter fluxit discusso *cortice sanguis*
$$(Met. \text{ VIII}, 753)$$

Furthermore, the parallel use of *obstupui* (*Aen.* III, 48) and *obstipuere* (*Met.* VIII, 756) and the elaborate simile of the slain victim (cf. *haud aliter...quam*, etc., *Met.* VIII, 753, with *Aen.* IV, 669 *non aliter quam*, etc.) have an obviously Virgilian ring. Most striking of all is the 'un-Ovidian' use of spondees, caesurae and diaereses in the passage. For once, Ovid checks his fluidity and apes Virgil.

Yet K. J. McKay (*The Poet at Play, Erysichthon*, 1962 (Supplementa VI and VII to *Mnemosyne*)) has argued that Callimachus was really familiar with Ovid's version of the story (Mestra, the bleeding tree, hypostasized Hunger, etc.) and that the new Hesiodic fragments and the contemporary folklore of the Dodecanese show the pre-Callimachean provenience of Ovid's source. Callimachus was, according to McKay, subtly parodying it. I have discussed the validity of McKay's thesis elsewhere (*AJP*, 1964, pp. 423–9). All that needs to be said here is that even if Ovid had another (or ostensibly non-Callimachean) version or source for most of the legend, he deliberately chose it and deliberately chose to put it in a Virgilian-epic garb. The 'epic' tone and manner of his *Erysichthon* is assuredly intentional. Much the same thing can be said of the 'idyllic' tone and manner of his *Baucis–Philemon* though here the reference to Callimachus is obviously much more tangential.

XII. BYBLIS (IX, 447–665)

The best discussions of the sources are in E. Rohde, *Griechische Roman*, 3rd ed. pp. 101–3 n. 1 and Dietze, pp. 37–9. The following seem to be the chief versions or sources:

(1) Nikainetos (given in Parthenius, *Erotica Pathemata*, XI). He makes Caunus the lover, Byblis the beloved. When Byblis was obdurate, Caunus left home, wandered through Ionia and Caria and founded a city. Byblis bewailed his absence, like a mournful frog or owl (ὀλολυγόνος οἶτον ἔχουσα... Καύνου ὀδύρετο νόστον). So too the source (obviously an Alexandrian or Hellenistic poem) mentioned by Nonnus (*Dionys.* XIII, 546–65). Nonnus mentions particularly Caunus' sophistical love-song (δολοπλόκον ἔπλεκε μολπήν) to Byblis with its mention of Hera's love for her brother Zeus, Endymion and Selene, etc. Cf. Ovid, 497 ff.

(2) The majority (οἱ δὲ πλείους) mentioned by Parthenius: these would seem to include Aristokritos in his Περὶ Μιλήτου and Apollonius of Rhodes in his Καύνου κτίσις (to judge from the MS. sub-title of *Er. Path.* XI) as well as Parthenius himself (his 'little epic' is quoted). Here *Byblis* falls in love with her brother, Caunus, appeals to him in words (λόγους αὐτῷ προσφέρειν), is rejected and left behind (Caunus wanders off to Caria) and then hangs herself (some, Parthenius adds, say that a spring ('Byblis') arose from her tears).

(3) The version of Nicander (Antoninus Liberalis, *Met. Syn.* 30) makes Byblis the daughter of Miletos and Eidothea. She had (like Psyche in Apuleius' *Golden Ass*) a plethora of suitors but loved only her brother Caunus. She concealed her love from her parents (and inferentially from Caunus himself) until, tormented beyond further endurance, she threw herself down from a high rock. But the nymphs rescued her and turned her into a hamadryad. The water that flowed down the rock was then called (by the natives) the 'tears of Byblis'.

There is little point in trying to reconstruct the exact version used by Ovid. It was certainly very close to Parthenius' 'little epic'. But Ovid very likely got details from the other (apparently numerous) versions of the story such as the sophistical love-song mentioned by Nonnus (its transfer from Caunus to Byblis would be easy), the Milesian origin of Caunus and Byblis and the wanderings of Caunus and Byblis (cf. here Conon, *Narrat.* 2). The discrepancy of names and places between the versions would not have bothered Ovid very much. He certainly was responsible for expanding the 'words' of Byblis to the elaborate letter and monologues and for making the metamorphosis an 'inevitable' outcome of Byblis' final plight rather than the elaborate rescue from a suicide leap that we find in Nicander or the hanging that we find in Parthenius, Aristokritos and Apollonius. There is no concealment (as in Nicander), no suicide (as in Parthenius) and certainly nothing like the legend recorded by Nikainetos and Nonnus. The best guess is that Ovid conflated Parthenius and Nikainetos (this is probably where Nonnus found his 'sophistical love-song') and perhaps added some detail (e.g. the Milesian origin of Byblis and Caunus) from Nicander. But the striking features (especially the letter and the metamorphosis) are his own. This is one of the episodes where we have quite good material on his sources (the quotations in Parthenius at least indicate actual poems, those of Nikainetos and Parthenius himself, that were almost certainly known to Ovid).

XIII. IPHIS (IX, 666–797)

Here there seems no reason to doubt that Nicander (reproduced in Antoninus Liberalis, *Met. Syn.* 17) is Ovid's principal or sole source. Ovid changed:

(1) The names Galateia and Lampros to Telethusa and Ligdus (but the Ovidian names (as Dietze, p. 34, remarks) are metrically equivalent to the Greek ($- \cup$, $\cup \cup - \cup$) and the provenience in both cases is Phaistos in Crete. Ovid, however, substituted *Iphis* (a name common to both sexes) for Nicander's *Leukippos*. He used it again in the quite different *Iphis–Anaxarete* (*Met.* XIV, 698–761) where he almost certainly reproduces Hermesianax's story of Arkeophon and Arsinoe).

(2) The social position of the father (in Nicander, Lampros is noble but poor (ἀνδρὶ τὰ μὲν εἰς γένος εὖ ἔχοντι, βίου δὲ ἐνδεεῖ); in Ovid (670–2) Ligdus is *ignotus nomine...ingenua de plebe...nec census in illo nobilitate sua maior*).

(3) The intervening goddess, from Leto to Isis (but (see p. 186 above) Leto, unlike Isis, does not make an imposing appearance to the mother *before* the girl's birth).

(4) The reluctance of the father is wholly Ovidian.

(5) The *betrothal* of the disguised Iphis is Ovidian. Thus the fulfilment of Iphis' *love* is substituted for *dread* of the deceived father (see text, p. 186) as the motive of the metamorphosis.

(6) The refusal of Iphis to countenance an unnatural (homosexual) amour is wholly Ovidian (cf. her soliloquy, 726–63).

The reason for the changes is clear and indicated above (pp. 186–9). Iphis is the 'good' antithesis of the unnatural Byblis; the heterosexually inclined opposite of the homosexual Orpheus (after Eurydice's death) and boys of Book x (86–219), thus a complement of the 'good' Pygmalion (who is likewise contrasted with the 'unnatural' Propoetides and Myrrha). Each is a miracle story. See pp. 185–92 above.

XIV. PYGMALION (x, 243–97)

Philostephanus is cited by Arnobius (*Adversus Gentes* VI, 22) and Clement of Alexandria (*Protrepticus* IV, 57). The Cypriot legends of this part of the book (x) are (the transition from Sparta to Cyprus comes at line 220): *Cerastae, Propoetides, Pygmalion.* Myrrha is not really Cypriot, as we shall see (p. 392 below). It is thus highly probable that these three indecent legends stood (probably close together) in Philostephanus' *Kypriaka.* That it was Ovid himself who changed the indecent or pathological agalmatophily (sexual relation with a statue, as, e.g., in Aristaenetus II, 10 and the Posidippus story cited by Clement and Arnobius in connection with Pygmalion) to the idealistic love of this episode is, it seems to me, overwhelmingly probable. We have but to consider the order of Ovid's episodes at this point (diagram on p. 390).

The 'miraculous' metamorphosis was suggested by its 'correspondent', the Iphis story. Ovid used the obscene Cypriot legends of the Cerastae and Propoetides to introduce it, then altered the originally obscene *Pygmalion* of Philostephanus to fit the *Iphis* and be a contrast (primarily) with the *Byblis* and *Myrrha* and (secondarily) with the lighter but still 'unnatural' homosexuality of the Cyparissus and Hyacinthus stories. So far as I can tell, this very revealing transformation of Philostephanus by Ovid has never been clearly described by commentators. Fränkel (pp. 93–7, 219) alludes to it rather tangentially and without full attention to its context though his treatment is far more satisfactory than that of previous commentators. I do not see that Ovid was influenced here by Euripides' *Alcestis* (348 ff.) or the story of Laodamia, as Fränkel (p. 219) seems to imply. Douglas T. Bauer ('The Function of Pygmalion in the *Metamorphoses* of Ovid', *TAPA* 93 (1962), pp. 1–21) tries to explain the *Pygmalion* as a sort of pivot or centre of the whole poem because it combines stone imagery, the love motif and the theme of fine arts and because it breaks the whole *Metamorphoses* into a perfect 'Golden Section' of 0·618 (the ratio of the preceding 7377 verses to the succeeding 4554). I cannot see that such observations shed any light on the episode. The fact that the *Pygmalion* deals with love, art and stone imagery does not explain why it segmentally divides the whole poem, nor do the three decimal places of the 'Golden Segment' mean much or anything unless we can also explain the plan of the *Metamorphoses* in much more detail and with much more precision than Bauer provides. The *Pygmalion* is a charming episode, but I can see no particular reason for exalting it above the *Iphis*, *Byblis*, or, above all, the *Ceyx–Alcyone*.

Book ix, 447–665	⌐ Byblis (incest, unnatural passion)
666–797	⌐Iphis (miraculous salvation of the innocent lover from unnatural passion)
Book x, 1–219	⌐ Orpheus–Eurydice (homosexual *amores*)
220–42	⌐ Cerastae–Propoetides (unnatural love)
243–97	└Pygmalion (miraculous reward of innocent lover)
298–502	└ Myrrha (incest, unnatural passion)

XV. MYRRHA (x, 298–502)

There can be no doubt that Ovid here had in mind the *Zmyrna* of C. Helvius Cinna. That Ovid could possibly have written on the same subject without having in mind the most famous poem of the New Poets to whom he, poetically speaking, owed his origin and inspiration, is quite inconceivable. Yet it is, for this very reason, inconceivable also that Ovid should have slavishly copied the *Zmyrna* or, indeed, failed to show his originality by diverging from it at several important or conspicuous points.

We can gain some notion of Cinna's *Zmyrna* from (a) the pseudo-Virgilian *Ciris* and (b) the digest (24) of the story in Antoninus Liberalis.

(1) That the *Ciris* is indebted to Cinna's poem in several respects is all but certain. Sudhaus (*Hermes* 42 (1907), pp. 469–504) has shown this in sufficient detail. Not only the rare genitive *tabis* (Charisius, 119 B., 93 Keil, attributes it to the *Zmyrna*) at *Ciris* 254 but the echo of the *Zmyrna* lines (schol. Virg. *Georg.* 1, 288):

Te matutinus flentem conspexit Eous
et flentem paulo vidit post Hesperus idem

at *Ciris* 351–2:

Quem pavidae alternis fugitant optantque puellae,
Hesperium vitant, optant ardescere Eoum,

and, above all, the similarity of the Scylla–nurse scene to Antoninus Liberalis and Ovid's *Myrrha* can hardly be coincidental. Thus our previous comparison of the *Ciris* with Ovid's *Scylla* (pp. 62–5 above) can *mutatis mutandis* be applied here. Ovid's *Myrrha* shows a dramatic continuity, based on empathetic penetration of Myrrha's *psyche*, that we do not find in the *Ciris*, especially in that portion of the *Ciris* (the dialogue of Scylla with her nurse Carme) which seems to derive from the *Zmyrna*.

(2) There are remote but unmistakable echoes of the *Zmyrna* in Ovid himself. Thus compare the *Zmyrna* (Morel, p. 88):

At scelus incesto Smyrnae crescebat in alvo

with Ovid (470, 503–5):

Semina fert *utero* conceptaque *crimina portat*

* * * * * * * *

At male conceptus sub robore *creverat* infans
quaerebatque viam, qua se genetrice relicta
exsereret. Media gravidus *tumet* arbore *venter.*

(3) The typically Euripidean nurse scene is common to the
Ciris, Ovid and Antoninus Liberalis.

How Ovid altered the *Zmyrna* is, however, more or less of a
mystery. Only two things seem reasonably certain: (1) that the
Zmyrna, like the *Ciris*, had a long central scene based on the
dialogue of Myrrha and her nurse (here the relatively crude *Ciris*
would be a more literal copy of the *Zmyrna* and would preserve
the static quality of the neoteric *epyllion*, see pp. 62-4 above)
but that Ovid shortened the scene (in proportion to the rest of the
episode); and (2) that Ovid himself emphasized the horror of the
story both to make it the climax of his episodes of *furiosa libido* and
to establish a contrast with the *Pygmalion*. Its dramatic and epic
narrative style is also (as we have just seen) Ovidian or Virgilian,
not neoteric. The (inconsistent) connection of Myrrha with
Cyprus is merely a consequence of the liaison with *Pygmalion* (see
pp. 189 f. and 389 f. above).

XVI. CEYX AND ALCYONE (XI, 267–748)

Probus (commentary on *Georgics* I, 399: *dilectae Thetidi alcyones*)
mentions two versions of the story:

(1) one in which Alcyone is daughter of Sciro, an Attic
brigand, and is made a bird after her enraged father had tossed her
into the sea (Ovid refers to this version at *Met.* VII, 401 ff.);

(2) the version we are here concerned with, which Probus
attributes to Nicander.

Dietze (p. 50) distinguishes two variants of this latter version:

(*a*) the Homeric scholium AB on *Iliad* IX, 562, Eustathius on
Iliad IX, 538 (p. 776) and Apollodorus (I, 52) contain the com-
moner variant. In this, Ceyx and Alcyone perished (ἀπώλοντο)

because of their insolent pride (δι' ὑπερηφάνειαν) in attributing divine qualities to themselves: Ceyx called Alcyone Hera; she called him Zeus. Presumably the metamorphosis itself was their 'destruction' or punishment, though in Eustathius Zeus is represented as taking pity on the birds by establishing the halcyon season for their nesting.

(b) Dietze's second variant is represented by Hyginus (65), pseudo-Lucian (*Halkyon*), Theocritus (7. 51 ff. with scholium *ad loc.*) and Dionysius paraphr. (*Poetae bucolici*, etc., ed. Didot, p. 218). Here the metamorphosis is seemingly motivated by Alcyone's grief at the loss of her husband. In pseudo-Lucian, she is changed by divine will (διά τινα δαιμονίαν βούλησιν) into a bird so that she could thus conclude on sea the quest (for her husband) she could not accomplish on land. In Hyginus, Ceyx is shipwrecked as in Ovid; Alcyone in her anguish then leaps into the sea and the pair are made halcyons *deorum misericordia*. Dionysius says the same: the metamorphosis is due to the humanity (φιλανδρία) of the Nereids when they observe Alcyone's grief at her husband's shipwreck (ἐν τῷ πελάγει διαφθαρέντα).

But the difference between the variants (a, b) is probably only apparent or rather conceals an original version perhaps reproduced in a scholium on Aristophanes' *Birds* (line 250, cf. White, *The Scholia on the Aves of Aristophanes* (1914), p. 307 and introduction, p. xxxiii) or, rather, in two MSS. of it (Ambrosianus L 39 suppl. = M and the second hand of Laurentianus XXXI 15 = Γ) and the *editio princeps* (an Aldine of 1498). Here the impiety of Ceyx and Alcyone is described as in variant *a* but the *punishment* for this is not the metamorphosis but the *storm* that drowns Ceyx. The metamorphosis, *per contra*, is motivated (as in variant *b*) by Zeus' pity for Alcyone's extreme sorrow (ἄγαν περιπαθῶς ὠδύρετο).

It is highly probable that this latter (Aristophanes scholium) variant was Ovid's principal or sole source. This is shown not only by his unmistakable references to Juno (Hera) and the *impiety* of Chione (see pp. 231 f. above) but by the evident fact that Ceyx and Alcyone could hardly have become *sea*-birds without some reason other than their sheer impiety. The true reason for the *maritime* metamorphosis is the previous shipwreck and drowning of Ceyx. Furthermore, the halcyon season is the obvious opposite of storm. It is at least a good guess that Cicero's *Alcyone* (cf. Morel, p. 56) represented a version very close to the Aristophanes scholium. It is evident that only *Lucifer* can fit the missing foot of the fragment:

> $- \cup \cup$ hunc genuit claris delapsus ab astris
> praevius Aurorae, solis noctisque satelles,

and that Ovid was therefore adhering to the same genealogy as Cicero.

XVII. PYTHAGORAS SPEECH (xv, 60–478)

I have little to add to my discussion in the text. The Posidonian–Varronian origin of the doctrines is not very clear (Schmekel, *De Ovidiana Pythagoreae Doctrinae Adumbratione*, Diss. Greifswald, 1885 and Lafaye, ch. x, pp. 191–223, have stated the case fairly, but cf. Alfonsi in *Ovidiana*, p. 265). The fact is that Ovid was not expounding any sort of consistent theory but a patchwork 'philosophy' based on the available lore at his disposal. Theories of his own pythagoreanism (cf. Crahay and Hubaux in *Ovidiana*, pp. 283 f.) seem to me quite unprovable and altogether unlikely. He was not a philosopher: he did not intend this philosophical display-piece to be treated as a profound explanation of all the metamorphoses set forth in his extremely variegated poem. Ovid did not mean us to scrutinize his very eclectic stoicism and pythagoreanism with a view to determining his personal philosophy. That he saw the wider implications of change or metamorphosis and was ready to treat philosophy and mythology as more or less convertible explanations of nature does not imply anything more than that he was a reasonably educated man of his time.

INDEXES

426

INDEXES

VIRGIL

Aeneid I (I), 14; (34–156), 244; (37 ff.), 131; (46–8), *137*; (82 ff.), *239*; (130 ff.), (148–53), 245, (148–56), 99; (204–7), *327* (208–9), (740 ff.), 377.

III (33, 48), 386; (588–683), 73; (630–5), 75; (588–691), 290; (631–3), 76

IV (1–55), 59; (23–7), *59*; (54–5), *59–60*; (169–72), *71*; (172), *61*; (279–86), *70–1*; (441), 415; (669), 415

VI (129), 19

VII (45), 195; (293 ff.), 131; (323 ff.),

131; (586 ff.), 240 n.; (593 ff.), *161*

VIII (185–9), *25–6*; (189 f., 200–1), 26; (228–30, 241–2), 27; (249–61), 29; (268), 27; (359–61), *20*; (370–406), 125

IX (136–8), *161*; (551 ff.), *241*

X (1–4), *96*; (5), 98

Eclogues, 4: 94; 6 (31–6), *48–9*; (31–40), 377; (41), 349; (74–81), 407; 7 (38–9), 287

Georgics I (145–6), 100 n.; (399), 421

IV (347), 377; (453–527), 74, 184

Schol. *Georg.* I (288), 420

2 GENERAL INDEX

accent-ictus coincidence in Ovid, 40 f., 76

Accius, 6, 194, 195; his *Tereus*, 406

Achaemenides, 85, 163, 289 f., 350 f., 361, 376; treatment in Virgil compared, 73 f.

Achelous, 168, 194 ff., 200 f., 330, 349, 369 f.

Achilles, 278, 282 f., 359

Acis, 70, 278, 286 ff.

Aconteus, 348

Acoetes, 80, 139 f., 400

Acrisius, 346

Actaeon, 80, 84, 87, 89, 117, 129, 130 n., 133 f., 134 n., 135, 141, 145, 147, 152 f., 158, 165, 206, 230, 261, 318, 338, 342, 368, 376, 387; compared with Callisto, 117; with Pentheus, 140; in *Tristia*, 145 n.; Actaeon–Diana, 132; relation of episode to sources, 133 f., 134 n.; sources, 396 f.

Adonis, 168, 170, 183, 186, 324, 343, 371

Aeacus, 168, 170 f., 174 ff., 181 n. 2, 182, 324, 327, 372; Aeacus–Cephalus, 173, 183; displayed, 181

Aegeus, 168, 174

Aegina, 168, 174 f.; pestilence, 170 f.

Aeneas, 47, 85 f., 88, 132, 164, 167, 199, 278 f., 286, 288, 291 f., 300, 331, 344, 347, 359 f.; bearing on Romulus, Caesar, 28; on Virgil's Aeneas, 281; his ships, 291

Aeneid, recalled, 159 f., 281; used or imitated, 96, 131, 143, 334, 350 f.

Aeolus, 233 ff., 244, 246 f., 255, 258 f.

Aerope, 270

Aesacus, 84, 168, 231

Aeschylus, 267; *Niobe*, 148, 404

Aesculapius, 85, 119 f., 278, 293 ff., 303, 388, 344, 360

Aeson, 168, 170 f., 173, 181 n., 2, 327

Agenor, 314

Agenorids, 137

ages, 93; the four, 94 ff., 377

Aglauros, 120, 154, 156, 158

aition, 30, 31, 119; *Aitia*, of Callimachus, 5, 48, 333; Roman, 45

Ajax, 283, 284, 330, 359

Alcestis, in Euripides, 267

Alcithoe, 129, 156

Alcyone, 156, 207, 234, 238, 266, 270, 273, 277, 286, 357, 421; *Alcyone*, of Cicero, 232

Alexandria, -n, 1, 4, 362, 371

Albrecht, M. von, 306 n.; 335

Hubaux, 423
human approach in *Metam.*, 59; to the
gods, 125
Hyacinths, 168, 183, 185 f., 189 f.,
225 f., 324, 343 f., 352, 371, 419
Hyale, 134
hybris, 146 f., 148 n. 2, 149, 320, 343,
406
Hyginus, 133, 139, 176 f., 180
Hylas, 25 ff., 36 f., 42, 333
Hypnos, 246
Hypsipyle, 264
hypsos (of style), 334

Ianthe, 186 f., 365
Icarus, 217
Icelos, 250
ideology, Augustan, 43; attacked by
Ovid, 18
Ilioneus, 149
Inachus, 104 f., 350
incongruity, 56, 104, 106, 110, 114,
124, 281, 283, 285; of god and
lover, 102; of *maiestas* and *amor*,
122 ff., 341
Ino, 70, 79, 87, 97, 117, 123, 130 n.,
131, 138 f., 142 ff., 152 f., 158, 165,
318, 322, 342, 352, 368, 376;
motif echoed, 213; sources, 401 ff.
Introduction (Bk. 1), 301
Invidia, 341
Io, 47, 87, 89, 104 ff., 116 f., 120, 147,
172, 206, 261, 269, 379, 381, 386;
relation to Callisto, 116; to
Daphne, 105; to Europa, 122;
sources, 379 ff.
Iolaus, 168
Iole, 197
Iphis (1), 166 ff., 170 f., 183 ff., 192 ff.,
201, 225 f., 229, 231, 262 t.,
268 f., 272, 278, 327, 329, 341,
352, 365, 371 f., 413, 419; relation
to Byblis, 311; sources, 186, 417 f.
Iphis (2)–Anaxarete, 293 f., 417
ina deorum, 313, 315, 318, 354
Iris, 246 ff., 295
Isis, 171, 186 ff., 192, 268, 365, 418

Ismenus, 149
Itys, 79, 211, 213 f., 408
Ixion, 143, 201 f.

Janus, gate of, 295
Jason, 173, 216, 367
Julias, 123
Julio-Augustan finale, 294
Julius, 301, 304, 331
Juno, 87, 105, 130 ff., 137 ff., 142 f.,
145, 171, 176, 232 f., 244 ff., 257,
291, 386, 422; jealousy, malevolence, vengeance of, 117, 132,
145, 152, 157, 366, 386, 401
Jupiter, 92, 138, 157, 171 ff., 199 f.,
202 f., 280, 292, 295, 304, 380,
395; loss of dignity, 104, 153, 357,
ff., 369; in Virgil, 125; Jupiter–
Callisto, 91, 93; Jupiter–Europa,
91, 93, 146, 156; Jupiter–Io, 78 f.,
84, 91, 93, 105 ff.

Kienzle, H., 130 n.
Kleinknecht, 397
Klimmer, W., 80, 130 n.
Knaack, G., 389, 394 f.
Knight, W. F. J., 40 n. 1, 76 n., 77
Kreydell, 394
Kypriaka (Philostephanus), 189

Lacey, De, 377
Laestrygonians, 290
Lafaye, G., 395, 413, 423
Lampetides, 161, 348
Lampros, 417
Laocoon, 281
Laodamia, 236 f., 265, 271, 419
Lapiths, 280 f., 283; Lapiths–Centaurs,
81, 85, 278, 282 f., 285, 330, 349 ff.,
358 f.
Latinus, 131 f., 161, 347
Latium, 279
Latona, 87, 146, 148 ff., 404
Latte, K., 410
Lavinia, 131 f., 291, 347
Leander, 264
Learchus, 142, 144, 403

435

436